W9-BWF-220

THE LIBRARY
T. MARY'S COLLEGE OF MARYLAND
ST. MARY'S CITY, MARYLAND   20686

BBC Hulton Picture Library

MARX
AS
POLITICIAN

David Felix

SOUTHERN ILLINOIS UNIVERSITY PRESS
Carbondale and Edwardsville

Copyright © 1983 by the Board of Trustees, Southern Illinois University
All rights reserved
Printed in the United States of America
Edited by Stephen W. Smith

83 84 85 86 87   5 4 3 2 1

Library of Congress Cataloging in Publication Data

Felix, David, 1921–
    Marx as politician.

    Bibliography: p.
    Includes index.
    1. Marx, Karl, 1818–1883.   I. Title.
HX39.5.F397 1983   335.4′092′4 [B]   82–10507
ISBN 0–8093–1073–2

For Georgette

Also by David Felix

Protest: Sacco-Vanzetti and the Intellectuals
*Walther Rathenau and the Weimar Republic: The
Politics of Reparations*

CONTENTS

PREFACE

Marx is one of the greatest thinkers in world history. His masterpiece, *Capital*, is the most profound study of industrial society ever made and a classic statement of the human condition. It rises upon the massive foundations of the *Communist Manifesto*, the *Economic-Philosophical Manuscripts of 1844*, the *Grundrisse*, the *Critique of Political Economy*, and the Inaugural Address of the First International. All social scientists beginning with economists and including sociologists and political scientists draw upon him, but no more so than do philosophers, literary critics, and historians.

It is the thesis of this book that Marx was primarily a politician and not a thinker; the word "politician" is used in its neutral sense, that is, man of politics. As great as Marx was as thinker, I shall argue that he was a greater politician.

Marx belongs with such politicians as Pericles, Alexander, Caesar, Augustus, Constantine, Cromwell, Napoleon, Lincoln, Disraeli, Gladstone, Bismarck, Lenin, Gandhi, Roosevelt, and Charles de Gaulle. We have only to look around us to see his colossal presence.

His friend, Friedrich Engels, put the two characters of Marx in proper order in his graveside talk: "An immeasurable loss has been sustained both by the militant proletariat of Europe and America, and by historical science, in the death of this man." Engels emphasized carefully: "Marx was before all else a revolutionary. His real mission in life was to contribute, in one way or another, to the overthrow of capitalist society."[1]

With genial political instinct and urgent will to command, Marx had functioned as a leader of men, completely the master of his life situation, since his early twenties. He had determined policy as editor of influential German newspapers; he was an active provincial politician during the Revolution of 1848 and head of various revolutionary organizations from the Communist League to the First International. It is also true that none of these activities was important in his own time. Marx was ahead of his time. By necessity he was a miniaturist of political operations, perfecting a tiny image which he accurately and gigantically projected onto the future. Where are his contemporaries among the leaders—men like Gladstone and Bismarck—now?

Marx had subordinated everything, his thought most particularly, to the action of making revolution. The thought became a political operation using ideas. Inevitably, his powerful intelligence collided with opposing facts and ideas, but he developed great skill in using it against itself—to arrive at his political, instinctively determined goals. This explains the incoherences and contradictions in *Capital*, but also the book's power over men. Marx taught revolution with its errors as with its insights. The thinker had penetrated to the monstrous truth of capitalism and the politician set out to master it. He died before he succeeded. But he succeeded.

Jacques Barzun, Sir Isaiah Berlin, Robert Payne, Maximilien Rubel, and Robert C. Tucker have given me invaluable counsel at various points in my direction-taking and research. Benjamin Brody, Christoph M. Kimmich, and my colleague James D. Ryan read parts of the manuscript and suggested improvements. George J. Lankevich, also a colleague, read all of it and functioned as an exacting editor. The final draft, as much in what it left out as in what it said, owes an immense debt to his judgment. To all I express my best thanks. I cannot say how much the book and I owe my wife, Georgette.

I am grateful to Mme. Anne Gruner Schlumberger for permission to make use of the Fonds Guizot. The following institutions, where I carried out my research, were most helpful: New York Public Library and Butler Library of Columbia University; International Institute of Social History, Amsterdam; Archive de la Ville de Bruxelles and Archives Générales du Royaume de Belgique, Brussels; British Museum and Marx Memorial Library, London; and Archives Nationales, Bibliothèque Nationale, Archives de la Préfecture de Police, Archives des Affaires Etrangères, and the Institut Historique Allemand, Paris.

The City University of New York, the State University of New York, and the American Council of Learned Societies assisted the project with generous grants.

David Felix

New York, New York
March 14, 1983

MARX AS POLITICIAN

ONE

BEGINNINGS

CIRCUMSTANCES AND FAMILY had made Karl Marx a consciously political being very early. His home area, the Rhineland, had undergone a succession of radical changes of authority in the generation just past. He was born in Trier, then a town of 15,000, on May 5, 1818, three years after Waterloo and during the beginning of the Restoration.[1] Before that, for two decades, France occupied the Rhineland and had granted its people the new rights won during the French Revolution. For Heinrich Marx, Karl's father, this had meant a perfectly timed opportunity to make a better life for himself.

French law permitted Jews to enter previously forbidden occupations, and Heinrich Marx became a prosperous lawyer, president of Trier's bar association, and an official of the district's High Court of Appeals. In 1815, however, the Congress of Vienna awarded the Rhineland to Prussia. A Prussian decree forbade Jews to exercise a number of professions, including the law.

Heinrich Marx resisted with skillful advocacy. Less than a month after the annexation was announced, on June 13, 1815, he addressed a protest to the regional *Generalgouverneur*. Like many emancipated Jews of the time, he saw his own people much as the Christian community did, and was willing the apologize for the usurer and speculator. But he reminded the official of the Prussian claim of tolerance, argued that discrimination would drive Jews into reprehensible practices, and permitted himself explicit sarcasm. "And why? Just because they are circumcised and eat unleavened bread at Easter?"[2] His temerity neither helped nor hurt. In 1816 the chief justice of the Provincial Supreme Court asked the Prussian minister of justice to make an exception of Marx and two other Jewish lawyers. The minister refused. That year, in fact, the discriminatory decree was applied to Jewish elementary-grade teachers, pharmacists, and officers, who had previously been unaffected.[3] Heinrich Marx converted to Lutheranism.

The conversion took place at about the time of Karl's birth, probably a year or two before.[4] In 1824 the seven Marx children living at the time were baptized; their mother, Henriette Marx, followed the next year.[5] Politics, associated with religious, social, and other public issues, had entered deeply into young Karl's personal life.

Great emotional violences lay at the heart of the alienation that had led to Heinrich Marx's act. His wife was the granddaughter of a rabbi, and he himself was the son of the late chief rabbi in Trier and the brother of his successor. No record of relations between the brothers exists, but Heinrich Marx and his family evidently had no contact with the other Jews in Trier[6] and were formally accepted as part of the Protestant community, itself a minority in the Catholic town. If Heinrich knew how to fight, he had also known when to stop. The conversion had been a compromise, and now he used his best skills as professional compromiser to contain and limit its effects. Everyone else in the family followed his example except Karl.

Karl found himself with a problem he would spend his entire life solving. Part of it was the unusual amount of freedom granted him to determine *who* he was. He took advantage of his situation to deny that he was a Jew, but then he could never wholeheartedly admit he was a German; he would seek himself in all humanity, the international community of dissidents, and the proletariat. He would never settle on one identity. He would, however, draw compensation in the intoxications of his extraordinary freedom.

In this way the political affected the personal in Karl Marx, while the personal, as it developed, would begin to direct itself back toward the political. Then there was the element of personal causation.

One experience of Heinrich's mixed the political and the personal in equal parts as influences on Karl. An emancipated Jew, Heinrich had inevitably been a liberal; in January 1834, as a member of a club of like-minded gentlemen of Trier, he helped organize two mild demonstrations in the form of political banquets, typical for that time. At the first, Heinrich, chairman of the banquet committee, gave the main speech and respectfully begged the king of Prussia to increase popular representation. At the second, the club members emphasized their politics by singing the "Marseillaise" and kissing the French revolutionary flag. In Berlin the government expressed its anger, the Rhineland authorities began surveillance of possible sedition, and the liberals fell silent. Karl, who was sixteen, was old enough to appreciate his father's humiliation. On the evidence the story of his father's part in the liberal demonstration and its aftermath left more of an impression with him than did Heinrich's brave, earlier stand on discrimination. The evidence was thrown up ten years later when young Marx, attacking an insufficiently radical former friend, compared his attitude to that of the old liberals. Remarking contemptuously on the failure of their demonstrations, the journalist Marx would write, "*Not a single* soldier was needed to crush the desire of the entire liberal bourgeoisie for freedom of the press and a constitution."[7] But Karl Marx never consciously connected his contempt for the liberals in general with his feelings for the liberal gentleman Heinrich Marx.

On a purely personal level Heinrich and his wife gave Karl another difficult problem, that of resolving contradictions emanating from them. Within the closeness of their union, man and wife were profoundly different from each other. Heinrich, moreover, was two persons: loving, tender, understanding, cultivated, and generous; judgmental and punishing. The tender Heinrich indulged Karl and the judgmental Heinrich punished him for taking advantage of it. As for Henriette, she was a cramped, self-centered being, parsimonious with affection, frightened, whining, ignorant, hard, and stubborn. In her hardness and stubbornness she was more like her strong-willed, egocentric son than he could ever admit or conceive. Their similar temperaments had to clash. Father and son appear to have conspired to uphold a higher public opinion of Henriette Marx than they really had. When Karl was a student at the University of Berlin, a letter of Heinrich's referred to "your admirable mother . . . whose whole life is a continuing sacrifice of love and faithfulness."[8] A few months later Karl responded with references to his "angel mother . . . this great, magnificient woman."[9] On either side the phrases rang hollowly. Heinrich surely forgave his wife for her inadequacies, the rhetoric serving to cover a necessary compromise. Doubtless because of Heinrich's negative example, compromise was impossible for Karl.

Heinrich died when Karl had just reached twenty, before the son could take the opportunity to fight out their conflicts openly. Arrested at this point, permanently his father's prisoner, Karl never became a completely mature person.[10] He never admitted to feelings for Heinrich other than love and worshipful respect, while he quickly swung to the simplest contempt and hatred for his mother, as expressed in repeated references in his letters. (When Henriette died, in 1863, the forty-five-year-old Marx rushed from London to Trier, although ill at the time, and writing to his wife, gave precise details on his mother's will without adding one word of regret for her passing.)[11] He had dealt with the problem of being the son of Heinrich and Henriette Marx by taking recourse in the absolute, loving or hating, bonding or breaking. He would act in the same extreme way in the world of politics, where making strong personal relationships is essential, and where breaking them, almost as much so.

Among the Marx children Karl had been established as the leader and favored one—the *Glückskind*—the "golden boy." The eldest surviving son, he had been endowed with physical vigor and the best intelligence. The three other sons were sickly and died early; the daughters never thought to challenge Karl's primacy, although Sophie, senior to Karl, was a personality of considerable strength and assurance. Karl had the self-confidence, spirit, initiative, and sheer power to make himself overwhelmingly attractive despite a forthright ugliness. He tyrannized over his younger sisters beyond the point of pain. As they remembered in later years, he would make them his horses, harness them with ropes, and drive them down a hill near their home. He would then get them to eat patties his dirty hands had molded of dirty dough. They complied, they said, because he told them such marvelous stories as a reward.[12] At school, however, he despised the other boys as country clods and made no close friends. At least he established his ascendancy over them. In the words of his daughter Eleanor, he later remembered that they "loved and feared [him], loved because he was always ready for boyish pranks and feared because of the ease with which he composed satirical verses and lampoons against his enemies."[13] He had early learned to identify certain others as enemies. The man—the political man—is acutely recognizable in this boy who took his pleasure in providing his sisters and other comrades with another sort of pleasure, one that compounded humiliation within itself. Young Karl had learned that a dollop of sadism makes leadership more seductive.

The man is similarly recognizable in the seventeen-year-old secondary-school student. In the compositions which were required for graduation and which have been fortunately preserved, young Marx clearly or ambiguously, depending on the sensitivity of the subject, articulated the principles of his most important future thought and action—his politics.[14] Of course the politics was not differentiated from such other concerns as poetry, philosophy, and private ambition. His German essay, "Reflections of a Youth on Choosing an Occupation," mixed the various elements characteristically. Marx was passionately concerned about remaining true to his ideals and keeping his honor unsullied, as well as the value of freedom, the danger of failure, and his need for personal fulfillment. As for the last, he emphasized that it required practical political action as well as abstract thinking. While nature directed the behavior of animals, "the Godhead gave man a universal goal, to purify humanity and himself, but divinity left it to man to find the way himself." Such freedom was an awful responsibility. Failure to exercise it would lead to self-contempt, "a snake, which, eternally burrowing, gnaws at the breast, sucks the lifeblood from the heart, and mixes it with the poison of despair and hatred for man."[15] "The poison of despair": this boy knew it already. Karl had felt more deeply and reasoned with more sophistication than most experienced and reasonably intelligent adults.

Now, however, Karl had to save the situation; he was writing for the eyes of respectable authority as represented by his teachers. But then he also had the optimism of youth. One could escape despair by entering "a profession which affords us the greatest honor, which is grounded on ideas, of whose truth we are completely convinced, which offers us the widest field to serve humanity . . . " The sentence rushed on passionately, losing its grammatical subject and lurching out of control. In his last thought Karl innocently remarked on the value of such a profession as "a means [to achieve] completeness."[16] He rephrased the thought at the end of the essay: "The chief guide which must lead us in the choice of a profession is the common welfare, our own completion."[17] "The common welfare, our own completion": young Marx had confounded himself with all humanity.

The theme of the Latin composition, an argument for or against the emperor Augustus, called up Karl's thoroughly conscious political sense. He was doubtless aware that his discussion related to contemporary Prussian politics. A few days later, after graduation, Karl paid farewell visits to his teachers, but failed to see one of them, the Latin professor. This deeply hurt the man, Karl's father reproachfully wrote him.[18] Earlier, following the liberal demonstrations, the Latin professor had been named joint headmaster as a control over the original headmaster, a founder of the liberal association. Clearly, Karl, who would become an expert in the art of political insult, had made *his* demonstration.[19]

The essay on Augustus was both purposefully and helplessly ambiguous. Karl could not expect that a denunciation of absolute rule would be well received. But then he was not clear about the alternative to the absolutism of Augustus. Karl began one train of argument with evident approval. "His [Augustus's] reign was distinguished by its clemency. Although all freedom and even the appearance of freedom had disappeared, the Romans still thought they were governing themselves." Karl seemed to be suggesting that power could institutionalize the lie as the truth. He did not rest there. His sense of irony cut through. "This is indeed a great truth of clemency if the citizens are uncertain who is the ruler—whether they themselves rule or are ruled." Karl caught himself, however, and concluded clumsily but with more decisiveness than his argument had justified. "The genius of Augustus succeeded in improving the institutions and laws which he created so that the badly shaken state could be transformed into a better condition, permitting the effects of the civil wars to be eliminated. . . . If a people has become enervated . . . an emperor rather than a free republic can give it liberty."[20] The future expert in Hegelian contradictions had left one unresolved in the essay like a bubble suspended in glass.

In his essays on private career and public administration, Karl had been passionate, forceful, and realistic enough to give sharp edge to his adolescent idealism. He dealt with "The Union of the Faithful with Christ," the subject of his essay on religion, as he dealt with his mother at the time: he heaped hyperbole over his subject. He began with effusive commonplaces of the Christian faith: "When we consider . . . the nature of man, we immediately see a spark of the divine in his breast and enthusiasm for the good, a striving after knowledge, a desire for truth." This could not fail to please the town pastor, who gave religious instruction in the school. But the essay made a turn into less conventional arguments. Karl would not rest on the surface of self-congratulating piety. A harder substance appeared. In earlier ages, he wrote, the pagans always suffered from "a fear of the wrath of the gods, an inner conviction of their reprehensible state." In the Christian era, however, the danger for man was still "the alluring voice of sin [as] heard above the enthusiasm for virtue. Sin mocks at us . . . and the baser striving after earthly goods frustrates the effort toward knowledge, and the knowledge of the truth is extinguished through the sweetly flattering power of the lie—" The result was man's terrible loneliness in the universe: "—and so man stands there, the unique being in nature whose purpose is not fulfilled. He is the only member of the whole of creation who is not worthy of the God who created him."

It was a fine existential moment, but, as in the case of his essay on choosing an occupation, Karl was too politic to halt there. He would save the situation again; he would find Christian hope in hopelessness. Eruditely citing passages from the Gospel According to St. John, he argued that perdition could be reversed into salvation. "But the good Creator cannot hate His own work. He wishes man to raise himself and sent His own son, and allows us to be called through Him." Karl rephrased the thought. "This union with Christ consists in the deepest, most living communion with Him. . . . We turn our hearts at the same time toward our brothers." In a last paragraph Karl repeated, "Thus union with Christ contributes to inner uplift, consolation in sorrow, quiet confidence, and a heart which is open to love for mankind and for all noble and great men, not out of ambition or love of fame, but through Christ." And again, "Thus union with Christ produces a joyfulness."[21] The pastor, while appreciating a "statement that is rich in ideas, captivating, and powerful," was nevertheless not persuaded by its argument, which he found "only imperfectly demonstrated."[22]

Karl graduated eighth in a class of thirty-two.[23] The general evaluation mentioned "excellent promise."[24]

For Karl, graduation meant leaving home and quickly distancing himself from his family. Entering the University of Bonn in October 1835, he wrote rarely, neglected his studies after an ambitious start, drank perhaps too frequently, got into a dueling scrape, and overspent his allowance. He was acting like the mirror image of the Jewish stereotype, and Heinrich Marx might have wondered what he had wrought when he made a Christian of his son. Correctly anticipating worse—Karl would spend the rest of his life in debt as well as disorder—Heinrich, complaining and compromising, thereupon arranged to send him to the University of Berlin, known for its sobriety, in the fall of 1836. Inevitably, it meant a wider separation of Karl from his family.

That summer, Karl acted out what could be seen as another effect of Heinrich Marx's conversion. He returned home and, barely eighteen years old, precipitously and successfully proposed to the town beauty. The engagement was at first kept secret from the parents of Karl's fiancée, a fact suggesting all manner of difficulty. Jenny von Westphalen, whom Heinrich knew very well, was of such unexceptionable quality and attractions that he had every right to be doubly apprehensive. Why should a twenty-two-year-old aristocrat want to marry this much younger, ugly youth of Jewish origins and doubtful and necessarily tardy prospects? The question, romantic formulas being unacceptable to an experienced lawyer, had to remain unanswered. Recalling the Bonn extravagances, Heinrich brooded over his son's immaturity and wondered if some "strange demon . . . of spiritual or Faustian character" did not dominate his son, endangering his chances for "domestic felicity."[25] History has not been able to answer other questions about the other persons concerned. Jenny's elderly father, Baron Ludwig von Westphalen, was a neighbor and friend of Heinrich's, and, like him, a man with progressive views of the Enlightenment. It is not known what the baron, who had earlier liked to converse with the precocious boy about intellectual matters, thought of the engagement. Surely it was a hard test of his principles, but he gave his formal approval a year and a half later, when the secret was out.

Heinrich Marx fell ill early in 1837, and his correspondence, always worried about his son's lack of measure, became heavy with foreboding. In mid-August he wrote at length from Bad Ems, where he was taking the cure, that he had been having bad coughing spells, that Karl's ten-year-old brother, Eduard, was ill and afraid he would die, as the boy did, toward the end of the year, and that both Jenny von Westphalen and Karl's sister Sophie, who was a friend of Jenny's, were ill as well. Heinrich begged his son to mend his ways for the sake of his family and fiancée.[26] On December 9, in a long letter, Henrich reported on his illness and complained that Karl had failed to write for months. He found Karl's behavior going from one extreme to the other, from the "wildness" of Bonn to the "gloomy floating about in all areas of knowledge, gloomy brooding by the dim study lamp, a reversion to barbarism in a scholar's dressing gown." Reviewing his son's prodigality and other failings, Heinrich reminded Karl that he claimed to "honor his father and idealize his mother," that Sophie, who had supported the engagement, was unhappy that "you don't think of her when you don't need her," that Karl had received the best of everything and that "yes, you have a great debt to repay." Repayment consisted of the impossible, Karl's living sensibly and responsibly.[27]

The last known letter in the father-son correspondence, dated February 10, 1838, expresses Heinrich and Henriette Marx's disappointment that Karl was not planning to come home that Easter.[28] It is possible that he did come after all, according to a letter of Jenny's, but he was in Berlin when, on May 10, 1838, Heinrich died.[29] The surviving correspondence suggests that Karl did not return home for the funeral. The next mention of Karl in Trier puts him there in the summer of 1839.[30] After that, his letters provide no evidence that he returned before January 1842, although it is likely that he made an undocumented visit or two in the interval. In any case, he did not stay with his family in 1842, but with the Westphalens, the baron occupying just that time—January to March 1842—in dying.[31] If Karl's stay with the Westphalens indicated his growing alienation from his own family, his next appearance, after brief visits with friends in Cologne and Bonn, resulted in virtually total alienation. Staying in the Marx home for six weeks in June and July 1842, he demanded money from his father's estate and quarreled bitterly with his mother and sisters when he failed to get it.[32] His future relations with his mother consisted in renewed efforts to get money from her. He would never again have anything to do with Sophie, the only sister to whom he had been close. While he had occasional contact with his other sisters, they meant little to him. By July 1842 he was free of his family.

Young Marx spent nearly six years as a university student. In Bonn, despite his irregular life, he had begun by attending classes regularly; in Berlin, his appearances in class were rare. He was learning, but in his own way. Karl had told his father about it a half year before Heinrich's death in a letter taking up seven printed pages, a three-month-late reply to the unhappy letter of Bad Ems. As he would all his life, Karl wildly and unnecessarily exaggerated his real accomplishments. Upon arriving in Berlin he had cast off old friends, he wrote. Preceding the rejection of his family, it was an early instance of his lifelong pattern of broken relationships. Karl's letter went on to report: He had planned to study law, but was also interested in philosophy, history, and languages. He became a Hegelian, a cataclysmic event in his intellectual life. At first, as he wrote Heinrich, he had resisted but then, overcoming his earlier Kantean-Fichtean idealism, surrendered to the philosopher's "grotesque, craggy melody." Assimilating Hegelian materials to his other resources, he composed dozens of poems, a 300-page preface to a study of the philosophy of law, a new metaphysical system that was a denial of all his earlier beliefs, and a philosophical dialogue on art and science. He then fell into a nervous collapse, which required a convalescence of six months.[33] Illness would continue to be an important and dramatic part of Karl Marx's life.

The surviving writings of those Karl had mentioned in his letter, which comprised poems and fragments of a verse-play and a novel, were ill-favored but promising. Karl lacked the poet's or novelist's eye, ear, taste, and discipline. His images were the romantic commonplaces of his reading, nature torn from the printed page. Yet at eighteen and nineteen he had a powerful imagination that could conceive of enormities and a literary range that could begin, at least, to approach them. One poem, dedicated to Henrich Marx, raises him up as the self-created god-and-patriarch of all mankind; in another, an old man at the seashore dances to the moon until the waves wash up to him and strip the flesh from his bones. In another, the poet finds heaven populated with gaunt old women and makes such a disturbance that Gabriel, on God's orders, throws him out. Other poems deal with revenge, Faustian pacts, corruption, damnation, self-blinding, suicide, and various other romantic horrors. The verse-play treats a homosexual intrigue, an extraordinary subject at the time, as if it were a stock theme of drama, but Marx was either not interested in homosexualty or did not know what to do with it, and went on to a grander subject. A Promethean character soliloquized: "I will howl gigantic curses at mankind/ . . . we are clockwork, wound up blindly, mechanically,/Nothing but calendar figures of all time/ . . . And we are chained, shattered, empty, frightened,/Eternally chained to this marble block of being/ . . . . We—apes of a cold god." The novel, meant to be humorous, broke off with the prescription of an enema.[34]

The young man impressed and even awed elders as well as persons of his own age. A philosophy lecturer remembered him in verse: "Who comes rushing in, wild and impetuous?/Dark fellow from Trier, monster on the loose/ . . . leaps upon his prey/In a mad fury."[35] In 1840 another scholarly friend dedicated a pamphlet to Marx and wrote to him, "You are a storehouse, a factory of ideas, or to put it in proper *Berlinerisch*, a stuffed sausage of ideas."[36] Moses Hess, one of the first German socialists and six years older than Marx, described him in a letter to a friend as "the greatest, perhaps the only living philosopher who can honestly be called a philosopher. . . . The eyes of all Germany will be upon him. . . . Dr. Marx—as my idol is named—is still a very young man. He will be the one to kill off medieval religion and government. . . . Imagine Voltaire, d'Holbach, Lessing, Heine, and Hegel united in one person—I say united and not jammed together—this is Dr. Marx."[37] At the time, 1841, Marx was an unemployed university graduate aged twenty-three.

Having bonded himself permanently to Hegel, Marx found his way to the Young Hegelians, also known as the Left Hegelians. In Berlin a group calling itself the Doktorklub took to meeting in cafés. Perfect intellectual comrades for Marx, its members were carrying through a philosophical revolution. Using Hegel's ideas to criticize religion and state, they were beginning to translate that revolution from thought to practice. Marx's dissertation was a part of their movement.

Marx's doctoral work was not, in truth, a dissertation. It was an exercise in literary virtuosity, an essay covering forty printed pages. Although its sixty pages of notes demonstrated impressive learning, Marx did not trouble to prove his thesis as a proper scholar. Instead, he had put it arbitrarily and made it a starting point for other arbitrary statements. He did not earn his doctorate. He had submitted an outpouring of early genius instead of a complete study, however mediocre, that met scholarly standards.

The work, entitled "A Comparison of the Natural Philosophy of Democritus and Epicurus," was a Young Hegelian polemic using the materials of Greek and Hellenistic philosophy to prescribe action in the present.[38] Marx, referring generally to the Hellenistic philosophies and specifically to Epicureanism, stated his thesis: "These systems taken together form the complete structure of self-consciousness."[39] Marx saw Epicurus as self-evident precursor of Hegel and fellow partisan in the Young Hegelian battle for German freedom. Marx then moved on to other unproven theses. At the end, without having attempted to develop the logic of any statement, he affirmed with emphatic underlinings (here represented by italics): "In Epicurus, the *atomic conception* with all its contradictions has been realized and completed in its ultimate sense as the natural science of the *self-consciousness.*"[40] In this way, according to Marx, Epicurus had produced human subjectivity out of the concreteness and contradictions of the atom—had made the leap from lifeless object to sentient and free humanity. Marx was joining with Epicurus against the pre-Socratic Democritus. At issue in antiquity was the latter's conception of reality as an absolutely determined flow of atoms in a straight line. Epicurus accepted determinism and the straight line but then argued that the atoms could nevertheless swerve spontaneously. Epicurus was qualifying the plain determinism of Democritus with a sublime contradiction. Marx, agreeing as a good Hegelian, ruled against Democritus: "For Democritus, on the other hand, the *atom* is only the *general objective expression of empirical natural science.*"[41] For Marx, the atom of Democritus, expressing only objective reality, was too impoverished a thing to represent life. Marx had entered into the old, unending conflict between theories of freedom and determinism, or, to give them their theological names, free will and predestination. It was a problem at which he would strain all his life. He wanted to believe in determinism—to have history and reality on his side—but he wanted to be free as well. The Hellenistic philosopher provided him with a saving formula and he seized upon it as an established truth: Epicurus had perfected the flawed determinism of Democritus by consolidating freedom into it. Escaping like the atom of Epicurus from the "blind necessity" of Democritus, man (and Marx) could create a better world.[42] The world requiring improvement was the order of things as fixed in place by the Restoration.

Marx was using the dissertation to transform his relations with father and religion. When he had first gone off to the University of Bonn, Heinrich Marx had advised him of the various advantages of a proper faith: "True belief in God is a powerful moral force. You know that there is no one less fanatical than I am. But sooner or later such a belief becomes a necessity of every man. . . . Everyone should submit to . . . the faith of Newton, Locke, and Leibniz."[43] With his professional skill Heinrich Marx had carefully avoided the fundamental question of whether religion expressed the truth. Karl could not endure such life-easing hypocrisy. In the appendix to the dissertation, irrelevant to its theme, he hurled himself upon the question of religion: "The proofs of the existence of God are nothing but *proofs for the existence of the actual human self-consciousness*. . . . In this sense all proofs for the existence of God are proofs for his *nonexistence, refutations* of all conceptions of a God."[44] Marx was too politic to expound unqualified atheism and endanger his doctorate, but his sense was clear enough. He now had another all-consuming belief that eliminated any need for religion, and he turned against it contemptuously. He was not aware that he was turning against his father with as little respect.

The dissertation's philosophical excursion showed unerring political sense as well as overwhelming intellectual and literary power. While it was not published during Marx's lifetime, its arguments provided valuable resources for immediate use. They would serve as a rationale of demands for political rights and popular representation, the platform of the liberals and the more radical democrats. Marx followed his ideas into contemporary politics.

The dissertation brought Marx's apparent aimlessness to an end. He had been impelled to act decisively by Bruno Bauer, a close friend who was ten years his senior, a crypto-atheistic theology lecturer, and a member of the Doktorklub. After first driving Marx to write the dissertation, Bauer then got him to resign from the University of Berlin and submit it to the newly founded University of Jena; Bauer had a friend on the faculty there. The new university, trying to establish itself, was eager to award degrees. Marx mailed the dissertation to Jena on April 6, 1841. The dean of the university transmitted it to the faculty of philosophy on April 13. By mail the university awarded Marx the doctorate, dated April 15.[45]

Legitimizing him, Marx's doctorate served his practical purposes admirably. The conventional title of Doctor of Philosophy gave him additional force with which to attack conventional society. The authorities were persuaded to treat him more gently, while in the revolutionary world that he would presently enter, his scholar's credentials gave him an advantage over his rivals. He began, however, with much more than formal advantages. He would build on the foundation of his real ability as philosopher and writer. He became editor of the *Rheinische Zeitung*.

A remarkable product of the German situation, the *Rheinische Zeitung* was founded on January 1, 1842, by an alliance of capitalists and philosophers. Capitalism was a progressive force in a Rhineland still dominated by medieval survivals and agricultural interests, and the capitalists included philosophers and men interested in new ideas generally. One member of the newspaper's board of directors was the industrialist Ludolf Camphausen, a sympathetic reader of French communist writers,[46] who would become chancellor of a revolutionary Prussia. Two wealthy directors, both bankers' sons and lawyers, who together formed the de facto executive committee, were the former members of the Doktorklub and friends of Marx, Georg Jung and Dagobert Oppenheim.

The Prussian government had supported the founding of the *Rheinische Zeitung* because of the needs of economic and political progress. Prussia had to modernize or be outstripped by its rivals. Economically, the newspaper was to encourage the Rhineland's commercial and industrial spirit so imaginatively represented by people like Camphausen and Marx's wealthy friends. Politically, it was to broadcast the message of a Prussian unity that could comfortably contain this very different region in western Germany. In both cases, the *RZ* would counter the influence of the well-established *Kölnische Zeitung*, the organ of Catholic particularism and agricultural traditionalism. There was more to progress, however, than the Prussian authorities wanted, and they knew they were taking a risk. They could not know how much of a risk.

At first, Georg Jung and Dagobert Oppenheim managed the *RZ* with the help of Moses Hess. Marx, still trying to find his vocation, was working at a number of unpromising literary projects, moving restlessly from Trier to Bonn and Cologne and back, and giving advice to his friends at the *RZ*.

Marx's first service to the newspaper was a failure. He had recommended Adolf Rutenberg as editor. Rutenberg was a friend of his from the Doktorklub and a brother-in-law of Bruno Bauer. A geography teacher dismissed for drunkenness, the new editor had been under police surveillance for his radicalism, and gave the authorities reason to be suspicious of the newspaper. Moreover, he drank so much and asserted his authority so little that the overburdened Jung and Oppenheim had to continue managing the newspaper.[47] In May 1842, meanwhile, the *RZ* carried Marx's first published article, actually a six-part series. It was a long celebration of the freedom of the press that combined literary aptness, Hegelian formulas, and legalistic reasoning.[48] With its philosophic content it was hardly the usual kind of journalistic writing, but all the more effective for it. Marx was particularly clever in putting the Prussian government on the defensive. A few months earlier, the stringent censorship law of 1819 had been relaxed. To an autocracy trying to be somewhat less autocratic but not unreasonably cautious, he put the demand for unqualified press freedom. The effect was exhilarating. Located precisely in the center of the field of tension between the best hopes of the best people and the mediocre imperatives of administering the country, the article immediately established Marx as a force in public opinion. It was widely republished in the German press, and Ludolf Camphausen got a letter from his brother: "Who is the author of that superb article?"[49] In early October 1842 Marx was invited to come to Cologne. On October 15, having written off his old friend as "impotent,"[50] he succeeded Rutenberg. Marx was twenty-four years old.

Marx showed himself to be as precisely suited to the *RZ*'s editorial requirements as he was generally representative of the Young Hegelian movement. He quickly condensed clear, hard policy out of great ideational clouds, the decisive manner of a leader out of a gregariousness complicated by hostility. He had the instincts and skills of a great editor.

The editor Marx began with statesmanlike realism and moderation. He avoided a frontal attack on authority. Several members of his old Doktorklub had organized themselves into a new group, the Free Men (*die Freien*), and having veered into anarchism, nihilism, and communism all at once, were causing scandalous disturbances in cafés, brothels, and churches. Earlier, in late August, Marx had defined his editorial policy negatively in relation to them. It was his first experience with a left deviation. In a letter that may have assured him the editor's position, he had written Oppenheim, "Such a clear protest against the present pillars of the state could only result in a tightening of the censorship and suppression of the paper."[51] The Free Men had been "smuggling communist and socialist ideas into casual theater reviews." Finding it "unsuitable, even immoral,"[52] Marx rejected their contributions, and the group thereupon broke off relations with him. Marx was more sympathetic to communist ideas themselves. Moses Hess, who had been the *RZ*'s correspondent in Paris, had contributed articles mentioning the French communist writers favorably, and when another newspaper criticized the

Hess dispatches, Marx responded like a Hegelian diplomat. "The *RZ*, which cannot even admit the *theoretical reality* of communistic ideas in their present form and can even less want their *practical realization* or deem it possible, will submit the ideas to thorough criticism." Clearly, Marx found them attractive but he would not commit himself. "Writings such as those by Leroux, Considérant, and above all Proudhon's penetrating work, can be criticized only after long and deep study." [53] It was a Hegelian flirtation, but only a flirtation, and the authorities could not very well object.

(The italics in the above quotations, an early example of his frequent use of such devices, are Marx's. He also used huge headlines, large-sized and spaced-out characters, boldface, and, on a notable occasion, blood-red ink. Underlinings suggested a similar topography in his hand-written letters. All such emphases will be replicated or indicated in the quotations here. Marx, a leader always engaged in leading, is reaching out from the page to seize the reader's lapels and physically *impress* the correct opinion on him.)

Marx did not remain content to exercise his leadership within the limits set by authority. In truth, he had never accepted those limits, or any others, but he needed to consolidate his position at the *RZ*. He did so very soon. Within the organization he was much more than an editor engaged by the board of directors. He was the chief ideologist and policymaker. He had developed a close relationship with Jung and Oppenheim, who both felt he was expressing the urgent and minimal demands of a liberal movement now come of age. He had convinced a group of otherwise hardheaded businessmen that it was the *RZ*'s duty to attack authority—to put itself into jeopardy. After having made a point of avoiding just that, Marx drove the newspaper into a series of confrontations with the government. This was infinitely more serious than the irregular sorties of the Free Men. Marx's supporters, nobly losing their investment, remained loyal to the end.

The communist writers had suggested a new area of concern for Marx— social and economic questions. He moved beyond the Free Men. The censor, reading the *RZ* carefully, was tolerant for the moment, and Marx published a series of abrasively sarcastic articles. The government was introducing a new law to stop a typical misdemeanor of the poor, the theft of wood from the forests. This gave Marx the chance to condemn the insensitivity—the hardheartedness—of authority. In his articles, he went on to suggest that private property was unjust by definition if its protection required further impoverishment of the poor.[54] The logic could offend the *RZ*'s businessmen shareholders as well as the government, but they were slow to react. Marx did not stop here.

The inner fury, which had made Marx "a monster on the loose" to his university friends, asserted itself more and more as he entered into other socioeconomic issues. The newspaper's tone became increasingly sarcastic and plainly accusatory. Another important article by Marx, a four-part series published January 15–20, 1843, dealt with the situation of the Moselle winegrowers, who were suffering from new competition. Marx made the government responsible. "The *emergency situation of the Moselle* is at the same time an *emergency situation of the administration.*" He moved from righteous indignation to an unabashed demand for power. "The press takes on the position of communicator of information about the condition of the people, but also, and just as much so, as an expression of popular feelings. . . . Its language is therefore not only the rational language of interpretation . . . but also the passionate language of the conditions themselves." As the voice of the truth, the press claimed the position of collaborator in government.[55] Expressing the feelings of many lonely dissenters throughout the German states, the *RZ* increased its circulation from less than 1,000 to 3,300 and became almost a national organ of opinion. This did not mean profitability but only increased expenses and losses. The newspaper had few subscribers in Cologne itself, and advertisers had little use for it.[56] Moreover, the success it did have, which can be expressed precisely as a *succès d'estime*, was conditional upon its swift death.[57]

The editor Marx had become a dangerous critic of state and church. The *RZ*'s effect extended beyond the Rhineland and even Prussia; one article, an early expression of Marx's feelings about the country and its ruler, attacked Russia and czar violently, and Nicholas I expressed his displeasure.[58] The censor, scolded by Berlin, refused to approve a greater number of articles or parts of articles.[59] Nevertheless he was soon recalled. The next censor, arriving at the end of January 1843, was a man of superior rank with another mission. Ministerial Secretary Wilhelm von Saint-Paul was to help suppress the *RZ* without irritating regional sensibilities too much. In a message of January 21—ten days before Saint-Paul made his first report from Cologne[60]—the minister of the interior communicated the governmental consensus to the chief administrative officer of Cologne. "The *Rheinische Zeitung* has for some weeks once again permitted itself a language which if anything, surpasses the insolence of its earlier manner, and a bias which quite openly presumes to attack and undermine the established order in state and church." Consequently, the Prussian king and his cabinet, meeting two days earlier, had decided to forbid publication of the newspaper after March 31.[61]

At last the *RZ* shareholders began to resist their editor. They held a special meeting, which endured through two three-hour sessions on February 12, and the majority protested Marx's extremism. Among the directors, Jung and Oppenheim, however, immovably supported him.[62] Jung insisted: "The *RZ* was and had to be a partisan newspaper. . . . The *RZ* has become the citadel of the liberal movement in Germany."[63] Marx, who had written a reply to the government, submitted it to the shareholders as his statement to them. It was a legalistic, uncompromising, and aggressively provocative rebuttal of the reasons given by the stop order. "The *RZ* furthermore . . . has never abstractly portrayed the state as opposed to the people, but rather has defined the crimes of the state as equally the crimes of the people."[64] Firm about essence, the Marx group was accommodating about face-saving verbalisms. Marx and his supporters signed two petitions that admitted nothing, the most conciliatory statement going no further than to promise "to insure that the tone of the newspaper [be] moderate and dignified and that every possible offense [be] avoided."[65] The protesting shareholders let themselves be mollified, but the authorities did not.

Marx gratuitously provided more arguments for suppressing the *RZ*. Having allowed Saint-Paul to become friendly with him, he could not resist the seductions of discussing his philosophy with a representative of authority who was also a man of subtle intelligence. For his part, Saint-Paul reported in a letter to his superior on March 2: "Dr. Marx is certainly the master of doctrine here, the living source of the newspaper's theories. I have made his acquaintance; he would die for his principles."[66] A few days later Saint-Paul wrote: "We have had several exhaustive talks. . . . Dr. Marx is just as certain of the correctness of his ideas . . . as it is certain that they are based on a deep philosophical error, which I have made every effort to demonstrate to him on his own theoretical ground." Saint-Paul concluded that right reason could not move Marx.[67] The Prussian government affirmed the stop order.

Marx, refusing to await the inevitable at month's end, resigned on March 17, 1843.[68] On March 21 Saint-Paul wrote, "There is in fact no personage who could maintain the newspaper in its earlier hateful eminence and champion its principles with such energy."[69] Marx had been editor less than a half year. In that short time he had established himself as a remarkably effective member of conventional society but, at the same time, had driven through it and beyond. That society was unbearable, as he explained to a friend: "The atmosphere is getting too oppressive for me. It's hard, doing the job of a lackey, even for the sake of freedom. . . . I got tired of the hypocrisy, the idiocy, and the raw arbitrariness—and of our own bending, bowing and scraping, and hairsplitting."[70] On March 17, 1843, he declared his separation from society as he found it. By that act he was separating himself from progressive associates willing to work within the society they wanted to change. He was also expressing his private being, with its great negatives. With their antimatter, making his person his politics, Marx proposed to construct another world. He had become a revolutionary although he had not defined his revolution or found his fellow revolutionaries.

TWO

THE
REVOLUTIONARY
MATERIALS

THE REVOLUTIONARY MARX BEGAN with three sets of materials: the politics of the French Revolution, the economics of the Industrial Revolution originating in England, and the concepts of the German philosophical revolution.

Growing up as the son of Heinrich Marx in Trier had established young Marx's connection with the French Revolution. Various renewals of French revolutionary thought and action made the connection stronger.

The Revolution of 1830 in France, which took place when Karl Marx was twelve, had made revolution a continuing contemporary process. King Louis Philippe, who succeeded the Restoration monarch, was a liberal whose father had supported the great revolution. Louis Philippe doubled the vote, but from the tiny base of 80,000 electors in a nation of 30 million, and granted more freedom, but kept various restrictions on it. Of course nothing he did could satisfy those who wanted a pure republic. A succession of republican societies made war on his government.[1]

"This was the aim: keep up the momentum of 1830 . . . unceasingly breathe anger and courage into spirits softened by apathy. Everything was set in motion—collections of funds for political prisoners or suppressed newspapers, street-corner speeches, communications with provincial groups," Louis Blanc wrote. "The revolution had its government, its administration, its geographical regions, and its army—in the midst of the legal state."[2] Louis Blanc, republican-and-socialist journalist and historian, was making propaganda for revolution as much as he was describing it. He was accurately pointing to its two components of real revolutionary action and the equally real and important legal activities of the fellow travelers of the period. The legal action included criticism, fair and unfair, by newspapers, the manufacture of sympathy for conspirators at their trials and afterward, demonstrations at the funerals of republican heroes, and operations of such front organizations as the Society for the Defense of the Press. But Louis Blanc was claiming a much more complete structure and greater effectiveness than was the case. Another writer more accurately called the republican movement "a system of permanent agitation."[3]

Revolutionary operations began upon the momentum of the Revolution of 1830. In September 1830 the Society of the Friends of the People called a public meeting in Montmartre, denounced Louis Philippe's government of two months as illegal, and prescribed revolution. Officials calmly ordered the arrest of a few of its leaders and drove it underground. By 1832 it had disintegrated and another organization, the Society of the Rights of Man, tried bravely to do more. On April 13–14, 1834, a few hundred fighting members challenged several thousand soldiers, who swept over their barricades in a working-class section of Paris. The organization was reconstituted before the end of the year as the Society of Families and, in March 1836, was defeated without a battle; police had discovered a gun shop that supplied its arms. It was reformed under a new name, the Society of the Seasons.[4] On May 12, 1839, 300 members captured the Palace of Justice and the City Hall in Paris. Failing to win popular support, they held the first for a few hours and the second for two days. This was the best the republicans could do. Their leaders captured, fragments of the Seasons subsisted in the 1840s under shadowy deputies, one of whom was a police agent.[5] The Revolution of 1848 would show the extent and limits of the accomplishment of the republicans. While their efforts had prepared the nation for it, that revolution, as spontaneous as its predecessor of 1830, took them by surprise and left them behind.

The republicans failed because they represented an idea whose time had come in the past. Losing themselves in a mystique of unceasing violence, they looked back to the idealized image of the revolutionary First Republic of the 1790s. Their ideas, besides frightening the bourgeoisie, lacked sufficient content. A few republicans were beginning to realize that socialism could provide that content.[6] Their longest-enduring leader, Auguste Blanqui (1805–81), however, never understood socialism and went on attempting vain coups d'état on the example of the great French Revolution. He spent thirty-three years in prison.[7]

Socialism had emerged naturally from the first revolution as a demand for social equality as well as political democracy. One of the first socialists was Gracchus Babeuf, a symptom more than an influence, who wanted to socialize the land, distribute food equally, and execute anyone who would resist.[8] He himself was executed for rebellion against the revolutionary government in 1797, and his undeveloped conception flickered out.

The next generation of socialists, the utopians, consciously began to add the Industrial Revolution's social dimension to the revolutionary tradition.[9] But, remembering the Terror and its guillotine, they rejected the idea of revolutionary violence. During the Restoration, Count Henri Saint-Simon (1760–1825) advocated an economic parliament led by industrialists and advised by experts ranging from artists and poets to mathematicians and biologists. Saint-Simon refused to think of his parliament as political in any sense; he trusted it would make decisions on the scientific basis of the self-evident good of the nation. He did not go so far as to advocate common ownership and he rejected the idea of class conflict, but his vision of economic coordination was a long step toward socialism, and some of his followers got closer to it by demanding the end of inheritance of wealth. Other utopians conceived of communes. Charles Fourier (1772–1837) envisioned the phalanstery of 1,700 to 1,800 persons living in cooperation but not equality. The Welshman Robert Owen (1771–1858) founded a commune similar in principle, the parallelogram, in Indiana in 1825. It soon failed. Fourier had not got even that far, although the celebrated Brook Farm in Massachusetts went from transcendentalism to Fourierism in 1845 before disbanding in 1847. In France, again, Etienne Cabet (1788–1856) published a book in 1839 that inspired short-lived colonies in Texas and Illinois. Another book, appearing in France in 1843, took up Fourier's ideas but urged the workers to reject paternalism and organize their own communities.[10] Its effect was lost and the author, Paul Gauguin's remarkable grandmother Flora Tristan, died the next year. All the utopians, believing that the self-evident superiority and equity of their systems would eventually win out, refused to face the question of conflict. "No violence, no revolution. . . . Develop insurance measures against bankruptcies, against unemployment, against poverty," Etienne Cabet told his followers, " . . . and you will arrive at your socialist community."[11]

A minority among the socialists, however, had moved easily enough from republicanism to the idea of revolution. Louis Blanc (1811–82), writing a history glorifying the great revolution, was also advocating workshops run by workers and supported by credit granted by a sympathetic government. Pierre-Joseph Proudhon (1809–65) was more important and fundamentally more revolutionary. Marx, who mentioned him respectfully in the *Rheinische Zeitung*, liked his pamphlet, published in 1840, which asked in its title, "*What Is Property?*" and replied in the text: "Theft."[12] Proudhon advocated mutualism, a combination of socialism and anarchism to be achieved by associations of producers, that is to say, workers. The government, while exercising no authority over the associations, would provide them with unlimited free credit. Angry and judgmental, Proudhon believed in class conflict but, functioning purely as writer, had no organizational following.[13] During the reign of Louis Philippe the sum of socialist rebelliousness was words, capable of much but not of revolution: the republicans had failed and the socialists never tried.

Marx became aware of the Industrial Revolution darkly, laboriously. The full title of Marx's newspaper had been *Rhine Gazette for Politics, Commerce, and Industry*[14] and defined it as a capitalistic agent of the Industrial Revolution. Marx, however, had no sense of that, and his articles ignored commerce and industry. He had, in fact, approached economic issues, thus the situation of the Moselle winegrowing peasants, but only when they gave him another reason for attacking the Prussian government as unjust. Presently, however, he would begin, somewhat like Saint-Simon, to see the Industrial Revolution for itself and as an event paired with the French Revolution.

Revolution had to do with power, and the Industrial Revolution manufactured the purest form of power in acceleratingly larger and larger multiples. The power came into existence first in the simple form of steam power. In 1760, when the Industrial Revolution began, England's steam engines produced a few hundred horsepower; a century later they developed the power equivalent to that of 6 million horses or 40 million men.[15] From 1760 to 1840, with British industry in its great period, production had multiplied twenty times; it doubled in the next twenty years.[16] The cotton mill generated much of the early progress as production improvements in weaving and spinning followed the introduction of steam power. In 1860 there were 2,000 mills with 300,000 power looms, 21.5 million spindles, and 500,000 operatives in Lancashire and Cheshire.[17] (In 1860 Marx's friend, Friedrich Engels, was a profit-sharing executive in the business office of one of the Lancashire spinning mills.)[18] Associated with this, as we know, were coal and iron production, steel refining, steam-powered transportation on sea and land, and the proliferation of new products from the slide rule to the steam hammer. The agricultural revolution should not be forgotten, nor the demographic revolution. World population went from 700 million in 1750 to 1.1 billion by 1850, while the Industrial Revolution found a use for the greater numbers in the factories. The old artisanal class had defended its interests by actions that included the destruction of machines. The new social group, the industrial proletariat, passively endured infernal factories and noisome slums while manufacturing wealth and power for others.

The philosophical revolution in Germany had dangerously assimilated the effects of the French Revolution. In 1807, after Napoleon's victory over the Prussians at Jena, Hegel's *Phenomenology of Mind*, a culminating statement of the German response, celebrated the period as a "birth time" and a "widespread revolution in manifold forms of spiritual culture."[19] It is one of the greatest contradictions in Hegel's contradictory thought that the book and his other writings tried to contain these effects peaceably. In his lifetime Hegel (1770–1831) succeeded.

The *Phenomenology of Mind* demands direct study because it was important to German thought generally and to Karl Marx's thought in particular. In it, Hegel pursued the World Spirit, the only reality, *realizing* itself through division and synthesis—dialectically. The beginning was the stage where knowing was "free from conceptual comprehension," like a child's sensual grasp of things. The next stage swung over into the opposite when the subject began to understand himself. The result was a "freedom of thought [which] takes only pure thought as its truth, and thus lacks the concrete filling of life."[20] A number of other stages follow until the Enlightenment, when, with politics added to philosophy, reason becomes universal and "finds its complete reality in fulfillment of the life of a nation."[21] But the dialectic operates again, and reality divides into a materialistic self-alienated world, and another raised to "the ether of pure consciousness."[22] This could mean the divisiveness arising out of the French Revolution. God repairs the break, but He represents only the penultimate stage of the World Spirit's progress. At this point God fails. "The spirit manifested in revealed religion has not yet surmounted its attitude of consciousness as such."[23] The World Spirit rises further. "The last embodiment of spirit—spirit which at once gives its complete and true content the form of self . . . this is Absolute Knowledge. It is spirit knowing itself in the shape of spirit."[24]

For Hegel, all reality was in a constant, dialectical cycle of dividing and unifying, always transcending itself. Divided, reality was thesis and antithesis striving against each other; united, it became synthesis as conflict was resolved. Everything implied its opposite: conflict and peace, beginning and end, unity and division, truth and falsity, matter and spirit.

It could encourage a political revolutionary to think that the solidity of established society was only an alternate aspect of its evanescent character.

The Industrial Revolution meant enormous but always measurable and finite power, but the dialectic promised infinite power. According to Hegel, "This is the process which consciousness executes on itself . . . in the sense that out of it a new and true object arises."[25] Consciousness, using the dialectic, could change an object upon which it had directed itself—could create reality. Hegel implied this also when he found religion inadequate at a point short of the ultimate. God's failure was due to the fact that the "actual self-consciousness" of the "spirit manifested in revealed religion . . . is not at this stage the object it is aware of."[26] Hegel's aim, thus, was to fuse thought and object of thought into a unity. Thinking about a billiard ball should move to the point where thought and ball become one. "This is Absolute Knowledge."[27] Herbert Marcuse, so much clearer than Hegel, reexpressed Hegel's ideas in a way that made their claims unmistakable. In his *Reason and Revolution*, Marcuse explained, "Reason could lead beyond the brute fact of what is, to the realization of what ought to be."[28] The "ought" becomes as real as the "is" because it *must* be *realizable*. The "ought," furthermore, gives an active aspect to the effort to understand reality. The thinker must do more than passively experience objects and report on what he experiences. His thought must deny the "brute fact" and go on to produce a better fact.

In bringing the "ought" into the dialectic, Hegel and Marcuse (and, between the two, Marx) compounded a powerful judgmental element into it. The dialectic's action was necessary and therefore absolutely moral. To resist it was absolutely immoral. The master of the dialectic had the right to compel and punish.

The World Spirit,[29] overrunning God in its dialectical movement, had eliminated religion as a serious matter for many thoughtful Germans: Hegel's effect upon religion was to be as revolutionary as it would be on the government. In fact, since the church lacked the state's repressive power, religion came under attack first.

Upon Hegel's death the Young Hegelians, splitting off from the peaceable Right and Center Hegelians, began to apply his ideas aggressively. The way for Bruno Bauer's atheism was prepared by David Friedrich Strauss, whose *Life of Jesus* (1835–36) denied the historicity of the Gospels and supernatural acts, and by Ludwig Feuerbach, who doubted that spirit was the beginning of all. Others began to examine government. In

1838 the obscure Young Hegelian August von Cieszkowski published a book vaguely advocating political action as a way of realizing the Hegelian idea. "We must not be afraid to say it, philosophy will begin to be applied from now on." He explained, still vaguely, "Consciousness now feels the justification to express itself in real deeds."[30] This was put more concretely by Arnold Ruge, who had spent six years in prison for revolutionary conspiracy but had later become editor of the scholarly journal *Hallische Jahrbücher*. In 1840 he began to publish articles bitterly critical of the political order. He explained, "The development is no longer abstract; the age has become political."[31] In 1841 Ruge moved the *Jahrbücher* to Dresden, in Saxony, to escape the Prussian censor. He did not move it far enough. In early January 1843, under pressure from Prussia, the Saxon government suppressed Ruge's journal. Three weeks later the *Rheinische Zeitung* got its stop order. This common experience of the censorship brought Ruge and Marx together in a joint assault on authority. They were leaders in a movement which one expert observer found seriously threatening. In mid-1843, writing from Frankfurt, an informant of the French foreign minister described a Young Hegelian journal, published in Swiss freedom, as written *"dans l'idiome barbare des terroristes."* He concluded, "All Germany is like a house invaded by a rain of sparks."[32] He was exaggerating, but not by much.

When Marx had resigned from the *Rheinische Zeitung*, he already had before him the seductive prospect of a field of operations situated in freedom. In January 1843, nearly two months earlier, he had written to Arnold Ruge to tell him of the *RZ*'s impending suppression.[33] Ruge immediately responded by offering Marx the coeditorship of his *Jahrbücher*, which he planned to revive in a more hospitable locale.[34] As publisher Ruge brought in a third man, Julius Fröbel, a German professor of mineralogy who was publishing the inflammatory Swiss journal deplored by the informant of the French foreign minister. Ruge and Fröbel, both men of some resources, invested money; Marx, contributing his talents, was promised a substantial salary and royalites.[35] Ruge had at first planned to move the *Jahrbücher* to Fröbel's location in Zurich, but Switzerland was showing itself unfriendly to such journals. Ruge would soon decide on Paris.

Marx, with his professional future in the process of being assured, wrote to Ruge four days after he had resigned from the *RZ*: "As soon as we have signed the contract I intend to . . . marry and spend a month or two at my bride's mother's place, since [the *Jahrbücher*] . . . must have some articles ready. . . . I can assure you that I am head-over-heels in love and in dead earnest about it." [36] He had fitted work and love firmly together, as he would for the rest of his life with Jenny von Westphalen. Already twenty-nine years old, Jenny had waited very nearly seven years for him to find the moment appropriate to his needs and ambitions. While she had passively accepted his determinations in principle, she had made pressing demands in the form of recriminations, long silences, and suggestions of suicide. Karl, himself neglecting to write out of distractedness, could also attack on her level, and he once took the initiative to quarrel jealously over her fondness for her brother. [37] But the bond between them had become stronger from year to year. On June 19, 1843, they were married.

Returned from their wedding trip, the couple stayed with Jenny's mother in her temporary residence in Kreuznach, not far from Trier, and Marx read and wrote ferociously though the summer. Marx's readings centered on Hegel and the French Revolution. [38] He would presently undertake the research for a history of the Convention, the governing body during the revolution's most radical period. In Kreuznach, he did not pursue French radicals to the extent of studying the socialists among them, probably because he had already made up his mind about them and felt they had nothing more to teach him. As for Hegel, taking extremely detailed notes, Marx read his *Philosophy of Right*, which dealt explicitly with political and social issues. These notes were a quarry for two articles, excellent specimens of Hegelian dialectics, to be published in the new journal. They were first sightings of capitalism and socialism, but as components of a moral problem. He was still ignorant of economics and only vaguely aware of the Industrial Revolution as a meaningful phenomenon. During his summer in Kreuznach, unaware quite of what he was doing, he had begun the process of fusing political, economic, and philosophical revolution.

THREE

MARX IN PARIS:
THE PRACTICE AND
THEORY
OF REVOLUTION

MARX WENT TO PARIS TO LEARN revolution. He had revolution in mind as early as March 1843, immediately after he had left the *Rheinische Zeitung*. He had then written his new associate, Arnold Ruge, that Germany was like a ship being driven toward its fate. He specified, "That fate is the revolution awaiting us."[1] Ruge later said that his own interest "in the political and social movement unconsciously" brought him to Paris.[2] By "political and social movement" he meant revolution, although, as it turned out, not Marx's kind.

Nothing Marx ever wrote showed the slightest response to the city's wealth of culture and its marvelous entertainments. He was interested only in revolutionary materials. He lunged at them clumsily, his experiences in Paris composing themselves into anticipations proven unreal and absurd. France, for her part, received Marx nonchalantly and as nonchalantly sent him on his way. But he got what he wanted from her.

Marx spent his time in Paris—from mid-October 1843 to February 3, 1845—alternating between practicing and thinking revolution. As for the thinking, it went into two articles for the *Deutsch-Französische Jahrbücher*, the journal he would publish with Ruge; it addressed itself to the study of economics and discovered the powerful conception of materialism, and it expressed itself in the writing of the famous *Economic-Philosophical Manuscripts of 1844* and his first book, *The Holy Family*. Meanwhile, he established an active presence in the revolutionary capital of Europe.

PRACTICE

Louis Philippe's government, having been established by revolution, had to exercise a certain tolerance of the idea itself, even though its life was

thereby threatened daily. Fortunately for it, the republican revolutionaries had outrun public opinion in their failed uprising of 1839. Still,
republican newspapers like *Le National* and *La Réforme* were permitted
to keep up another, more dangerous form of attack. *La Réforme*, founded
two months before Marx arrived in Paris, looked beyond republicanism
toward a suggestion of socialism, its *Programme du journal* promising a
"discussion approfondie sur les principes vrais et naturels d'organisation
sociale."[3] For Marx Paris was a locale of friendly theory.

The French government extended its tolerance to cover foreign revolutionaries. France pullulated with Germans, Poles, Spaniards, Italians,
Russians, and others plotting to imitate her revolutionary example at
home. In 1840, one estimate put the number of political émigrés in the
whole country at 18,000 to 20,000, with 12,000 in Paris. This hospitality
mollified the liberal opposition, which was always ready to accuse the
government of betraying the generous principles of the great French
Revolution. Mollifying their home governments, Louis Philippe's officials kept a careful watch over these foreign revolutionaries and reduced
their desperation with pensions—9,000 in 1841.[4] During this time revolution was a lively and paying international enterprise.

Besides the revolutionaries, a substantial colony of 15,000 to 20,000
Germans inhabited Paris. Most of them were artisans without political
concerns who were tracing out a classic life pattern. The city was an
attractive stopover during their *Wanderjahre*, when they developed new
skills in foreign parts. They were all the more encouraged to come because France was prosperous while Germany was comparatively poor
and overpopulated;[5] most of the street cleaners in Paris were German.[6]
Among the artisans, to adapt a metaphor of Mao Tse-tung's, swam a
few revolutionaries like fish in a pond. The nonpolitical workers, learning to appreciate France's liberal institutions, were at least sympathetic
to the revolutionaries and open to their persuasions; both groups were
thrown together in the same lodgings, cafés, and German clubs. It was
an ideal situation for the growth of a revolutionary movement, since the
innocent clubs could serve as front organizations, while their members
could provide a continuously renewed stock of proselytes.

The history of German radicalism in France went back to 1834, when
some members burst out of the patriotic and middle-class German Peoples
Club (*Deutscher Volksverein*) of Paris and organized the League of the
Outcasts (*Bund der Geächteten*). They began to enroll artisans and established an uncertain relationship with the republican revolutionary societies.[7] Apprentices in revolution, the Germans of the League of the Out-

casts advanced beyond their French associates at one point. By the mid-1830s the league began to adopt communist ideas. Karl Schapper, a former forestry student, built a following among its more radical artisans and organized them as the League of the Just (*Bund der Gerechten*) in 1837, leaving behind an enfeebled League of Outcasts. The Seasons' abortive rising of 1839 threw both German groups into disarray. Schapper was arrested and held for a few months. He then made his way to London, which was becoming a more important German center than Paris. In 1840 he founded the German Workers' Educational Society of London, which was just what its name said, an organization for innocent educational and recreational activities. But it was also a front for a revived League of the Just. In Paris German revolutionary activity remained quiescent during the 1840s.

In Paris the Marx residence was located at the center of a number of geographical, social, political, and theoretical contradictions. Marx and his bride lived in the rue Vaneau, which had been named for a student rebel killed in the Revolution of 1830, but was in a section of the Left Bank inhabited by aristocrats and well-to-do bourgeois. It was near the even more aristocratic Faubourg St. Germain and a few hundred meters from the Palais Bourbon, seat of the Chamber of Deputies. Arnold Ruge, preparing the way for the *Deutsch-Französische Jahrbücher*, had found the rue Vaneau. Adapting the communal conceptions of utopian socialism, he proposed to organize, as he put it, "a *ménage*—a bit of communism," with three or four families and one kitchen.[8] The wife of the radical poet Georg Herwegh, another associate, anticipated the problems and persuaded Herwegh to settle elsewhere. Within two weeks the wives of Marx and Ruge were quarreling, and Karl and Jenny Marx moved to rooms a few doors away, still on the rue Vaneau. By then, however, Marx had made the acquaintance of the poetaster Germain Mäurer, who was a fellow resident in Ruge's ménage. Mäurer was connected with the German revolutionaries.

Like most foreigners, Marx remained caught in the surface tension of Paris. He did not make one French friend. Arnold Ruge had, in fact, counted upon finding friends and cooperation for the *Jahrbücher*. This, besides French freedom, was why he had decided to locate the journal in Paris, as he wrote his wife in August 1843. Ruge had visited the offices of *Démocratie Pacifique*, the Fourierist newspaper, "a salon where you can meet people in a free and pleasant way," and whose editor, Victor Considérant, expressed good will to Germany.[9] In a pleasant way Ruge met the poet Alphonse de Lamartine who was also an historian of the great

French Revolution and a future revolutionary foreign minister, the utopians Flora Tristan and Etienne Cabet, the socialist-minded editor and
former Saint-Simonian Pierre Leroux, the communist writer Théodore
Dézamy, the Catholic socialist Abbé Robert de Lamennais, and Louis
Blanc, the radical journalist and historian.[10] Louis Blanc promised an
article for the *Jahrbücher*, but it later appeared in a French journal, and the
atheists Ruge and Marx would have found it unacceptable since it was
an attack on atheism.[11] Lamennais had sounded a realistic note, telling
Ruge straightly, "You won't get what you want here."[12]

After the first courtesies, Ruge saw that Lamennais had been right.
"France is the whole world to the French."[13] Louis Blanc was not the
only disappointment. As Lamennais might have predicted, not one French
contribution appeared in the *Jahrbücher*. In the salon world of Paris, Marx,
like Ruge, continued at least to enjoy light contacts with French radicals.
He probably was in the home of Countess Marie d'Agoult, sympathetic
to radicals and briefly the mistress of his friend Herwegh. On March 23,
1844, Marx attended a banquet of French and foreign radicals at which
Louis Blanc and Pierre Leroux were present,[14] but it was another of those
empty demonstrations substituting for real relations. Marx did meet the
revolution-minded Proudhon, but then Proudhon, while intransigent and
important, was a theorist and not an activist. He did not improve upon
acquaintance, particularly since Marx was beginning to see a rival in him.
(When Proudhon died in 1865, Marx, asserting his primacy, remembered cruelly in an obituary article, "I infected him with Hegelianism to
his great injury in the course of long debates that often lasted through
the night."[15] Proudhon, for his part, did not take note of Marx in his
diary, although he mentioned Marx's friends.)[16] In May 1844 Ruge complained, "Foreigners find themselves isolated here."[17]

Marx had no contact, or virtually none, with the real masters of revolution, the republican revolutionaries. In a recollection in 1860, he claimed
to have known the leaders, as he put it, of "most of the French secret
workers' societies." Auguste Blanqui, first among the republican leaders,
however, was imprisoned at the time, while the others were also in prison
or exiled. The police agent who was then active as a second-rank surrogate in the leadership did not mention Marx in the book he wrote about
the republican movement.[18] Furthermore, no republican organization could
properly be called a *workers'* society. Although it used some workers as
foot soldiers of the revolution, the republican movement was as petit
bourgeois in character as its leader Blanqui. In any case, Marx went on

to volunteer the fact that he had not joined any French society.[19] Marx's elaborately unspecific memories suggest an effort to enrich his revolutionary qualifications without committing himself to a disprovable statement. In the event his luck had been precisely bad. He was in Paris at just the wrong time for open revolutionary action, after the failure of the 1839 action, during an anodyne period of prosperity, and before the unexpected Revolution of 1848.

Marx had begun in Paris as an editor bearing the message, only slightly disguised, of international revolution. His *Jahrbücher* failed in general and in detail.[20] Marx must accept the greater responsibility: Arnold Ruge had fallen ill shortly after Marx's arrival in Paris, and Marx, as de facto editor-in-chief, published one issue at the end of February 1844. Besides Marx's two articles, which were important and brilliant, it carried two prophetic articles on economics by Marx's future friend Friedrich Engels, and fine poems by the great lyric poet Heinrich Heine. Its readership, however, was insignificant, and, particularly because of Marx's provocative opinions, the journal managed to alienate those few who saw it among the radical German émigrés in Paris.[21] Ruge and the co-publisher Julius Fröbel, refusing to lose more money, let the *Jahrbücher* perish. The authorities expressly prohibited its sale in Prussia; Marx thereupon smuggled two shipments, one of 214 and one of 100 copies, into the Rhineland, but they were discovered and confiscated.[22] Seeking a nonexistent international brotherhood of nations, Ruge and Marx had lost touch with their own country and contemporaries. This was the defect of the journal's great virtues. It had addressed itself to the future with genial familiarity.

Marx refused to be too much disturbed to find himself in the first of the innumerable financial crises of his life. His salary stopped. He had been paid at the annual rate of at least 550 Prussian thalers (the thaler was worth about 75 cents), a comfortable middle-class income for the time;[23] He expected help and got it. Wealthy friends from Cologne took up a collection and sent him the substantial sum of 1,000 thalers in mid-March.[24] Nevertheless Marx was "struggling as ever against financial embarrassment" and unrealistically trusting that his salary would be continued, Arnold Ruge reported on May 14.[25] A few weeks later one of the Cologne friends sent more money, 800 French francs (the franc was at 20 cents), as his way of making up for what Marx had presumably lost when the *Jahrbücher* shipments were confiscated.[26] (Just before his departure from Paris, moreover, Marx would capture another substantial sum,

1,500 francs as an advance on a book he would never write.) His financial problems alleviated, although far from solved, he could concentrate on his revolutionary concerns.

The *Jahrbücher* and its failure directed Marx toward his real objectives. Trying to be a revolutionary, he had departed Germany of his own free will, with all the rights of Prussian citizenship. The *Jahrbücher* changed that. On March 8 the Prussian minister to Paris noted that the journal had attacked the king of Prussia and that Marx had hinted at violent revolution. Two weeks later a high official evaluated the *Jahrbücher* in Berlin, concluding "the editors' objective is insurrection of ideas as a means to revolution."[27] Marx would have agreed. The Prussian minister of the interior ordered the arrest of Marx, Ruge, and two lesser collaborators if they returned home. By the early spring of 1844 the status of Marx had changed from émigré to exile. He was free to devote himself to the exploitation of the revolutionary materials at hand.

Marx's most important activity in Paris was not editorial or journalistic, although he would go on from the *Jahrbücher* to a newspaper. It was the development of associations with persons and groups. All these relationships had to do with making revolution in one way or another. Even his errors, as in the case of the *Jahrbücher*, spun out new associations leading to his real aims.

Marx found a new center of operations in the newspaper *Vorwärts!* Heinrich Börnstein, an enterprising theater manager, had founded it providentially in the beginning of 1844. Serving the German colony of Paris, *Vorwärts!* had begun as a banal gossipmonger. In mid-May Carl Ludwig Bernays, an émigré journalist like Marx and a contributor to his *Jahrbücher*, displaced the original editor and solicited articles from talented radicals. Besides Marx, they included the Hegelianized Russian revolutionary Mikhail Bakunin, and the poets Heinrich Heine, Georg Herwegh, and Georg Weerth. Börnstein, who was converted to socialism by his writers, proudly recalled in his memoirs, "And now *Vorwärts!* had a constellation of editorial capacities which no other newspaper could very well claim."[28]

The newspaper's editorial conferences became an important stage in the development of revolutionary socialism. Börnstein had granted hospitality to the penniless Bakunin, and the meetings were held in his tiny quarters in the *Vorwärts!* building. Börnstein captured the moment. "There would be a dozen or fourteen people in Bakunin's room, some sitting on the bed or [his] trunk, some standing or shifting about—all the while seriously, excitedly, and passionately smoking and debating." Afraid that the "vehement bellowing" would have drawn a mob, Börnstein dared not open the windows, although the smoke became so thick that the debaters became unrecognizable. Two of the most passionate were Karl Marx and Arnold Ruge. In the haze and noise of ideological battle the "socialist-communist vision showed itself more and more sharply and harshly against the pure humanistic philosophy, and Ruge simply could not come to any kind of understanding with the socialists and communists. Marx brutally criticized Ruge's writings, and Ruge and the more moderate persons began falling away. An out-and-out radicalism came out on top." [29] Now, among his newer friends, Marx had established himself as leader.

This was the moment, in mid-1844, when Marx totally committed his life to making revolution. In the offices of the newspaper, without quite realizing it, Marx had begun to organize a revolutionary party. It did not matter that most of the party's members would quickly fall away. The associations made in the offices of *Vorwärts!* would lead to others, even more appropriate.

Breaking relationships was nearly as important to Marx's operations as making them. Arnold Ruge provided a fine example of someone who had been an enormously useful friend but who would serve as an equally useful enemy. In May 1844, even as he was beginning to debate with Ruge in the offices of *Vorwärts!*, Marx took offense at a critical remark of Ruge's about their friend Georg Herwegh. [30] Ruge sensed that this was only an excuse, but then there was the more serious question of money. Marx felt, as he had told Ruge, that Ruge was obligated to keep the *Jahrbücher* going despite their experience with the first issue. [31] But there was more to it than money. When Marx had objected to Ruge's criticism of Herwegh, he had told Ruge that he "could no longer work with me as I was only conventionally political, while he was a communist." [32] If Ruge had failed to follow him into communism, Ruge must be in a state of moral error—even though he had spent six years in prison for lonely dissent in the 1830s.

Two months after the rupture, Ruge gave Marx an ultimate reason for enmity. Ruge wrote an article in *Vorwärts!* on the famous strike, on June 4–6, of the Silesian weavers, [33] which Gerhart Hauptmann took as the subject of his classic play of 1892. Sympathetic and unhappy, Ruge correctly judged their cause to be hopeless. To Marx, who regarded principle and personality as different expressions of the same essence, the article confirmed Ruge's vileness: this kind of defeatism was betrayal of the heroic weavers. Argumentum ad hominem was the appropriate counter-measure. In *Vorwärts!*, on August 7 and 10, Marx accused his former friend of possessing a capitalist's nature, treating the weavers "with contempt," and (in Marx's italics) indulging in *"literary charlatanry."*[34] Ruge's dishonor was part of Marx's argument. Marx mentioned the "genial writings" of a peripatetic member of the League of the Just, the ladies' tailor and autodidact Wilhelm Weitling. These were "the giant baby shoes of the proletariat," compared with the "dwarflike and worn-out shoes of the German bourgeoisie" as represented by Ruge's writings.[35] Weitling's pamphlets were vaporous with love for humanity and Rousseauist religion, but Marx found him likable for the moment. It took Ruge a few months to realize quite what his former friend was doing to him. He concluded, "Baring his teeth and sneering, Marx would slaughter all those who get in his way—Marx the new Babeuf."[36] Marx had not only disposed of a man who had become useless to him but had pulped and ground him into his revolutionary mortar as the bourgeois enemy.

Marx, meanwhile, could take satisfaction from such new friends as Heinrich Heine. In the poet's person he was granted a valuable opportunity. While enjoying the role of fellow poet, he could experiment in the management of art for political purposes. It was just before the break between Marx and Ruge, and Ruge had actually abetted Marx. The two men proposed to sharpen Heine's poetic expression into political satire. Years later Ruge boasted: "He owes this orientation to Marx and me. We told him, 'Give up your eternal moaning about love and show the satirical poet how to do it—how to use the whip.'"[37] On July 10, 1844, Heine celebrated the rising of the Silesian weavers in *Vorwärts!*: "No tears in their glowering eyes/They sit at the loom and show their teeth!/Germany, we're weaving your shroud,/Into it we're weaving the triple curse—/We weave, we weave!"[38] Earlier, in January, he had written a long poem, his classic *Germany: A Winter's Tale*, begging pathetically for what Marx was demanding angrily: "There's plenty of bread down here/For all the children of men. . . ./The lazy belly better not carouse away/What busy hands have earned."[39] In September, after revising the poem, Heine, on a visit to Hamburg, sent it to Marx, and Marx had it published in one of the last issues of *Vorwärts!* According to the reminiscences of Marx's daughter Eleanor, he gave active advice to Heine on revising one or two of the poems, going over every line carefully.[40] Collaboration with a person as dominant and antilyrical as Marx must have bruised both poetry and poet. Marx soon vanished from Heine's life, and, despite an older sympathy with socialism, Heine firmly rejected the revolution and socialism itself. In his *Confessions*, written in 1853–54, he called Ruge, "his still more obdurate friend Marx," and the other radicals "godless, self-appointed gods." In fact, "our whole civilization, the fruit of the noblest work of our predecessors, is threatened by the victory of communism."[41] With Heine, Marx had set a precedent for communism's use of the artist, but Heine had set the precedent for the artist's resistance.

Another relationship which began in Paris, Marx's friendship with Friedrich Engels, was more central and successful. Establishing that friendship was Marx's most important action in Paris. Without Engels, Marx is not Marx.

Engels, two and one-half years younger than Marx and as precocious, had also been rebelling against his bourgeois origins, also in the Rhineland. Even before Marx himself, Engels had moved from philosophy to socialism. Marx and Engels had already met. In the fall of 1842 Engels visited the offices of the *Rheinische Zeitung*, but he was a member of the Free Men, and Marx received him coolly. The Paris meeting was different. Engels' arrival at the end of August 1844 had been preceded by favorable signs and substance. He had spent twenty-one months in England in a branch of his father's firm as an already dedicated socialist. There he had made contact with Karl Schapper's revolutionary League of the Just and sent the *Rheinische Zeitung* dispatches on the economic crises he had observed. He then submitted his two articles to the *Jahrbücher*; one had discussed English industry, poverty, and proletariat, while the other advanced into theory, suggested by the title, "Outline of a Critique of Political Economy."[42] Marx, beginning with his *Economic-Philosophical Manuscripts*, thoroughly assimilated both into his equipment, praising the second precisely as "a brilliant outline."[43] (This article, Marx neglected to say, had encouraged him to apply himself to economics in Paris, as one can see from what he subsequently wrote.) After a talk in the Café de la Régence, much frequented by the German émigrés, Marx took Engels home with him. (Jenny Marx was away. On May 1 she had given birth to their first child, also named Jenny. In June she had taken the baby, who had been intermittently ill, to the Rhineland, where she would stay with her mother for three months.) In Paris, Marx and Engels talked through ten days, established their complete agreement on principle and action, and defined their relationship for the rest of their lives. Marx was commander-in-chief of the revolution; Engels, executive officer. Engels then moved on to Germany and began to carry out his first revolutionary assignments.

Such relationships were all well and good, primary, even. Nevertheless, Marx needed his popular base. While his ideas were driving ahead

to discover the theory of the proletariat, he was moving to meet its reality, or the closest thing to it, the German artisans of Paris. A proletariat
in the sense of industrial workers—factory workers—was not at hand,
but the radicalized craftsmen of the *Wanderjahre* would do even better.
Marx's association with them, however, was not quite as he drew it.
Claiming an unsubstantiated acquaintance with *French* workingmen, he
wrote to a correspondent on August 8, 1844, "You would have to attend
a meeting of French workers to be able to appreciate the virginal fresh-
ness, the nobility that blooms in these workworn people."[44] In the *Economic-
Philosophical Manuscripts*, written at the time, he described them. "Smoking, drinking, eating, and so on, are no longer there to bind the union
. . . coming together is good enough for them." The workers had taken
"study, propaganda and so on as their first objective."[45] In his next work,
the book composed later in 1844, Marx redrew the image. "You have to
get acquainted with the study, the thirst for knowledge, the moral energy, the drive for self-improvement of the French and English workers—to get an idea of the noble humanity of the movement."[46] He had
never seen English workers. In any case these are hardly descriptions of
real workers, or human beings, for that matter. Marx had absorbed his
artisans into his fantasy. He did more. The workers who had rejected
facile pleasures for self-improvement and propaganda were following
the orders of a revolutionary leader. Seeing himself as that leader, Marx
was writing not to inform but to command.

The reality of Marx's experience of workers in Paris was scant and
ambiguous. He arrived at his goal by way of Germain Mäurer, the chance
member of Ruge's short-lived ménage of the rue Vaneau. Mäurer was in
contact with two fragments of the old revolutionary artisanal groups,
fifty members of the League of the Just, and perhaps twenty claiming
membership in the League of the Outcasts. A friend of Mäurer's, the
former doctor and struggling writer Hermann Ewerbeck, gave both groups
what little leadership they could tolerate. An attempt to unify them had
failed in 1840.[47] In July 1844 Ruge, observing Marx from the distance,
wrote, "Marx has dived into the local communism." Ruge wondered,
"He can't take those wretched doings seriously."[48]

Marx applied his imagination and will to these unpromising materials.
On February 1, 1845, two days before he left Paris, a police agent reported having seen Marx and his friends, including the publisher Börnstein and the poet Herwegh, at meetings of "sometimes thirty, often one
hundred to two hundred Germans." The meetings took place in a wine
shop in the workingclass quarter near the Porte de Vincennes, at the

eastern extremity of Paris, where many of the artisans lived. As the agent saw it, Marx and his friends were "intriguers [who] take advantage of the poor German artisans, and also young business-people and clerks, to seduce them into communism." The speakers, whom he did not identify, "made speeches in which they openly advocated regicide, the abolition of all private property, the elimination of the wealthy classes and religion."[49] Marx had found his revolutionary army, and, impatiently, was beginning to give his orders.

The leader may not have uttered a word, and the army was a small, shifting mass of the malcontent, the indifferent, and the uncomprehending. The group included commercial employees who would one day become business executives and capitalists, and the workers were craftsmen organized in guilds that operated in the spirit of medieval economics.[50] The fact that Marx was able to work with such associations begins to suggest the quality of his genius.

Unconstrained by the mediocrity of his physical situation, Marx's mind, meanwhile, had made blazing progress. In Paris he sketched in the main elements of his world-historical view.

THEORY

Seeking his revolution in Paris, Marx had brought with him, as shaped by a summer of readings and ruminations in Germany, a lopsided but considerably developed conception of it. Although he had much to learn, the student understood the subject better than his French masters.

Marx had found inspiring suggestions in French history, but his most important instruction came from Hegel. The *Phenomenology of Mind* had given Marx his world view; Hegel's *Philosophy of Right* now provided the narrower, more purposeful social-political focus. Marx, showing easy command of a philosopher's technical skills, wrote "The Critique of Hegel's *Philosophy of Right*," as editors have entitled it, a commentary on the second work that filled 130 closely printed pages.[51] Concentrating on politics, he examined the last part of the *Philosophy of Right*, which discussed the state. He was still a Hegelian—he would remain one all his life—but he struggled against Hegel as he used him. Marx got ideological support from the Young Hegelian philosopher Ludwig Feuerbach, who was enjoying a brief renown at the time. Marx found particularly apropos an article of Feuerbach's which Arnold Ruge had published in the collection of like-minded work, *Anekdota*, appearing in February 1843.

Feuerbach, developing the Young Hegelian variant, argued that Hegel had made the mistake of beginning with thought and then proceeding to being; it was necessary to reverse the direction.[52] Early in his commentary, Marx seized upon Feuerbach's revision: "It is significant that Hegel makes the idea the subject everywhere and the real subject itself . . . the predicate." The result was that the "real subjects . . . become empty *names*, so that you get only the appearance of true perception."[53] Building upon Feuerbach, Marx devoted several pages to establishing his own philosophical position in detail.[54] In this way he drove closer to his own "real subjects," the political and revolutionary realities.

Marx nevertheless used the Hegelian political materials, abstract as they were, as he found them. Hegel, drawing upon Adam Smith and Rousseau, conceived of the state mediating the conflicts arising among competitive private interests in "civil society." This took place under a monarch and by way of a professional bureaucracy, the state defending the general interest because of its "more elevated point of view."[55] Marx objected here, but he did not inquire just how a specific government functioned. Instead, operating on Hegel's ground, he used hostile abstractions to attack abstract ruler and his equally abstract agents. Marx had already dismissed the monarch: "Monarchy is only form, and a bad one at that. Democracy is substance and form."[56] As for the bureaucrats: "The spirit of the bureaucracy is the 'formal spirit of the state.' . . . Since the bureaucracy transforms its 'formal' purposes into its content, it hurls itself everywhere into conflict with its 'real' purposes."[57] Particularly concerned to contest its impartiality, Marx returned repeatedly to the bureaucracy. He aided his argument with the ad hominem: bureaucrats were "*Staatsjesuiten und Staatstheologen*," who were using the state's purposes to serve their private interests.[58] With better logic, Marx questioned the capacity of "a special class to dedicate itself to the universal class." The bureaucracy, this "special class," simply would not do. The imperative, he concluded, was the "capacity of the universal class to be really universal."[59] Marx then wound through several pages of abstractions, dealing chiefly with the legislative function, before attempting to identify the "universal class" further. He approached it by way of another, unnecessary and clumsy abstraction. "The characteristic aspect [of contemporary civil society] is simply this: *propertylessness* and the *class dependent* on working, on concrete work, do not so much form a class of civil society as they serve as the basis on which society's elements rest and move."[60] Behind "propertyless*ness*" was the vision of a class that could be more than a class. This meant revolution. Marx had moved beyond Hegel.

After raising up the class of the propertyless, Marx attacked the principle of private property. Insensibly, thus, he had shifted from the essentially political considerations of an examination of the state to social and explicitly economic issues.

Marx dealt with private property carelessly but absolutely.[61] He began with primogeniture because Hegel happened to begin with it. "*Primogeniture, the superlative of private property*," dehumanized human relations; the state demeaned itself by protecting it. Then there was "the *raw stupidity* of unentailed private property."[62] Beyond that, Marx made no effort to develop an argument against the idea of private property; he simply treated it as a self-evident evil. The state had already been condemned for failing on its own political terms. Now it stood doubly condemned for its relation to property. In fact: "What power does the political state have over private property? *The power of private property itself*—its being brought into existence. What is left for the political state independent of this being? *The illusion* that it is the determining agency when it is actually being determined."[63] The state had disappeared into the exponentially expanding mass of private property, the fundamental evil of society. Marx had transformed politics into economics by making the state vanish. This was his political method.

A few pages later, close to the end of his commentary, Marx rushed into the future in the first of a number of his suddenly ignited, far-traveling anticipations. Unembarrassed by his inconsistency, he restored explicitly political considerations and returned to the theme of representative government. "It is only in *unlimited* suffrage . . . that civil society *actually* rises to an abstraction of itself, to *political* existence as its true, universal, and essential existence." Marx moved on swiftly. "But the realization of this abstraction is the transcendence of the abstraction at the same time. By making its *political* existence as real as its *true* existence, civil society also makes its civil existence *inessential* in contrast to its political existence; and with the one element removed, the other—its opposite—falls away." Thus, with the Hegelian dialectic, Marx had arrived at the goal which he would spend the rest of his life straining to reach. "Thus, within the *abstract political state, the reform of voting* means the demand for the state's *dissolution*—and similarly for the *dissolution of civil society*."[64] The state vanished again, now as absolutely as had private property, the essence of civil society. This was as far as humanity could go: socialist anarchy.

Marx's other readings in Germany, approaching revolutionary politics through history, gave harder point to his ideas.[65] He studied the papers of Robespierre and a history of the French Revolution by a German scholar, and once again discovered a class bearing revolution with it. Robespierre and his Jacobins had sought, and for a while achieved, "power for the poor, the *sans-culottes*, because they made up the majority on earth." Marx adjusted history to suit his policy, including economic policy; Robespierre had demanded "true equality, that is equality of possessions." Marx also found an enemy against whom all measures could justifiably be taken; he warmly approved "arming the *sans-culottes* against the bourgeoisie, from whom all the internal dangers come." Other works he had read were a miscellany that might fall under the eyes of any intellectually curious European of the time. One was Machiavelli's commentary on Livy, but out of it Marx seized for his last note, "'United, the people is brave; divided, it is weak.'"[66] All his thoughts converged on revolution.

From March to September 1843, meanwhile, Marx had been articulating the objectives of the *Deutsch-Französische Jahrbücher*. He did it in the form of letters to Arnold Ruge which were published in the journal as a programmatic statement. Marx proposed that the *Jahrbücher* unite French revolutionary experience, French socialism, and German philosophy.[67] The German homeland had to be saved from itself. Marx began with contempt. "Germany has plunged headfirst into the muck and will only dig its way deeper into it."[68] Beyond Germany there was the world itself. Marx introduced his ultimate objective by deprecating it. "If the construction of the future . . . is not our affair . . . "[69] Construction of the future, however, required a great deal of destruction, but Marx felt as great an affinity for it. "What we have to accomplish at present is . . . *the ruthless criticism of everything existing*, ruthless in the sense that the criticism must not be afraid of the results it produces and must even less be afraid of the struggle with the powers that be." He would not stop at words. "Philosophy has made itself worldly . . . the philosophical consciousness has been drawn . . . into the agony of battle."[70]

Violent with genius, Marx's two articles carried him a long way. Both drawn from his commentary on Hegel, "The Critique of Hegel's *Philosophy of Right*," they were closely related to each other despite their misleading titles. They were "On the Jewish Question," begun in Germany and completed in Paris, and, immediately following, "A Contribution to the Critique of Hegel's *Philosophy of Right*: Introduction"[71] (this latter not to be confused with his commentary on Hegel).

Parts of the first article might have been reprinted without change in a Nazi publication. "What is the earthly foundation of Jewry?" Marx asked and replied: "Practical need, self-interest." He played with the conception: "What is the worldly religion of the Jew? *Petty trading*. What is his

worldly God? Money." He concluded, "We recognize in Jewry a generalized *contemporary anti-social* element." Two pages later he repeated: "What
was the real basis of the Jewish religion? Practical need, self-interest. . . .
Money is the jealous God of Israel."[72] Yet in a sense a lawyer would
appreciate, those who excuse Marx are correct:[73] it was not an anti-Semitic
exercise. Thus, after his characterization of the Jews, Marx drew another
conclusion: "Emancipation from *petty trading* and from *money*, that is to
say from practical, real Jewry, would be the self-emancipation of our
era." He explained: "The God of the Jews has secularized himself, has
become God of the world . . . Jewry reaches its heights with the completion of bourgeois society."[74] "Jewry" became another word for capitalism, Marx's real subject. With this identity, which the absolutist Marx
made absolute, his logic had simply annihilated the humanity, in fact the
existence, of the Jews. With nothing left for anti-Semitism to attack, his
anti-Semitism had transcended itself. "On the Jewish Question" had logically eliminated the Jewish question.

More remains to be said about Marx's anti-Semitism, but we note that
in his ruthlessness he had discussed the Jews in the article as if they were
a race strange to him. Turning against himself as well, Marx had simultaneously denied his own existence.

Marx's starting point had been two articles by Bruno Bauer, his old
university friend, on the question of Jewish emancipation. Bauer, not
unsympathetic to the Jews, had argued that Christians as well as Jews
were repressed in contemporary German society. The objective, he said,
was emancipation for all, not only Jews; this would come only with the
disappearance of all religion. In "On the Jewish Question," Marx objected, criticizing Bauer mildly and impersonally, if firmly. Marx's thought
was running in the same direction, but he wanted to go further. Not
only should religion be eliminated, but, he hinted, the state as well. He
repeated a thought from his commentary on Hegel, "We humanize . . .
the view [that sees a] contradiction between state and religion in general
by means of [the view of] the contradiction between the state and its
premises in general."[75]

"On the Jewish Question," identifying the Jew-capitalist as the antithesis in a new dialectic, had been on the negative side of the Hegelian
equation. Like Hegel, Marx was a master, as Herbert Marcuse has said,
of "the negative character of reality."[76] The second *Jahrbücher* article,
the explicit analysis of Hegel's *Philosophy of Right*, developed the positive side.

The two articles would have been more correctly entitled "The (Jew)

Capitalist" and "The Proletariat." The first looked back to the French Revolution and then swept forward, almost to the creation of the proletariat. In one powerful sentence Marx revived the unfulfilled promise of that revolution. "The state can and must proceed to the *elimination of religion*, to the *annihilation of religion*—in the same way it proceeds to the elimination of private property, to the [Law of the] Maximum, to confiscating property, to the progressive income tax—as it moves on to the elimination of life—to the *guillotine*." The great revolution had been a failed promise; the synthesis at that point in history had reestablished religion and fixed a new dominant class, the bourgeoisie, in place. Victory had turned into defeat.

In another of his early flashes of anticipation Marx saw ahead: the political process must "declare the revolution *permanent*."[77] With its wonder-working ambiguity, the conception "permanent revolution" had begun life, and Marx and many other men, Leon Trotsky among them, would make varied use of it. The capitalist-proletariat dialectic would continue its work, this time to the end, as Marx had conceived. In the second article Marx explained how.

The proletariat would supersede the capitalist class. It would be the "universal class" which both the bureaucracy and the bourgeoisie had failed to be, the class that would mean the end of all classes. It was the only one "which could hurl at its enemy the defiant battle cry: '*I am nothing and I am to be everything*.'" Marx conceived his proletariat: "For the *revolution of a people* and the emancipation of a *particular class* of civil society to coincide, for *one* estate to represent the estate of the whole of society, another class must concentrate in itself all the failures of society, a particular estate must be the estate of general humiliation, the incorporation of the general enslavement. A particular social sphere must stand for the *notorious crime* of the whole society—so that emancipation from this particular sphere shows itself to be the act of general emancipation." Marx celebrated its triumph: "When the proletariat announces the *dissolution of the existing world order*, it simply announces the *secret of its own existence*, because it is the *effective* dissolution of this order."[78]

Of course the proletariat was perfectly the least-who-would-be-first of the Judeo-Christian imagination. All of Marx's thought rested on a thick, dark religious substratum and raised itself upon stages of religious logic. His atheism was an integral component of his faith. As punishingly moral as Jeremiah, as authoritative as Christ, he was the last of the Hebrew prophets.

Expanding upon a theme from one of the programmatic letters, Marx looked back at his own country and found it a proletarian among nations. He began with hostility; he would have a "*declaration of war* on the German state of affairs. *By all means!*" He proceeded to contempt. "This state of affairs is *beneath the level of history*; it is *beneath all criticism*, but it is still an object of criticism, as the criminal who stands beneath the level of humanity remains an object of the *executioner*." The identification of Germany with the proletariat, however, raised her out of her moral wretchedness and punishable guilt. Marx stopped short in the midst of denunciation. "They begin to commence in Germany what they begin to complete in France and England." Insinuatingly, he asked, "Can Germany arrive at any action *à la hauteur des principes*, that is to say, a revolution that will raise it not only to the formal level of modern nations, but to the *human level?*" [79]

Marx's elevation of Germany expressed a drive of such force and purity in him that he was doubtless unconscious of it, the drive for primacy—the need for it. He was a leader; he had to make himself first. He would have to make Germany first with him. Primacy would explain much of his important action and thought throughout his life. It would explain his quarrels with Ruge and others, and his method of correcting and patronizing a thinker, Hegel most prominently, as he appropriated the man's ideas. Yet Marx was too statesmanlike to attempt too much, and, representing Germany, accepted less than parity with France for the moment. "When all the concrete conditions are fulfilled, the *German day of resurrection* will be signaled by the *crowing of the Gallic rooster*." [80]

The failure of the *Jahrbücher* early in 1844 gave Marx the time to study economics, the one important deficiency in his education. In May Arnold Ruge reported on him to the philosopher Ludwig Feuerbach. "He works with extraordinary intensity. He has a fresh talent, which lets itself go for the moment in an arrogant dialectic that tries to explain too much. But he finishes nothing. He breaks off again and again, and dives once again into a shoreless sea of books." [81] Ruge was intelligent enough to appreciate Marx's great ability but too reasonable to recognize his genius and its method.

In his readings Marx moved swiftly from the politics of the French Revolution to the economics of the contemporary world. For a few weeks he planned to write a history of Robespierre's government, but his passion, as was already evident, was too much engaged in the present and in more than politics. In July Ruge said that Marx had apparently given up the history project, although he "had done a tremendous amount of reading." (He had spoken so convincingly of it that an informant said he was still working on it in Brussels almost two years later. The informant, obviously well acquainted with him, told the prefect of police of Paris more accurately that Marx's conception of the revolution was "*sous le point de vue social.*")[82] Marx's surviving notebooks contain notes on just one book about the revolution compared with fifteen on economics, printed on 16 as against 147 pages in the first Marx-Engels edition. By this time Arnold Ruge was experiencing the effects of these readings in the debates at *Vorwärts!*

In his last glance at the French Revolution Marx sought out its economic essence. Again, as in his readings in Germany, he sided with Robespierre's Jacobins against the Girondins. He condemned the latter for confining their concerns to "violations of the laws of private property and threats to its existence," thus for defending the selfish interests of the bourgeoisie.[83] He did not, however, forget his politics for a moment. He found that the Girondins were as incompetent politically as they were reprehensible in matters economic. They "could not put up effective resistance to the people's movement. Their theories restricted themselves in practice to speeches and declarations which maximized their unpopularity without having the slightest influence on developments." On the other hand the Jacobins "recognized in anarchy the only *mobile d'action*, in the enthusiasm which they inspired, the substitute for a complete organization, the only resource for resistance externally and internally."[84] In the distances of history as in the immediacies of present action, Marx had an unerring eye for the essential, economic or not, in revolutionary politics.

Marx's attack on Ruge in *Vorwärts!* was itself an exercise in revolutionary politics. It is worth examining again because it shows the connection of thought and action in Marx and his ability to compact a number of meanings in one movement. Reinforcing the effect of the *Jahrbücher* articles, it economically asserted primacy in three overlapping forms: Marx over Ruge, proletarian over bourgeois, and, going beyond the earlier, more modest claim of near-equality, Germany over France (and England, as well): "The Silesian rising begins precisely at that point where the French and English risings *ended*, with [its] self-consciousness of the essence of the proletariat."

Marx spun the logic arguing his point out of one negative and one positive fact. Thus the ferocious fighting song of the weavers, "The Court of Blood," had not been so parochial, so limited in its self-consciousness, as to mention "hearth, factory, district." But, affirmatively, the weavers *had* destroyed the account books, "the titles of possession," of the mill owners. This meant that the proletariat had appeared in its pure character as the "antithesis of a society based on private property." The weavers, Marx concluded eloquently, had "cried out" this definition of their being "strikingly, keenly, relentlessly, powerfully."[85] Marx went on to dismiss any facts that did not fit his thesis. Thus the weavers, imitating the English Luddites of 1811–18, had broken up the power looms that were eliminating the need for their skills. To Marx, socialist generalizer of the factory system, this was a reactionary act, and the weavers' heroism and honest despair did not justify sympathy. Yet he saw something else. This minor economic episode could be re-created as a grand inspiration in the politics of revolution. Marx's *Vorwärts!* article began the process.

During the spring and summer that year Marx's economic readings flowed directly into the writing of the *Economic-Philosophical Manuscripts of 1844*, also known as the *Paris Manuscripts*.[86] While his notes had paid close albeit brief attention to the French Revolution, the *Manuscripts* ignored it completely, as if Marx had resolved all the issues associated with it. He quickly identified the themes that would come to final expression in *Capital*: wages, profit, rent, labor and alienated labor, the division of labor and the relation of the division of labor to trade, use and exchange value—the discussion on value adumbrating the idea of surplus value—and money and credit. To these recognitions Marx angrily added a moral dimension. In his notes he had been sardonic that Adam Smith would temper laissez-faire with "reasonable" wages for workers: "Lovely concession!"[87]

Although Marx accorded considerable respect to Adam Smith and David Ricardo as well, he objected that classical economics merely described. Its "statistical averages are only insults," he burst out, "humiliations heaped upon individual human beings."[88] The *Manuscripts* continued the theme: economics as taught "had the effect of reducing the worker to a product—to the most wretched product, of reducing the worker to a situation that is in inverse ratio to the power and magnitude of his production."[89] In the notes Marx had quoted Ricardo: "'The nations have become workshops, a man is a production and consumption machine, human life a capital; the economic laws rule the world blindly.'" To Marx this meant that "humans are nothing for Ricardo, the product is everything."[90] The scientist and his science had accepted unacceptable reality. Marx condemned the scientist and denied the science.

All of Marx's economic writings, *Capital* as their ultimate expression, were written against economics as studied by the unengaged scientist. Marx had fixed his position in the notes. "The usual reversal of econom-

ics. Objective: freedom of opinion. Therefore mindless serfdom of the
majority. . . . Objective: marriage. Therefore prostitution of the majority. Objective: property. Therefore propertylessness of the majority."[91]
One thoughtful student of Marx, the political scientist Robert C. Tucker,
has argued that Marx was never an economist but a critic of economics.
Tucker granted Marx "an arresting vision of something real [although]
the reality that Marx apprehended and portrayed was an inner reality."[92]
Yet Marx was a man of action, and still another reality confirmed his
sense of inner reality.

Marx's subjectivity coexisted with the world's objectivity in a field of
great tension. The title, *Economic-Philosophical Manuscripts*, originating
not with Marx but with Soviet editors, reflects that tension. Marx was
inevitably, insensibly combining his philosophy, while transforming it,
with the economics he was just beginning to comprehend. He had undertaken an impossible task, and the *Manuscripts* was a flux of decaying
and developing elements. It was all the richer for that.

In his sublime egotism Marx wanted man self-created and anterior to
the world, which man himself had brought into existence. Marx attempted to argue self-creation by way of an innocently-pruriently comic
analogy. "You must . . . keep in mind the *circular movement* sensibly apparent in that process whereby man reproduces himself in procreation;
thus man always remains the subject." Dissatisfied with this, Marx then
attempted an act of verbal legerdemain that would make the question
vanish. He countered an instantly created interlocutor. "You postulate
[nature and man] as *non-existent*, and yet you want me to prove them as
existing. Now I say to you: Give up your abstraction and you will also
give up your question. Or if you want to maintain your abstraction . . .
think of yourself as non-existent."[93] Underlining the key phrases (here
italicized), Marx gave himself the victory in a perfect circle of reasoning.
"But since for socialist man the *entire so-called history of the world* is nothing but the creation of man through human labor . . . so he has the
visible, irrefutable proof of his *birth* through himself, of his *process of
coming into existence*."[94]

The *Manuscripts* furnished still more evidence of the ability of Marx
the philosopher to use his professional skills to subvert thinking. Thus
he derived alienated labor from private property, although, he conceded,
"it becomes clear . . . that private property . . . is rather its conse-
quence—" At that point Marx was colliding with the common wisdom
that if *A* gave birth to *B*, *B* could not very well give birth to *A*. He
preferred to disagree. In the same sentence he continued his movement

through and beyond the objection: "just as the gods are *originally* not the cause but the effect of man's intellectual confusion." He concluded, "Later the relationship becomes reciprocal."[95] Availing himself again of analogy, Marx had achieved the impossible once more.

The fundamental philosophical issue of the *Manuscripts* was alienation. Marx got it from Hegel naturally enough. Hegel's dialectic was a series of alienations between spirit and matter. Ludwig Feuerbach had turned the conception against itself in such works as *Principles of a Philosophy of the Future* (1843). He argued that Hegel had been rationalizing the self-alienation of man, which occurred when man shifted his attention from himself, his real concern, to God, an imaginary concern: religion destroyed the humanity in man. Feuerbach defined his position as humanist. Marx's two *Jahrbücher* articles used this view without reservation, and the *Economic-Philosophical Manuscripts* now applied it to economics.

The *Manuscripts* is seen today as an expression of the humanistic Marx. Associated with the idea of alienation in this way, "humanism" as a word more than as an idea has attracted and consoled twentieth-century Marxists unhappy with Stalinism and other distressing phenomena of their world. The most cultivated minds of recent Marxism, thinkers of the stature of Georg Lukács, Karl Korsch, and Herbert Marcuse, worked their way back to the early Marx.[96] What is the quality of Marx's "alienation" and "humanism"? We must first remind ourselves that humanism, as we normally understand the word, means a culture associated with the Renaissance and its individual, all meanings unfolding from his human singularity. Feuerbach, leading his minor philosophical movement of the nineteenth century, had made off with the word to describe something absolutely different. For Feuerbach man was not an individual, but the accidentally encountered incorporation of the species, the "species-being" (*Gattungswesen*). The person was a point in the life of the species, and the species was the irreducible reality. While trying to save man from God, Feuerbach had sacrificed him in the name of the species humanity. In Marx's "Theses on Feuerbach," written a year after the *Manuscripts*, he would assert that the "human essence" was "the ensemble of social relations."[97] His worker was as collective and abstract as Feurbach's social man, and his humanism as deadly.

Marx the leader was instinctively demanding that the individual lose himself in the ensemble of social relations, "the masses" of future slogans: obedience before human essence.

Marx nevertheless developed a conception of alienation meant to save man from the world as Feuerbach proposed to save him from God.

Alienation was not in the world of the religious imagination but in the economic world. Feuerbach's man as modified by Marx in the *Economic-Philosophical Manuscripts* was a worker manufacturing things and his own alienation. "The object which labor produces, its product, confronts the worker as *an alien being*, as a *force independent* of the producer. . . . This realization [or, as it is often translated, "reification," that is, "thingifica-tion"] of work appears . . . as *annihilation* of the worker . . . as the *loss* of the worker's *being*, as his *slavery to the thing*—the appropriation [i.e., by the capitalist] as *estrangement* and *alienation*."[98] Marx concluded, "The worker transfers his life into the object."[99]

Marx's conception of alienation is as special—as social—as his human-ism. Absolutely reductive, he had defined alienation as purely an effect of the production process. He did not recognize the unqualified aliena-tion of the individual in his total life situation, where he lives trapped forever in the existential moment: the agony of an Augustine who loses his friend and his spiritual confidence, the child who needs his mother so he can sleep, the boy who is abandoned to the blacking warehouse by his father, a Nietzsche with his headaches and invading psychosis, a Marx with his cosmic needs. Marx had vulgarized human suffering, including his own, into a mechanical part of the economy. Yet his suffering, in the course of being denied, had been as evident, as true, as Augustine's or Nietzsche's. It was similarly creative.

As defined by Marx, moreover, alienation was an insecure construct. It begged the question: What is the sense of producing, if not to create something independent of yourself? Should the watchmaker hoard his watches, the singer remain dumb? Marx seemed to want to turn the individual life into pure solipsism. Of course he defended himself against this charge with the word "communism." In a communist society the new social definition of the productive actions of watchmaker and singer would remove their alienating character. A second abstraction, commu-nism, might render the first one harmless.

Never forgetting the political imperative of primacy, Marx expressly rejected various forms of communism advocated by others. The more moderate forms he found corrupted by unsuppressed aspects of private property. The radical sects represented an "entirely raw and mindless communism," which he accused of what he himself was doing when he defined man as an "ensemble of social relations": "It denies the personal integrity of the human being." Similarly, he projected his greed and envy onto his rivals: he argued that while private property was based on greed, raw communism was hardly an improvement as "only the ultimate expression of . . . envy."[100] Marx was being utterly ruthless and destructive, but it would be difficult to argue that he was wrong about mild or mindless communism.

Marx immediately described his own vision of communism: "*Communism* as the *positive* transcendence of *private property*, which is *human self-alienation*: communism therefore as the real *appropriation* of the *human* essence through and for man; communism therefore as the complete return of man to himself as a *social*, i.e., human being—a return become conscious and accomplished within the entire richness of the social development up to this time. This communism as fully developed naturalism equals humanism, as fully developed humanism equals naturalism; it is the *genuine* resolution of the conflict between man and nature, and between man and man, the true resolution of the struggle between existence and essence, between reification and self-confirmation, between freedom and necessity, between individual and species. Communism is the riddle of history solved and knows itself to be this solution."[101] It is a great statement. Marx had found his voice.

The statement marks a brilliant advance in Marx's creative powers. In a burst of brassy lyric he had summarized all his thinking and longings to date: his adolescent equation of serving humanity and achieving completion, as expressed in school essays, his passage through romantic poetry as a university student, the formal philosophizing from idealism to "humanism," the considerations of politics, the conflicts and contradictions, his unrecognized or repudiated suffering. This was perhaps his finest moment in Paris.

A rising affirmation of the best hopes of men, the statement also marks a brilliant advance of the human spirit. But its greatness remains its greatest failing. It verbally solved all the philosophical problems with which Marx had struggled, and anticipated all the solutions to all the new problems—political, economic, and social—he was in the act of formulating. In his new field of operations he was now approaching the production process, the grimy, concrete details of work. Yet the statement does not describe a single visible action. Functioning as a philosopher, Marx was arranging abstractions, human representations indistinguishably mingled among them.

Marx did not improve the statement by going on to assert that the great resolution reached into every physical part of the individual being. It would repair each of the hitherto alienated "*human* relations to the world—seeing, hearing, smelling, tasting, feeling, thinking, observing, experiencing, wanting, acting, loving."[102]

The greatness of the statement remains. The whole of Marx's life and works would provide the substance to fill out its abstractions.

The substance was promptly suggested by the great organizing idea of Marx's thought, materialism. "He told me that the whole idea came upon him, as he was studying in Paris, like a flash," H. M. Hyndman, founder of the first English Marxian party, recalled from talks during Marx's last year of life. Another remark to Hyndman showed the power, early and late, of Marx's single-mindedness. "The conception once formed in his mind . . . all the rest became merely a matter of the exposition of the theory."[103] In fact, Marx's recollection had transformed the hard-won insight of another man into his own personal revelation.

In 1844 Marx had read, and approvingly quoted in the *Manuscripts*, a book that argued the materialist thesis but without his reductiveness.[104] He developed his own conception in his writings of 1845–48. In 1859 he then carefully constructed a massive definition which has become a valuable part of Western thought.[105] But he did arrive at its essence, as he said, in Paris, and it can be expressed in a sentence. The mode of production, that is, the material order, determines *all* else, society, politics, and consciousness. Having just discovered economics, Marx had made it the source of everything. The world's material character was its First Cause. He saw in it no contradiction with his theses of the self-creation of man and man's consequent creation of all reality. Marx rested his case with materialism. That established, he would no more permit anyone to go behind materialism than a Christian theologian could admit anything behind the divine. The materialist conception itself would serve as the theoretical fulcrum by which Marx, as agent of the First Cause, would move the world.

It is not extraordinary that Marx discovered materialism in the course of a great swing away from the transcendence of the *Economic-Philosophical Manuscripts*. He spent his life joining the abstract and the concrete. The unregenerate philosopher had seized upon the abstract first.

The dialectic of materialism and transcendence is one among innumerable conceptual conflicts in Marx. Another important contradiction, the problem of free will and determinism, appeared within materialism, which posited inevitable progress to the ultimate. If the final resolution was indeed inevitable under the laws of materialism, why dedicate your life, as Marx was doing and calling on others to do, to accomplish it? But then Marx's mind throve on such impossible problems.

Leaving it incomplete, Marx broke off the *Manuscripts* to write his first book, *The Holy Family or A Critique of Critical Criticism: Against Bruno*

Bauer & Company. *The Holy Family* showed him at his worst: vulgar, egregiously insulting, disorderly, lacking all sense of proportion.[106] Yet it made sense in what it said and did. The purpose of *The Holy Family* was to combat Bruno Bauer's ideas, then being propagated in a new Berlin journal. Bauer had given up on the majority of the people as hostile to thought and was advocating an intellectually fastidious inaction. Of course Marx had to combat such a position, as he agreed with Engels during Engels' stay in Paris. Once again Marx turned against an old friend, his most important and helpful friend before Engels. The project, it was assumed, merited a brochure which he and Engels would write in collaboration. Engels left his share, some 15 pages, before he departed, but Marx, in his characteristic boundlessness, expended three months to produce a 300-page book. At the end of November 1844 he was just finishing it when its immediate *raison d'être* vanished, Bauer's journal having failed. Marx did not, however, stop with that. He would give up his plan to write a study of politics and economics for which he received the generous advance just before leaving Paris, and, in his next residence, write still another book attacking Bauer.[107] It all made sense.

The Holy Family was a cluster of associations stirred up by a random selection of the journal's articles. At one point Marx was moved to protest the absurdity of referring to romantic love as a "cruel goddess"; at another he debated for fifty pages with a contributor on *Les Mystères de Paris*, the interminable popular novel of Eugène Sue.[108] But the novel had a political and economic point to it, Sue having used socialism as its deus ex machina. Marx was contemptuous about Sue's conception of a Bank of the Poor, really a dole for the unemployed, and his vision of a commune. Drawing upon his economic studies, Marx pointed out that the bank could not support more than a tenth of the poor in one Paris *arrondissement*, while the commune's members worked twice as hard and ate six times as much as normal workers.[109] Socialists, as Marx would presently demonstrate in the case of Proudhon and many others, were easy to ridicule; Bauer's quietism, discouraging to the revolutionary spirit, represented the greater danger at the moment. Marx, too indignant to develop a coherent argument, thrashed about and applied the argumentum ad hominem ad nauseam.[110] He used the already questionable Proudhon for purposes of invidious comparison. Proudhon was a printer-become-writer of peasant background, but Marx provided this definition: "He himself is proletarian, worker. His work is a scientific manifesto of the French proletariat and therefore has a totally different meaning than the literary gimcrackery of any critical critic."[111] More logically, Marx attempted to counter Bauer by raising up the proletariat as the new agent of the historical process, but its passivity—he forgot the desperate heroism of the Silesian workers—defeated him. Logically, *The Holy Family* was a failure. Barely touching upon Marx's newly discovered materialism, moreover, it represented little advance in his thinking.

Nevertheless, Marx's genius flashed here and there. He plunged back into the French Revolution and brilliantly interpreted its Delphic utterances. The bourgeoisie had succeeded and the proletariat had failed because only the first could match its "interest" or "life principle" with the "life principle of the revolution." For the moment he refused to be judgmental; the bourgeoisie could be excused for claiming too much. "Every great, historically victorious 'interest,' when it first strides upon the worldly stage . . . goes far beyond its true limits and identifies itself with the interest of humanity."[112] Clearly, although he was still vague about the details, Marx proposed to complete the old revolution by bringing into play a class with no limits, his "universal class." To these insights he added a fair approximation of his own life principle, the fusing of thought and action. "To carry out ideas you need men who can summon up effective power."[113]

Coordinated with Engels' mission in the Rhineland, *The Holy Family* was part of a rational political action. Wretched thing that it was, it was published in February 1845 and had some slight value in reducing Bruno Bauer's influence within the community of German intellectuals. The book was another signal that Marx was ready to leave Paris.

THE RESOLUTION

Marx's reasons for staying in Paris had dwindled away after he got his directions operationally and intellectually. The French radicals remained sealed off from a foreigner like him, while the communist artisans represented suggestions more than realities. He had conquered *Vorwärts!* for his uses, but it was a wretched vehicle in a dead season of revolutionary fortunes. It served him in another way. His connection with it led to his leaving France. The departure was unplanned but in no sense accidental.

Making the best of things at *Vorwärts!*, Marx had been driving it into more and more intransigence. When the newspaper expressed regret at a failure, on July 26, 1844, to assassinate King Friedrich Wilhelm IV, the Prussian government made representations to the French government. François Guizot, head of government, feared left-wing protests in the

Chamber of Deputies and delayed action as long as he could. *Vorwärts!*, like the *Rheinische Zeitung*, would not desist from its provocations. In December, finally, Guizot closed it down. The next month, for good measure, he ordered Börnstein, Ruge, Heine, Bakunin, and Marx to leave the country. The French police, however, were quite dégagé about carrying out the order. Anyone requesting a postponement got it and stayed on indefinitely. But Marx had had enough of France. On February 3, accompanied by a young *Vorwärts!* collaborator, he left for Brussels, where he knew he would find other revolutionaries.[114] Jenny Marx followed a few days later, after selling off what possessions she could. The expulsion was another perfectly timed step in Marx's revolutionary career.

FOUR

BRUSSELS: ANTICIPATING REVOLUTION

ONE OF MARX'S EARLY ACCOMPLISHMENTS in Brussels, where he remained for three years, was to compose a theory uniting idea and object in the service of the revolution. He was using a Hegelian mode to arrive at a point Hegel would have found frighteningly alien. Marx had arrived in Brussels as a full-time professional revolutionary. He was master of all the important conceptions in approximate form, and a set of relationships comprising a revolutionary table of organization. He could not have got so far if he had not sensed the unity of his enterprise. He had to translate that feeling. He did it in his "Theses on Feuerbach."

Marx's unifying theory looked back at Hegel's dialectical objective, as set in the *Phenomenology of Mind* (discussed here, ch. 2), where the self-consciousness of the spirit becomes "the object it is aware of." The "Theses," written in the spring of 1845, were eleven statements covering less than three printed pages.[1] Marx may have formulated them as points to be developed in the book *The German Ideology*, begun a half-year later. If so, the "Theses" were the only truly worthwhile part of the project, but then they were more than simply worthwhile. They were expressions of genius.

Marx seized Hegel and Feuerbach with either hand. He began by remarking that Feuerbach's improvements on Hegel had introduced new error. "The chief defect of all hitherto existing materialism (that of Feuerbach included) is that the thing, reality, sensuousness, is conceived of only in the form of the *object or of contemplation*, but not as *sensuous-human activity, praxis*, not subjectively." The point was to get back to unity, but not to the Hegelian case where the thought of the billiard ball and the ball itself merged into each other. The fusion was not in thought but in action. Feuerbach, as Marx put it to conclude Thesis I, "does not grasp the significance of 'revolutionary,' of practical-critical activity." Revolutionary activity, accomplishing the necessary fusion, was the ultimate reality.

Marx looked at his great idea from several angles, but they added little to the first viewing. While he touched upon other ideas of Feuerbach, he always came back to the first statement. In Thesis II "man must prove the truth, i.e., the reality and power, the this-sidedness of his thinking in praxis." Thesis III, lest anyone forget, returned to revolution. "The concordance of the changing of circumstances and of human activity or self-improvement can be conceived of and rationally understood only as *revolutionary praxis*." If Hegel lost himself and his thought in thought, Marx would lose himself and his thought in action.

Marx's first objective, like Hegel's, was to reach a state of exaltation in which he felt himself in communion with the ultimate truth beyond reason. In action, as fusion became complete, the mind grasped transcendental blur. Marx had made incomprehensible, hence could ignore, the question, "How can you *know* that your activity is correct in your revolutionary sense?" Marx was claiming to know without registering experience in the mind, without thinking.

If we make Marx's claims mediocre, if we restore human proportion to them and eliminate the absolute, we can get back to usable meaning. Most of our knowing is not registered in the conscious mind. Marx, who innocently thought he knew everything worth knowing, sensed much more of the truth than any other man in important areas of experience. His achievements at this point in his life prove his instinctive or, to use his own (and Hegel's) word, sensual grasp of reality: he had won ascendancy over men, captured an influential newspaper, and maneuvered himself into a position of leadership in an intellectual-and-political movement. Unthinking action, as much as his powerful intelligence, had been responsible for his effectiveness.

The sum of Marx's instincts expressed itself as a powerful will: at the core of the "Theses on Feuerbach" is the rationale for the unbrooked will of the leader.

Marx went on to state the absolute truth of fusion variously in Theses IV to X, and then put the corollary in Thesis XI, an explicit demand for revolutionary action upon the world. "The philosophers have only *interpreted* the world in various ways—the point is to *change* it." Like Hegel's identification of his intelligence with the World Spirit, Thesis XI is a remarkably pure concentrate of egomania and megalomania. Marx, having corrected Hegel and Feuerbach, was claiming that he had completed all the world's essential thinking. It remained only to transform the world in accord with the established truths, those truths which Marx alone among all mankind completely understood. He doubtless would impatiently agree that some thinking of the second order was necessary to mediate between the great ideas and the details of the moment's worldly circumstances: it was to be understood among those who had accepted the truth that he himself was the mediator, the master of applied theory as well. It was to be understood, finally, that Marx was to be chief of operations in changing the world.

In his writings in Belgium Marx made aggressive political use of his ideas as he developed them. He would smite a rival with a new conception and proceed to fix it in place in his steadily rising ideological structure.

Marx made great progress with the idea of materialism in *The German Ideology*, written with Engels' unobtrusive collaboration from September 1845 to August 1846; *The Misery of Philosophy*, begun at the end of 1846 and finished by April 1847; and in the *Communist Manifesto*, written for the most part evidently in January 1848. In the first, anticipating his ultimate statement of 1859, he established his theoretical position solidly.

> The production of ideas, of conceptions, of consciousness, is at first directly interwoven with the material activity and the material intercourse of men, the language of real life. Conceiving, thinking, the intellectual intercourse of men still appear in this stage as the direct product of their physical behavior. The same applies to intellectual production as expressed in the language of politics, laws, morality, religion, metaphysics, etc., of a people. Men are the producers of their conceptions, ideas, etc., etc.,—real functioning men, as they are conditioned by a specific development of their productive forces. . . . It is not consciousness that determines life, but life that determines consciousness.

Marx moved, skillfully managing materially conditioned determinism and morally irreducible freedom, to revolution, "the driving force of history." While a philosopher like Feuerbach had relapsed into helpless idealism, the "communist-materialist sees the necessity and at the same time the precondition of a transformation of industry as well as the social order."

Marx captured a few more insights beyond his revolutionary materialism. With economy he sketched the revolution as internationalized and proletarianized at the same time.

> This development of productive force in general (which itself implies the empirical existence of men in their *world-historical*, instead of local, being) is an absolutely necessary practical premise because without it *want* is nearly made general . . . and furthermore, because only with this universal development of productive forces is a *universal* intercourse between men established, which produces in all nations simultaneously the phenomenon of the propertyless mass (general competition) . . . and finally puts *world-historical* and empirically universal individuals in the place of local ones.

Beyond that, Marx dealt with the division of labor, which he denounced as another aspect of private property. In the spirit of the *Economic-Philosophical Manuscripts* he found that it truncated humans into machine parts and concluded that it should be eliminated. He saw the solution in the communist-materialist future. "Society regulates the general production and thus makes it possible for me to do one thing today and another tomorrow, to hunt in the morning, fish in the afternoon, rear livestock in the evening, and criticize after dinner, without ever becoming hunter, fisherman, shepherd, or critic."[2] At this point Marx was clearly better as critic of the present than builder of the future. Nevertheless his materialist conception and even his less practical views were rich in potentials for thought as well as action.

The discussion of materialism and related philosophical and economic subjects had been a small fraction of *The German Ideology*, 60 out of more than 500 pages. Of the rest all was polemics: more than 300 pages devoted to an obscure Young Hegelian, and somewhat less than 100 to the True Socialists, a new grouping of German socialists led by Moses Hess, among others.[3] This was the book that he wrote instead of the political and economic study he had contracted to undertake. In August 1846 he tried to impress upon the unhappy publisher, who correctly feared for his advance, the sense of his change of plan. "It seemed to me to be very, very important to prepare the way for my development of a positive program with a polemic against German philosophy and against the contemporary German socialism."[4]

In *The German Ideology*'s preface, referring to the Young Hegelians, Marx had begun with an insult that he proceeded to generalize: "The first volume . . . has the objective of unmasking the sheep who take themselves for wolves, to show how their philosophical bleating only echoes the conceptions of the German bourgeoisie, [and to show] how the boasting of the philosophical expositors simply mirrors the wretchedness of the real conditions in Germany."[5] Max Stirner, the Young Hegelian who had aroused Marx, presented a perfect target, in fact too perfect. In late 1844 he had published a brilliant but self-destructive work, *The Ego and His Own*, which proposed to annihilate society for the sake of the individual.[6] Marx could not endure a philosophy that rejected massed humanity and action on its behalf, and he contemptuously entangled Stirner's theses in endless syllogisms and sterile word play. As for the other object of attack, the True Socialist group believed it could win power by persuasion, preached altruism, and denied the existence of class conflict. That would have paralyzed action, and Marx responded with more sarcasm and insult. Whatever sense might be attributed to either of Marx's critical assaults, the means, a distended conglomerate of a book, were grossly impractical. More than a half-dozen publishers rejected it, and Marx abandoned it unfinished. The book was not needed to accomplish his ends: Stirner was quickly forgotten, and the True Socialists broke up in the stresses of the Revolution of 1848.

In 1859, in the preface of the *Critique of Political Economy*, Marx tried to transform the failure of *The German Ideology* retroactively. "We gave the manuscript over to the gnawing criticism of the mice all the more freely because we had achieved our main purpose—self-clarification."[7] That was untrue, since self-clarification had not been the main purpose. It had, however, been the main result, and the result was infinitely more important. Within two years, using its ideas, Marx had made good the failure by an immeasurable margin.

Marx's second book was also a polemic, this one directed against Pierre-Joseph Proudhon, his old Parisian acquaintance. In 1846 Proudhon published the two-volume *System of Economic Contradictions or The Philosophy of Misery*. Proudhon's first title suggested an imitative threat to what Marx regarded as his double monopoly, Hegelian philosophy and economics; the second title let him begin the counterattack by playing a pointed and insulting word game in the title of his book. *The Misery of Philosophy*,[8] a quarter of the length of *The German Ideology*, was a much more efficient savaging of a rival set of beliefs. Marx wielded his materialism, now to be accepted as the plain truth, not only against Proudhon's Hegelianism but also against Hegel's Hegelianism as well. Both philosopher and incompetent pupil made the mistake of beginning with the idea: "As a true philosopher M. Proudhon puts matters upside down and sees in real relations only the materialization of those principles, those categories, which, again M. Proudhon the philosopher tells us slumber in the lap of the 'objective reason of humanity.' "[9] Marx satirized the Hegelian-Proudhonian use of the dialectic in a scintillating exercise which could be turned against his own dialectic.

> The yes becoming no, the no becoming yes, the yes becoming yes and no at the same time, the no becoming no and yes at the same time, the contraries balance off each other, neutralize each other, paralyze each other. The fusion of these two contradictory thoughts constitutes a new thought, which is its synthesis. The new thought doubles itself again into two contradictory thoughts, which in turn fuse into a new synthesis. Out of these birth pangs is born a new group of thoughts. This new group of thoughts follows the same dialectical movement as a simple category, and has a contradictory group as antithesis. From these two groups of thoughts is born a new group of thoughts, which is their synthesis.[10]

Marx tried to protect his own dialectic against such criticism by arguing that the dialectic began and ended with the empty idea for Hegel and Proudhon. On the contrary, as Marx's thought system recognized, everything was economics, and "the economic categories are only the theoretical expressions, the abstractions, of the social production relation."[11] Behind this was Marx's "Theses on Feuerbach," in which he had proven for himself that philosophy had been transcended.

In attacking Proudhon's anarcho-socialist economics, Marx fortified the materialism of *The German Ideology* with Ricardo's classical theory. The lessons of his Paris readings made it easy to ridicule the Proudhonian ideal of free associations of workers freely producing abundance with abundant free credit. Marx was willing to concede that "certainly Ricardo's language is only too cynical," but still, "Ricardo shows us the true movement of bourgeois production, which constitutes value."[12] For the moment Marx was happy to accept the findings of a neutral observer. But then Proudhon, himself using Ricardian reasoning, had argued that union action to increase wages would simply raise prices and fail to benefit the workers. Marx dropped Ricardo. He erased Proudhon's calculations from the blackboard with a sweep of his left hand; prices would remain stable if the organized workers simply forced the capitalists to settle for lower profits. But the real issue, after all, was not economics, as it had not been philosophy. Proudhon (and, incidentally, Ricardo) stood corrected.

The *raison d'être* of unions began with aggressive efforts to increase wages—strikes—and "in this battle—a true civil war—all the [progressive] groups unite and develop themselves for a future battle. Once arrived at this point, the trade union takes on a political character."[13] Leaving this out of account, Proudhon, besides failing as an economic theorist, had made a grave *practical* error. The essence of economics was politics, and true politics was only revolution.

Marx, although desperate as usual for money, financed the publishing of *The Misery of Philosophy* himself. Most of the edition of 800, appearing in Paris and Brussels in July 1847, remained unsold.[14] The fact that Proudhonian ideas were dominant among French workers for the rest of the century nevertheless proved that it was worth the trouble and expense. Small salutary effects were better than none at all.

With these writings and the practical activities associated with them, Marx enriched and refined the ideas entering into the *Communist Manifesto*. The *Manifesto* would mark the end of his Brussels period.

Marx was active as a revolutionary leader from his first moment in Brussels. Engels, in the complacency of his later years, recalled their aims: "We had absolutely no intention of whispering the new scientific insights exclusively into the ears of the academic world by means of thick books. Quite the contrary. We were already deeply established in the political movement. . . . If we were obliged to prove our view scientifically, it was equally important for us to capture the European, and, first, the German proletariat for that belief."[15] To achieve these general objectives, Marx and Engels had four specific tasks: (1) attach themselves to the German communist-revolutionary artisanal movement, especially the London and Paris groups, but also the lively Swiss and the covert and feeble organizations in German, (2) maintain and improve their connection with the radical German intellectuals at home and abroad, (3) create a working revolutionary organization out of these two very different sets of persons, and (4) enforce their conception of materialist socialism upon the revolutionary organization. The ultimate stage meant the fusion of all the above into the operational unity Marx and Engels had planned from the beginning.

Engels had commenced operations upon leaving Marx in Paris in September 1844. He returned to his home area to make speeches and organize dissidents. His home was in the town of Barmen, near Düsseldorf in the Rhineland, and he was temporarily and loosely prisoner of his father and the old businessman's money power. In late 1844 and early 1845 Engels was reporting enthusiastically on communist activity in Cologne and Bonn, as well as in the Barmen area. In October 1844, mentioning Elberfeld, a few miles distant from Barmen, he wrote, "Turn to the left, turn to the right, you find yourself stumbling over communists."[16] Five months later, a letter dated February 22–March 7, 1845, was even more enthusiastic. Every day new members were joining, and Elberfeld had had three communist meetings, the last with 200 in attendance. "All of Barmen and Elberfeld was there, from the patricians to the grocers." He added innocently, "Only the proletariat was missing." Three days later, in the second of four differently dated notes in that letter, he reported abruptly that all future meetings had been forbidden.[17] This was the end of communist activity in the Rhineland. In a month Engels had settled in Brussels.

But useful connections had been established with middle-class radicals in Cologne, where Marx still had friends, and elsewhere in the Rhineland.

If Engels had failed to accomplish the impossible, he was nonetheless accomplishing a maximum of the possible. He was always writing. In the Rhineland he was writing a substantial book, *The Condition of the Working Class in England*.[18] He reported to Marx, "At the bar of world opinion I charge the English middle classes with mass murder, wholesale robbery, and all the other crimes in the calendar."[19] Published in Leipzig before the end of 1845, the book was much more successful than Marx's two books of the Brussels period. Engels had artfully blended hasty research, plagiarism, and cruel facts collected during his Manchester stay. The result was great propaganda but more than propaganda; the book was widely reviewed, reprinted within three years, and used as a model for studies of working classes in other countries.[20] This was not all that Engels was doing for the cause. As he had done for some time and would continue to do for the rest of his life, he was sending an occasional article in the appropriate language (he was effortlessly polyglot) to radical newspapers and periodicals in England, France, and Germany. All this would give more materiality to Marx's organization-in-becoming.

Another service of Engels was to take Marx to England, where they spent some six weeks in the summer of 1845. Although Marx occupied most of his working time in a hospitable library in Manchester, his friend led him to London and introduced him to Karl Schapper and the other leaders of the old League of the Just in the German Workers' Educational Association. Engels was a contributor to the Chartist weekly newspaper, *The Northern Star*, and Marx also met its editor, Julian Harney. These personal relations were of little immediate value; the Germans had never accepted Engels and found Marx a similarly alien, bourgeois nature, while Harney's greater friendliness offered little to exploit.[21] But by the next year the leadership of the revolutionary artisanal movement would pass from the unstable groups in Paris to Schapper's sufficiently united organization. The connection could be developed over time. By the next year Marx had *his* organization.

The organization, created in February 1846 and the first institutional expression of Marx's revolutionary leadership, was the Communist Correspondence Committee, named in self-conscious filiation to the correspondence committees of the American and French revolutions. In it Marx gathered together perhaps a dozen and a half followers, most of whom would fall away in the next few years. The committee's activities consisted essentially in Marx's mailing out and receiving a few letters. Unknown to many sympathizers, frequently ignored by those who did know of it, the CCC nevertheless functioned usefully as a communications switching point for revolutionaries in Germany, France, Switzerland, and England, besides Belgium itself.

In Brussels Marx found a populous German community that was composed chiefly of artisans but enriched by a number of dissident intellectuals. Among the latter was Ferdinand Freiligrath, a poet supporting himself comfortably as a businessman, whom Marx had attacked in the *Rheinische Zeitung* for excessive respect to authority. Affected by the increasingly radical spirit of the 1840s, Freiligrath subsequently wrote less respectful poems and made himself persona non grata in Germany. Now in Brussels, Marx turned his charming side upon him and won him for a friend and, presently, CCC member. There were other friends in Brussels and elsewhere.

The Belgian political situation was hospitably similar to the French. Belgium, which had been united to the Netherlands at the Congress of Vienna, then won its independence by its Revolution of 1830, and revolution was respectable there. The prudent Leopold I, an uncle of Queen Victoria, reigned as constitutional monarch over a conservative but hardly reactionary government. The liberal opposition was vocal, if not vigorous. Belgium permitted the greatest freedom of expression of any country on the Continent, and its radicals were friendly and helpful to the revolutionary exiles. Conveniently close to Germany, its capital was an excellent operational base.

The situation of Marx and Engels as revolutionaries was heroically absurd. This was an early moment in the life of a movement of a very few persons. The movement included such barely possible members as a lonely tailor in London going to the German Workers' Educational Association for companionship or choir practice, and finding himself listening to an outraged account of the Silesian weavers' strike, or a school-teacher in a small German town falling upon a Swiss-published periodical justifying his hatred of the local landowner. Marx and Engels built with odd scraps.

Marx's capacity for leadership always showed itself to be in advance of the powers he commanded. In mid-1846, responding to an overoptimistic correspondent in the Rhineland, Marx advised hard work, hard thinking, meticulous organization, and, especially, caution. As for a statement of principles or a petition, which his correspondent had wanted, Marx's genius glittered: "A statement can have effect only when Germany has a strong and organized communist party." Adding a new element, he repeated the thought: "A petition is only useful when it presents itself at the same time as a threat, behind which there stands a compact and organized mass."[22]

Marx's correspondence, most particularly the letters written to him, showed the masterly, intensely personal character of his leadership in this period.[23] From Paris, the former doctor Hermann Ewerbeck, still struggling to guide the radical German artisans of the League of the Just, writes a gossipy letter in October 1845: Bernays, editor of the old *Vorwärts!*, is rusticating wretchedly in a town outside Paris after a prison stay, Heine sends greetings, "the people of 'our party' . . . are often enough to drive you to despair," and "when is your big book coming out?"[24] Bernays wrote a few times between March 1845 and April 1846 to describe a book he said he was writing, complain piteously of his situation, and successfully beg for money.[25] In March 1845 Georg Jung, Marx's wealthy supporter in Cologne, promised to send 400 French francs, enclosed a small sum in Dutch money, and pressed Marx to confirm receipt of money already dispatched.[26] At the beginning of 1846 the doctor Roland Daniels, another friend from Cologne, passed on a warning signal about Jung himself. Jung was moving to Berlin, and, without saying goodbye to the communists, had enjoyed a farewell dinner given by his bourgeois friends.[27]

The next month, in February, a communist ally of Daniels named Heinrich Bürgers discussed personalities and party politics. Obviously responding to opinions already expressed by Marx, he denounced Moses Hess as a person with questionable theories and friends.[28] In the letters one could see a clear image of Marx as a leader who gave much of himself to his followers, but who required quick and sensitive obedience. Obviously, also, Marx emphasized the value of receiving intelligence. The intelligence reports, particularly the one from Bürgers, accurately reflected the fact that Marx was planning to undertake an important action. On March 24, 1846, Jenny Marx wrote her husband from Trier, where her mother lay seriously ill. She said she was glad that the "radical break didn't take place until I was away."[29] It was the first Marxian purge.

In the month following its creation, Marx used the Communist Correspondence Committee to begin to purify socialist doctrine. Jenny was referring to the attack, still covert, on Moses Hess. While publishing futile radical journals in the Rhineland, Hess had spent part of 1845 in Brussels in close personal and working relations with Marx. In fact, Marx's correspondents sometimes addressed letters jointly to Marx, Engels, *and* Hess.[30] It was doubtless the personal character of the "radical break" that made Jenny so uncomfortable; she had been characteristically hospitable to Marx's friends who would no longer be friends.

The first overt action took place six days after Jenny's letter. The victim was Wilhelm Weitling, whom Marx had found conveniently praiseworthy less than two years earlier. Weitling had just turned up in Brussels after wandering from Switzerland, where he had been briefly in prison, to England, where he had been welcomed but then dropped by Schapper and his friends. Weitling, identifying himself with Christ, had begun to advocate a mystical communism that would capture power behind an army of 40,000 brigands. If Schapper had found this reason to reject Weitling, Marx proposed to do more than that. In his sublime arrogance, he took upon himself the responsibility and authority of cleansing the international movement of such dangerous nonsense. On March 30, 1846, Marx invited Weitling, who had been taking daily lunch at the Marx home, to a "conference being called in order to determine . . . the overall mode of operations of the leaders of the workers' movement," according to a fortuitous and fortuitously impartial witness. Weitling had walked into a trap.

The witness saw Marx:

> Marx himself was a man of the type made up of energy, will, and invincible conviction. . . . He had a shock of deep black hair and hairy hands. His coat was buttoned crookedly, but he looked like a man with the right and power to demand respect. . . . His sharp metallic voice was wonderfully adapted to the radical judgment that he passed on persons and on things . . . categorical pronouncements over which still reigned . . . a certain shrill note. . . . This note expressed his firm conviction that it was his mission to dominate men's minds and to legislate over them. Before me stood the democratic dictator incarnate such as one might imagine in a daydream.

The witness did not remark upon Marx's age. Marx was twenty-seven years old. Weitling, who had been trained as a ladies' tailor, was frail, blond, delicately bearded and elegantly dressed.

The witness, whom Marx had also personally invited, was the Russian liberal Pavel A. Annenkov, a friend of many of the leading personalities of the time. The liberal was a species-being Marx easily despised but the visit of this distinguished traveler was flattering. Furthermore, the visit was validated by a letter of recommendation from a Russian landowner, an odd acquaintance of Marx's Paris days. Also present were six of Marx's followers, Engels functioning as chairman of the meeting.[31]

Engels had opened the meeting with a little speech on "the necessity for people dedicated to the cause of transforming labor to expound their views and establish one overall doctrine which would serve as a standard for all their followers who had neither the time nor the opportunity to concern themselves with theoretical issues." He was making more sense than any liberal, then or now, would like to admit.

Marx thereupon intervened in a manner and with a substance that, beginning with his friend Engels, economically insulted three persons. He abruptly interrupted his friend and shouldered him aside to take command of the proceedings. Marx began, "Tell us, Weitling, you people who have made such a commotion in Germany with your communist preachings, you who have won over so many workers with the result that they have lost their work and their bread, with what fundamental principles do you justify your social-revolutionary agitation?" Marx pointed to Annenkov: "Look here, we have a Russian with us. In his country, Weitling, your role might be suitable. There, associations of nonsensical prophets and nonsensical followers are the only things that can be put together and made to work successfully." With the inevitable contradictions Marx would think this about Russia for the rest of his life.

Marx's first words to Weitling had been accusation-and-condemnation. He continued, "But in a civilized country like Germany you should realize that nothing can be achieved without solid and concrete doctrine, and up to the present all you have got is noise, harmful excitement, and the destruction of the very cause you claim to represent." The perfect arrogance of Marx's assumption of authority threw Weitling into confusion. By implication recognizing Marx's right to act as he did, he began defensively, pleading "justice," "solidarity," and "brotherly love."

But then Weitling caught himself and went over to the attack. He was a proletarian, he reminded himself and the others, and here was an intellectual seeking to impose his bookish theorizing on real workers who were experiencing injustice in their daily lives. Weitling's logic was as perfect as Marx's arrogance. Marx saved himself by stopping all logic. He flew into a rage and "struck his fist on the table so violently that the lamp shook. Jumping to his feet, he shouted, 'Ignorance has never helped anybody yet!'

"We followed his example and rose to our feet, and the conference came to an end."[32]

In a letter written the next day to his fellow victim Moses Hess, Weitling described the end of the scene differently. "There was a complete uproar and everybody was jumping around the room." Before then, as Weitling heard it, Marx had demanded that the communist movement "be sifted" to eliminate both "philosophical communism," meaning True Socialism, and the "artisanal communism" of the League of the Just in Paris and London. Marx had also communicated the threat that he would make use of the power given him by the support of wealthy patrons; he was referring to people like Georg Jung, just then in the process of disappearing from his life, and publishers who still thought him profitably publishable. With this help, Weitling understood, Marx proposed to cut off funds from communist heretics and assure the propagation of the correct doctrine.[33] Although Weitling had certainly not been an impartial observer, his report overlapped Annenkov's without contradiction and showed Marx in characteristic action.

As for the heretic Hess, although Marx denounced his True Socialism, Marx did not attack him directly and personally. That left an ambiguity to which Hess accommodated himself. From a small Belgian town near the Rhineland, where he was directing his journalistic enterprises, he wrote a letter remonstrating with Marx about Weitling: "You have driven him completely crazy and now you wonder that he is. I won't have anything more to do with the whole business—it makes me throw up. Shit flying in all directions."[34] At the end of the month he wrote: "I would still like very much to keep on seeing you yourself, but I don't want to have anything to do with your people."[35] This sketched out the outlines of the Marx-Hess relationship for many years to come.

Weitling himself still had possible revolutionary uses, a contradiction appropriate to the dialectic, and the Marx *ménage* continued to receive him at lunch. About five weeks after the meeting Weitling was invited to support the purge *in absentia* of another heretic, also indefinably connected with the Communist Correspondence Committee. The man, Hermann Kriege, had wandered off from Brussels to the United States and into True Socialism, and was publishing a short-lived newspaper that advocated universal love and the equal division of the land. To Marx this was a denial of class war and, worse, encouragement to the American proletarians to become agricultural capitalists. The purge took the form of a series of CCC resolutions denouncing Kriege, and reported in a circular letter written by Marx and signed by most of the members present at the Weitling condemnation. Weitling resisted for Kriege as he had for himself, and the circular explicitly stated that he had "voted against" the resolutions.[36] Shortly thereafter, Weitling, for his part, accepted his own purge and left for America—on Kriege's invitation.

Marx tried to reach out to the League of the Just in Paris to attempt still another liquidation. Doubling his literary attacks on True Socialism, he had selected as his new victim the True Socialist Karl Grün, a university friend going back to his year in Bonn, because of Grün's recently established ascendancy over the German artisans in the league. A few weeks before Marx saw Proudhon's book in 1846 and began to write his polemics against *him*, Marx invited Proudhon to become Paris correspondent of the CCC. At the same time he tried to turn Proudhon against Grün. Marx explained the CCC's purposes: "exchange of ideas and nonpartisan criticism" among English, French, and German socialists. He appended the postscript: "I hereby warn you about Herr Grün in Paris. This man is nothing more than a literary swindler, a kind of charlatan. . . . Moreover, this man is *dangerous*. He *exploits* his acquaintance . . . with well-known authors. . . . He dares . . . to call himself Proudhon's tutor [and] . . . *makes fun* of his writings. Watch out for this parasite."[37] Marx was assaulting a relationship that was stronger perhaps than he realized. Grün was Proudhon's German translator. Proudhon defended Grün loyally, and himself intolerant and a vicious polemicist, lectured Marx virtuously. "Let us together seek, if you wish, the law of society . . . but, for God's sake, after having demolished all the *a priori* dogmas, do not let us in our turn dream of indoctrinating the people. . . . Let us not . . . pose as the apostles of a new religion. . . . Let us gather together and encourage all dissent." Proudhon mentioned his new book and speculated on the possibility that he might "receive a caning from you."[38] Marx accepted Proudhon's letter as a refusal to join with the CCC and was presently engaged in writing *The Misery of Philosophy*. As for Grün, Marx attacked him from another flank.

Engels, after assisting Marx variously with the CCC and their literary projects in Brussels, went off to Paris in mid-August 1846. His first mission was to destroy the influence of Karl Grün. In fact, Hermann Ewerbeck, after giving up what little leadership he had exercised, now had become a supporter of Grün's. On the day before Engels left for Paris, Ewerbeck, overwhelmed by private miseries, wrote to Marx, "I can just barely make it—I've pulled out of all the old administrative rubbish."[39] At least Ewerbeck was so diminished that he was little hindrance to Engels, who set manfully to work. He reported on his progress formally to the CCC and privately to Marx. In the tone of a boastful adolescent two Committee Letters recounted a pair of successive triumphs, but the second trimph was necessary to recover from a mysterious and unexplained defeat that had rendered the first one naught. On September 16, 1846, he told how he had dominated a meeting. On October 23, however, he wrote that he had had Grün's followers driven from the meeting hall. The action was successful, Engels announced, and his Marxian resolutions won out.[40] But by December he was writing to Marx in discouragement and on March 9, 1847, he wrote he was not seeing any workers.[41] Yet Engels returned to the attack and achieved one signal success.

The truth of the matter, as told by a German companion of Engels in Paris, was that Karl Grün had remained the most influential leader among the German workers. The companion was Stephan Born, a typesetter who spent almost every evening in Paris with Engels. According to Born, the artisans disliked this young bourgeois on family allowance and preferred Grün and Grün's softer version of socialism. It was Stephan Born who enabled Engels to accomplish his one saving deed. As meeting chairman one evening, Born maneuvered the recalcitrant members into sending Engels as the Paris delegate to the founding congress of the Communist League. He did it by nominating Engels and asking if anyone objected; no one was assertive enough.[42] Engel's attendance at that congress, in June 1847, was a historical event.

During 1846, following the founding of the CCC, Marx's activities made him a substantial presence in the international community of revolutionaries. He was, however, an intellectual with no experience of revolutionary struggle. Whatever Engels accomplished in Paris, Marx and his group had to be accepted by the professionals, the leaders of the League of the Just in London, who commanded the only effective, revolution-minded organization. His meeting with Schapper and Schapper's most important colleagues, the shoemaker Heinrich Bauer and the watch-maker Joseph Moll, had produced no palpable results. Marx had had no organization himself at the time, no compelling force; but the leaders of the League of the Just lacked precisely what Marx had. The surviving minutes of some of their discussions from February 1845 to January 1846 express enthusiasm for their cause and bafflement over the mediocrity of their gains. In their thinking they had not got beyond the old communal socialism of Fourier or Cabet plus the idea of revolutionary action in the French tradition. The league leadership, however, was prudent enough to hesitate about commencing the revolutionary action. Against the insistences of Hermann Kriege and Wilhelm Weitling, then in London, Schapper and Bauer had, in fact, argued that the League could not very well make a revolution yet.[43] But what then did Schapper and his friends have in mind? They were intelligent as well as prudent; they realized they needed to have more in mind. They were responsive when Marx the editor and bookman wrote to them in mid-May 1846. Writing as an equal, Marx suggested joint action.

On June 6 Karl Schapper replied. He had read Marx's letter to his colleagues and, having their concurrence, organized a committee "to enter into communication with you and to support you in your objective." Indicating what Marx had said in *his* letter, which has not survived, Schapper went on, "A broad organization of propaganda [and] an exchange of ideas among the communists of all countries are so needed that every true communist would be glad to cooperate." He opposed a demurrer to an objection Marx had made, "As far as conspiratorial ideas are concerned, we have long since gotten over such silliness." He gave a detailed account of activities in London—describing not the tiny core represented by the League of the Just but the German Workers' Educational Association, to which he ascribed a membership of 250. If he was according approval, he was also seeking it. Then Schapper put the demand: "And finally we ask you to tell us more about your plans. It is true that you have told us what you want, but you haven't said how you think you will go about achieving it." In a postscript Schapper criticized the harshness of Marx's attack of Kriege. "Couldn't you do something more productive than turning out a circular denouncing the man?"[44]

Another exchange emphasized both the seriousness of the correspondents—and their differences. Marx wrote again on June 22. On July 17, after going into more detail about the operations in London, Schapper responded again in detail. He defended the spirit of brotherly love, a commonplace of utopian socialism, against Marx's contempt. Beginning with irony, he could arrive at an expression of contempt himself. "You proletarians of Brussels still have the professors' arrogance in a high degree." Nevertheless, he enthusiastically concurred with Marx's suggestion of a communist congress.[45] In early September Schapper was astounded, as he wrote Marx, not to have heard from him since June.[46]

At this moment, as Hermann Ewerbeck withdrew and the movement in Paris faltered, Schapper's London group announced its primacy to the communist world. In November 1846, calling itself the People's Executive of the League of the Just, it broadcast an urgent message. Taking up Marx's idea, it issued a call for a communist congress for the following May. But the People's Executive had not consulted Marx; moreover, it warned against irresponsible bourgeois theoreticians.[47] If Marx was right in establishing relations with Schapper when he did, he had failed to develop them appropriately.

In Paris Engels evaluated the situation coolly and precisely. In a long letter to Marx he expressed the theoreticians' reaction for both of them. Engels referred to Schapper and his friends with the slang word for peripatetic artisan, *Straubinger* (singular and plural), which he used pejoratively, but with an undertone of grudging respect, as in "working stiff(s)." (Engels and Marx would frequently use the word in that sense when these allies were being difficult.) "This business with the London people is annoying . . . because . . . they were the only ones with whom one could try to make a real connection straight off, without *arrière-pensée*," he wrote. The league leaders' "eternal jealousy against us as 'professors'" was particularly discouraging. Engels balanced two courses of action: the CCC could either attack the London initiative with ridicule or let the connection become dormant. But he had to admit that both were bad. "We can take a position . . . against intellectuals, but not against working stiffs. After all they're a couple of hundred strong, accredited to the English by Harney, advertised by the *Rheinischer Beobachter* throughout Germany as a ferocious and by no means feeble communist society. . . . We can't afford to tangle with the *Straubinger* so long as there is no real organization in Germany. . . . These fellows set themselves up against us as 'the people,' 'the proletarians." On the other hand, the CCC needed the League of the Just as active ally, nothing less and nothing less positive than that.[48] But the League of the Just was arriving at a reciprocal evaluation of its situation.

One earlier signal of the inevitable rapprochement was the presence of Wilhelm Wolff, a selfless and dedicated professional revolutionary, in Brussels and in the CCC membership. Wolff was of the same generation and type as the league leaders. The son of a Silesian peasant, he became a university student, joined the student revolutionary movement of the 1830s, and experienced his share of imprisonment. After his release, supporting himself as a teacher, he then continued his rebellious activities among the peasants of his home province. In the 1840s he could achieve little. The existence of the CCC promised more. He arrived in Brussels in the spring of 1846, in time to sign the denunciation of Kriege, and placed himself under Marx's orders.

On January 20, 1847, the League of the Just authorized Joseph Moll to discuss cooperative efforts, and sent him to Brussels with credentials which have survived.[48] According to Marx, Moll requested the Brussels CCC to join the league. Marx said he "raised objections" to the league's vague utopianism, and Moll, indicating that he was sympathetic to Marx's views, suggested that Marx could best persuade the league to adopt the correct ideas by entering it and helping to overcome its retrograde element. "So we joined."[50]

The League of the Just held its congress a few days later than originally planned, from June 2 to 9. At this congress it changed its name to "Communist League."

Marx did not attend the founding congress of the Communist League. Engels, nominated by his friend Stephan Born, attended as delegate from Paris. Marx had written to Engels: "I'm not going to London. The funds don't permit it. We have to send Wolff over. And that ought to be enough, with both of you there."[51] Marx and Engels swung so easily from truth to fiction that Engels doubtless translated Marx's lie automatically. Money had not kept Marx from London, since he planned to send Wolff and did find the money. It was a statesman's discretion. Had the London congress turned out badly, Marx the leader would have kept his prestige intact by repudiating his representatives. The results of the congress were a compromise. The more Marxian slogan "Proletarians of all lands, unite!" replaced the softer "All men are brothers." But the first article of the new bylaws could have been written by a True Socialist. "The League aims at the abolition of man's enslavement by propagandizing the theory of the community of goods."[52] Marx, however, correctly decided that he could trust the weight of his purposes upon the compromise.

On August 5, 1847, Marx formally transformed the Communist Correspondence Committee into the Brussels branch of the Communist League, with himself as president. A note in his own handwriting recorded the change.[53] Marx immediately dealt with the London leaders as an equal. In a formal communication the next month, the Brussels branch took exception to the Central Committee's policy of forbidding league members to join other political organizations, thus national or progressive parties. "We see this as unpolitic because you thereby rob our people of any chance of influencing these groups."[54] Within the league, in fact, power had shifted, and was continuing to shift, toward Marx. With his instinct for leadership, he took advantage of it and made difficulties. On October 18 a beseeching letter from London signed by Schapper, Moll, and Bauer—the membership of the Central Committee—documented the change and Marx's tactics. "Since the distressing misunderstanding, which we hope is forgotten, your letters seem to be very precisely pondered and cold. Why so—you ought to know best." The situation was critical. "Right now there is such disorder and confusion in the League. . . . We have come to a complete break with Paris. . . . All hell has been let loose in Switzerland." The *tour d'horizon* concluded: "London and Brussels are the pillars of the league at the present moment." With underlinings, here represented by italics, it insisted: "It is *absolutely necessary* that Brussels send delegates to the next congress, and in concert with London surgically cut away the 'rotten flesh,'" that is, the ideas and machinations of the followers of Wilhelm Weitling and Karl Grün. To that end "we would be very happy *if Marx could come to the congress.*"[55]

A recent discovery by Soviet archivists, the letter seems almost too perfect to be real, but it does express the sense of the situation. In any case Marx agreed that a second congress was necessary and that he should attend. It was held in London from November 30 to December 8, 1847. Seconded by Engels, he could cooperate with the London group in establishing a measure of order in the league and, at the same time, use his strengthened position to impose his will on it. The point was correct doctrine. Everything else, including Marx's position in the organization, was subordinate to that. With correct doctrine he could bide his time; with false, he could simply not remain a member. The statutes were, in fact, thoroughly revised, and Article 1 gave the measure of Marx's progress since the first congress. It was purely Marxian. "The purpose of the league is the overthrow of the bourgeoisie, the rule of the proletariat, the transcendence of the old bourgeois society presently based on class contradictions, and the establishment of a new classless society without private property."[56] The triumph of his theory was further guaranteed when Marx and Engels were given the assignment of formulating the league's program in what became the *Communist Manifesto*. Marx was the master of theory, while Schapper, Moll, and Bauer were elected as the total membership of the Central Committee, thus recognized as the operational leadership of the Communist League.

The whole of 1847 had meant a steady and palpable accession of strength for Marx. He retroactively merited one stroke of fortune, the support of an émigré newspaper. Adalbert von Bornstedt, a former officer and a specimen of the pararevolutionary species, had founded the twice-weekly

Deutsche Brüsseler Zeitung on January 3. According to the Belgian police records, Bornstedt, after having been cashiered from the Prussian army for "unnatural acts" and then expelled from the French foreign legion for counterfeiting, had at one time vainly offered his services as a spy to the French minister of the interior, and was "generally regarded as a spy for the Prussian Legation." [57] According to police archives in Germany, Bornstedt was also a spy for Austria and perhaps for some of the smaller German states. Many of these facts were known to Marx's friends. [58] Marx knew and refused to know. The *Brüsseler Zeitung* had recommended itself to him by publishing increasingly radical and (was this an effort to combat suspicion?) anti-Prussian articles. Consistent with his career's inconsistency, Bornstedt had been the first editor of the Paris *Vorwärts!*, and had lost his position to Marx's friend, Bernays, because of insufficient radicalism. By the summer of 1847, choosing not to inquire where Bornstedt had got the money to found his newspaper, Marx was using it for his purposes. [59] In a letter at the time, carefully avoiding the matter of espionage, Marx defended Bornstedt vaguely against other vague and milder accusations. Given "an uncensored opposition newspaper . . . whose editor . . . shows himself to be accommodating to everything progressive," Marx asked, "could one do anything else besides exploiting this opportunity?" [60] A newspaper was too essential a revolutionary instrument to be spurned, even if the enemy also made use of it. Marx was certain he was the more skillful exploiter.

From September 1847 Marx and Engels published a series of articles in the *Brüsseler Zeitung*, chiefly attacks on the True Socialists. The last article, by Engels, in the issue of February 27, 1848, celebrated the Revolution of 1848 in France and called for neighborly revolutions in Germany. [61]

Before that time Marx had added other valuable elements to his operations. In late August 1847, a fortnight after he had transformed his CCC into a branch of the Communist League, Marx organized the German Workers' Educational Association of Brussels around it. This was on the classic revolutionary model of the front organization, to function like Karl Schapper's similarly named association in London. In Brussels, the president was a typesetter who was an old member of the CCC. The vice-president was Moses Hess, whom Marx and Engels were still alternately chastising as a True Socialist and patronizing as a useful ally. Wilhelm Wolff, suggesting to the members the appropriate way to think, gave a weekly review of politics, and Marx himself lectured occasionally on economics. [62]

Marx was also developing relations beyond the German groups. He had made one real friend among the Belgians, an archivist named Philippe Gigot, who became the secretary-treasurer of the Brussels branch of the Communist League. Gigot had his various uses for Marx: he had been a cosigner of the letter to Proudhon denouncing Karl Grün. Marx broadened his Belgian connections in a roundabout way in 1847, but to good effect. This was through the international community of progressives, an association of those who still hoped to achieve the egalitarian ideals of the great French Revolution. In 1846 Engels' friend Julian Harney had organized the Society of Fraternal Democrats, which brought together his English Chartists and Schapper's German revolutionaries. The Fraternal Democrats were little more than a sponsoring organization for an occasional meeting in the spirit of international radical fellowship, but they kept the spirit alive. On the day before the opening of the second congress of the Communist League, the Fraternal Democrats called one such meeting to commemorate the Polish insurrection of 1830. The meeting was held in the same hall, and Marx and Engels both spoke. Marx took the occasion to lift the Polish nationalist cause, a favorite among all progressive-minded people, to his level of internationalism. He was not interested in reviving "the old Poland." Poland's salvation would be achieved by "the victory of the proletariat over the bourgeoisie," which was the "signal to free all oppressed nations."[63] At this time Marx was already an officer of a fraternally international Belgian-German organization, the Democratic Association of Brussels.

The Democratic Association had been organized two months earlier, evidently on the initiative of Adalbert von Bornstedt. As it happened, Engels was in Brussels, where he had been staying since the end of July, while Marx was not. Engels was being useful in the activities of the Communist League and the Workers' Association, and Marx, again in need of money, had gone off briefly to Holland to see relatives in a complex negotiation. (Earlier, he had got a loan from a brother-in-law, among others, but his finances remained in a critical state, and he wanted to get an advance on the money he would inherit from his mother.)[64] Engels, paranoically suspicious, thought that Bornstedt was trying to overwhelm the Workers' Association with a superorganization, but in fact, while Bornstedt remained only one of the dozen members of the governing committee, Engels was elected one of the Democratic Association's two vice-presidents.[65] As Engels diplomatically wrote to Marx after the election, he thereupon told the president that he was planning to return to Paris as soon as possible and strongly urged that Marx, as the leader of the German community of democrats, should replace him. " 'Ce ne serait donc pas M. Marx qui m'y remplacerait, c'était plutôt moi qui à la réunion ai remplacé M. Marx.'" However paranoid, Engels had carried out his seconding with great skill, and the association duly elected Marx as a vice-president in November.[66] Marx found it convenient to operate as an international democrat at times, although he would unabashedly remind his bourgeois allies that he represented the only true wing of democracy, that is, communism. In the next weeks he made good use of the Democratic Association. Marx's revolutionary apparatus was complete.

Returned from the London congress, Marx found himself engaged in a complex of activities, all integral to his revolutionary purposes. He was commanding, instructing, giving speeches, writing articles—and trying to write the *Communist Manifesto*. He procrastinated with the latter, as he always did with important writings. He could see only too clearly the effect he wanted to achieve. The leaders of the Communist League grew impatient. In the idiom of their rough trade they wrote him late in January 1848 that if they did not have the manuscript by February 1, "measures would be taken against him."[67] It arrived in time to be published as a twenty-three-page pamphlet in London toward the end of February.[68]

Commissioned to meet the practical needs of a revolutionary organization, the *Communist Manifesto* was informed with the most daring dreams of the Western mind. With it, Marx achieved a real fusion of idea and action as impossibly promised in the magical formulas of the "Theses on Feuerbach." Marx, not yet thirty years old, had reached greatness. The voice, which he had first found in the *Economic-Philosophical Manuscripts*, was now a great bronze bell.

The *Communist Manifesto* is a masterpiece of many dimensions. Timely and timeless, equally specific and general, it is also marred by vulgarity, envy, resentment, infantile demands, sadism, and lies. But the baseness is transformed, transcended. With the *Manifesto* Marx entered the revolutionary guild as a master.[69]

Marx began with a boastful lie, which he would make true in the next generation. "A specter is haunting Europe—the specter of communism. All the powers of old Europe have entered into a holy alliance to exorcise this specter: pope and czar, Metternich and Guizot, French radicals and German police-spies. . . . Communism is already acknowledged by all European powers to be itself a power."[70]

In fact communism frightened no sane person at the time. The governments were well enough informed about it, and knew that the league had only a few hundred half-organized adherents. Czar, Metternich, and Guizot were much more concerned with the danger represented by liberals and nationalists. Communism would become a frightening specter, but only a specter and not a reality, when the Paris Commune erupted in 1871—and Marx's fictions would be largely responsible. Communism's feebleness in 1848, however, justified Marx all the more. His first purpose was to convince his fellow communists that they were frightening enough to take themselves seriously.

While it gave an efficient summary of Marx's economic ideas, materialism, and the rest, the *Manifesto* was, before all else, an inventory of the materials for the seizure and exercise of power. Marx had assimilated the sense of the Industrial Revolution into his thought. "Steam and machinery [have] revolutionized industrial production," he wrote. There were now "whole industrial armies" to command.[71]

Marx could not withhold his admiration for the present leaders of the industrial armies, "the modern bourgeois." He saluted these "bourgeois" and their class. "The bourgeoisie, historically, has played a most revolutionary part." The first of the four sections of the *Manifesto*, "Bourgeois and Proletarians," enthusiastically celebrated the middle-class creation of the contemporary world. The bourgeoisie "has been the first to show what man's activity can bring about. It has accomplished wonders far surpassing Egyptian pyramids, Roman aqueducts, and Gothic cathedrals; it has conducted expeditions that put in the shade all former exoduses of nations and crusades."[72]

The *Manifesto* was important in giving the industrial working class its identity, but Marx brought it only to partial and passive life. The proletariat appeared as what the bourgeoisie was not. Revealing his underlying realism, the working class existed here as the feeble negation of a satanically splendid affirmation.

Also realistically, the revolutionary politician Marx anticipated problems in the proletariat's mundane behavior and carried out a Hegelian operation on it. He split it in two: an unqualified proletariat that remained a blameless abstraction and the *Lumpenproletariat*, the "scoundrelly proletariat" ("*Lump*" means "scoundrel" or "wretch"). While Marx attributed no origins to the pure proletariat, the lumpenproletariat was "this passively rotting mass of the basest layers of the old society"— dispossessed members of the lower middle class, small manufacturers, shopkeepers, artisans, and peasants.[73] Whenever proletarians failed to act appropriately, Marx would throw them into the category of the lumpenproletariat. One instance would occur in less than a half-year. In Paris,

unemployed workers, having been driven by need to join the Mobile
Guard, shot down their fellows in the June Insurrection in Paris, and
Marx would condemn them pitilessly.

The third section was an appropriately nasty and deliberately misleading denigration of all the rival socialist groups that had come to Marx's
notice.[74] He had begun the section with a category he had invented, "Feudal
Socialism," which was really a social-welfare movement led by aristocrats and conservatives to succor the workers and win their support.
Marx condemned it along with Christian Socialism as a cold-blooded
political maneuver.[75] Beginning this way, he facilitated the workings of
guilt-by-association upon the authentic socialists that followed. Again
Marx attacked True Socialism, which he categorized along with "Feudal
Socialism," under "Reactionary Socialism," and at the same time defined
more specifically as "the bombastic representative of the petit-bourgeois
Philistine." As for its ideas, they made up a "robe of speculative cob-
webs, embroidered with flowers of rhetoric, steeped in the dew of sickly
sentiment."[76] Again Marx attacked Proudhon, placed here under the
heading "Conservative, or Bourgeois, Socialism" for denying the class
struggle and trying to transform the proletariat into a new bourgeoisie.[77]

Beyond these old competitors, Marx went through the list of socialists
meticulously. Petit-bourgeois socialism, as he defined it, "dissected with
great acuteness the contradictions of the conditions of modern production" and "proved, incontrovertibly, the disastrous effects of machinery
and the division of labor." But its solution, industrial guilds and a patriarchal agricultural system, was both reactionary and utopian.[78] Marx also
found the Utopians Saint-Simon, Fourier, Owen, and Cabet usefully
critical, but they sought "to deaden the class struggle" and build "duo-
decimo editions of the New Jerusalem . . . castles of the air."[79] Marx's
objective with this review was clear enough. He was trying to make the
other socialist ideologies too ugly to be able to seduce his present or
potential followers.

The second and fourth sections defined the relations of the communists respectively to proletarians and to the various political parties of the
opposition. With his strategic genius, Marx established the communists,
that is, the Communist League, as "the most advanced and resolute section of the working-class parties of every country; . . . they have over
the great mass of the proletariat the advantage of clearly understanding
the line of march."[80] In that one sentence he gave his party the exclusive
leadership over the proletariat and the future. It was sleight of hand of
the highest order: he had identified a political party with a social class

and then, by attributing superior understanding to the party, confided to it the function of thinking and acting for that class.

As for the other parties, Swiss radicals, Polish nationalists, and German middle-class liberals, the communists would cooperate with them whenever such action led to progress: "But [the communists] never cease, for a single instant, to instill into the working class the clearest possible recognition of the hostile contradictions between bourgeoisie and the proletariat."[81] Marx correctly understood that he lost nothing in telling his middle-class allies that he intended to use and then destroy them. He ended greatly and almost honestly: "The communists disdain to conceal their views and aims. They openly declare that their ends can be attained only by the forcible overthrow of existing social conditions. Let the ruling classes tremble at a communistic revolution. The proletarians have nothing to lose but their chains. They have a world to win. WORKING MEN OF ALL COUNTRIES, UNITE!"

The sheer power of the *Communist Manifesto* brought Marx to a point within one step of the leadership of the Communist League. The French Revolution of 1848, breaking out on February 22, 1848, permitted him to take that step. Schapper, Bauer, and Moll, as the league's Central Committee, found themselves separated from the great events by the English Channel. Marx was on the Continent, close to Paris. Entrusting Marx with all of Europe's revolutionary promise, the Central Committee formally transferred all of its authority to him. It was less an act of self-abnegation than an acceptance of the reality of the political situation, although it was also an implicit recognition of Marx's capacities. The committee gave him "the discretionary power . . . to administer the league's interest according to his own judgment."[82] Marx now incarnated idea and action.

FIVE

COLOGNE: MAKING
REVOLUTION

WELL PREPARED FOR THE ENCOUNTER, Marx went out to meet the revolutions sweeping Europe. He began in Brussels, badly. In his revolutionary optimism he lost himself in a fantasy of 1789 repeating itself, lunged about planlessly, flung away desperately needed funds, and quickly managed to get himself arrested and expelled from Belgium. He had made a fool of himself. Always adept at explaining away his mistakes, however, he covered over the fool with a martyr's gloss in his public complaints: he and his wife were victims of police repression, he wrote in a letter published in *La Réforme* of Paris.[1] In Paris, at his next revolutionary station, he oriented himself immediately, and during the month he spent there acted with remarkable effectiveness and economy. He made no mistakes in Paris. Then, unfolding the wealth of his revolutionary genius, he spent a year back in Cologne as a leader of the German Revolution.[2]

In all of Marx's operations, the instructive Belgian fiasco excepted and excused, what he did not do was as important and successful as what he did. He did not let himself be arrested at a critical moment. In action as in thought he was a master of the negative.

In Brussels, Marx began by trying to make a Belgian revolution. His recent trip to the Netherlands had been successful; he had belabored his mother into advancing him 6,000 francs. From that sum, he proceeded to contribute 2,100 francs to arm the Belgian workers, according to a Belgian police report.[3] The Belgian Democratic Association, with Marx's enthusiastic concurrence as a vice-president, then held a mass demonstration that surrounded the city hall on the night of February 27–28. One of the demonstration's more conspicuous leaders was Wilhelm Wolff. Calling for a republic, it demanded that the government cooperate in its demise by arming a civic guard made up of workers. Troops dispersed the demonstrators easily enough, and Wolff was arrested along with other foreigners, held in prison for about a week, and expelled from Belgium.[4] Marx had preceded him.

At 5:00 P.M. on March 3 Marx was handed an order to leave Belgium within twenty-four hours. No reason was given in the curt note, but the Belgian archives have a copy of an undated order to expel Marx "for conduct compromising the public tranquillity."[5] Marx was arrested for other reasons a few hours after he got the formal expulsion order. The episode took place in the early morning of March 4, and he was kept in prison until noon. Marx and the police differ on the details. Marx said the police invaded his home.[6] A police report said that Marx and about a dozen foreigners had called attention to themselves when they uproariously celebrated the French revolution in a café. At the approach of police officers most of the others scattered. Marx, however, remained, and when requested to do so, handed over some papers he had been holding. On reflection he clumsily tried to snatch them back. He was thereupon arrested.[7] Whatever the truth, the Belgian police found it expedient to release Marx and conduct him to the French border before the day was over.

A few days earlier, drawn by the center of revolutionary action, Marx had requested the new French government to rescind his banishment of 1845. He got his reply the day that Belgium gave him the expulsion order. It was a warm welcome from Ferdinand Flocon, editor-in-chief of *La Réforme* and a member of the provisional government.[8] This was one more example of Engels' great services to the cause. He had, of course, interceded with Flocon, who had been publishing Engels' articles.

On the day of his arrival in Paris Marx spoke at a meeting of the revived Society of the Rights of Man, which he had joined. "I am a revolutionary. I want to march in the shadow of the great Robespierre."[9] This was sentimentality and diplomacy. Marx was not interested in the French revolution *en soi*. He proceeded to make use of it as a base for *his* revolution, concentrating on the German situation both in Paris and in Germany. Again, one of his most important actions was negative. Before his arrival, his old friend, the poet Georg Herwegh, and his associate of only yesterday, Adalbert von Bornstedt of the *Deutsche Brüsseler Zeitung*, had begun to organize a German legion of some 2,000 among their compatriots. Certain that it was a dangerous mistake, Marx refused to have anything to do with it. He did not change his mind in mid-March when a series of revolutions broke out in Germany. The German legion marched out of Paris on April 1 and was promptly annihilated when it crossed the Rhine.[10]

Earlier, on about March 12, Marx had tersely reported to Engels, who was still in Brussels: "The Central Committee has been constituted here. . . .I have been made president."[11] This confirmed the shift in leadership and formally recognized the primacy of Marx and his lieutenants over the London group. The new Central Committee comprised: Marx, Engels, and Wolff; and the original members, the former forestry student Karl Schapper, who had been *primus inter pares*, the watchmaker Joseph Moll, and the shoemaker Heinrich Bauer. Schapper accepted the post of secretary.

Marx then proceeded, in what had become the classical communist revolutionary method, to organize a German workers' association as a reserve for new league members. He was in effective command of the kind of force he thought appropriate to make his kind of attack on the old order. The Provisional Government of France was providing funds to the foreign revolutionaries, partly out of feelings of solidarity, but chiefly to rid the country of an excess of foreigners. Bornstedt and Herwegh had enjoyed this questionable benefit. So did Marx, and he used the money to send several scores of league members and hastily recruited candidate-members into a Germany now open to revolutionary enterprise. They were armed with the *Communist Manifesto* and another statement of principles, "The Demands of the Communist Party in Germany," which Marx and Engels, the latter now in Paris, drew up. The statement was an aggressive jumble of Marxian and pre-Marxian ideas calling for a republic with some socialist measures. It was meant to appeal to the lower middle class and the peasants as well as to the workers.[12] At the beginning of April Marx, accompanied by Engels, set out for Cologne, which would be his revolutionary capital. He had got all he wanted from France and her revolution.

One of Marx's earliest actions in Cologne was a ruthless denial of his own revolutionary optimism of February. He dissolved the Communist League. At a meeting of nine leading league members two months after he arrived, he got his way over the objections of the rigidly optimistic Schapper and Moll. Marx argued that the league was superfluous, since the right of assembly and freedom of the press, now general in Germany, permitted action that was revolutionary without being illegal.[13] Behind his decision was the estimate of the revolutionary potentials he had already made in Paris, as expressed, for example, in the formulation of the

"Demands of the Communist Party." What he now saw in Germany confirmed him in his judgment. At the moment the revolutionary movement belonged more to the middle class than to the workers, most of the latter artisans in any case, and not industrial proletarians. Furthermore, the peasants had to be considered. The league, which would inevitably fail if it tried to make a proletarian revolution, could keep its integrity for future operations only by dissolving itself now. Another negative factor reinforced Marx's arguments powerfully: most of the men the league had dispatched to Germany simply disappeared, and not one effective league section had been organized outside of Cologne itself, where the league section antedated the revolution.

There was one apparent exception. Stephan Born, Engels' companion in Paris, had been remarkably successful when he began as the league's representative in Berlin. On May 11, 1848, he diffidently wrote Marx, "I am pretty much at the head of the workers' movement here." He was, however, concentrating on the economic welfare of the workers, a policy obedient neither to the league's principles nor Marx's leadership. Born understood Marx's actions better than Marx's followers did. Like Marx, he had found the Communist League irrelevant in the circumstances. "As far as the league itself is concerned . . . I can't tell you a thing. Nobody really has the time to organize it in the old style. The league has dissolved—it is everywhere and nowhere." [14]

Born's activities suggested the limits to Marx's only too clearly, but Marx refused to take offense. In early 1849 Born visited Cologne and, despite the heresy he represented, Marx welcomed him warmly. At the time, after his early successes in Berlin, Born had established himself even more successfully in Leipzig. He was editor of *Die Verbrüderung*, the twice-weekly organ of the Workers' Brotherhood, a union of thirty-four workers' associations in northern and eastern Germany, which he had helped organize. The brotherhood wanted social measures, not socialism, the ten-hour day, production cooperatives, and employment bureaus. Born had accompanied Jenny Marx to Paris the day before Marx was expelled from Brussels, but it was surely more than gratitude that led Marx to receive Born so well. It was respect for a leader who had a substantial *workers'* organization behind him. Born's memoirs do not report what he and Marx said to each other. [15]

In Cologne, Marx's command post was a newspaper office. Upon his arrival he found that the local radicals, including Moses Hess and Heinrich Bürgers, the latter having cast off his hostility to Hess, were engaged in founding a newspaper. Marx, with his experience and undoubted ability, and with the power given him by his league followers, overwhelmed the Hess group and began publishing the *Neue Rheinische Zeitung* (dated June 1) as editor-in-chief on May 31. (Hess presently went off to Paris, where he was ineffectively active in the radical German community.) Engels, Marx's second-in-command, later described his management as "pure dictatorship."[16] Marx, correctly calculating that he could win Bürgers wholly from his other loyalties, accepted him as one of his editors. The other members of Marx's editorial staff were all friends or followers from Brussels, Wilhelm Wolff, the journalists Ferdinand Wolf and Ernst Dronke, and the poets Georg Weerth and (arriving later in 1848 from Brussels) Ferdinand Freiligrath. With this absolute control of one revolutionary force, Marx could maneuver skillfully among the other revolutionary forces.

The *NRZ*'s financing was a series of miracles. Engels said that the first issue, which attacked the Frankfurt Parliament, drove away half the original shareholders, and the other half gave up in June, when Marx reacted with characteristic fury to the suppression of the uprising of the Parisian workers.[17] This is doubtless an approximation of the truth. Engels did not explain where Marx found the money to keep the *NRZ* alive, but Marx sought it on time-consuming trips, one to Berlin and Vienna from August 24 to September 11, 1848, and another to Hamburg and northwest Germany from April 14 to May 9, 1849. The second trip was an odd and inexplicably extended failure during the German Revolution's last days, but the first had produced a fair sum from a Polish group happy about the *NRZ*'s support of its cause and desirous of keeping it.[18] Probably Marx contributed the last of the money he had gotten from his mother.[19]

The *NRZ*, always trying to move from reporting events to making them, was more than a newspaper. It was a political organization exercising power and proposing to use that power to mount another revolution upon the German Revolution of 1848. Marx and his editors, holding other, specifically political positions, were the general staff of the second revolution. The dissolution of the Communist League had been a technical maneuver. It had, however, been absolutely necessary.

The *NRZ*, avoiding name and issue, was not a communist newspaper. In fact, it carried the subtitle *Organ of the Democracy*, meaning the left-wing liberal but incorrigibly bourgeois Democratic Party. Engels later said its policy concentrated on two major objectives: "a single, indivisible, democratic German republic, and war against Russia."[20] With patriotism meant as the generator of other changes, it was an adaptation of

Robespierre's policy of the French Revolution. As for the other changes, the *NRZ*'s articles advocated reforms that would emancipate the middle class while granting modest benefits to the workers and peasants. By this policy Marx and the *NRZ* were recognizing the fact that the industrial proletariat, as distinct from the pre-industrial skilled workers, scarcely existed in Germany. Nor did the *NRZ* make any great effort to attract the skilled workers, who preferred other newspapers. (A recent analysis has said that the *NRZ*'s sophisticated language tended to repel working-class readers.)[21] Failing to appeal to the peasants as well, the *NRZ* was thrown back on the middle class and its dreams of a great and united Germany. Marx could not forbear to hint that the initial objectives would be transcended in the apocalyptic events, but such sulfurous whiffs only made the newspaper's patriotism more interesting. Increasing its circulation to 6,000, it became one of the largest and most passionately read newspapers in Germany.

Marx, meanwhile, was functioning not only as head of a somewhat secret revolutionary organization and as a prominent editor but also as a political leader within the limits of legality—as a Democrat. The Democratic leader Marx had considerable weight in Cologne and the Rhineland, and his influence extended, although attenuated and belatedly, as far as Berlin. When he had arrived in Cologne in April, however, he had found a rival, also armed with a newspaper, commanding enthusiastic support among the city's artisans. The situation called forth Marx's subtlest capacities.

The rival was the Jewish doctor Andreas Gottschalk, described by a contemporary, much as the Russian Annenkov had seen Marx, as "made to be a dictator . . . with the sharp intelligence of a guillotine, a living portrait of Robespierre."[22] Gottschalk had organized a small section of the Communist League in Cologne in the summer or fall of 1847. The section comprised perhaps fewer than a score of intellectuals and other nonworkers. Its members, all of whom would have more or less important relationships with Marx, included the former officers August von Willich and Friedrich Anneke, and the doctors Karl d'Ester and Roland Daniels. On March 3, 1848, as the news of the revolution in France was taking effect, the Cologne section of the Communist League organized a mass demonstration at the city hall. Troops were called, clashes took place, and a few persons were killed and wounded. Gottschalk, Willich, and Anneke were arrested and spent three weeks in prison.

Gottschalk, his revolutionary stature heightened by many cubits, proceeded to found the Workers' Association, which quickly expanded to a membership of some 5,000 or more. His position on the left of Marx was so embarrassing to Franz Mehring, the German Social Democrat who was Marx's first biographer, that he did not mention Gottschalk's existence at all.[23] Marx was not embarrassed. He cooperated with Gottschalk and Gottschalk's workers. Furthermore, he did it in the character of a bourgeois politician. A few days after coming to Cologne, Marx had helped organize the city's Democratic Association, which had a membership of middle-class radicals, and he led it into a coalition with the Workers' Association. While he maneuvered between bourgeoisie and workers in this way, he also had to deal with a third group as part of the coalition whose name was a denial of his fundamental belief in the class war. This was the Association of Workers and Employers, composed of small businessmen and master craftsmen along with their employees. Although it presently faded away, its support was most convenient to Marx for a few months. The three groups tried to act together to the extent of opposing the majority liberals and conservatives.

In Germany at large, liberals responsibly attempted to master and direct the revolutionary unrest. Throughout March more or less violent and successful insurrections had taken place in Vienna, Berlin, and elsewhere. Among the results was the formation of the Frankfurt Parliament for all of the thirty-nine states of Germany, and the Prussian Assembly in Berlin. Few radicals close to Marx's position were elected to these bodies, where mild and mildly progressive bureaucrats, professors, lawyers, and businessmen tried to match the desirable with the possible in the almost incomprehensible complexities of the new situation. The complexities included the demands of the aroused middle class as well as the workers and peasants, the competition among equally aroused national interests in a German-dominated area that included millions of non-Germans (three-quarters of the population of the Austrian Empire was non-German), and the resistance of the landowning aristocracy which provided the officers of the army. Marx the editor held to his newspaper's simplistic program while Marx the politican traced an appropriately qualified tactical pattern.

Marx, making no mistakes, was able to exploit the mistakes of others. In June Andreas Gottschalk, particularly dangerous to Marx's revolutionary position because particularly revolutionary, proposed a complete union of Cologne's three left-wing organizations. The idea was all too obviously Machiavellian: Marx's Democratic Association and the Association of Workers and Employers together would have been outvoted by the much more numerous membership of Gottschalk's Workers' Association. Marx did not have to think long to refuse for the Democrats. Coordination—a "united front"—against common enemies was nevertheless advisable. Marx's solution was to cooperate in creating an executive organ, the Committee of Six, with two representatives from each of the three associations. Marx was one of the two Democratic members.

Another Machiavellian action of Gottschalk's, combined with revolutionary naïveté, proved self-defeating. He had taken advantage of the great revolutionary energy of Marx's men, Karl Schapper and Joseph Moll, to use them in his Workers' Association. Perhaps he could seduce them away from Marx. But on July 3, shortly after the Committee of Six was formed, the police arrested Gottschalk. In his revolutionary élan Gottschalk had been urging his Workers' Association, the police said, "to use violence to establish a republic."[24] Gottschalk was imprisoned for six months, a tremendous stroke of fortune for Marx. Schapper and Moll, undisturbed by the police, proceeded to capture the presidency and vice-presidency of Gottschalk's Workers' Association, thus the association itself, and placed it at Marx's disposal. Marx reached the height of his political power in mid-August, when the Committee of Six, which he now dominated, called a congress of Rhine Democrats in Cologne.

Carl Schurz, who later became secretary of the interior in the United States, was a student at Bonn in 1848, and attended the congress as a delegate. He remembered Marx as "the recognized head of the advanced socialistic school . . . [who] at once attracted general attention." But the congress also suggested the limits to Marx's persuasions. He could not win popularity with a bearing, as Schurz described it, that was "so provoking and intolerable" toward those who disagreed with him. To the middle-class delegates it must have been extraordinary to experience "the cutting disdain with which he pronounced the word *bourgeois*."[25] The congress passed its vague resolutions, including one expressing concern about the peasants, and laid plans for a future that never came. Beyond the Rhineland, the Democrat Marx managed to have some influence in the governing committee, in Berlin, of all the German Democratic associations. The committee chairman was actually Hermann Kriege, the True Socialist returned from his American adventure, but he was overshadowed toward the end of 1848 by the Cologne doctor Karl d'Ester. Marx's powerful attractions as a leader, meanwhile, had won d'Ester away from his attachment to the imprisoned Gottschalk. The Democratic associations remained a scattering of weak groups, but they gave Marx and his *NRZ* somewhat greater effect upon events.

As politician and editor Marx managed his contradictions masterfully.

As either he kept his policy prudent, however reckless his behavior and language. For the while, Marx remained true to the conception of a united front, which sternly ignored the workers' demands. He might insult bourgeois Democrats who would not follow him in transcending their class origins, but he went on working with them. Nor did Marx change when the workers' insurrection in Paris roused his revolutionary temper. In late June several thousands of radicalized Parisian workers rose up against the bourgeois republican government of France. This was the social revolution within the political revolution, which Alexis de Tocqueville, aristocratic, liberal, and frankly frightened, had identified as clearly as had Marx. Hundreds of workers were shot down and hundreds of survivors later transported.

Marx reacted with pure revolutionary anger and an acute sense of the economic and social issues. "The momentary triumph of brute force has been purchased at the cost . . . of the dissolution of the whole antique republican party—with the cleavage of the French nation into two nations, the nation of proprietors and the nation of workers." His style, stuttering with dashes, reproduced his incoherent rage. "The fraternity, the brotherhood of opposing classes, of whom one exploits the other . . . —its true, undisguised, prosaic expression is—*civil war*, civil war in its most frightful aspect, the war of labor and capital." With merciless revolutionary justice he would offer "no tears, no sighs, and no words of regret for the victims in the ranks of the National Guard, the Mobile Guard, the Republican Guard, and the regiments of the line who fell before the anger of the people. The state will look after their widows and orphans, pompous decrees will glorify them."[26] But this had to do with France. In Germany, Marx continued to overlook the class war and contain his hatred, if not his contempt, for his middle-class associates.

Marx released his editorial recklessness only in the area of international politics. Here he could operate, as Engels' statement of the newspaper's policy indicated, with another of his great simplifications. An unsigned article gave the logic: "Only the *war with Russia* is the war that revolutionary Germany should fight . . . spreading civilization through the sacrifice of her sons and freeing herself within, while bringing freedom without."[27] But the Russian war, comparatively modest as it was, remained another unattainable ideal. Russia, fearing revolutionary energy, avoided confrontations, and Germany had neither the resources nor the will for such an action.

In fact, Prussia, thrust into the leadership of all Germany by the circumstances, backed down in a dispute with the insignificant force rep-

resented by Denmark. Engels could only condemn this cowardice before
"a brutal, dirty, piratical old-Nordic nationality."[28] Marx ceaselessly
scourged the Prussian government, headed originally by Ludolf Camphausen, the liberal Rhine industrialist who had been one of the founders
of his old *Rheinische Zeitung*. Camphausen, caught between left and right,
resigned in June, and Marx's attacks intensified against the succession of
decreasingly liberal chancellors. Marx was contemptuous of the Frankfurt Parliament, scorning even its far left group of twelve, of which his
old associate, Arnold Ruge, was a member. This greater German assembly, lacking military forces or even an administration, was seldom a serious object of his concern as it helplessly discussed such problems as the
inclusion or exclusion of the Austrian Empire. Marx and his newspaper,
functionally irresponsible, demanded the impossible and condemned the
responsible leaders who would not attempt it.

In September the editorial staff of the *NRZ* sallied out in its truer character as a revolutionary general staff. Disorders in Cologne provided the
occasion. On September 13 Prussian troops rioted, following outbursts
of patriotic anger over the Danish affair. Wilhelm Wolff organized a protest demonstration, which several thousands attended, in the main square.
The speakers included not only Wolff, but also Engels, Bürgers, and the
insignificant Dronke. They demanded a new civic guard of workers under a Committee of Public Safety, an old revolutionary name that promised a new revolutionary authority. The demonstrators thereupon elected
thirty-two members to the committee, including Marx, who was evidently not present, and most of his close associates.

On September 17 the committee organized a meeting of some 10,000
in the village of Worringen, ten miles north of Cologne. The announced
objective was to urge the impotent Frankfurt Parliament to unite all Germany in an action that would, in effect, overwhelm Prussia within a war-
united Germany, while taking up its action, suspended by an armistice,
against Denmark. The committee also hoped to draw the local peasants
into the revolutionary spirit. The meeting was noisy and helpless. Schapper presided, and Engels, among many, made a speech. Marx did not
attend. When violence also broke out in Frankfurt, the authorities began
to react carefully. In Cologne, on September 25, the Prussian government ordered the arrest of Engels, Wolff, and two other friends of Marx,
but not Marx himself, since he had most prudently not gone to Worringen.
The radicals in Cologne reacted by raising a few barricades; the authorities countered by declaring a state of siege; the populace permitted itself
to be quickly calmed.

Newspapers had been suspended from September 26 to October 3, when the state of siege was lifted. The *NRZ*, however, did not reappear immediately because Marx was too short of funds and staff. Desperately signing promissory notes, he resumed publishing only on October 12. Schapper was imprisoned for two months and most of the other staff members had fled. Engels "seems to have lost his nerve," according to his latest biographer,[29] and escaped to Belgium. Put on a train to Paris as a vagabond, he proceeded to act like one, and walking for the most part, enjoyed an idyllic interval in the countrysides of France and Switzerland. He returned to Cologne in mid-January. Marx, meanwhile, had managed to keep the newspaper going with his two poets, Weerth and Freiligrath.

The revolutionary actions of September, new examples of attempts at the impossible, had crippled Marx's operations. Yet, again, he had made no mistakes. He had had to test the revolutionary potentials but, as chief of staff, could not expose himself. He had properly given his lieutenants the mission. Moreover, the actions would have their value in the future. No one could accuse the Marx group of lacking revolutionary energy and daring.

With Schapper's arrest and Moll's flight, Marx found himself with another leadership responsibility. Replacing Schapper, he was elected president of the Workers' Association and gave it distracted attention. The association was, however, becoming less important. Gottschalk, still in prison, was helpless to take advantage of the situation; he became no more effective when he was released in January 1849. By that time Schapper, freed a month ealier, had resumed daily control of it, although Marx remained president in name until February. Gottschalk, in his frustration, departed Cologne for Brussels and intrigued vainly through a few remaining lieutenants against Marx's domination. The struggle ended at a meeting of the executive committee on January 29. Schapper and his friends reorganized the association and removed the editor of its newspaper, a lieutenant of Gottschalk's who had been attacking the alliance with the Democrats.[30] Whatever the association was worth, it remained Marx's tool.

In November 1848 Marx had led the *NRZ* into a new editorial campaign. The king of Prussia, in a dispute with the Prussian Assembly, dismissed a mildly liberal general who had been head of government, and replaced him with a conservative aristocrat. The assembly was ordered to leave Berlin, where the radical workers were intimidating it, and meet in the town of Brandenburg, thirty-five miles to the west. Most of the assembly's members resisted the decision. Troops thereupon evicted them. As a revolutionary countermeasure, Marx urged the Rhineland to organize a people's militia and refuse to pay taxes. In the issue of November 14 he roared in italics and boldface, "*Now the battle seems unavoidable* and it is the **duty of the Rhineland to hurry to the help of the National Assembly with men and weapons.**"[31] The king, his authority becoming stronger daily, dealt with the legislature easily enough in December. When a quorum failed to appear in Brandenburg, he dissolved it and granted a constitution that preserved his essential powers. The *NRZ* and its recalcitrant editor were a local problem, and the government of the Rhineland indicted Marx for incitement to rebellion.

Marx was not deterred. The fall of revolutionary Vienna to Austrian imperial troops at the end of October had further enraged him. An article of his, coolly announcing his revolutionary strategy, identified the enemy and the enemy's crime: "the *Bourgeoisie. . . . Treason* of all kinds saw to it that Vienna fell."[32] He concluded, leaning on both materialism and revolutionary free will, that "the fruitless slaughter since the June revolution . . . the cannibalism of the counter-revolution itself will persuade the nations that there is only one way *to shorten,* to simplify, to abbreviate the murderous birth pangs of the old society, the bloody birth pangs of the new society, only *one way—revolutionary terrorism.*"[33] A month later, on December 10, a huge headline urged: "NO MORE TAXES!!!" The article, by Marx, went on: "We have never made a secret of it. We do not stand on legal ground; we stand on revolutionary ground."[34]

In the New Year's issue of 1849 Marx responded to the frustrations of the first revolutionary year with a transcendent vision for this next one. He theorized: Great Britain's leadership would intervene against a continental revolution, but a new series of actions would erupt out of the tradition of the great French Revolution. The workers would rise again in France. The tremors would shiver Britain's foundations and the Chartists would join in the renewed revolution. Having convinced himself, Marx ended in boldface: **"Revolutionary rising of the French working classes, world war—that is the table of contents of the year 1849.**"[35]

The extremity of Marx's editorial optimism was the measure of his desperation. Marx the politican knew better than to believe Marx the editor.

In February Marx could, at least, enjoy a personal triumph, indeed, a triumph doubled, as he twice superbly defended himself in court. He had helped himself by packing the courtroom with his supporters. On February 8, at his first trial, he swept quickly to acquittal of a charge of libel committed against state officials. After a skillful use of legalistic arguments to deal directly with the charge, he fixed his position above it with easy arrogance. "I . . . assure you, gentlemen, that I prefer to study the great issues of the world, I prefer to analyze the historical process— rather than wrestle with provincial personages, police, and courts." He explained, however, that such small men as he had attacked in the *NRZ* conveniently lent themselves to his analysis; he was frankly revealing his conscious use of the *argumentum ad hominem.* As editor he took his authority from history, he concluded, not from the temporary legal structures justifying the unjust. "The first duty of the press now is *to undermine all the foundations of the present political order.*" The sympathetic courtroom applauded.[36]

At the second trial on the next day, Marx defended himself against the charge of sedition by attacking the legal basis of the Prussian government. He was correct, since Prussia was operating with a mixture of prerevolutionary and revolutionary laws. He turned the charge upon his prosecutors. "If the Crown carries out counterrevolution, the people has a right to respond with revolution." He had first taken occasion to give a lecture on materialism. "Society is not based on the law . . . [which] must be the expression of society's common interests and needs as they arise from the material methods of production."[37] Marx won another acquittal, the jury foreman thanking him for an illuminating exposition,[38] and both speeches were published in a pamphlet. They would serve a greater cause than defense in legal actions.

Marx was returning to revolutionary social and economic issues as the political revolution declined in Germany, but his maneuvers were too subtle for his associates. In the *NRZ* on January 22 he had still defended political cooperation with the middle class. "Our cry to the workers and the lower-middle class is: You should prefer to suffer in a modern bourgeois society whose industry creates the material conditions for a new society that will free you all."[39] This called up a tellingly pathetic rebuttal from Andreas Gottschalk in Brussels. "Why should we, men of the proletariat, spill our blood? . . . Should we really . . . Mister Preacher . . . escape the hell of the Middle Ages only to precipitate ourselves freely into the purgatory of decrepit capitalistic rule?"[40] But this had little effect.

Later, in the spring of 1849, however, Marx had to withstand an attempt by some of his own followers to change direction. Joseph Moll, after fleeing in December, had gone to London. There, with Heinrich Bauer, he had organized a new Central Committee of the formally non-existent Communist League. Now Moll returned to Cologne, and winning the support of Schapper, among others, demanded the reconstitution of the league. Marx refused in two tense meetings. With the press still free, he said firmly, the situation did not call for conspiratorial tactics. His strong will maintained his authority. Moll moved on to other cities in Germany on a mission that became more and more senseless.[41]

Marx was moving to the left, but after his own fashion. The issues of the NRZ from April 5 through 11 carried a series of articles entitled "Wage-Labor and Capital" which were drawn from the lectures he had given to the Workers' Association in Brussels in late 1847.[42] Marx explained that tactical needs had dictated his concentration on politics but it was now necessary to return to the "*economic relations* [as the] material basis of the present class struggles."[43] On April 15 the NRZ carried the curt announcement that Marx and his associates, including Schapper and Wolff, were resigning from the Rhineland Committee of Democratic Associations. The committee, the article said, represented "too many heterogeneous elements to allow of an activity profitable to the aims of the cause."[44] Marx could now act as a frank revolutionary through his one remaining affiliation, his membership in the Cologne Workers' Association. It was beside the point that the association was now weak, isolated, and suffering continuing losses as the disillusioned followers of Gottschalk fell away. The point was revolutionary purity.

The German Revolution was ending. In early May a rising in Dresden, in which the oddly assorted Bakunin and Richard Wagner participated, was put down. The authorities were encouraged to consolidate their position. On May 11 Marx was ordered to leave Prussian territory. He had renounced Prussian citizenship while he was living in Belgium, probably to avoid the danger of arrest, and now he had no recourse but to obey. The last issue of the NRZ, dated May 19, appeared on May 18. Marx printed 20,000 copies in red ink. It was the famous Red Edition, an act of revolutionary defiance. On the first page, with the voice of Ferdinand Freiligrath, the NRZ cried: "With hate and straining scorn on my lips,/ With my glittering dagger in my hand,/In my act of dying calling out, 'Rebellion!'/ . . . . Now farewell you swords and spears! . . . /Soon will I rise up again with clattering weapons,/Soon will I return—all the greater!"

Marx nevertheless counseled caution to the workers of Cologne. "Finally, we urge you to avoid any attempt at a putsch. What with Cologne's military situation you would not have a chance." The only result would be a state of siege and a profounder humiliation of the Rhineland. The workers would do better to do nothing. "Your calm will drive the Prussians to despair." On another page Marx reiterated Freiligrath's promise to return. Speaking for the revolutionaries and not for the workers they had to leave behind, he addressed the authorities with uncompromising intent. He repeated his statement of the first trial. His policy, he said, had always been aimed at "*undermining all the foundations of the established order.*" He made it clear. "*We are ruthless, we ask no mercy from you. When our turn comes we will practice terrorism without trying to prettify what we do.*"[45] Marx left the German Revolution of 1848 with his own revolution inviolate.

Marx left Cologne with Engels. After some adventures, including a few days of imprisonment in Darmstadt and Frankfurt, they separated. In Baden, Engels joined revolutionaries commanded by August von Willich, fought in a last, futile operation as Willich's adjutant, and escaped to Switzerland. (Joseph Moll, after his vain efforts to revive the League, also joined the Baden revolutionaries and was killed in action.) Marx went on to Paris, where the duly elected president of the Second Republic, Louis Napoleon, was skillfully smothering the French revolution. A feeble demonstration by the remaining radicals in Paris in mid-June, a few days after Marx arrived, gave the government the excuse to move against all radicals. In August Marx was told to leave Paris; he could settle, if he liked, in a small town in Brittany. On August 23 he wrote to Engels, who was in Lausanne, that he was going to London. He told Engels to join him there. "We'll do business in London."[46]

SIX

THE PERMANENT REVOLUTION

In 1875, AFTER SO MUCH MORE revolutionary achievement and failure, Marx reflected on his early period in London: "The shattering crash of a revolution leaves the heads of its participants in a state of shock—I mean those who have been flung into exile, away from the field of action at home. The shock robs even the ablest person of the ability to think straight for a shorter or a longer time. He cannot locate the course of history."[1] Marx was referring to another revolutionary but he was inevitably talking about himself.

Yet Marx had already made himself so much a part of history that he never quite lost his way. He kept his somnambulistic security in all the shock and confusion. He had long since developed his saving idea, the conception of the permanent revolution, which had been first expressed in the *Deutsch-Französische Jahrbücher*. All the apparent contradictions and changes of direction in revolutionary circumstances, Marx believed, had an inner coherence. He continued to lead his permanent revolution.

For Marx the wretched situation of the revolutionary refugees in London represented a duty and an opportunity; he made no distinction between the two. The German Workers' Educational Association in Great Windmill Street, Soho, was his first base of operations. There, in November 1849, Marx had joined a committee to assist refugees, and, while struggling incompetently and distractedly to care for his own family, gave himself to the needs of his penniless and bewildered fellows. In November, also, Engels had arrived in London, and Marx brought him and August von Willich, both survivors of the Baden action, into the committee. Marx and Engels would soon have their difficulties with Willich, but now he was their ally in dealing with noncommunist committee members. In January 1850 Marx and his friends drove them out. The refugee community was an unstable mass, and the purged committee had to maintain itself against several other competing groups. It survived long enough to help some hundreds of arrivals and give Marx a starting point in his professional activities. In the course of 1850, while thus engaged, Marx adjusted his conception of the permanent revolution to the real circumstances.

In London, Marx had found a more or less operative Central Committee of the Communist League. While he had dissolved the league in Germany in 1848, the circumstances were different now. Had Joseph Moll not reconstituted it behind his back, Marx would doubtless have done so himself when he arrived in London. He rejoined the Central Committee and brought in Engels and, on Engels' recommendation, Willich. Karl Schapper, reappearing a little later, also rejoined. In 1850, on the revolutionary afterwave, the Central Committee members agreed that the next revolution would come soon and be theirs.

On the Continent, in the debris of revolution, some small, broken revolutionary life stirred. Schapper, in fact, had organized a tiny communist group in Wiesbaden after his release from prison, but the town authorities discovered and annihilated it, expelling him in June 1850. They could not, however, eradicate all worker organizations, and here and there one continued to meet. In Cologne, Gottschalk's old Workers' Association transformed itself into the Workers' *Educational* Association under the formal leadership of the cigarette worker Peter Gerhard Röser. Actually, its real leader was the old friend of Marx's, the doctor Roland Daniels, and most of its members, like Daniels, were middle-class intellectuals, doctors, lawyers, and journalists. Marx, writing officially to Röser in January 1850, ordered him to organize secret sections of the Communist League in Cologne and elsewhere in southern Germany.[2] Röser complied, but succeeded only in Cologne. In Hamburg and a few other cities, communist groups managed to survive, often with the help of police agents who wanted to have something to report. Other German communists kept up some kind of organizational existence in France and, more actively and numerously, in a more tolerant Switzerland. In London the Communist League had work to do, however petty and frustrating, which justified its existence.

In March 1850 the Central Committee of the league sent out its orders. The March Address was a tiny, deceptively clear beacon in the postrevolutionary murk.[3] In Marx's language and expressing his irreducible revolutionary optimism, it reaffirmed the policy he had pursued since the spring of 1849, when he had broken with the German Democrats. The address was directed ostensibly to communist workers, but actually, since there were almost none such, to revolution-minded intellectuals. Marx ordered them to create their own "independent, secret, and public organization." Clearly talking to leaders and not to the masses they would lead, Marx went on to mix daydream and realism in his advice. "Far from opposing the so-called excesses, the expression of the people's revenge committed against hated persons or public buildings to whom hateful memories are attached, you must not only tolerate such expressions, but also assume the leadership over them."

A projection of the characteristics of past revolutions into the immediate future, the fantasy also expressed Marx's internal violences and affinity for external ones. Happy to assume that such actions would necessarily occur, he looked ahead to the next step, when the communist leadership would limit them by a "calm and cold-blooded comprehension of the circumstances." Nor, in his immediate revolution, did Marx give immediate victory to the communist workers. While warning against the machinations of the petit-bourgeois Democrats, the address assumed that they would first control events. "You must maintain your own revolutionary worker-governments side by side with the official governments." These latter would be "observed and kept under threat by a leadership behind which the whole mass of workers stands." Only then did the address arrive at the final stage, when the proletariat would assume all power. "Your battle cry must be: the permanent revolution." [4]

During the next month Marx explored a larger fantasy. With five others he constituted the World Society of Revolutionary Communism as a superior level of revolutionary authority. The World Society's membership would include only the leaders of the operative organizations. Such a group might coordinate all action against the established governments. Yet its only reason for existence, as given in the founding statement,[5] was its negative character. Besides Marx, Engels, and Willich, the signatories of the statement were two followers of Auguste Blanqui, republican revolutionaries but not communists, and the Chartist leader Julian Harney, who was neither a revolutionary nor a communist. The first article, calling for a "dictatorship of the proletariat" and, again, for the "permanent revolution," was purely Marxian. The statement then proceeded with the "principle of republican fraternity," which Marx had contemptuously transcended. With such regressive contradictions, the society could hardly affirm anything besides a demand for power.

Marx did not take the Blanquists seriously. Not long after he signed the statement, he coldly reviewed two books by French republican con-

spirators. "Their activity consists precisely in anticipating the revolutionary process . . . in improvising a revolution in the absence of revolutionary conditions. . . . They are the alchemists of the revolution."[6]
Marx may have distractedly attended a few meetings of the World Society, but his final word on it showed how little it had meant to him. On
October 9, 1850, he wrote a curt note to the Blanquist members. He said
the society had long since been dissolved in reality, and he invited them
to join him the following Sunday, four days hence, in burning the founding statement.[7] Marx was always willing to use alchemists, but he had
found these alchemists useless and could indulge himself in the pleasure
of insulting them.

Closer to reality, Marx was using his position within the Communist
League to pursue his real objectives. The June Address of the Central
Committee, which was bombastic in a way uncharacteristic of Marx,
pressed hard for action in Germany while admitting the power of reaction and ubiquity of police spies.[8] In the earlier part of July evidently,
Marx personally wrote to Roland Daniels and remonstrated with him
about a "lack of energetic activity" in Cologne.[9] Late that month, however, Marx warned the Cologne section that August von Willich was
trying the anticipate the revolution like the Blanquists.[10] Here was an
issue of absolute seriousness.

In the summer of 1850 the military man Willich challenged the ideologist Marx. It was Willich whom Marx would see in 1875 as a victim of
revolutionary shock, but Willich had never done enough thinking to have
suffered real shock to his mental processes. Used to giving orders, Willich now found a new field for action. His hunger for power justified
itself with reckless hope, and he could easily seduce those others who
demanded more hope than Marx would dispense. Willich, overshadow-
ing the other leaders of the Communist League, presently had a greater
following than Marx in the Workers' Educational Association, the refugee committee, and the league itself. Karl Schapper humbly became his
ally. Willich then attacked Marx's last position of authority, the Central
Committee of the Communist League. A gourmand of action, Willich
was simultaneously advocating alliances with Democrats and a workers'
dictatorship. At a meeting of the Central Committee on September 1
Willich and Marx quarreled violently, and Willich challenged Marx to a
duel. Marx had too much moral courage to enter into wasteful bravado,
but a young follower accepted the challenge for him. Marx, with his
ruthlessness and capacity for hatred, made no effort to discourage his
champion and may well have hoped that the duel would eliminate his

grossly inconvenient rival. Willich's shot, however, grazed the young man's head, causing him to lose consciousness and become the subject of a death report. Quickly recovered, he reappeared miraculously in the Marx home the next day.[11] This was a mad prologue to a coldly sane action by Marx.

The action took place at the next meeting of the Central Committee, on September 15.[12] Among the nine members present Willich had only two supporters. On his authority, however, he was calling an assembly of the whole London section of the league, confident that he could command a majority there. The meeting gave Marx his opportunity before the assembly could elect a new Central Committee which Willich would inevitably control. Marx began by questioning his right to convoke an assembly of the London section. Abruptly, Marx made a motion, which began, "The Central Committee is transferred from London to Cologne; the Central Committee of the Cologne section becomes the Central Committee of the league as soon as this meeting of the Central Committee today is closed."[13] The point was clear to all: Marx dominated the tiny Cologne section through his friends; furthermore, the Prussian government, stiffened by reaction, would see to it that the section attempted no adventures.

As for the Willich group, Marx recognized and minimized it in the same phrase. The motion called it the "minority," an unfair word since Willich's followers formed a majority in both the London section of the Communist League and the Workers' Educational Association. The motion then provided for two London sections unrelated to each other directly, but connected with the Communist League in Cologne, which, according to Part One of the motion, would be the active authority of the league.

In his perfect arrogance, Marx justified his decision by citing himself as the ideological authority on the revolution. The dissidents were violating the fundamental ideas, materialism and revolutionary internationalism, of the Communist League as expressed in the *Communist Manifesto*. Willich and his followers, Marx specified, had put revolutionary will above materialism. "While we tell the workers, 'You have fifteen, twenty, fifty years in which to endure the civil war in order to change the conditions,' you say, 'We must arrive at leadership immediately.'" That would reduce the revolution to an empty word—destroy it. Marx sharpened his reasoning. "I believe I have found the way to permit us to separate without annihilating the party."[14] Marx was sincere. He did not want to destroy the Willich group, with its considerable numbers, since the damage to the revolutionary cause would be too great. The best policy would be to try to render it harmless and keep it in a state of suspended existence until conditions justified overt action.

Marx's opponents were as helpless against his arguments as they were against his majority of the moment. There was a brief discussion, hardly a debate. Only Karl Schapper spoke against the motion. (Heinrich Bauer, the other surviving leader of the League of the Just, silently supported Marx.) Schapper took his stand on faith. "I am above all an enthusiast on this issue."[15] He went on to accuse Marx of putting himself above the proletariat. Marx replied, "I have always scorned the proletariat's opinion of the moment."[16] Willich and his other follower left without a word. Schapper protested his friendship for Marx and regretted the principle driving him into opposition. He expressed his own conflict by remaining to the end but refusing to sign the minutes that gave the victory to Marx.[17] For Marx it was a joyless victory, but nonetheless valuable.

Marx had fitted together the elements of his mature definition of the permanent revolution. As he told the Central Committee, he saw it as a process that would persist until it had worked itself out. No one could predict how long that would take, and the revolutionary party must have the courage to confront a delay of fifty years. The revolutionaries must not destroy themselves by overrunning reality. They had the duty to survive, at the same time pressing forward continually toward the socialist future. The revolution would be permanent until consummated.

Marx had begun developing the sense of the permanent revolution in a series of articles written through most of 1850. In London, he had continued his journalism. With money he could not afford and uncertain financial support, he had founded the *Neue Rheinische Zeitung: Politisch-Ökonomische Revue* in London. This was to begin as a monthly journal and become a daily newspaper when the revolution resumed. He got out three issues from March to May 1850, and a final, double issue in November.

Through its four issues the *Revue* carried Marx's study *The Class Struggles in France, 1848–1850*.[18] He was asking why the Revolution of 1848 had failed. At first view it might be surprising that he took the French experience as part for the whole, despite his daily experience of the *German* Revolution. Indeed, he returned once again to the French revolution in another study, *The 18th Brumaire of Louis Napoleon*, published two years later.[19] One reason would seem to be that Marx knew too much about the revolution in Germany: the facts in his head were too numerous and anarchic for him to dominate. Engels suggested an analogous reason.

"France is the country where . . . the changing political forms are stamped out in the sharpest outline,[20] that is to say, the June rising in Paris had most clearly acted out the proletarian-bourgeois class struggle. The French had obligingly performed in a way more suitable to Marx's revolutionary logic and imagination.

Marx's view of the French experience, strictly consistent with his tactics as a leader of the Communist League, changed over the summer. The fourth and final article of the study of 1850 was much closer in sense to *The 18th Brumaire*, published in 1852, than to the preceding three articles.

In his first article, written very early in 1850, Marx looked squarely at defeat—"*defeat of the revolution!*"—and denied it with the help of the dialectic. "It was not the revolution that was overcome in these defeats." He explained, "It was the prerevolutionary traditional survivals, the products of social conditions, which had not developed themselves to the cutting edges of class contradictions." Out of this came revolutionary progress in the form of a "united, powerful counterrevolution," which would transform the "party of rebellion" into a "true party of revolution."[21] In the May issue the third article found substance for hope in the recent election of three left-wing candidates, none of them even socialists, to the French Assembly.

The substance was infinitesimal, but Marx saw the "French proletariat gather[ing] more and more behind the leadership of *revolutionary socialism*, behind *communism*." This was the "*declaration of the permanence of the revolution*."[22] In June, while struggling with his communist rivals, Marx took a reader's ticket to the Reading Room of the British Museum. He wanted to undershore his next article with economic data. Writing it in October, he found the data perversely discouraging. The Western economies, further assisted by the discovery of gold in California the year before, had recovered exuberantly from the recession that had begun in the late 1840s. In the final issue of the *Revue* Marx concluded, "There can be no thought of a real revolution . . . in the face of this genuine prosperity."[23] Adding more materialism to the dialectic, Marx saw hope not lost but surely delayed.

When Marx began *The 18th Brumaire of Louis Napoleon* at the end of 1851, he had settled more deeply into patience. In a remarkably mellow passage he reviewed the facile successes, as he insisted upon seeing them, of the eighteenth-century bourgeois revolutions. The proletarian revolutions of the nineteenth century had infinitely greater responsibilities and problems. The new revolutions found themselves flung back "only to begin again from the beginning. Cruelly and thoroughly, they administer contempt to the insufficiencies, weaknesses, and wretchednesses of their own first initiatives . . . shrink back continually before the unbounded immensity of their own objectives—until the conditions are created which make any retreat impossible, and the conditions themselves call out: '*Hic Rhodes, hic salta!*' "[24]

Yet the revolutionary will would be weakened if immature material conditions could be blamed for revolutionary failure. As a leader depending on the morale for his followers, Marx could not permit resignation to matter, even if matter was all. More important, he had to deny resignation to himself. Once again he had to solve the problem of determinism and free will. Both *The Class Struggles in France* and *The 18th Brumaire* leaned dangerously toward both. *The Class Struggles in France*, while attacking various personalities, had emphasized the force in given conditions. *The 18th Brumaire* began with a denunciation of Louis Napoleon, Louis Blanc, and others seen as leaders who crucially and nefariously influenced events. Immediately, however, Marx drew away from that logic. "Men make their own history, but not of their own free will, not under circumstances they themselves have chosen, but under the immediate effect of anterior, given, and inherited circumstances."[25] Still an apt pupil of Hegel, arranging to have both the support of history and his freedom from it, Marx had produced a skillfully fused contradiction. In 1869, in his foreword to a later edition of *The 18th Brumaire*, Marx covered the operation with a complementary contradiction: he attacked a pamphlet by Victor Hugo for making the outcome of the Revolution of 1848 depend on Louis Napoleon, and one of Proudhon's for surrendering helplessly to determinism.[26] For the practical needs of his revolution such a dialectic would serve well enough.

In November 1850, with his pessimistic last article in the *Revue*, Marx had definitively rejected the immediate revolution which Willich and Schapper claimed. Refusing to recognize the transfer of authority to Cologne, the dissidents won the support of most Communist League members in London, founded a new Central Committee, and made their control of the Workers' Educational Association absolute. Marx, who had withdrawn from the refugee committee, formally resigned from the association as well.[27] (He would quietly rejoin the latter at the end of the 1850s, when newer hopes would begin to rise, but he would never again accomplish much with it.) For a while Willich speculated on the opportunities provided by a dispute between Austria and Prussia, when Prussia made an effort to dominate the revived German Confederation. He sent out messages commanding a rising in Germany that would inspire a new French rebellion, the united German and French workers then marching into Germany and proclaiming a German workers' republic.[28] Prussia all too prudently backed down before an Austrian show of force, but a war, unlikely in any case, would surely have offered no opportunities for a proletarian or quasi-proletarian revolution. Marx left Willich and Schapper to their retribution, although, again, he had to be sternly patient.

At the meeting of September 15, when Marx split the Communist League in London, he had accurately defined his position: "I affirm that . . . I want twelve persons at most in our group—as few as possible."[29] On February 11, 1851, writing to Engels, he bravely insisted: "This suits me fine—this widely known and authentic isolation in which you and I find ourselves. It is entirely appropriate to our position and our principles. We're through with this system of reciprocal concessions, with half-truths accepted for the sake of appearances, and with the duty of publicly admitting to our share of the absurdities perpetrated by these asses."[30] While Marx believed this honestly and wisely enough, he could not help feeling differently. A few days later some hundreds of émigrés held the huge Banquet of the Equals in London to commemorate the outbreak of the Revolution of 1848. From his isolation Marx had sent two of his young followers as spies, and they were recognized as such. Marx reported to Engels, "It is one A.M. About an hour ago Pieper landed here in a heap, hatless, all messed up, in tatters." Shouting "spy, spy," Marx's enemies had leaped upon Pieper and the other young man, who were "thrown out of the hall and thrashed in the process, their hats torn, and then outside, in the courtyard, they were kicked and trampled on, their ears were boxed, they were almost torn into pieces, handfuls of hair torn out, etc."[31] It was the lowest point in Marx's revolutionary career.

During the 1850s Marx remained splendidly isolated. There always was a Marx Party, but Marx had spoken only too accurately when he mentioned twelve persons as sufficient. Of the original leaders of the League of the Just and the Communist League, Schapper had gone over to Willich, Moll was dead, and Heinrich Bauer, although remaining loyal to Marx and his purposes, would presently lose heart and emigrate to Australia in 1851. In 1853, in a letter to Engels, Marx mentioned nine followers in all. Three of them were not even in England, but in France, Germany, and the United States, and most of the other six were of no great quality. "We must recruit our party completely from scratch." [32] With these exiguous materials, as before, Marx accomplished the necessary.

There were a few steadying elements in Marx's situation. Engels had left for Manchester in November 1850 to become an executive in a cotton-spinning mill partly owned by his father, but a heavy correspondence between the friends made up most satisfactorily for the loss in daily personal contact. Indeed, it was probably safer because of Marx's great sensitivity about his own feelings and lack of it for those of other persons. Engels as capitalist, furthermore, was able to provide Marx with the financial support which Marx never could manage for himself. At home, Marx drew heavily upon his wife and children for human support.

Another steadying and saving element was journalism. In August 1851 Charles Dana, editor of the New York *Daily Tribune* and a Fourierist, asked Marx to write a series of articles on Germany. Marx, whose English was poor, got Engels to write the German series, a total of eighteen articles. Dana liked the articles so much that he made Marx the *Tribune's* London correspondent on British and world affairs, a position that Marx kept for eleven years. At first, Marx wrote his articles in German and sent them to Engels to be translated. By January 1853, Marx had mastered the language well enough to risk sending in an article in English, [33] and, failing any negative reaction, continued to do so. He had developed an excellent, even a formidable, if always Germanic style. Although he still assigned some articles to Engels, he wrote most of the rest himself. Sensitive to economic forces, imaginative in his suspicions of government leaders, unexpected in his evaluations, Marx was a fascinating and valuable correspondent despite his frequent errors of judgment. Yet Dana, unaware of the partnership's operations, preferred Engels' articles. [34] Marx earned badly needed income, and he could slip in propaganda for the cause or attacks on his rivals. Anticipating his pleasure, he wrote Engels, "This means a marvelous opportunity to scourge the émigrés." [35] Marx's work as a correspondent served his revolution quite well.

The permanent revolution was put on trial in the persons of the Cologne communists toward the end of 1852. On May 10, 1851, a member of the Cologne group aroused police suspicion in Leipzig. Examination showed that he lacked proper papers but was carrying documents of the Communist League, including names and addresses of its members. The Prussian police thereupon arrested all the communists it could find. The original charge was vague, while Prussian authority was hardly a monolithic block of reactionary anxiety. The Cologne appeals court decided that the evidence of illegal activities was insufficient. But more police work persuaded a higher court to indict and try eleven members of the Cologne group for "conspiracy . . . to overthrow the state [and] begin a civil war."[36]

The accused, faced with a mass of league documents, could not deny action to change society, but they said it was restricted to propaganda and education. Actually, they had done little more than hold the usual type of meetings with discussions of social issues. Granted, they had studied the *Communist Manifesto*, but if that led to revolution, then revolution became a natural event. Again, this was Marx's conception of the permanent revolution as a series of stages in which the earlier stages might be less than treasonable attacks on the state institutions. This was the sense of the stream of legal instructions which Marx himself was sending to the chief defense lawyer, Karl Schneider, who had been a Democratic ally of his during the 1848 Revolution (and a codefendant in one of *Marx's* trials in Cologne in 1849). Marx put the argument contemptuously in his book on the case: "The defendants operated on the frivolous assumption that the present Prussian government would fall even without their efforts. Therefore, they did not set up an organization to overthrow the present government . . . they were not guilty of conspiracy to commit high treason." He arrived at his modulation, however, only after refusing to deny his ultimate objective. Marx and his Communist League were dedicated to the "overthrow of society . . . by means of political revolution." All this was true enough, but "it meant the overthrow of the Prussian state as an earthquake meant the collapse of a henhouse."[37] Determinism was the real agent of revolution.

Against such an argument, expressed much more moderately in the court in Cologne, the presiding judge quoted the statutes of the Cologne League, which called for the use of propaganda, but "as a means . . . for the destruction of the old society [and] the implementation of the communist revolution." Peter Gerhard Röser as formal head of the Cologne communists was asked to explain. He could only say that he had wanted to add the phrase "by all legal methods," but had been persuaded by an associate that that was understood.[38] The court found itself dealing with Marx's old problem of free will and determinism, but the joint action of court and defendants buried it.

Marx had accompanied his philosophical precisions with ruthless argumenta ad hominem, particularly against Police Councillor Wilhelm Stieber, who had prepared the case.[39] The prosecution piled up questionably relevant information, some of it tending falsely to suggest a direct connection between the Marx and Willich groups—thus blurring the distinction between immediate and permanent revolution, the arbitrary and the inevitable. In February 1852, there had been a trial in Paris of a group of German followers of Willich; ten of the thirteen defendants were convicted. The Cologne court, ignoring the fundamental issue, asked the jury to decide a complex of questions about degrees of guilty action, by definition treasonous, to overthrow the government, or assistance to such action, in circumstances that might or might not be extenuating in character. The jury's response and the judge's decisions produced three six-year sentences, three five-year sentences, one three-year sentence, and four acquittals. In all the confusion, Marx's own contributing, Marx's hard sense of the issues was lost. But all was far from lost.

The trial, which took place from October 4 to November 12, 1852, was a constructive operation of the permanent revolution itself. Initially, the existence of the Cologne group had permitted Marx to keep his revolution out of Willich's hands. After the split, the Willich-Schapper Central Committee had failed utterly. In 1852 Willich and Schapper quarreled. Schapper foundered in the refugee underworld. (He was later reconciled with Marx, but in a humiliatingly subordinate position.) In early 1853 Willich gave up on the revolution and emigrated to the United States.[40] The activities of the Cologne group, however mediocre, had kept a pure revolutionary movement alive after the failures of 1848–49. Arousing sympathy among nonradicals, the trial then added a new chapter to the revolution's martyrology. The convictions, given the seriousness of the charges, were absolution as much as punishment, recognition of the reality in Marx's objectives as much as a rejection of his fantasies.

Most of the convicted, after serving their sentences, went on to respectable careers appropriate to their talents.[41] Röser became a leader in the workers' movement that led, after his death, to the creation of the Social Democratic Party. One of the other defendants, a lawyer and publisher, became a leader of the National Liberal Party and successively mayor of Dortmund and of Cologne itself. A journalist among the defendants also became a prominent National Liberal. Another defendant became a leader of the First International as an associate of Marx's. In character with its contradictions, the Communist League in Cologne, Marx in command from London, led to reform *and* revolution: the permanent revolution.

Meanwhile, Marx descended all the deeper into his pit of discouragement. Five days after the Cologne trial ended, Marx's small London group of communists, which had been meeting every Wednesday evening, dis-

solved itself on his motion.[42] Of course this did not end the life of the
Marx Party, which the will of its leader and his ascendancy over others
kept in being. Marx would nevertheless avoid active organizational work
until the time of the First International, beginning in 1864. He wrote a
book on the case, *Revelations on the Communist Trial in Cologne*, as another
effort to rewrite reality and transform a defeat, if not into a victory, at
least into an affirmation of the justice of the cause. He had copies printed
in Switzerland and smuggled into Germany; they were all discovered
and confiscated by the police in 1853.[43] The book would have its value,
but only in the long run. And so Marx settled into the long run.

Marx's revolution still lacked its core, a theoretical statement of its
whole promise. On February 13, 1851, three months before the Cologne
arrests, Engels wrote Marx, reminding him once again of the need. Marx
must publish serious journals, or better, "thick books": "What would
happen to all the gossip and nonsense when you answer it with your
economics?"[44] Marx was back in the British Museum, and indeed earlier
had demanded Engels' opinion of an interpretation of Ricardo's theory
of rent. When Engels did not reply immediately, the postscript to another letter of Marx's, written by young Wilhelm Pieper, said that Marx
was getting impatient. Pieper added: "Marx lives very much out of it.
His only friends are John Stuart Mill [and other less well-known econo-
mists], and when you visit him, you are met not with proper courtesies
but with economic categories."[45] Yet the Cologne trial, the seductions of
émigré intrigues, Marx's need to find money to live, and his rage to
command, let away from consistent work on his great theory. In a letter
to Engels on February 13, 1855, Marx made the first mention of his
economic studies in many months. He had reread his old notes; he could
not do more because of an eye inflammation.[46] He had kept his revolution permanent and inviolate, but it was moving very slowly.

SEVEN

THE PERMANENT REVOLUTIONARY

SEE MARX, THIRTY-ONE YEARS OLD when he arrived in London, in the full force of precocious maturity. His brow is monumental. He has thick black hair and a patriarchal beard, which are just beginning to turn gray. Black hair sprouts from his nostrils and ears. He is ugly, short, and stocky, "a cross between an ape and a cat," one alienated friend called him, but, the man added, Marx's blazing spirit could make him attractive.[1] Marx's linen is probably stale and his shirt dirty.

A man with the experience and intelligence to evaluate Marx the revolutionary leader saw him at one of the turning points, already recounted here, in Marx's operations. The former lieutenant Gustav Techow, who had participated in the Baden action, found himself the object of Marx's intense interest. Techow was precise enough to record the date of a talk with Marx in a London public house. It was, he said, August 21, 1850. Marx wanted him to act as military counterweight to August Willich, who claimed command of the future revolutionary army. Marx and Willich would quarrel openly a few days later. Marx was probably balancing alternatives when he spoke with Techow. Marx, Techow said, drank port, Bordeaux, and champagne indiscriminately, and became "completely drunk. That was exactly what I wanted. . . . I found out the truth about certain things which would otherwise have remained mere suppositions. In spite of his drunkenness Marx dominated the conversation up to the last moment." Techow was impressed. Marx was "someone possessing a rare intellectual superiority . . . a man of outstanding personality. If his heart had matched his intellect, and if he had possessed as much love as hate, I would have gone through fire for him, even though at the end he expressed his complete and candid contempt for me." Marx's contempt, as Techow experienced it, was generalized. "He laughs at the fools who parrot his proletarian catechism, just as he laughs at communists like Willich and over the bourgeoisie. . . . Engels and all his old associates, in spite of their very real gifts, are all far inferior to him, and if they should dare to forget it for a moment, he would put them in their places with the arrogance of a Napoleon." Marx respected only the aristocracy, whom he meant to displace with his army of workers. "Accordingly, he has tailored his sytem to them." If Techow's characterization of a man as complex as Marx was too simple, it was consistent with everything we know about him, and Techow had recognized Marx's quality. "He was the first and only one among us all to whom I would entrust leadership, for he was a man who never lost himself in small matters when dealing with great events."[2]

We see Marx in the bosom of his family as a Prussian police spy saw him in 1852 or 1853. "As father and husband, Marx, in spite of his wild and restless character, is the gentlest and mildest of men. Marx lives in one of the worst, therefore one of the cheapest quarters of London. He occupies two rooms. . . . In the whole flat there is not one clean and solid piece of furniture. Everything is broken, tattered and torn, with a half-inch of dust over everything and the greatest disorder everywhere. . . . But none of these things embarrasses Marx or his wife. You are received in the most friendly way and cordially offered pipes and tobacco and whatever else there may happen to be, and eventually a spirited and agreeable conversation arises." Yet, agreeing with Lieutenant Techow, the spy had also seen a man of "wild and restless character," and he went on to remark that Marx's "large, piercing, fiery eyes have something demonically sinister about them."[3]

Another witness, the Social Democratic leader Karl Liebknecht, described the Marx home as a "dovecote, where many and all manner of peripatetic, escaping, and fleeing creatures of the refugee community flew in and out. . . . Moreover, it was a natural center for the comrades in residence."[4] "Dovecote," with its pacific connotations, was a deliberately misleading word used with hagiographical intent. The home was, as Liebknecht had nevertheless hinted, the command post of the permanent revolution, and the family members were part of the staff.

Family life was a succession of Victorian tragedies, interrupted by social evenings and Sunday picnics on Hampstead Heath in north London. With money his wife got from her mother, Marx had first settled the family in an expensive flat in the more prosperous Chelsea. They were evicted six months later for nonpayment of rent. In December 1850, after brief stays elsewhere in Soho, they established themselves at 28 Dean

Street, where they remained until 1856. Soho was already a shabby and cosmopolitan quarter, where many émigrés had lighted. At first there were three children, Jenny, born in Paris, and Laura and Edgar, born in Brussels. In November 1849, very soon after arriving in London, Jenny Marx gave birth to another son, Edmund, called "Guido." Jenny Marx was again pregnant a year later, when Guido had convulsions and died. A third daughter, Franziska, was born on March 28, 1851; the flat was so crowded that she was boarded out with a wet nurse. Franziska died of bronchitis the next year, and her mother had to borrow £2 from a French émigré to bury her. In April 1855 Edgar, seven years old, died, evidently of tuberculosis.

Whatever pain these deaths caused—Marx experienced, he wrote Engels, "the most frightful agonies"[5] when Edgar died—they could be accepted as natural occurrences, particularly in that earlier age, with its high rate of infant mortality. But Marx was responsible for another event that introduced an almost unbearable strain into the family. Their housekeeper, Helene Demuth, gave birth to a son in June 1851, three months after Jenny Marx's daughter Franziska was born. Marx was the boy's father. Helene, called Lenschen, who had been with the family since Brussels, was indispensable because Jenny and Karl Marx were equally incompetent in household management, and she continued to serve during her pregnancy. She placed her son in foster care. Marx did not acknowledge his parenthood; it never occurred to Lenschen to make demands on him. (The boy grew up to become a skilled metalworker.) Jenny Marx retired to her bed. But the Cologne communists had just been arrested. She joined the struggle to help them, and could begin to forget as she copied out Marx's illegible letters in her clear handwriting. The strain lessened with other distractions and time.[6] In January 1855, shortly before Edgar died, Eleanor, who with Jenny and Laura would survive childhood, was born. In July 1857 a female child was stillborn.

Marx had been extraordinarily fortunate in his wife. Jenny Marx's letters and a brief memoir she wrote in middle age show a woman who had entered totally into her husband's imaginative and real world. As if her life had begun at that moment, she began her memoir: "June 19, 1843, was my wedding day." But then she had waited seven years to marry a man of undefinable promise. She never questioned the rightness of that decision, although she could turn the bare light of honest awareness on her life with Marx. Mentioning Willich and perhaps referring to Lenschen's pregnancy, she wrote that as a frequent guest he "had tried to coax out the worm that hides in every marriage."[7] Scolding, weeping, communicating a reasonable amount of her suffering to her husband, she forgave him as she punished him. In this way she maintained an irreducible dignity in the worst of her humiliations. With her warmth and hospitality, she created the kind of home the private and public Marx needed.

Marx's revolutionary family extended beyond wife and children. Liebknecht, entering it as a young émigré, was in the Marx home almost daily for a dozen years. Marx was genuinely kind and generous to such émigrés, although he expected them to repay in obedience and services. Liebknecht penetrated to the home only after Marx and Engels had sharply tested him at the German Workers' Educational Association: "I was suspected of petit bourgeois 'democratic ideology' . . . [and] South-German sentimentality by my two examiners." He passed the test after accepting "very sharp criticism. . . . Marx tried to assure and reassure himself about his people." Liebknecht's services included running errands, generally aiding in Marx's operations, and helping to look after the children. Young Wilhelm Pieper had been functioning as Marx's agent when he was thrashed at the Banquet of Equals; he made himself useful as a secretary before he went off to a teaching post and was lost to the cause. For periods Marx sheltered and fed Pieper despite his own great poverty. Liebknecht remembered gratefully, "Being at home in this family . . . saved me from foundering in the wretchedness of the émigré underworld."[8] For these young men and others the price paid for Marx's hospitality was more than fair. For the members of the Marx family the price was higher.

Marx's initiative, imagination, and erudition were great family resources. Homer, Aeschylus, Sophocles, Dante, Shakespeare, Goethe, and Balzac, among others, entered into the family's private language. Marx gentled his powerful sense of humor to the point where it generated jokes, games, and nicknames. Everyone had a nickname. In instinctive accuracy the children called their saturnine father "Moor," "Devil," or "Old Nick"; Engels' letters often saluted Marx as "Dear Moor." Jenny Marx was "Möhme," "Mummy" as a German might speak it. Her daughter Jenny was "Qui-Qui, Emperor of China" and "Di." Laura was the "Hottentot" because she was fairer than the other children, and "Kakadu" after a character in a novel. Eleanor was "Tussy," "Quo-Quo, Successor to the Emperor of China," and the "dwarf Alberich" of the *Niebelungenlied*. With his military preoccupations, the family friend Engels was "General."[9] The nicknames suggest the spirit of play that made family intercourse stimulating and dramatic. The play covered over, but thinly, the unresolved problems of life with Marx.

Marx was the very nearly perfect egomaniac, and his family suffered accordingly. He was the classic *monstre sacré*; one thinks of Victor Hugo, Richard Wagner, Pablo Picasso, flooding and sometimes drowning the lives around them with too much life and meaning. One psychological study concluded that Marx remained infantile in his emotions.[10] During all of his life he showed the egoism of the infant who feels that he should be given everything while giving nothing in return or, at best, giving what he chooses to give. This is in accord with the ideas of alienation and reification in his *Economic-Philosophical Manuscripts*, where he had seen the product of man's labor as stealing away man's life. Identifying himself with the worker, Marx defended himself against reification by withholding everything important. He never completed, never quite handed over to strangers, his greatest work, *Capital*. He might be generous with money, but he did not understand it and repaid a debt only under extreme duress. Money, moreover, was not nearly as important to him as power, and he would have died rather than share it with anyone. Overriding the independent needs of the other people in his life, he incessantly tried to increase his power: Marx's defense against his own reification was to turn others into objects. The worker himself, with whom Marx had virtually no contact, remained an abstraction and instrument to him. He could shake off a reminder of dissident opinion when he split the Communist League by quoting Horace, " 'I hate the vulgar mob and drive it away.' "[11] As for his own family, he had led it without second thought into poverty, insecurity, and the darkness of his private torment. If his wife could defend herself at least partially, his children could not, and became unhappy women. Eleanor and Laura would become suicides; Jenny, sad and always ailing, would die of cancer at thirty-nine. They had been Marx's beloved objects.

Another sufferer was Engels,[12] but he had accepted his role as freely as had Jenny Marx. The Marx-Engels relationship,[13] with its powerful homoerotic undercurrents, was paramarital. If Marx was plainly heterosexual, Engels, consorting with prostitutes or working girls, was only pathologically so. In Manchester he lived with Mary Burns, a young woman of the working classes, and, when she died, replaced her with her sister Lizzie. To Engels Marx was infinitely more important than any woman reserved for given delimited functions. Marx was the Old Testament or Victorian husband, originating, dominating, and law-giving; Engels, as passive as Jenny Marx and more efficient, tidied up Marx's genial disorder, nagged, and manipulated. Engels was a practiced masochist, a splendid match for Marx the sadist, and this deepened the hold either had on the other.

Indeed, their one recorded quarrel shows how far Marx and Engels, respectively, would go in inflicting and receiving humiliation. In early 1851 Marx had asked Engels' opinion on an economic question, and Engels had been slow in replying. When he did write, he mentioned that he was studying physiology.[14] Marx, perhaps because he was irritated at the delay, inquired, referring to Engels' mistress, "Are you studying physiology on Mary?"[15] Engels did not respond to Marx's joke, which was all the more painful because the proper Jenny Marx had always refused to receive Mary Burns in her home. Twelve years later Mary Burns died. In his next letter after receipt of the news, on January 8, 1863, Marx remarked on the death casually and moved on to a recital of his latest money problems.[16] In his reply Engels burst out: "You find this the appropriate moment to trot out the superiority of your coolly scientific mode of thinking. So be it!" As for Marx's troubles, Engels said he could not spare any money until the next month.[17]

Marx waited more than a week to reply. He tried to excuse himself by emphasizing the direness of his situation, and went on to apologize and make one of his few admissions of error. "I was very much in the wrong." He returned to his problems. He would declare himself bankrupt, send Lenschen Demuth away, place his two eldest daughters in service as governesses, and, giving up the house into which they had moved after leaving Soho, take his wife and youngest daughter to live in a working-class flat.[18] Marx's threat of a kind of self-destruction, his family obediently cooperating, was both blackmail and a temporary exchange of sadist-masochist roles with his friend. Was Marx serious? The words were enough for Engels. By return post he accepted Marx's apology. He was sending £100. He did not have the money, but he had, at considerable risk, taken it from the company funds.[19]

Marx, his ego demanding all, did not know how to be grateful. Yet his arrangement with Engels was entirely equitable: either did what he could do best to serve the revolution, and Engels' money certainly could not outweigh Marx's genius. The money was considerable. In the main, Engels supported Marx from 1851 to the end of Marx's life. The Marx-Engels Institute in Moscow calculated that he gave Marx more than £7,500, a huge amount for those days.[20] Marx could be described as poor only during the first two or three years in London, before Engels was established in his Manchester position and able to send him larger and larger amounts of money. Thereafter, Marx's income grew from a minimum of £150 annually, more than sufficient for a family of the lower middle class, to that of a fairly prosperous bourgeois family. In 1869 Engels, while paying all of his friend's debts, bought an annuity of £350 for Marx.[21] During all those years, and afterward, Marx's debts and demands for money increased more than his income.[22] In his boundlessness Marx was a greater Micawber than Dickens conceived.

Marx was the hero of an epic struggle against bankruptcy. He had various money sources besides Engels. For eleven years from 1851 he had a fairly steady, if small, income as the *Tribune's* London correspondent. He wrote articles for other publications as well. Material blessings descended upon him. He inherited money, as did Jenny Marx. They came into £270 when Jenny's mother and uncle died in 1856. In 1864 Marx got £700 when his mother died at last and unmourned, *plus* £824, willed to him by his old revolutionary comrade Wilhelm Wolff, who had saved that astonishing sum by giving lessons and living ascetically.[23] The first stroke of fortune permitted the Marx family to move from Soho to a seven-room house in Hampstead, in north London; with the second they moved to a larger house, also in Hampstead. Each time they found themselves living beyond their means, a situation that was worsened as Marx financed another hopeless action or his wife arranged another set of private lessons for their daughters.

Marx undertook various expedients while signaling to Engels, who, however, learned that a certain intensity of wretchedness in the Marx household and threats of angry creditors were necessary to restrain Marx, if not to halt him. Accordingly, Engels doled out one, two, or five pounds almost weekly, and effected a rescue with a greater sum when Marx's cries of disaster were loud and credible enough. Engels had an ultimate defense against being dragged into bankruptcy along with Marx: his employment contract, perhaps on his own initiative, forbade him to sign notes. But then Marx could transcend the ultimate. He got third persons to sign notes on Engels' unbinding promise to send them the money if Marx failed to make payment before the notes came due. In the end it was Engels who paid. Meanwhile, however, Marx had to expend time and great nervous energy in these subtle and complex negotiations, which he called "I.O.U.-riding" (*Wechselreiten*), as he postponed the inevitable one more time. His desperation was no less real for being absurd.

One person refused to be victimized by Marx's desperation. He was Ferdinand Lassalle, the first important socialist leader in Germany and one of the few competitive egos in Marx's life. In the summer of 1862 Marx persuaded Lassalle, on the occasion of a long visit in Marx's home, to sign a note for £60. Marx, however, cashed it before he had arranged for the security that the businesslike Lassalle demanded. Also, envious of Lassalle's success and prosperity, Marx pursued his guest with insulting letters. Lassalle thereupon belabored Marx for having violated their agreement and remarked on Marx's use of "all manner of twisty insinuations" in "such a sarcastic, sour letter that strides in here under ponderous escort of quotation marks."[24] An accurate description of Marx's letter of August 20,[25] Lassalle's masterfully insulting language might be mistaken for Marx's own. Such a reaction from a man who was indispensable to Marx's plans for Germany shocked Marx into total defeat: he apologized, adding that his situation was so bad that he felt like "putting a bullet through his head," actually begged Lassalle not to break off with him—and returned the £60.[26] It was another instance of the bully become pitiable when all else had failed. Of course Marx had spent the money, but he got an emergency loan from Ferdinand Freiligrath, who was manager of the London branch of a Swiss bank. Engels, in his accustomed role, repaid Freiligrath.[27] At his weakest in his dealings with money, Marx could not command and fell back upon manipulating. But in this, too, he showed extraordinary capacity, in fact, genius in getting what he wanted.

Marx's ego was somewhat restrained in its claims upon his wife, Engels, or other person he needed, but it could go over to the attack on family members or friends no longer useful to him. Early examples were his unfeeling rejection of his mother combined with renewed efforts to get money out of her, and his savaging of former friends like Arnold Ruge and Bruno Bauer. Similarly, Marx had pillaged the ideas of the utopian socialists and classical economists, and then proceeded to insult ideas and thinkers. Similarly, praising and denouncing the bourgeoisie at the same time, he directed his force to expropriate its material achievement, modern industry. He raised ingratitude to the level of a principle of action.

Marx's ego indulged itself in cruelty for cruelty's sake. The boy who forced his sisters to eat dirty cakes of dough and who ridiculed his schoolmates grew up to do more of the same with newer victims. The adult Marx happily recounted to Engels how he added humiliation to humiliation in a quarrel with his poet friend Georg Weerth. After Marx had been unpleasant to him, Weerth allowed another friend to persuade him to return two days later. Marx thereupon "gave him something of a dressing down" and "he straightened himself out and became the old Weerth again."[28]

On another occasion, writing to Engels, Marx complained of Ferdinand Lassalle's tactlessness. Using the same idiom, Marx looked forward with pleasure to the occasion when "I will give him a dressing down." Marx was all the more anxious to punish Lassalle because Lassalle was helping him out. As the letter reported, Lassalle, among other things, had arranged for Marx to become correspondent for a leading Viennese newspaper.[29] Marx never quite got the chance to humiliate Lassalle. When, in 1861, Marx had been the guest of the prosperous Lassalle in Berlin, he contented himself by responding to him with "a continuing irony . . . which wounded his vanity."[30] He had needed Lassalle too much to attack him openly, but his skills in sadistic punishment had found a way to achieve the maximum possible effect in the constraint of the given circumstances.

Engels himself experienced more of Marx's sadism than any other friend. Lieutenant Techow and Stephan Born were among the many witnesses reporting how Marx treated him. When Marx was editor of the *Neue Rheinische Zeitung*, Born saw him "give Engels the kind of tongue-lashing you administer to a street urchin." Marx then left, slamming the door shut, and Engels muttered, "I'll make him pay for that."[31] There is no record that Engels ever did. He got his satisfaction in other ways.

Marx's cruelty flowed naturally into policy. In 1850, in the March Address of the Communist League, he had woven into his fantasy of a new revolution "the so-called excesses, the expression of the people's revenge." In 1856 Marx made one of his rare public speeches. At a celebration of the anniversary of a Chartist newspaper he looked back at the failure of the Revolution of 1848 and, looking even further back, saw a suggestion for the future. "To revenge the misdeeds of the ruling class, there existed in the Middle Ages, in Germany, a secret tribunal called the '*Vehmgericht*.' If a red cross was seen marked on a house, people knew that its owner was doomed by the '*Vehm*.' All the houses of Europe are now marked with the mysterious red cross. History is the judge—its executioner, the proletarian."[32]

Marx's destructiveness—his deadliness—had earlier been directed against his own people in "On the Jewish Question." The logic of the article may very well have functioned with the moral neutrality of a garbage-disposal machine, but Marx was privately an impassioned anti-Semite.[33] Sir Isaiah Berlin, whose distinguished scholarly work includes a finely appreciative biography, has called Marx's anti-Semitism "one of the most neurotic and revolting aspects of his masterful but vulgar personality."[34]

Dispensing with even the appearance of neutrality, Marx attacked Jews privately and publicly for the rest of his life. In 1848–49 the *Neue Rheinische Zeitung* mixed anti-Semitism into its editorial content, and Marx called the contributions of his Vienna correspondent, who made a specialty of Jew-baiting, the best the paper was receiving.[35] Indeed, an angry reader of the *NRZ* signing himself David Levy Elkan canceled his subscription, accusing the newspaper of spreading religious hatred "expressly against the Jews . . . by throwing around accusatory words like 'spies, false democrats,' etc., etc."[36] In 1850 Marx added a dash of anti-Semitism to the ingredients of *The Class Struggles in France*: the phrases "finance Jews" and "stock-jobbing Jews."[37] Marx's letters to Engels contained large volcanic lumps of anti-Semitic hatred, contempt, and disgust. Ferdinand Lassalle, in particular, brought them down upon his head because he threatened Marx's primacy in the socialist movement. Engels defined that object of hatred in a letter to Marx in 1856. Echoing Marx, he called Lassalle a "true Jew of the Slavic border . . . always poised to use anyone for his selfish interests under the excuse of party duty . . . that oily Breslau Jew with his pomade and rouge."[38] The friends, doubtless drawing upon Marx's inventiveness, often referred to Lassalle with nicknames suggesting Jewish stereotypes: "Ephraim Gescheit" (i.e., "Smart") and (mocking Lassalle's social successes) "Baron Gescheit," "Itzig" (the favored epithet) and "Baron Itzig," "Kike [*Jüdel*] Braun," and "Isidor Berlinerblau."[39] "Kike" was frequently added for emphasis. On one occasion, Marx, finding no nickname adequate, specified: "the Jewish Nigger Lassalle."[40]

Marx drove himself to an infinitely more violent expression of anti-Semitism in the case of an infinitely less important person. He was Moses Joseph Levy, editor of a London newspaper, who otherwise had no relation to Marx's concerns, but had strayed into the cross fire of a battle between Marx and an émigré named Karl Vogt. Levy's newspaper, the *Daily Telegraph*, had published an article, drawn from a German newspaper, that gave Vogt's side of the story. In 1860 Marx published a book accusing Vogt of various delicti, but he reserved his worst for Levy. In the book Marx sneered at Levy for having changed his name from Levi;[41] Levi was the family name of Marx's father. Marx made much of Levy's nose, which he found crookedly Semitic. Leaning on *Tristram Shandy*, with its famous passage on noses, Marx wrote:

> I have been at the promontory of Noses; and have got me one of the goodliest and jolliest. . . .
> There was a Greek epigrammatist who described the nose of a certain Castor, which served all kinds of purposes. It could be used as a shovel, a trumpet, a sickle, or an anchor. . . . The great art of Levy's nose consists in the fact that it caresses foul odors.[42]

Marx opened up cloacal depths.

> By means of a hidden and artificial sewer system all the lavatories
> of London spew their physical filth into the Thames. By means of
> the systematic pushing of goose quills the world capital spews out
> all its social filth into the great papered central sewer called the
> *Daily Telegraph*. . . . Over the gates leading to this central sewer
> made of paper there can be read these words written *di colore oscuro*:
> "*Hic . . . quisquam faxit oletum*," or as Byron so poetically expressed
> it: "Wanderer, stop and—piss!"[43]

Marx, drawing his family into it, continued to struggle with his Jewish question. In 1869, when his daughter Jenny was twenty-six, he wrote
her about a Jewish lady whose "voice had the guttural sound, the curse
with which the chosen people is burdened"[44] Marx appears to have acknowledged his Jewish origins in just one recorded instance. In 1864, in
a letter to a rich uncle from whom he succeeded in extracting money, he
remarked on "our kinsman *Benjamin Disraeli*."[45] In a letter in 1875, the
aging, ailing Marx remarked to Engels from Karlsbad (in the old Austrian Empire), where he was taking the cure, on an encounter with a
"sly-looking kike."[46]

Marx's public anti-Semitism, however, had declined. Originally, in "On
the Jewish Question," he had used it on a strategic level, where it carried
through a major theoretical operation. The anti-Semitism of the *NRZ*
had been tactical; the anti-Semitism of *The Class Struggles in France* had
been less than that, offhand rather. The eruption against Levy was private
in its real character; in any case it was part of a psychotic episode and
had nothing to do with Marx's theorizing. By the uses Marx did not
make of anti-Semitism as time went on, he showed his statesmanlike
judgment that it would not bear much weight of idea or action. *Capital*
is innocent of anti-Semitic logic, although Marx permitted himself one
erudite joke that was too good to give up. "True trading nations exist in
the ancient world only in its interstices, like the gods of Epicurus, or like
the Jews in the pores of Polish society."[47] The joke did not change the
fact that while the mature Marx remained anti-Semitic, mature Marxism
was not.

The ego, loving or hating, life-giving or destroying, obtruded in all
these concerns of Marx. His egomania expressed itself politically as the
will of a leader, one of the strongest wills known to history. A will of
that force inevitably demanded too much. In the case of Marx's anti-
Semitism, it was trying to crush the facts and eradicate his Jewish character. In other cases it drove Marx to the borderline of psychosis. Yet

Marx retained too much sense of reality during his worst moments ever to commit himself to attempting the impossible in any important enterprise. Defending or advancing his position as circumstances required or permitted, Marx worked incessantly to gain the power to satisfy his will.

Bismarck once said, "I have observed in myself that my will decided even before my thinking was over."[48] Similarly, whenever Marx's intelligence attempted to contradict what he wanted, the will overwhelmed it. The will, as we have already seen, led Marx, with easy virtuosity, to expand, contract, disguise, or deny selected parts of reality. A word was not safe in his hands. Thus in *Capital*—anticipating the analysis in the next chapter—one can see Marx characterizing the work of a capitalist or merchant as a "function which is fundamentally unproductive, but a necessary element of the production process."[49] He had annihilated the meaning of the word "productive" in order to keep his argument consistent with the a priori claim that the capitalist or merchant contributed nothing to society.

Similarly, an equation did not have to mean equality. In *Capital*, again, he began one argument, "Nothing can be sillier than the dogma that the production of commodities necessarily implies an equal balance of sales and purchases because every sale is a purchase and vice versa." He went off into a learned disquisition, but then conceded, "No one can sell unless someone else purchases." In his next sentence, however, he seemed to withdraw the concession, "But no one is therefore bound to purchase, because he has just made a sale."[50] The important word here is "but." This last sentence did not deny the identity of sale-and-purchase, *but* the "but" suggested that it did. Thus, it is true that a person who has made a sale need not buy anything, *but* his refusal to buy does not change the identity in the sale-and-purchase which had previously taken place or could take place in the future.

Argumentation of this kind produced confusion, first in Marx's head and then, if the reader were not careful, in his head as well. One can observe Marx preparing another such confusion during his early economic studies, when he was writing to Engels in 1851. Dealing with Ricardo's theory of rent, Marx had to face the fact that the best land necessarily paid a premium—rent—to the owner. Marx could not admit the sense of rent, although he granted the existence of unequal fertility. One could properly object, he went on dangerously, that differences in fertility would remain in socialist production. But then he caught himself in the same sentence: "—although, the best soil would no longer produce a product as costly as the poorest, which is the case under a bourgeois regime."

If you accept Marx's reasoning, you would have to believe that under socialism a given bushel of wheat, for example, would sell for a higher or lower price than another bushel of wheat indistinguishable from it—but originating from, respectively, a less or more fertile farm. Marx, himself, refusing to see what his words were saying, did not follow his own reasoning: he had achieved perfect confusion. His next and final sentence on the problem was abruptly and arbitrarily satisfied. "This objection vanishes in view of the above."[51] Elsewhere, Marx wrote, "Ricardo himself often falls into confusion."[52] Many of the great verbal storms in Marx's writings are confusions, the last defenses thrown up by his will against the logic of the enemy, his intelligence.

In the area of action, daily responses to the details of his life situation, Marx's will expressed itself even more extremely. This was most pronounced during his early London years, when Marx the leader had few materials upon which to exercise his personal powers. Having surrounded himself with people who lacked the strength to say "no" very strongly, he could insist upon altering reality to the point of losing contact with it. Trying to help the defendants in the Cologne trial in 1852, for example, he often appeared to extract the ultimate truth from documents rather than from the facts they were supposed to represent. Nevertheless, his book about the case, whatever fantasy was mixed into it, made usable propaganda.

If Marx's will could not alter the real nature of the world, it could take powerful effect on persons. It never relented in attempting to impose its primacy. Those who would not yield to him were defined as hostile and subjected to uninhibited attack. The spy who had described the Marx household also reported on Marx's professional character.

> He is jealous of his authority as head of the party. He is vindictive and inexorable toward rivals and opponents; he will not rest until he has ruined them. His dominant characteristic is his boundless ambition and love of power. . . . Up to now his greatest, in fact, his exclusive task has been to overthrow his rivals and destroy their parties. To him every means to do this was good. Sometimes he would intrigue secretly; sometimes he would try to make the leaders of the other party look ludicrous or contemptible by speaking publicly about their faults and weaknesses; sometimes he would incite the members of one faction against another and in this way cause a split; and then again he would try to insinuate some of his

own secret comrades into the inner circle of his opponents with instructions to keep him informed about the opponents' plans, which he would secretly thwart. Then, after the plans had failed, he would scourge his rivals with his fearsome satire.

Yet the spy noted: "All this, however, concerns only his secret activity, and the secret sections. At public meetings of the party, he is, on the contrary, the most liberal and popular of them all."[53] But in the shadows, which he now preferred, Marx went on pursuing what his will demanded as ruthlessly as ever.

Primacy was the point of the Bangya affair. In 1852, after the Cologne arrests but before the trial made real demands on him, Marx became friendly with the Hungarian officer János Bangya. Marx recognized the man as a spy, but insisted upon defining him as a spy in the service of the revolution.[54] Marx had been similarly naïve about Adalbert von Bornstedt, when he found Bornstedt's newspaper so useful in Brussels. Now, in London, Bangya told him that a German publisher was interested in a pamphlet about the leaders among the London exiles, and Marx spent some enjoyable weeks in the spring of that year producing a manuscript entitled "The Great Men of the Emigration."[55] Bangya passed it on to the Prussian police.[56] The manuscript consisted of a series of attacks on the accomplishments, character, and appearance of its subjects: Arnold Ruge of the "weasel face" produced "daily literary diarrhea," August von Willich was "pinheaded," and another revolutionary leader had a "silly-sly pop eye."[57] Marx found it possible to ridicule the six years of imprisonment Ruge had suffered.[58] The police most probably found the manuscript useless, but its potential for damage cannot be excluded. The damage might have been worse if the pamphlet had been published, instead of remaining in the police files, since it also included simple slander. Thus, on no evidence whatsoever but able to manufacture or deny suspicion at will, Marx identified the popeyed man as a Russian agent.[59] As Marx's personal Prussian spy wrote, Marx would not rest until he had ruined his rivals.

Primacy was also the point in Marx's furious quarrel with Karl Vogt. It was a useless, senseless primacy. In 1852, when Marx had sought to destroy his rivals through Bangya, émigré politics was still fairly close to the realities of the revolution just experienced, and men could rationally contend over issues and prospects. The Vogt quarrel arose in 1859, after revolution was a bare, deserted battlefield. Marx's intelligence had known and acted on this since 1850, but his will went mad for lack of sustenance and it seized upon Vogt as a substitute for a rival. A full decade earlier, in 1848–49. Vogt could have been seen distantly as such, since he had been a left-wing Democratic leader in the Frankfurt Parliament. Still another person was dragged along with the editor Moses Joseph Levy into the affair: Louis Napoleon. Perhaps Marx's personal sense of rivalry with the man who had given the coup de grâce to the French Revolution of 1848, as expressed in *The 18th Brumaire* and his letters to Engels, explains why he created the Vogt affair in the first place. Vogt himself had become a geography professor in Switzerland entirely lacking in political interest for Marx. The fact that he was so far away, furthermore, had prevented any collision in the course of Marx's ambulations.

The quarrel began when Marx, repeating what he had done in the Bangya affair, gratuitously denounced Vogt. At the time, painfully losing money in the undertaking, Marx controlled an ephemeral German-language newspaper in London. In it, having plucked one of the innumerable rumors out of the émigré air, he published the report, which was repeated in the German press, that Vogt was an agent of Louis Napoleon. Vogt's services, the report specified, included various conspiratorial actions in cooperation with Russian agents. In reply Vogt wrote a book that denied any French or Russian connection, and counterattacked by characterizing Marx as the leader of a gang of revolutionary bullies.[60] If questionably accurate and vigorous enough, the rebuttal was well-contained according to standards of émigré polemics.

Marx could not contain himself. In February 1860 he turned away from the manuscript of *Capital*, which he had begun two months previously, and devoted more than a year and a half to the attempt to demolish Vogt. One part of the effort was the book *Herr Vogt*, written from August to November 1860 after a period of document-gathering, which has sufficiently characterized itself here in the quoted passages referring to Levy. Marx's assault on Vogt himself was as incompetent as it was incoherent.[61] The other part of Marx's demolition operation consisted of a series of expensive and futile lawsuits, financed by Engels, against the German newspapers carrying articles that seemed to put Vogt in the right.

To support the legal action Marx demanded that Ferdinand Freiligrath swear to a statement meant to assist his case, and when Freiligrath refused, broke off with him temporarily and permanently damaged their long friendship. He coerced a German compositor in London into going to a police station to sign an affidavit supporting another claim; the compositor had a criminal record, and Marx had threatened to tell his employer about it. Marx recounted the story of the affidavit triumphantly in a letter to Engels, as if the affidavit were the event and not a presumed account of the event as extorted by the intimidation detailed in the letter itself.[62] Neither Freiligrath nor the compositor, moreover, could have provided real proof that Vogt was an agent, the point at issue. At most all they could say was that a certain German émigré had originated the story in London in conversation with Marx or through an anonymous fly sheet—entirely questionable hearsay.[63] The story was also inherently incredible: Louis Napoleon lacked good reason to make use of an unimportant exile as an agent.[64] Marx's drive for primacy had veered out of the real world. Yet the action did make sense of a sort. Absorbing some of Marx's rage, it helped save him from madness. He could continue work on *Capital*, assume leadership of the First International, and guide the growing socialist movement in Germany.

In all of these activities of Marx one was absent: personal interaction with the workers for whom the revolution would be made. Marx had no contact with them except indirectly, through labor leaders whom he distrusted and despised. His published correspondence does not record that Marx ever inquired about the wages or working conditions of the 800 operatives of Engels' cotton-spinning firm. Actually Engels had little to do with them, since he worked in the business office in Manchester proper, where he was chiefly responsible for accounting and marketing, while the mill itself was located in a suburb.[65] According to the letters, the only interest shown by Marx in the firm was confined to such questions as depreciation, allocation of operating funds, and calculation of turnover time—all relating to his studies for *Capital*.[66]

The various sources put Marx in a factory twice in his life, although never in the mill of the Engels firm. The first time occurred when Marx was in Germany to see *Capital* through the press in 1867, and, as a distinguished visitor, was given a tour of a foundry by the manager. Writing to Engels, Marx mentioned the excellent machinery but not the workers.[67] In 1874 he observed and spoke to a worker in Karlsbad, in the old Austrian Empire, where Marx was taking the cure. The occasion was another sight-seeing expedition, this one in a porcelain factory. The worker's function was to hollow out cups, and Marx, learning from him that he never did anything else and drawing upon Marxian theory, commented as a social scientist to a companion, "In this way, through the division of labor, the human being becomes an extension of the machine and the intelligence vanishes into muscular memory."[68] If Marx's children were objects within the close perimeter of intimacy, the workers remained objects at a very great distance.

The distant champion of the proletariat was an almost pure capitalist. Except for the few pounds he earned as a correspondent, Marx lived on the surplus value, as *Capital* would call it, of the work of the operatives in the Engels firm. (Marx's various inheritances were all similarly unearned derivatives of the same surplus value). Engels, at least, was entrepreneur as well as capitalist, since he contributed considerable managerial labor for the rewards received; Marx contributed nothing. Yet this is too narrow a view.

Marx worked and sacrificed on a scale vastly greater than that applicable to the Engels company. If the economic system was not sophisticate enough to pay for such original services, Marx had every right to take his sustenance where he could. As to the relations with workers, recognition of their humanity would have distracted him from his world-historical task. He could not have functioned effectively without that selective indifference which is the professional deformation of the politician. A generation later Lenin would struggle against the tendency of Russian revolutionaries to lose sight of the revolution in concentrating on the workers' welfare, a practice he condemned as "economism." Lieutenant Techow's evaluation of Marx is relevant here. "He was a man who never lost himself in small matters when dealing with great events."

It was in the 1860s that Marx reached his full stature. Barely in his thirties, he had had the bearing and authority of a man of fifty when he had arrived in London, but his genius was still too raw, chaotic, and urgent for an undertaking of the magnitude it promised. In the early London years, furthermore, Marx lacked the materials with which to work. The hapless 1850s were a period to be survived; this should suffice as accomplishment. But then, while the moment did not offer itself for action, it need not have stopped a thinker from thinking. Marx failed to advance his great economics work very far. Perhaps he was suffering too much from revolutionary shock. Certainly he needed to be engaged in an activity that palpably gripped the world: he would *not* be a "pure" thinker. The italics and boldface of his pressing statements demanded responses. In the 1860s the world moved toward Marx. Meanwhile, he had learned to communicate with it more fluently.

Marx gained control of the peremptorily demanding infant within that had dominated him until his forties. He had been learning after his own fashion, as shown by his refusal to destroy himself in revolutionary adventures or to give up his life purpose. In the 1860s Marx set about a task that was infinitely more difficult than anything he had ever attempted: persuade the world rather than command it. The persuasion took three forms: the creation of *Capital*, grinding out its theoretical revolution patiently, the leadership of the First International, which was too loose and heterogeneous to follow orders, and the counseling, often humiliatingly disregarded, of the self-confident German socialists. Marx, the thunderer of the *Communist Manifesto* and the dictator of the *Neue Rheinische Zeitung*, became the meticulous scholar, amiable corresponding secretary for Germany, and adept of half-measures. Marx's personality had consolidated itself on a superior level.

Even as Marx arrived at the commanding heights of his life and work, a series of ailments worked away incessantly to hollow out and destroy him. They were obviously associated with his boundless will and his inevitable rages of frustration. The doctors might call attention to his excessive cigar-smoking and the ingestion of overspiced food, but in one of his few insights into himself Marx once said, "My illness always comes from my head."[69] After his breakdown as a youth in Berlin and minor complaints for the next few years, he began to suffer from a vast range of chronic maladies in his early thirties. His illnesses, eruptions of boils most particularly, were accurate metaphors of the anger in him. The boils first appeared in 1854,[70] and, attacking nearly every part of his body—lips, cheeks, back, bottom, and genitals—occurred most frequently in the 1860s, his most productive period. The boils were serious enough to make him seriously ill and require operations. In 1867, as he was preparing the first volume of *Capital* for publication, he wrote Engels, "In any case I hope that the bourgeoisie will remember my boils as long as it lives."[71] His anger was a prime revolutionary fuel. Marx also endured eye inflammations to the point of temporary blindness, a variety of stomach disorders, lack of appetite, gallbladder trouble, liver trouble, headaches, rheumatic pains, insomnia, and nervous exhaustion.[72] In the autumn of 1873, at the age of fifty-five and a year after his work with the First International was over, Marx, suffering episodes of uncontrollable trembling, fell into a deep depression. The doctor ordered complete rest for a period, and although Marx was somewhat restored with the help or distraction of an annual cure, he was never again able to do extended work. But he had accomplished all that he had set out to do.

The pettiness, cruelty, and even psychosis in Marx do not deny his greatness. Rather, it takes its force and edge from them. Institutions and accepted behavior supported but inhibited the masters of the contemporary world, a Bismarck, Louis Napoleon, Disraeli, or a Gladstone, for example. Constructing the future with his few shards, thus in his weakness, Marx had both greater freedom and a more pressing need to act upon that freedom. A slight error of doctrine or action, too easily made, could lead too easily to the destruction or the domestication of *the* revolution. Marx's ugly envy kept him on the alert to maintain his primacy. His sadism, useful in the exercise of power, was all the more necessary because so much of Marx's power was in his person alone. History agrees with Lieutenant Techow that Marx was the first and only one among the revolutionaries to whom leadership could be entrusted. In the boundlessness of his will and being he was proving himself equal to the greatest of events.

EIGHT

THE POLITICS OF
CAPITAL

CAPITAL WAS THE SUM OF "thick books" which Engels had demanded of Marx in 1851 to assure their revolutionary leadership. Marx took sixteen years to publish the first volume. The flaws in the whole of *Capital* and the delays in its creation have become—to use Marxian emphases—valuable parts of its *revolutionary magnitude*—its *overwhelming achievement*—its *colossal presence in history*.

In examining *Capital* we must begin with the elementary and define our terms. With Marx things are never quite what they seem. To call *Capital* a book in three volumes is formally correct, but inadequate. Even the attribution of *Capital* to Marx must be qualified. It is difficult to say *what Capital* is.

In one sense Marx was writing *Capital* nearly all his life, from adolescence to senescence. The student in secondary school wrote essays setting down its objective of creating a better world. The *Economic-Philosophical Manuscripts* introduced many of *Capital*'s themes briefly but in depth. The *Communist Manifesto* provided an outline of its powerful revolutionary statement. In his last letters Marx was extending its relevance to primitive communism in Russia and other forms of backwardness in regions like Algeria.[1] The three volumes labeled *Capital* and deriving from one huge manuscript cannot be separated from the mass of his other writings.

Capital consists of one volume which Marx saw through publication in 1867, and two posthumous volumes appearing in 1885 and 1894. Engels, who published the last volumes, said the manuscript left behind by Marx required considerable rewriting. Engels said that he himself had to write some passages on the basis of sparse notes, but loyally tried to minimize his contribution.[2] The reader, however, can see that volume 2 is written in his style, while huge lumps of volume 3 are more characteristic of Marx. In any case Marx not only wrote the original draft of volume 1, but spent an additional two years revising it. Marx put almost all of his best writing and ideas into it. Volume 1 is the masterpiece.

The sense and moral passion of all of *Capital* could have been put into a book considerably smaller than the 750-page volume 1. Furthermore, Marx's own logic virtually annihilated the *logical* justification for the last two volumes. The three individual volumes are subtitled, respectively, *The Production Process of Capital*, *The Process of Circulation of Capital*, and *The Process of Capitalistic Production as a Whole*. (This is in addition to the subtitle *Critique of Political Economy* for the entire work.) Yet Marx explicitly argued that "circulation," that is, trade and finance, contributed nothing to the economy. By Marx's own definition, volume 2 is a book about nothing at all, at least in the context of economic theory. Volume 3, proposing to integrate production and "circulation," promised to add nothing to something. In fact, Marx had little interest in trade and finance, and volumes 2 and 3, continually falling back into further disquisitions on the production process, gave "circulation" summary and distracted attention. Of itself volume 2, a flatland of stale ideas expressed in Engels' characterless language, is as worthless as it is boring. If volume 3 contains valuable Marxian ore, it adds little truly new or positive. Nevertheless, the later volumes served Marxism well, not by their substance, but by their existence.

Marx had been unclear about the extent and even the subject of his undertaking. In 1858, boundless, boastful, and creatively mendacious, he told Ferdinand Lassalle that he intended to cover a series of major economic and political topics *plus* the history of economic theory and socialism. Capital would be treated in just one of six books. Marx then proposed to go on to: landed property, wage labor, the state, international trade, and world market.[3] The fact that the last two subjects were identical suggests that Marx was not completely serious. But his loose talk fully discounted, he was irreducibly serious about attempting the impossible.

Capital came closely after two other works, while it is entangled in still another. The precedent writings were: the manuscript published as *Foundations of a Critique of Political Economy (Rough Draft) 1857–1858* by Soviet editors in 1939–41 and generally known as the *Grundrisse* from the first word of the German-language title; and the *Critique of Political Economy*, as published by Marx in 1859. The third work is his *Theories of Surplus Value*, edited and published between 1905 and 1910 from unused portions of the manuscript of *Capital,* by the scholarly German Marxist Karl Kautsky.[4] To dispense with the last and least important work for the moment, the *Theories of Surplus Value* was actually a series of Marx's comments on his economic readings and not restricted to surplus value or even value. Although Marx needed help to bring all these writings before the public, he had himself, beginning in 1857, accomplished almost incredible labors.

Always political, Marx was writing—or failing to write—in intense accord with events. He began what became the manuscript of the *Grundrisse* when an international business crisis in 1857 revived his revolutionary hopes. From August of that year to March of 1858 he wrote enough to make up 764 printed pages.[5] Drawing upon this and writing from August 1858 to January 1859, Marx produced his first explicitly economic book, the *Critique of Political Economy.* By then the crisis of 1857 had vanished, perhaps removing Marx's motivation, and the book's one distinction was its powerful definition of materialism, given in its preface. The *Critique* ended abruptly after some 160 pages and just two chapters, the first chapter on the commodity and the second on money. The reader has only to set it beside *Capital* to see how puny it is, and the least critical Marxists are embarrassed to refer to it. A few scholars like David McLellan have fallen back upon the *Grundrisse,* as they have upon the *Economic-Philosophical Manuscripts,* because of its Feuerbachian humanism and suggestiveness. In his biography of Marx, McLellan devotes more space to analyzing the *Grundrisse* than to *Capital,* fourteen pages as against eleven.[6] The most authoritative opinion on these works is Marx's own; he made little use of the *Grundrisse* in the *Critique,* for which that manuscript, after all, was to serve as a source. As for *Capital,* it would situate itself in the far distance from both. Neither Marx's ideas nor the moment had been quite ready.

After publishing the *Critique,* Marx went off into scattered activities, especially his campaign against Karl Vogt. But then his sense of timing seized him: a German socialist party and an international labor movement would presently be organized. Marx returned to his economic broodings and researches.

On June 18, 1862, as he labored, Marx wrote Engels another letter about his troubles: the £50 Engels had sent him had been spent in paying less than half of the family debts, the children were ashamed to invite their friends to the house because of its strident poverty, "my wife tells me every day she wishes she lay . . . in her grave." He added, "But otherwise I'm working full blast and oddly enough my brainbox in the middle of all the misery is turning over better than it has in years."[7] Marx had begun writing in August 1861, and by June 1863 he had raised up the Himalayan manuscript that comprised the first draft of *Capital* proper *and* the *Theories of Surplus Value*—1,472 quarto pages in his small, crabbed handwriting, or enough to fill more than twice that many printed pages.[8] Then Marx's literary creativity, occasionally interrupted by bursts of irrelevant or redundant research, lay fallow for three years. Engels claimed unconvincingly that Marx was working on *Capital*,[9] but Marx had other things to do. The First International was founded in 1864, and he was increasingly absorbed in its affairs. In 1866, pausing to read Auguste Comte contemptuously and Honoré Balzac appreciatively,[10] he confronted *Capital* once again, splendidly. In September 1867, after Marx had spent several weeks in Germany to oversee the beginning of the operation, volume I was published in Hamburg.[11] It was the right moment.

Capital contains so much that it might well be worth the risk of pretentiousness to speak of levels of meaning. Marx, however, was too disorderly to keep his arguments separate, and the work can be more appropriately seen as three loose bundles of meaning which are entangled in each other: the economic-metaphysical—in direct line with the *Economic-Philosophical Manuscripts* of his period in Paris, the humane-literary, and the political bundle. The last of these three is most to the point here since we are essentially concerned with *Capital*'s character as a revolutionary act. As the Marxian scholar Maximilien Rubel remarked: *Capital* "was born of the revolutionary passion which it proposed to arouse."[12] This emphasis, however, does not relieve the reader of his responsibility of trying to answer the question: how accurately does *Capital* describe reality?

THE ECONOMIC-METAPHYSICAL BUNDLE

The economic statement on which the great bulk of *Capital* rests is not in the book but in the *Critique of Political Economy*. It is Marx's long-pondered definition of materialism. Drastically summarized here earlier, it deserves full attention.

> In the social production of their life, men enter into definite relations that are indispensable and independent of their will, relations of production which correspond to a definite stage of development of their material productive forces. The sum total of these relations of production constitutes the economic structure of society, the real

foundation, on which rises a legal and political superstructure and to which correspond definite forms of social consciousness. The mode of production of material life conditions the social, political and intellectual life process in general. It is not the consciousness of men which determines their being, but, on the contrary, their social being that determines their consciousness. At a certain stage of their development, the material productive forces of society come in conflict with the existing relations of production, or—what is but a legal expression for the same thing—with the property relations within which they have been at work hitherto. From forms of development of the productive forces these relations turn into their fetters. Then begins an epic of social revolution. With the change of the economic foundation the entire immense superstructure is more or less rapidly transformed. In considering such transformations a distinction should always be made between the material transformation of the economic conditions and production, which can be determined with the precision of natural science, and legal, political, religious, aesthetic or philosophic—in short ideological forms in which men become conscious of this conflict and fight it out. . . . This consciousness must be explained rather from the contradictions of material life, from the existing conflict between the social productive forces and the relations of production. No social order ever perishes before all the productive forces for which there is room in it have developed; and new, higher relations of production never appear before the material conditions of their existence have matured in the womb of the old society itself. . . . In broad outlines, Asiatic, ancient, feudal, and modern bourgeois modes of production can be designated as progressive epochs in the economic formation of society. The bourgeois relations of production are the last antagonistic form of the social process of production— antagonistic not in the sense of individual antagonism, but of one arising from the social conditions of life of the individuals; at the same time the productive forces developing in the womb of bourgeois society create the material forces for the solution of that antagonism. This social formation brings, therefore, the prehistory of human society to a close.[13]

Dense with valuable truths and powerful with arguments for action, the statement immensely improved modern man's understanding and command of his society. He would henceforth be aware that production and production relations were important determinants of thought and behavior, and he would change his thought and behavior accordingly. Of course the definition's shattering insights destroyed as they revealed. They arbitrarily attenuated nonmaterial phenomena—ideas, feelings, social relations, politics—to shadows of the material; history was reduced down to a precise set of progressive dialectical encounters. Furthermore, the materialist logic had not proved its conclusion that social peace would inevitably follow what Marx insisted upon seeing as "the last antagonistic form of the social process of production." In fact, this metaphysical (even religious) promise of peace was a denial of that materialist logic. The contradiction would be followed by many more.

Capital itself begins and ends in metaphysics, its economics doubled as Hegelian dialectics at all the hinge points. The reader must remind himself of this from time to time since the discussion proceeds by way of great masses of economic data. A half-hidden metaphysical structure holds the book together.

The importance of metaphysics was recognized in the term "dialectical materialism," invented by the Marxian convert Georgi Plekhanov.[14] Marx and Engels never used it, but it remains the most accurate designation for Marx's style and system of thought. The adoption of the term by Marxists and Engels' failure to object to it were admissions that there is more to materialism than materialism. Most Marxian scholars have, in fact, insisted that *Capital* cannot be reduced to "pure" economics, the incorrigible metaphysician always dominating the emergent economist in Marx, although a few, including Marx himself, have made the attempt. The profound student of Marx's thought Maximilien Rubel has described Marx as a moral philosopher using sociological and historical as well as economic categories. After noting that "*Capital* is as much an ethical statement as a scientific work," Rubel went on to discuss the Marxian conception of value, which he recognized as central to Marxian theory. With the idea of surplus value, Rubel said, "Marx abandoned the terrain of political economy proper to function as historian, sociologist, and moral philosopher."[15]

David McLellan has said much the same thing. "What seem to be purely economic doctrines (such as the labor theory of value) are not economic doctrines in the sense that, say, Keynes or Schumpeter would understand them."[16]

Among the non-Marxists, the distinguished neoclassical economist Joseph Schumpeter himself included Marx as a worthy subject for a book entitled *Ten Great Economists*. In his long essay "Karl Marx, 1818–1883: The Marxian Doctrine," however, Schumpeter insisted that "Marxism *is* a religion," deftly set Marx's economics in a noneconomic category by calling his economic interpretation of history "doubtless one of the greatest individual achievements of sociology to this day," and concluded that Marxian sociology and economics interpenetrated each other inextricably.[17] Sociology, history, theology, philosophy, and very nearly every other discipline concerned with the human condition pulsate between Marx's economics and his metaphysics. In view of all this and since metaphysics claims to mediate all efforts to understand reality, we can proceed most economically by concentrating on the relation between Marx's economics and his metaphysics.

Marx began *Capital*, like the *Critique of Political Economy*, by devoting the first chapter to the commodity, but with a metaphysical difference. The opening sentence of *Capital*, using quotation marks to call attention to the earlier work, rephrased the *Critique's* first sentence to express the same thought. "The wealth of the societies in which the capitalistic mode of production prevails appears as a 'monstrous accumulation of commodities,' the individual commodity as its elementary form." In *Capital's* next paragraph Marx specified, "The commodity is an objective thing first of all." [18] As in the *Critique* we first see the commodity in its sheerly physical character, just as materialism, of which it was the elementary building block, began as only materialistic in Marx's original definition. But Marx, his powerful imagination lighted up, returned to the commodity some forty pages later in *Capital*. "A commodity appears at first view as a self-evident, trivial thing. Analyzing it shows that it is a very queer thing, full of metaphysical pedantry and theological gnats." Marx described one such commodity, a wooden table, "an ordinary material thing": "But as soon as it steps forth as a commodity, it transforms itself into a material immaterial thing. It does not merely stand with its feet on the ground, but in relation to all other commodities it stands on its head and produces fancies out of that wooden head that are matters for more wonderment than if it had spontaneously begun to dance." [19] Inserting consciousness into the table incidentally, or rather, not incidentally at all, Marx was making a complex Hegelian joke, but this was cover for a serious logical operation. He meant it when he attributed "metaphysical pedantry"—a metaphysical dimension—to the commodity. The further development of *Capital* shows it precisely.

In the first volume of *Capital* Marx was driving toward a Hegelian apocalypse. [20] He used many intermediary metaphysical and logical-paralogical devices to arrive there, most particularly the doublings and splittings of Hegelian dialectics, but also as we have seen in his other writings, the argumentum ad hominem, the arbitrary statement, the destruction of identity, the tautology, the elimination of huge lumps of reality, and the grand confusions. We shall inevitably experience them as we study *Capital's* economics, but examples of one category, the dialectical operation, can be summarily mentioned here to show how pervasive they are. Thus labor is simultaneously labor and labor power, and, as either, could be seen as abstract labor or concrete labor. Private property is defined as being different from an individual's property; production, on second view, is . . . production and *re*production. Value is similarly doubled and redoubled: unqualified value and surplus value, but also use value as opposed to exchange value. Price expresses or falsifies value. Surplus value is and is not profit. Surplus value, furthermore, is both relative and absolute, although the phrase means something *relative* by definition, that is, something *compared* with something else and thus found to be *relatively* greater. Not content with this, Marx insisted at one point: "Relative surplus value is absolute. . . . Absolute surplus value is relative." [21] We need not pursue him into these metaphysical regions. The denouement is Hegelian in the classic tradition. Capitalism will perish "by the action of the immanent laws of capitalistic production itself, by the centralization of capital."

This argument produces a perfect contradiction. "The centralization of the means of production and the socialization of labor reach a point where they become incompatible with their capitalistic integument. The integument is ruptured. The knell of private property sounds. The expropriators are expropriated." The economic-metaphysical process does not halt here. The dialectic moves from the past through the present into the future. "The capitalistic mode of appropriation, which arose out of the capitalistic mode of production, is the first negation of individual private property based upon the labor of the individual himself. But capitalistic production begets its own negation with the inexorability of a law of nature. It is the negation of negation. This does not reestablish private property, but the property of the individual based upon the achievements of the capitalistic era: cooperation and possession in common of the land and the means of production as created by labor." [22] Like Hegel, Marx circles back to the beginning which is and is not the beginning. In Marx the World Spirit triumphs again.

In volume 3, using Hegel's dialectical metaphysics, Marx peered at the world after the apocalypse. "Just as the savage must wrestle with nature to satisfy his wants . . . so must civilized man, and he must do so in all social formations and under all possible modes of production. With his development this realm of physical necessity expands as a result of his wants, but, at the same time, the forces of production which satisfy these wants also increase. Freedom in this field can only consist in socialized man, the associated producers, rationally regulating their interchange with nature . . . instead of being ruled by it. . . . But this nonetheless still remains a realm of necessity." Clearing away the intervening clauses in the last two sentences, we note the perfect Hegelian antithesis: freedom equals necessity. Marx concludes: "In fact, the realm of freedom actually begins where labor which is determined by necessity . . . ceases; thus in the very nature of things it lies beyond the sphere of actual material production. . . . Beyond it begins the development of human energy which is an end in itself, the true realm of freedom, which, however, can blossom forth only with this realm of necessity as its basis." As in the *Economic-Philosophical Manuscripts* Marx describes a vision which only he can see.

Then Marx the practical political leader returns brutally to the non-Hegelian present as an economic phenomenon. In his next and final sentence on a future characterizied by freedom he concludes, "The shortening of the working day is its basic prerequisite."[23] Or has the Hegelian Marx hidden a metaphysical-dialectical promise in the juxtaposition of the two thoughts?

Marx had very little more to say about the future in the whole corpus of his writings. In *The German Ideology* of his Brussels period he had casually sketched a communist society where everybody could change at will from hunting to fishing, to tending herd, to writing criticism. After *Capital*, in 1875, he was led to a new effort. This was in the *Critique of the Gotha Program*, a series of literally marginal notes written on a copy of the unification agreement of the two German socialist parties. Marx was protesting the unification itself, the terms of the agreement, and its adoption of some Lassallean ideas.[24] To give force to his argument Marx was led to provide another description of the future. Most of it was a less felicitous rephrasing of the passage on the realms of necessity and freedom of volume 3 of *Capital*. He did, however, try to be more concrete about such practical matters as distribution, but could offer little more than generalities about a process of contributions to and withdrawals from a common fund.[25] He concluded hastily: "Then can the narrow horizons of bourgeois law be crossed in its entirety and society inscribe on its banners, 'From each according to his ability, to each according to his needs!' "[26] Surely the instinct of Marx the leader kept him from giving a detailed view of the future and its economic order: he knew how easy it was, as these minor tentatives suggest, to provide documentation of foolishness.

The genius of Marx's economics as economics is not to be denied, although the economic theory seems at times naked and gaunt without its metaphysical integument. As Schumpeter has remarked, "If ever it is true, it is in this case that the whole is greater than the sum of its parts."[27]

It was the metaphysics that made up the difference in *Capital*. This can be most clearly seen in Marx's best statement of his purely economic theory elsewhere than in *Capital*, which he made in two talks before the General Council of the First International in 1865. He spoke in English, which he commanded superbly, although Teutonically, by then, from a concise and comprehensible manuscript entitled "Wages, Price, and Profit."[28] Here the economics is overwhelmed neither by the metaphysics nor its own excesses. The reader is cautioned not to let his attention wander, however, since Marx spoke like an experienced schoolmaster of a certain persuasion trying to indoctrinate at the same time as he was teaching. Marx's purpose in giving the talks, in fact, had been to rebut the view, which he found "theoretically false and practically [*sic*] dangerous,"[29] of an English member of the International's General Council. Marx dealt with some problems by refusing to admit their existence. With others he used the superior deception of frankness, winning trust by admitting momentary perplexity. He then moved on as if sheer mention had solved those problems, but they had less space in which to hide in this brief popularization. The manuscript, preserved and published in some forty pages, affords the one opportunity for anyone who reads English to approach Marx's essential economic thought without the mediation of translator or interpreter.

Marx had innocently added to *Capital*'s overpowering character by overloading it mercilessly. Always keeping in mind its world-historical task, he tried to deal with everything relevant to the boundless requirements, and almost everything seemed relevant. The more research he did, the more he had to write about, and the longer the writing took, the more time he had in which to discover new research materials, etcetera, etcetera. Moreover, he had the receptivity of the conscientious student, and he tried to use, as he corrected, all of the important ideas of his teachers in economics, from Aristotle to Ricardo. Indeed, the "pure economist" Marx has been most authoritatively categorized as a "minor post-Ricardian."[30]

Marx approached his great denouement through the conception of value, so important to him that he had enough material left over for the three volumes of *Theories of Surplus Value*. Value is the real subject of *Capital* to the extent that it is an economic-metaphysical work. In a theoretical sense Marx committed himself absolutely when he laid down his labor theory of value. It is, furthermore, the labor theory of value that gives *Capital* such tremendous force as a revolutionary act. The labor theory of value is the point of the pyramid of Marx's economic logic. The pyramid, however, is standing on its pointed head. The point, furthermore, is not in *Capital* or any other of Marx's writings, since Marx never defined value itself, nor did he make a real attempt to prove that labor was the sole source of value, whatever value might be, as the labor theory of value claimed. As for pure value, Marx explicitly disdained defining it in a letter to a friend. "The babble about the necessity of proving the concept of value arises from complete ignorance both of the subject itself and the scientific method."[31] Here is another example of Marx's method of dealing with important problems that threatened his arguments. He buried them under a mountain of scorn. The fact that value was central to his system was all the more reason to refuse to define it. All of *Capital* rests upon an empty conception of value. The point of the work's pyramidal logic not only lacks dimensions as in geometry; it does not exist.

In order to make sense of *Capital* we shall have to override Marx and provide a definition of value ourselves. The dictionary will give us a start. Value is "relative worth, merit, or importance." In another definition value is "equivalent worth or return in money, material, services, etc."[32] The operative words are "relative" or "equivalent," which suggest that value is not intrinsic, as the labor theory of value would require. Behind this lies the marginalist conception developed about 1870, to which Marx remained impervious and which is taught in every elementary course of non-Marxian economics today. Virtually no rational mind outside the Marxian community disputes the conception now. In effect the marginalist economists believed that the idea of *intrinsic* value was meaningless, because anything or any *thing* would have no worth in a universe without consciousness or life. One corollary would be the notion that value is nothing other than the price determined by the transaction between seller and buyer at the moment it occurs. An individual could attribute any personal "value" or "worth" whatever to an object or service, but such an attribution does not enter the economy until a transaction has taken place. An economy is a *social* phenomenon and economics is a social science. Thus, price, as far as we are concerned, is another word for value *in economics*, and it is determined by matching the intensities of the desires to sell and to buy, these intensities being expressed as "supply" and "demand." Stock and commodity exchanges illustrate the functioning of the marginalist theory of value precisely. Marx, supported by Aristotle, St. Thomas Aquinas, Adam Smith, and David Ricardo, would not have it so.

The labor theory of value posited an intrinsic value as determined by the amount of labor going into a commodity. We ourselves must unlearn the idea of intrinsic value, since we unconsciously validate all reality with our own consciousness. We are inclined to assume that diamonds are worth more *of themselves* than, say, rotten tomatoes, until we realize how the proposition would change if we imagined ourselves starving or dead in relation to diamonds and rotten tomatoes. Similarly, it seems reasonable at first to suppose the value of a commodity should increase as the labor going into it increases. If a man making shoes by hand produces and sells a given number of shoes in a month, the value of two months' work would seem to be twice that of one month's work. But if he cannot find a buyer for the work of the second month, the shoes will be worthless—valueless—*in the economy*. In the economy the shoemaker, however hard and well he works, cannot alone determine the value of his shoes. If the shoemaker produces for the second month, it was because he assumed he could find buyers at a given price. It was not his work that determined the price, that is, the value of the shoes, but the price, that is, the value, that determined his work. The labor theory of value reverses the sequence of cause and effect.

It never occurred to Marx to question the labor theory of value as found. Furthermore, Adam Smith provided him with a recent and persuasive confirmation. Actually, Smith's famous illustration of the theory showed that supply and demand were the real determinants of value, as Paul A. Samuelson has noted in his widely used textbook, *Economics*. Moreover, Smith, consciously or unconsciously, recurred to the logic of supply and demand, in his *Wealth of Nations*.[33] The labor theory of value was, however, central to Marx's personality. Superbly solipsistic, always imposing his will upon the world, he found it natural to identify himself with the worker-producer imposing his valuation upon the world.

Marx did more with Adam Smith's value theory. Smith had credited the work of the capitalist-entrepreneur in creating value along with that of the worker. Marx swept away that component in the theory by simply assuming that only the worker did the working: the words were the argument. Yet Marx was aware of what he was doing. He openly put the question about the capitalist-entrepreneur's function: "Hasn't he worked himself? Hasn't he done the work of inspection and superintendence of the spinner-operative? Doesn't this work also create value?" With his next sentence Marx threw up a cloud of irony and insult, and turned his back on his own question: "[The capitalist] couldn't care less. He leaves this and all such facile evasions and cheap tricks to the professors of political economy paid precisely for that. He himself is a practical man."[34] In his own evasion Marx had admitted that the capitalist had indeed contributed work and value to the economy. But then he went on as if he had never raised the question, and fled into the evasion. His thesis remained intact.

Marx's radical reductiveness on the subject of value did not stop here. Consistent with his elimination of the capitalist's work, Marx went on to annihilate all of nature in the production of value. Thus air, undeveloped land, meadows, and woods had no value, he specified. He explained that these nature-given materials were valueless because labor did not produce them.[35] His conception of value reduced itself down to this: value is that which is produced by work (of the worker alone), and work (of the worker alone) is that which produces value. This perfectly circular reasoning, moreover, eliminated all need for defining either term.

Marx contradicted himself on the labor theory of value before and after *Capital*. Earlier, in the *Critique of Political Economy*, he wrote, "Labor is not the only source . . . of wealth."[36] He proceeded characteristically in the book's argumentation from this point; he let the thought vanish and continued to assume that labor was indeed the only source of wealth or value. Later, with the *Critique of the Gotha Program*, he reverted to that abandoned thought. The first article of the Gotha unification agreement had begun with Marx's preferred variant, "Labor is the source of all wealth." In his comment, however, Marx wrote baldly and emphatically, "Labor is *not the source* of all wealth." He insisted that the statement was true only if it were "conditional" upon the fact that labor operated with nature-given materials.[37] Marx could propose the labor theory of value more easily than he could believe it.

Whatever its inherent problems, the labor theory of value had a corollary of great power, surplus value. If, according to the theory, the worker created all the value and if the capitalist enjoyed an income, this income must be the surplus of the labor-created value. Marx's logic did not need the conceptions of use *and* exchange value, and labor *and* labor power, which he developed at great length in *Capital*. The idea of surplus value could do all of the work. You had only to believe that the capitalist was unproductive to see the capitalistic system as organized injustice. Yet it would have been too simple, too banal, if the reader had begun here. Instead, blindfolded part of the way, he had made a dizzying tour of Hegelian philosophy and classical economics. Now he suddenly found himself in possession of an easily comprehensible idea. The burst of light provided by surplus value could mean revelation and conviction.

Before arriving at surplus value, however, Marx had expended many pages on use and exchange value, conceptions found in Aristotle. *Capi-*

tal's first chapter begins with a close discussion of use and exchange value in relation to the commodity. Marx went on to refer to value in these terms again and again throughout the whole work.[38] We can dispense with the definitions quickly enough (although superficially), since they mean (superficially) what they seem to mean: use value is the worth of a commodity to its user, whether he produces it or not, while exchange value is what the seller can get for it in the form of other commodities as mediated usually by money. For *Capital* the importance of the conceptions lies in their absolute insignificance in Marx's economic logic, despite all the attention he gave them.

The ideas of labor and labor power, which were original with Marx, developed redundancy in another direction. He defined the latter as "the essence of the physical and mental capabilities which exist in the bodily character, in the living individuality, of a person, and which he sets in motion whenever he produces use values of any kind."[39] Marx was splitting his worker into two. This was in order to be consistent with the generally accepted economic law that, as Marx put it, "on an average, commodities are *sold at their real values*."[40] Marx said that there had to be an equality of values in the exchange taking place between capitalist and worker.[41] Yet the capitalist made a profit. This was an impossibility or a paradox. Marx's logic explained it as a meaningful and soluble paradox by alternating between the conceptions of labor and labor power. As "labor," the worker was a *producer* of value; as "labor power," he was a *consumer* of values. But the worker produced more than he consumed, since he was paid, Marx argued, only a bare subsistence wage under the Iron Law of Wages, as propounded by Ricardo. In other words, the capitalist paid for labor power, that is, subsistence, while in return he got not labor power but labor, that is, the production of a total of commodities that included a surplus. The surplus was the source of profit. If labor equaled labor power, the process was consistent with Marx's law of equal exchange of values. If labor was greater than labor power, by definition did not equal labor power, the process produced a profit. Marx thus resolved his paradox by insisting upon the truth of contradictory phenomena: labor was simultaneously the same as labor power and different from it. Thus the worker and the capitalist made an equal exchange which nevertheless produced an unequal result, a profit for one of the parties. Here was another instance in Marx's reasoning when, as he would have it, equality equaled inequality.[42]

Why did Marx, so arbitrary with the meaning of words when he chose, get into such a scholastic tangle? The law of the exchange of equal values was sanctioned by the authority of Adam Smith, among others. But Marx had better reasons. The law seemed to confirm his a priori belief that labor was the sole source of value. Furthermore, equal-exchange-of-values permitted Marx to claim a cohesive force for his theoretical system, as with a natural law like evolution. It would give the economic world a "natural" equilibrium, if a law dictated that the value of a commodity was the basis of the terms of the exchange. Actually, just as Marx intermittently saw disequilibrium in the world, he went on to break his own law about the equal exchange of values. While straining more or less successfully to keep to it in volume 1, he discarded it in volume 3. His earlier obedience, however, had its advantages. Marx could claim scientific rigor. At the same time he had made the most of the mystifications on the route to the idea of surplus value.

The proper reader, having experienced the epiphany of surplus value, saw the capitalistic system as based on ineradicable injustice. Behind this lay a standard of good and evil and the shadow of a higher being who set that standard. Surplus value gave *Capital* tremendous moral power. Once again, Marx was a prophet of Zion denouncing evil ways and, since he always personified their agents, evil men. Arrived at surplus value, the argument of *Capital* was arraignment, condemnation, and execution in the name of the Inexpressible.

Yet surplus value was more than a form or an essence of injustice. To Marx justice was and was not all-important. Besides his morality, he also demanded his (material) materialism and his determinism. Surplus value also provided them because its character, establishing the character of capital, created the objectively revolutionary dynamics of capitalism. Surplus value would not only justify revolution, it would make the revolution inevitable.

Marx arrived at his materialistic-deterministic revolution through the conception of the organic composition of capital. Following the teachings of other economists, but again making his own corrections, Marx divided capital into two parts, constant and variable capital. Labor was variable capital, not because, as one might think, it varied with the production requirements. That would also have been true of everything except fixed plant, the physical facilities of a given size. Again using circular reasoning, Marx defined labor and only labor as variable capital because it "undergoes a change of value in the production process. It produces the equivalent of its own value and, in addition, produces an excess, surplus value, which itself may vary.[43] While labor was variable capital, fixed plant *plus* raw materials, fuel, and anything else consumed in production comprised constant capital.[44] As an economy progressed industrially, Marx reasoned, the production facilities expanded disproportionately compared to the labor force. He took as an example an economy changing the constant capital-variable capital ratio from 50/50 to 82/20.[45] The capitalists themselves would suffer because their profit rate, derived from surplus value, would fall in accord with that ratio. A lower proportion of variable capital, that is, labor as sole producer of value, would mean proportionately less value produced. The capitalists would defend themselves against lower profits by reducing wages and dismissing workers. Thus industrial progress meant progressive impoverishment and unemployment.

Meanwhile, the great capitalists could temporarily take advantage of their strength by concentrating capital in their hands and driving their smaller competitors into bankruptcy. Part of the capitalist class would suffer proletarianization as the proletariat fell into deeper misery. "Accumulation of wealth at the one pole is thus at the same time accumulation of misery, sweated labor, slavery, ignorance, brutalization, and moral degradation at the opposite pole." Marx had already announced in italics, "*This is the absolute, general law of capitalist accumulation.*"[46] After dwelling on other matters for a hundred-odd pages, Marx recapitulated his account of wretchedness and disorder. The process reaches its term: "The monopoly of capital becomes a fetter on the mode of production, which flourished with it and under it." We have now arrived at the Hegelian apocalypse already quoted, when the capitalistic integument is ruptured, the expropriators expropriated, and the workers take possession of the world they made.[47] Thus had surplus value worked in association with the organic conception of capital.

Marx's logic of capitalism's self-destruction is another example of the reductive character of his thought. Without entering into other objections, we can see that he has reduced out one phenomenon which invalidates the whole argument. The expanded use of the production instruments forming constant capital was a response to the fact that constant capital is more productive than variable capital, that is, ordinary labor. Thus the effect of increased constant capital is more and more production, consequently more and more wealth, and not more poverty.[48] History has massively contradicted Marx; one has only to read the statistics on increases in per capita income in industrialized countries. But then Marx contradicted himself as well. One occasion occurred during his debate in the General Council of the First International, when he used the argument of increased productivity and production to rebut his opponent on another point.[49] Marx was intermittently forced to deny what he was persistently proving. Only in this way could he prevent his theoretical machine from breaking down.

If a loyal Marxian scholar could forget increased productivity along with Marx, he would still be forced to admit that volume 1, which held very nearly all the important sense of the whole of *Capital*, had failed to resolve important theoretical problems. The organic composition of capital had a fatal contradiction in it. The definition necessarily meant that labor-intensive production would produce more surplus value, given the fact that only labor created value, than a process requiring a greater proportion of machines. Volume 1 left the reader to wonder why capitalists invested in machines in the first place, or, accepting that as an arbitrary starting point, why those capitalists receiving low returns from their machine operations did not shift into more remunerative economic sectors, that is, those employing a greater ratio of workers. Marx promised an answer in volume 3, but he could say little more in that volume than, "A complicated social process intervenes here, the equalization process of capitals, which divorces the relative average prices of the commodities from their values, as well as the average profits in the various spheres of production . . . from the actual exploitation of labor by the particular capitals."[50] But Marx could not *show* how this process of equalization worked. He would have you believe that inexplicable generosity or blackmail would impel the capitalists of the high-return capitals to share part of their profits with their less fortunate fellows.

The great Austrian economist Eugen von Böhm-Bawerk wrote, "Either products do actually exchange in the long run in proportion to the labor attached to them—in which case the equalization of the gains of capital is impossible, or there is no equalization of the gains of capital—in which case it is impossible that products should continue to exchange in proportion to the labor attached to them." In volume 3 Marx, as Böhm-Bawerk went on to point out, simply dropped his earlier assumption that commodities were exchanged according to their values.[51] Marx also redefined surplus value, profit, and price in a sense inconsistent with that of volume 1. All this led him into long exercises in mathematics and the construction of dozens of mathematical tables which demonstrated his innocence of that subject. As for the argument of volume 3, Böhm-Bawerk found the writing "demoralized," with Marx unsuccessfully trying to avoid "a retraction of the main argument of the original system." Böhm-Bawerk concluded: "This is the great radical fault of the Marxian system at its birth. . . . The system runs in one direction, facts go in another."[52]

Another wayward fact, and a huge one, was agriculture, which threatened not only to run away from Marx's system, but to run away with it. As we have seen, Marx had dismissed nature, since his definition of value required labor and only labor as the creator of value. Agriculture might be less bulky than nature, but it was perversely difficult to manage. Agriculture was confounded with labor, indeed too much of labor, since the overwhelming majority of the world population, the peasantry, worked in it. In a secondary maneuver Marx made off with the peasantry's clothes: he seized upon the word "masses" for the industrial proletariat, which made up an insignificant percentage of the population of the world and a modest one of the population of the few industrialized areas like Britain, the United States, and Western Europe at the time. His major action consisted of eleven chapters and 200 pages of volume 3 devoted to the annihilation of agriculture.[53] Marx's treatment of agriculture was one of his greatest negations.

For the modern world, as well as for Marx, progress has developed out of industry. Characteristically, Marx translated an emphasis into an absolute. Characteristically also, he personified an economic process.

Marx had conducted a vendetta against the peasants, confounding them with the landowners as the collective personification of the reactionary essence of agriculture. To him the peasants' demand for private land ownership was another expression of this reactionary essence. The *Communist Manifesto* remarked on "the idiocy of rural life."[54] When the French peasants supported Louis Napoleon, Marx's *18th Brumaire* described them as "a monstrous mass whose members live in the same situation but without having joined with each other in manifold relations." Creating his own rural sociology, Marx explained, "The peasant proprietors form no class—to the extent that they have only local connections, [and to the extent that] the isolation of their interests creates no community, no national order, and no political organization among them." This was the second successive sentence in which, with the same phrase, Marx asserted the nonexistence of a peasant *class*.[55] In *Capital* Marx repeated the charge: "small landed property creates a class of barbarians standing outside of society."[56] But this was a casual blow, almost an aside. In *Capital's* eleven chapters on agriculture, the greatest part of the discussion had to do with rent and the relations between landowners and industrial society. Marx used one repetitive argument in barely differentiated details: through rent, the announced subject of ten of the eleven chapters, the landowners made off with a part of the surplus value produced by the labor of others. Of course the others, besides the industrial proletariat, included peasant proprietors and landless agricultural laborers, but these last disappeared from view in the argument. The reader was left with the suggestion that agriculture was a swollen parasite on the corpus of an advanced economy. With that, Marx returned with relief to industry, the one true value-producer.

Besides assaulting such sizable realities as nature and agriculture, Marx wielded *Capital*'s destructive force against one terribly important idea. Originally proposed by Thomas Malthus, as truly simple as it remains important, it held that population tended to exceed food supply, and that starvation and malnutrition set limits to the number of people permitted to live. In effect Malthus argued that the world would always have a margin of the dying. In his *Essay on the Principle of Population*, first published in 1798, Malthus was questioning the promise of the Enlightenment that all men could attain the good life. Marx correctly read Malthus as a rebuttal of all that he himself promised, and he began attacking theory and theorist as early as 1844. Thus, in the *Vorwärts!* article that marked his break with Arnold Ruge, Marx struck an incidental blow at Malthus.[57] Volume 1 of *Capital* referred to Malthus more than thirty times. Malthus is a powerfully sprung and imperfectly contained jack-in-the-box reappearing again and again to Marx's always fresh surprise, a figure from a nightmare erupting into a dream. Against Malthus' theory, the best Marx could do was to assert arbitrarily that capitalism deliberately produced an excess population and that "this is a law of population peculiar to the capitalist mode of production . . . historically valid within its limits alone."[58]

But Marx was aware of the feebleness of his argument. Indeed, Marx admitted the existence of limits to population in the *Grundrisse*, but in nothing he himself made public. He could only suggest that the limits be pushed back, a palliation of their consequences and surely no denial of their reality.[59] The margin of the dying persisted in his logic, as it persists in the real world today. Failing with his argument, Marx fell back on the attack on the person. He continually accused Malthus of plagiarism, since others had anticipated him in touching, at least, upon so obvious an idea. One of Marx's attacks took the form of a footnote that raged in fine print over the greater part of three pages. Malthus had originally taken orders, and Marx now accused the body of English parsons of fathering children in a "truly indecent degree" to make the Malthusian prophecy self-fulfilling.[60] It was, as the classical scholar Marx might well say of another's literary effusion, the reductio ad absurdum of the argumentum ad hominem. In doing justice to the high seriousness of the issue, Marx had made himself a figure of high comedy, the great man in a tantrum.

At this point, when we see Marx at his most absurd, let us remember what we should have recognized from the beginning: *Capital* is the greatest effort of the imagination to comprehend the new capitalistic world created by the Industrial Revolution. More than any other man Marx confronted its achievements and potentials as well as its horrors. Responding to his sense of reality, Marx denied his own economic theory and produced a great work of economics.

Marx's negative sightings were often tragically accurate in detail and sweep. "The monstrous, jerky growth of the factory system and its dependence on the markets of the world necessarily beget feverish production, followed by market surpluses with the resultant crippling of production. The life of industry transforms itself into a series of periods of moderate activity, prosperity, overproduction, crisis, and stagnation. The insecurity and instability . . . become normal." Human beings become shuttlecocks in a game played by machines. "The workers are continually repelled and drawn back, hurled back and forth."[61] The famous chapter "The Working Day" is a 75-page heaping up of the horrors of capitalism: wretched wages, child labor, female labor, endless hours, foul working conditions, equally foul living conditions, industrial illness and accidents, and shortened lives.[62] Marx also flung up onto the heap a review of instances of adulterated food, a stricture on factory legislation, more disquisitions on surplus value, and a freshly outraged recapitulation of the June Days of the Revolution of 1848. The chapter ended abruptly as if Marx had exhausted himself in his outrage. But he returned to the horrors of industrialism again, more than 400 pages later, with greater force. "All means for the development of production transform themselves into means of dominating and exploiting the producer; they chop the worker into a fragment of a man, degrade him into an appendage of the machine, destroy the meaning of his work by the agony of it, alienate him from the spiritual wealth of the work process . . . turn his lifetime into worktime, hurl his wife and child under the juggernaut-wheel of capital."[63]

But then, in seizing upon these wretched facts, Marx could not avoid other facts that shouted, "Yes!" While he continued to attack the capitalistic division of labor as an evil, he had to admit that it had a "positive side," and made the workers more productive. Elsewhere, he described it as "a necessary developmental stage."[64] He condemned capitalism for causing the inevitable technological unemployment, but then saw new

jobs being created to build up the necessary infrastructure and he specified: canals, docks, tunnels, bridges, gasworks, telegraph lines, steam-
ship transport, railroad systems, and "photography."[65] He accepted child
labor as normal and even speculated on the factory system as "the germ
of the education of the future, an education that will, in the case of every
child over a given age, combine productive labor with instruction and
gymnastics . . . as the only method of producing fully developed human
beings."[66]

In volume 3, returning to the insecurity of capitalism as expressed in
business cycles, Marx veered off into contradicting his doom-saying. He
believed that English industry had undergone a series of ten-year cycles
from 1815 to 1870, and that each time "the maximum of the prosperous
period *before* the crisis then appeared as the minimum of the next period
of prosperity, [the cycle] once again to rise to a new maximum on the
next swing."[67] The great, if more than usually chaotic, chapter "Machinery and Industry" thrust upon the reader some 140 pages of the history
of industrial production from the age of the individual craftsman through
the period of small workshops to the tremendous presence of modern
industry—and more: an analysis of the dynamics of the new phenomenon.[68] Marx examined such marvelous new machines as the one that
could cut and fold 3,000 envelopes in one hour. He noted the specializa-
tion of machines, thus the beaters, combers, cutters, and spinning machines in the woolen industry; he described their coordination into an
"organized system of various kinds of simple machines" so that "passage
is effected not by the hand of man but by machinery itself."[69] He arrived
at the latest stage:

> The most developed form of machine operation is the coordi-
> nated system of machines, to which motion is communicated by
> the transmitting mechanism from an automatic master machine. In
> the place of the individual machine a mechanical monster takes over—
> a monster whose body fills the whole factory building and whose
> demonic power, at first concealed under the almost dignified and
> measured character of the movement of its giant limbs, finally breaks
> out into the feverishly mad dervish dance of its countless working
> organs.[70]

At this point Marx could only admire.

With its negative and positive elements, his profound understanding
of both the structures of a modern economy and the underlying reality
of all existence defines the aggressively wrongheaded theoretical econo-

mist Marx as a great institutional economist. Joseph Schumpeter suggested this when he emphasized the central importance of sociology in Marx's thought. Wassily Leontief, the creator of input-output economics, remarked that Marx's "rational theories . . . do not hold water," but credited him with a "great feeling for social structure and the social order—what the capitalist system is." In fact, "three volumes of *Capital* give the reader "more realistic and relevant first-hand information than you could possibly hope to find in ten successive issues of the United States Census, a dozen textbooks on contemporary economic institutions and even, may I dare say, the collected essays of Thorstein Veblen."[71] Marx the theorist had simply refused to recognize the character of *exchange*, which is the essence of an economy, while the institutional economist pondered marvelously about the production complex, necessary enough as a condition of exchange, but not of itself achieving *economic* character. That institutional economist remains peerless and inexhaustible.

The great machine of modern industry still needed its personnel. Furthermore, it required that such personnel be all the better organized. Marx fell easily into military metaphor: "Just as the offensive power of a squadron of cavalry or the defensive power of a regiment of infantry are significantly different from the sums of the powers of attack or defense taken separately, so the sum total of the mechanical forces exerted by isolated workers differs from the social force that is developed when many hands take part simultaneously in one and the same unified operation." The workers were an "army [with its] industrial officers (executives, managers) and noncommissioned officers (inspectors, foremen, assistant foremen), who give the orders during the working process in the name of capital. . . . The supreme command in industry is an attribute of capital, just as in feudal terms the supreme command in war and justice was the attribute of landed property."[72] Once again, working his way through to knowledge, in this case knowledge of the economic order of things, Marx had arrived at the sense of his real goal, power.

THE LITERARY-HUMANE BUNDLE

To make a point of its literary-humane character might falsely imply that *Capital* communicates the kind of warmth one feels in, say, *Hamlet* or *The Divine Comedy*. Written by a revolutionary who had no human contact with the specified beneficiaries of his revolution, it is a cold work. Its cosmic indignation overwhelms its feeling for human individuals, and when it does apprehend certain ones, it does so only to hate them. Otherwise, *Capital* lumps men into a mass which cannot be loved. Marx, furthermore, cannot contain his contempt for a proletariat that must be told to save itself and inherit the earth. Yet Marx was capable of great love. Indeed, an undertaking like *Capital* would have been impossible without a massive bond to humanity beginning with the persons in Marx's own life. Enough love undergirds *Capital*, however hidden and strained, however frequently reversed into hatred, to make it a literary-humane achievement of the first order.

Marx's greatness as a writer communicates itself to the reader through even the deadliest interpretation by the deadliest interpreter, Stalin, to take an extreme example. Marx joins the company of Aeschylus, Dante, Shakespeare, and Goethe, whom he frequently quoted. He felt and expressed the sense and the agony of the human condition as deeply as they. Indeed, it was through his literary imagination that Marx arrived at what he and his followers thought were scientific reports on the political economy. He had seen most truly as artist.

But then it is a commonplace that great art and great science tell the truth. We confirm this every time we listen to what any first-rate artist is saying. A few examples might illustrate the point, and, at the same time, emphasize the art and truth in Marx's work. (The fact that Marx was a great and artful liar is no contradiction at all.) Aeschylus communicated the spirit and mechanics of rebellion so well in *Prometheus Bound* that Marx liked to think of himself as a new Prometheus. In *Antigone* Sophocles balanced *raison d'état* precisely against family feeling. Shakespeare, in his way, understood power politics as well as the government official and social scientist Machiavelli, but then Machiavelli was an artful playwright. But then Shakespeare also understood the Oedipus complex, among other neuroses, as well as Freud. Nietzsche anticipated Freud so accurately that Freud has been accused of stealing his ideas. Dante built the *Inferno* as well as the rest of *The Divine Comedy* out of dense earthly materials: Italian and Florentine politics, parental and sensual love, ambition, treason, betrayal, hate, and so much more.

We might pause for a moment with Dante, whose *Inferno* can be compared to the world of *Capital*. Both works are visions of the inferno of reality. Dante, a political exile like Marx, saw politics much as Marx did. The poet figure finds Farinata degli Uberti, chief of the opposing party, in a burning tomb in the sixth circle of hell, where Dante the politican had put him. Farinata, recognizing Dante, continues their old quarrel and recalls that he twice drove Dante and his friends out of Florence. Dante the partisan retorts that his party returned twice. Farinata, as innocent as Marx in his partisanship and ruthlessness, demands: "Tell me: why is that populace so savage/In the edicts they pronounce against my strain?"[73] The reader need not believe in hell or Dante's cartography of it to accept the truth in the scene. Similarly, the reader need not believe in capitalistic evil or the labor theory of value to see the monstrous truth of *Capital*.

The literary-humane dimensions of *Capital* have been suggested in what has already been noted here. The chapters "The Working Day" and "Machinery and Industry" have not only given detailed plans of large areas of the industrial economy, but—recall the supermachine—have projected an image of the world as infernal workshop. The idea of alienation, accompanied by the word "alienate," has also been mentioned, thus when Marx anathematized capital for turning the worker into an appendage of the machine. A philosophical construct at first sight in the *Economic-Philosophical Manuscripts*, although it began to become more even then, alienation reappeared in *Capital* in a much more substantial character, properly characterized as literary-humane rather than as philosophical or metaphysical. This is worth exploring further: Marx the literary man made many of his greatest discoveries in turning and twisting around the theme of alienation.

Marx dealt with alienation deceptively in *Capital*. While he occasionally used the word, he carried out the unnecessary operation of giving the phenomenon another name, "fetishism." Yet, with all this, he did not truly develop the idea. Thus he entitled the last section of the first chapter of volume 1 "The Fetishism of the Commodity and its Secret,"[74] but the section dealt essentially with other subjects.[75] Before passing on, Marx defined fetishism in just part of one sentence, distractedly and awkwardly: "a social formation . . . in which the production process rules men, in which man has not yet won mastery over the production process."[76] Marx returned to fetishism explicitly at the end of volume 3, also in a fragment of a sentence: "It is not merely the products of workers turned into independent powers, products as rulers and buyers of their producers, but rather also the social forces. . . ."[77] But Marx did not need to continue. All of *Capital* was a metaphor of the idea of fetishism or alienation.

In his artistry Marx also made a game of his treatment of fetichism or alienation.

> Everything is for sale; everything is buyable. Commerce becomes a great social alembic into which everything is thrown, to reappear as gold crystals. Not even the lives of saints and still less those more delicate things which are especially sanctified, thus kept outside the commerce of men, can resist this alchemy. Just as every qualitative difference between commodities is extinguished in money, so does money the radical leveller wipe out all distinctions. But money itself is a commodity, an objective thing. . . . The social power thus becomes the private power of private persons. The society of antiquity therefore denounced it as the counterfeit of its economic and moral order.

From this Marx spun three footnotes, one a historical excursus on money and religion which ended with a reference to temple prostitution, a second quoting Shakespeare's *Timon of Athens*: "Gold, yellow, glittering, precious gold! . . . Thus much of this will make black, white; foul, fair;/ Wrong, right; base, noble; old, young; coward, valiant," and a third quoting *Antigone* on money as "the most shameful of evils."[78] If Marx said nothing new here, he showed how traditional belief, as documented in the classics, agreed with *Capital*'s conception of fetichism.

Referring with irony to the ideals of the French Revolution, Marx brought fetichism up to date a few pages later. He was no longer playing: "The sphere of commerce or commodity exchange . . . is in fact a very Eden of the inborn rights of men. Here, only freedom, quality, property, and Bentham give the orders." Marx particularly hated the utilitarian Jeremy Bentham as a spokesman of efficient capitalism. Furthermore, in the original German, the name Bentham was audially perfect after the word for property, *Eigentum*. Marx continued: "Freedom! Because buyer and seller of a commodity, say labor power, are constrained only by their own free will. They contract the terms of their exchange as free, legally equal persons. . . . Equality! Because . . . they exchange equivalent for equivalent." This was a reference to the distinction between labor and labor power, permitting Marx to reassert that equivalents were not, in point of fact, equivalent. Then, in the richness of his invention, Marx unconsciously undercut the alienation-fetichism thesis that things ruled the world. He fell into his reflex of personifying the enemy, in this case the forces manufacturing fetichism-alienation. "The man who has begun as the man with the money now strides forward as capitalist, the owner of labor power follows him as his worker; the one self-importantly smirking and all business, the other timid, holding back, like someone who is bringing his own hide to market and can expect nothing except— a hiding."[79] One might, with Marx, just as well say that men—evil men— ruled things and thus other men, the good men. Fetichism-alienation was all and not all. Once again, Marx's art scaled his findings to human proportions.

Sometimes the literary Marx gave himself to the joy of the polemic so completely that his statement outran his meaning, but then not too far for his purposes. Reviewing the failure of the Chartists, his account ig- nited at the associated memory of the events in France: "Soon after this the June Insurrection in Paris and its bloody suppression united, in En- gland as on the Continent, all factions of the ruling classes, landlords and capitalists, stock-market wolves and shopkeepers, protectionists and free- traders, government and opposition, parsons and freethinkers, young whores and old nuns—under the universal demand for the salvation of property, religion, the family, and society!"[80] Shopkeepers and young whores could hardly be classified as members of the ruling classes, but Marx had marched a motley cast of characters, villainous, suspect, and comic, across the stage, and the audience could amuse itself by hooting and whistling without thinking too much.

Marx's use of the *argumentum ad hominem,* the epithet, the insult, and the sarcastic rejoinder was play and more than play. As with the polemic, the sheer pleasure he took in exercising these literary skills evokes a reciprocal pleasure in the reader. Behind his excesses was hard, if always contestable, argument. Marx drew Jeremy Bentham as "the arch- Philistine . . . that insipidly pedantic, leather-tongued oracle of the com- mon bourgeois intelligence of the nineteenth century."[81] It was a recog- nizable caricature of the man and philosophy. Edmund Burke, not inaccurately, was "the famous sophist and sycophant."[82] Marx attacked others with less justice because their logic was less vulnerable. The French *philosophe*-economist Destutt de Tracy was a "fish-blooded bourgeois doctrinaire," who on another occasion aroused Marx to exclaim: "*Voilà le crétinisme bourgeois dans toute béatitude!*"[83] A fish-blooded person would lack feeling for humanity, and thus, Marx was suggesting, was certain to be in theoretical error. Another nonsocialist economist, Frédéric Bas- tiat, was "truly comical," but on a second thought, "the most superficial and therefore most typical representative of the apologetics of vulgar economics."[84] The latter remark was deadly serious. All nonsocialist economics after the time of Ricardo was "vulgar economics," a popular- ization that falsified important ideas of Smith and Ricardo like the labor theory of value. The inherent vulgarity of such economic thought being granted, Marx could speak confidently of the "bad taste of the boring J. B. Say."[85] But then even Smith and Ricardo fell into the error of their unworthy followers. Although they had developed the labor theory of value, they failed to understand what they had wrought. Smith was guilty of a "silly blunder . . . thereby opening the gate wide for vulgar economics," while "Ricardo fell into the superficiality of vulgar economics."[86] The reader got his instruction as well as his amusement. Part of the point of both was the superiority of the entertaining instructor over his rivals of the past, present, or future. Now Marx was no longer joking.

All of Marx's important epithets, like "vulgar economics," were products of strict logic and had precise meanings. They led to the final link in Marxian logic: revolution. "Exploiter" and "exploitation," for example, derived from the conception of surplus value, as exhaustively reasoned out in *Capital*. The exploiter, through the process of exploitation, "expropriated"—another highly charged word—the surplus value created by the worker. The epithets, thus, were conclusions of arguments and to be accepted as having been proven. Marx's most extravagant or trivial word games had their high seriousness.

The reader is always aware that Marx's play is the play of a giant of literature. His defects become virtues. His vulgarity, for example, is so monumental that it contributes to his greatness. His confusion and mystifications inspire belief and faith where clear sense *alienates*. For the rest, Marx seduces with the secret yet to be revealed. With his art and his vast powers, Marx was able to create a roomy cosmos in which millions would live comfortably and in which they would think they lived freely.

POLITICS

With *Capital* Marx had imposed a new structure on the new world of the nineteenth century, with its new class, the proletariat, as its creative force. The structure demanded a special leadership which only Marx and his followers could give. Only Marx and those who thought and acted like him could function in *Capital*'s field of tension between great truths and great deceptions. This meant power.

The subject of *Capital* is power. Marx exercised power incessantly: he intimidated his schoolmates, shaped an aristocratic wife and dependent children into revolutionary subordinates, overwhelmed his housekeeper to satisfy a sexual reflex, commanded others to support him emotionally and financially, and used all persons in his life as saving conductors of his rage. Most of his writings are concerned with power, the *Communist Manifesto* most explicitly so. Marx wrote *Capital* to attain power. He manipulated the reader, as he manipulated himself, through his own confusions and mystifications. *Capital* did not seek to elucidate the economics of the world. It set out to conquer the world through economics as understood and arbitrarily misunderstood by Marx.

Capital is also a conscious study of power, how to attain it and how to exercise it. This is clear in the passages where Marx reviewed the rise of capitalism and likened the factory system to a military organization. His captains of industry were armed with full powers and deadly discipline. The factory organization required no redesign whatever. Without changing the table of organization, Marx would put himself at the head of it and command its dervish machines to continue their dance.

The publication of *Capital* was timed negatively as well as affirmatively to achieve Marx's objective of power. Marx knew better than to hurl a great work into the deep trough of the 1850s. If he let his revolutionary optimism revive with the business crisis of 1857, his political realism reacted quickly to the resolution of the crisis. Thus in 1859 he would invest only the *Critique of Political Economy*, the meager residuals of his *Grundrisse*, in the revolution. It was not until 1861 that Marx felt the situation to be right: Europe, recovered from the wreck of the Revolution of 1848, was beginning to stir. The immediate result was his greatest labor, ending with the publication of volume 1 of *Capital* in 1867. Marx's failure to complete the whole of *Capital* was no less correct as a negative action. As Böhm-Bawerk remarked, volume 1 used the promise of the future volumes to fill out the gaps in his logic. The other volumes came too late to be tested by a fresh-minded reading. In 1896 Böhm-Bawerk could write, "Now a belief in an authority which has been rooted for thirty years forms a bulwark against the incursions of critical knowledge."[87] Furthermore, the inadequacies of the last volumes of *Capital* could be blamed on Engels.[88] *Capital*'s conquests began with the overwhelming inevitability of the careers of the New Testament or the Koran, or the armies of Constantine, Mohammed, Trotsky, and Mao Tse-tung.

The moment had also been perfect for the other of Marx's great labors, his leadership of the First International, which occupied him from 1864 to 1872. In 1868 the International's Brussels Congress, dominated by Marx's lieutenants, passed a resolution noting the appearance of *Capital*:

"Karl Marx deserves the very greatest credit for being the first economist to have subjected capital to a scientific analysis."[89] *Capital* gave Marx unsurmountable intellectual authority in the organization, while the International itself served to promote the book. The relation of *Capital* and the International, either helping the other, was a paradigm of Marx's fusion of theory and action, and superior to the promise of such a fusion in the "Theses on Feuerbach." Marx's style showed itself just as clearly in the International as in *Capital*, most particularly in the organization's precisely timed, precisely inconclusive demise. But then Marx's earlier writings and leadership activities had prefigured this matched pair of ultimate cases.

The center of gravity of the First International had been situated too far in the future for the organization to have any great immediate effect. *Capital*, however, operating through the Marxian movement in Germany, Russia, and elsewhere on the Continent very soon won real power. More than a classic study of the new industrial society, *Capital* was an instrument of power.[90] Its creation had been revolutionary politics of the highest order.

NINE

THE POLITICS OF INTERNATIONALISM

THEORY

MARX'S MASTER PLAN WAS TO ORGANIZE a revolutionary movement that would capture progressive Europe. The movement would lead it away from the survivals of medievalism and particularism through bourgeois nationalism to proletarian internationalism. Other regions would follow as their maturity permitted. The plan had to be large enough to cover all the various cases without being so diffuse as to mean anything or nothing. Sections of the plan have been examined in the *Communist Manifesto* and *Capital*, *inter alia*, and now the rest can be added. Actually, Marx provided an outline of very nearly all of it in the *Manifesto* itself, which was so well drawn that he never had to alter or even strain it. Of course he took positions as different as the different cases to be covered, but the dialectic accommodated itself to every one of them.

It was not extraordinary, given the world's contradictoriness, that Marx's international strategy not only tolerated but consciously used nationalism.[1] Any specific decision depended on how he could situate and manage a given aspect of nationalism in the context of his master plan. Marx was entirely consistent when his *Neue Rheinische Zeitung* demanded *"war with Russia"* as a war of *"revolutionary Germany"*[2] a half year after the *Communist Manifesto* had proclaimed that "working men have no fatherland."[3] The rationale of the Russian war matched that of Marx's alliance with the middle-class Democrats. In the *Manifesto* itself, the passage quoted had led to this precision: "Since the proletariat must first of all acquire political supremacy, must raise itself to the status of a national class, must constitute itself as a nation, it is itself national, though not in the bourgeois sense of the word." The last phrase had saved the proletariat from mere nationalism by a deft Hegelian splitting, Marx going on to promise that proletarian nationalism would mean the end of all national hostilities.[4] In the Revolution of 1848, thus, Marx could reasonably try to transform a medieval and particularistic Germany into a nation and, as he insultingly told his middle-class allies, move beyond that point.

But if Germany had the duty of exercising patriotism, an already national France was in a different situation, as Marx wrote in the *NRZ*. He had only contempt for *La Réforme*, the newspaper which had welcomed him to France when the revolution broke out. *La Réforme*, trapped in its bourgeois character, deplored both the June rising and its suppression, and blamed the tragedy on a failure of patriotism. Marx preferred to keep a spirit of that kind buried in the past as "precisely that gushing enthusiasm with which both classes smear a patriotic and nationalistic coat of whitewash over their specific interests and life situations." In the France of 1789 patriotism had been a force for progress, but "what was a living body then is saintly bones today."[5] This treatment of Germany and France suggested Marx's policy for and toward other countries: internationalism for the advanced part of the world and a provisional nationalism elsewhere.

Working outward from Western Europe and regarding the non-European continents as appendages of Europe, Marx assigned specific roles to certain large European nations and, in many cases, no roles at all to the smaller ones. Both Marx and Engels were clear and consistent on the principle, although they recognized exceptional cases. In the *NRZ* Engels wrote that only three nations in the Austrian Empire were "standard-bearers of progress . . . —the *Germans*, the *Poles*, and the *Hungarians*. Therefore, they are revolutionary." As for "the other greater or lesser tribes and peoples, they first have the mission of going under in the international revolutionary storm. For this reason they are counter-revolutionary."[6] A year before Marx died, Engels, trying to assuage the distress of two leading Social Democrats, twice explained the Marx-Engels policy in more detail. He wrote Karl Kautsky: "Whether I really have absolutely no feelings for your little Slavic peoples and rubble of peoples? . . . *Verdammt* little in fact." The principle remained. "Above all, an international movement is possible only on the basis of self-sufficient nations."[7] Two weeks later Engels told Eduard Bernstein, "Our objective, subordinating everything else, is to help in the emancipation of the Western proletariat."[8] At whatever cost Marx never relented in his drive toward the great objective.

Poland and Russia were perfectly opposed examples of nationalism, each raised to the highest power. For Marx Poland was the great national affirmation and Russia the great national negation of progress. Of course, aside from the fact that Poland was a captive of Russia (and Prussia and Austria), Marx knew very well that the two Slavic countries were quite similar: not simply nationalistic but chauvinistic, agricultural, backward, and divided between wretched masses of serfs and increasingly useless nobles. But Marx's dialectic dominated.

Poland was too perfect a cause to be rejected. All progressives sympathized with her, while the attainment of her freedom would be a great blow to Russia. The First International would be founded at a meeting demanding a free Poland. Marx had long been a supporter of Polish independence, thus his speech demanding it on the day before the second congress of the Communist League began. If his ruthless refusal to succor "old Poland" might have offended some,[9] The *Neue Rheinische Zeitung* associated itself with the Poles vigorously enough to receive a subsidy from them a few months later. Yet Marx's speech of 1847 expressed his real policy, an ideological *Realpolitik* that overwhelmed the facts of the virtual nonexistence of a Polish proletariat and the aristocratic character of the Polish leadership. Poland was useful to the revolution, thus Poland was revolutionary, as Engels' *NRZ* article would have it. In any event Marx's hatred of Russia would have dictated his attitude toward Poland.

The *NRZ*'s demand for war against Russia was one example of the public convenience Russia represented. All good men could unite in hating nation and ruler. From 1825 to 1855 Czar Nicholas I personified sadistic autocracy. He had opened his reign by personally examining the Western-minded Decembrist rebels after they abruptly tried to take power and he sanctioned the execution of five and the exiling of a hundred. Nicholas later sent troops to crush the Hungarian rebellion in 1849, the last tragedy of the Revolution of 1848, and ended his reign by a series of aggressions that led to the Crimean War. Polish nationalism was a beautiful dream; Russian nationalism rolled back European progress where it did not massively block it. As London correspondent of the New York *Daily Tribune*, Marx could use its columns to publish his ideas. In the issue of June 14, 1853, making rather free estimates, Marx recalled that since Peter the Great "the Russian frontier has advanced:

"Toward Berlin, Dresden, and Vienna about.......... 700 miles.
"Toward Constantinople about....................... 500 miles.
"Toward Stockholm about........................... 630 miles.
"Toward Teheran about .... 1,000 miles."[10]

In the Inaugural Address Marx wrote for the First International eleven years later, he called upon the members to influence their governments to resist the Russian threat: "The fight for such a foreign policy forms part of the general struggle for the emancipation of the working classes."[11] In this way Russia would serve Marx's revolution.

Marx's attitude toward Russia, especially during the period of the Crimean War, was another example of his beginning with hard sense and arriving at the borders of psychosis, paranoia in this case. In the *Daily Tribune* he might coolly and accurately analyze Russia's use of the role of protector of the Christians to seize smaller states, and warn that Turkey was to be the next victim.[12] But then, when the war did break out, he saw conspiracies everywhere and chastised the allied governments for failing to pursue it with loyal energy. He was convinced that Lord Palmerston, the powerful home secretary and future prime minister, had become, in effect, a Russian agent. Marx allied himself with a correspondingly fanatical member of Parliament, who happened to be a Conservative but who was a Turkophile and Russophobe. Marx proceeded to write enough articles on the Palmerston-treason thesis to fill out a book.[13] The allied victory did not end Marx's suspicions, since he felt that Russia had been treated too mildly.[14]

Beyond Europe Marx recognized countries to the extent that they showed signs of being eligible for the revolutionary dialectic. In the *Tribune* in 1853, for example, he published the article "The Revolution in China and Europe," but failed to keep the promise his title had made. He said little more about China than that the Opium War had usefully ended its "barbarous and hermetic isolation from the civilized world." China was still too retrograde for him, and he dropped that part of the subject. He went on to expatiate passionately and at length on Europe's revolutionary future.[15] Shortly thereafter he turned his attention, also in the *Tribune*, to the other great Asian country in an article entitled "The British Rule in India." Marx began severely: "The misery inflicted by the British is of an . . . infinitely more intensive kind than Hindustan had to suffer before." But, on second thought, that misery was improvement. England had brought about a social revolution in India: "Can mankind fulfill its destiny without a fundamental revolution in the social state of Asia? If not, whatever may have been the crimes of England, she was the unconscious tool of history in bringing about that revolution."[16] Wasting no indignation over imperialism as practiced, in fact tacitly propagating a socialist imperialism, Marx returned to his proletarian revolution in Western Europe.

One series of eight articles in the *Tribune* represents a limiting case in Marx's writings on world politics: objectivity. Studying Spanish revolutionary history, Marx described the rebellion against the Napoleonic occupation as "regeneration united with reaction." Marx had to admit that the Spanish masses, led by priests and nobles, were more conservative than the generals and bourgeoisie. The conception, drawn from a fair evaluation of the facts, paralyzed or even reversed the dialectic.[17] Here was a case of the dialectic failing to manufacture a popular revolution, and instead producing a positive effect by a reactionary mode. At the time Marx wrote the articles, in 1854, Spain, despite its proximity, was too backward socially, politically, and economically to have entered his field of revolutionary tension. He looked forward to the time when she would arrive there, but for the moment took on the role of a very nearly neutral observer.

Marx's impatient polemics helped move history in the direction his theory was predicting it would move. In 1864, with the First International, he found himself controlling an instrument with which to begin to apply the theory.

THE MACHINERY OF INTERNATIONALISM

The immediate history of the International Working Men's Association went back to the summer of 1862, when a delegation of 750 French workers visited London. They came to see the International Exhibition, another display of nineteenth-century industrial progress. The trip had been funded by Prince Victor Napoleon, a cousin of Louis Napoleon and a patron of a substantial trade-union movement in France. The prince's function was to serve the emperor's policy of succoring and taming the French working class, but Louis Napoleon could not always control the effects of his clever ideas. The French delegation fraternized with English union leaders and workers, and a formal meeting was planned for the following year. Before the second meeting during the next summer, the Polish revolution of January 1863 had broken out and been suppressed. The delegates took the occasion to express their new access of sympathy for the Poles and hatred for the Russian oppressor. They also decided to form a permanent organization the next year, with the objective of coordinating the operations of the national labor groups, supporting the Poles, and promoting world peace.

It was not until a few days before the founding meeting, on September

28, 1864, that Marx had anything to do with the First International. As he wrote to Engels more than a month later, he had received the visit of "a certain Le Lubez," who asked him if he could suggest a German workingman to speak at the meeting. The visitor, Victor Le Lubez, was a French salesclerk living in London and a mutualist follower of Proudhon who would presently differ with Marx and return to obscurity. Marx gave Le Lubez the name of the tailor Georg Eccarius, a former member of the Communist League and an old friend. Marx himself did not get an invitation, a curt note, until the day the meeting took place. He refused to permit the scant courtesy to offend him.[18] He wrote Engels, "I knew that this time there were real powers 'in play' on both the London and Paris sides, and so I decided to waive my otherwise standing rule to decline any such invitation." One may doubt that Marx had been receiving enough invitations as to require a standing rule. At the meeting he contented himself with being "a silent figure on the platform." Some 2,000 persons filled a hall near Covent Garden and confirmed his feeling about "real powers,"[19] a feeling that probably originated in his impeccable revolutionary timing.

A half-generation had passed since the revolutionary wave had receded. Trade unions were expanding in England, where the London Trades Council, which had been founded in 1860, provided leadership, and in France, Germany, and elsewhere, as governments accepted the fact that they could no longer maintain the reactionary policies of the 1850s. At the meeting, George Odger, shoemaker by trade and secretary of the Trades Council, made the usual remarks about Poland, but he also mentioned an objective that would give the new organization a practical task recommending itself to all. He wanted to prevent employers from shipping workers across national borders to keep down wages or break strikes. A provisional committee of thirty-four members, twenty-seven of them English, was elected. The others were three French, two Italians, and the Germans Marx and his man Eccarius. Additionally, a subcommittee of nine was elected to draft a statement of principles and the organization's rules. Marx was a member of the subcommittee as well.

Marx's invitation to the founding meeting had not been as fortuitous as it seems. The First International was the descendant of at least three organizations with which he had been associated: the German Workers' Educational Association, the Communist League, and the Society of Fraternal Democrats, the last having been sponsor of the protest meeting on Poland in 1847. Everything Marx had done since he became an international personage in Paris had helped to prepare the world for the First

International and himself for leading it. After the Revolution of 1848 the absurdities he had committed had, at least, kept his presence known in the right circles, and he had done nothing to disqualify himself, either by undertaking disastrous revolutionary action or by compromising with the established order. He had done much to make the opportunity that came so carelessly.

If the International began with real substance, it was not, however, of a quality easily amenable to Marx's ideas. The English members, restricting themselves to the modest objectives of better pay and working conditions, were not socialists at all. The French were chiefly Proudhonian anarcho-socialists, who ignored governments, rejected political action, and put their faith in cooperatives and free credit. The International was neither revolutionary nor, even with Proudhonians and Marxists lumped together, socialist. Yet the substance, the immaterial material, was there.

Marx's first actions showed how he could exploit the situation. He was hampered by illness, which kept him from important early meetings, but he almost immediately established a position of authority for himself. In his absence the subcommittee had produced a statement of principles and a set of rules, both unsatisfactory and both unsatisfactorily synthesized by Le Lubez. This was Marx's opinion, but most of the others agreed. Marx thereupon volunteered his services as editor. He scrapped the draft statement of principles and replaced it with his own. Known inaccurately as the Inaugural Address of the International Working Men's Association, it was accepted with minor changes by the provisional committee on November 1, 1874.[20] On Marx's initiative ten organizational rules had been appended to the address; they would assist his plan to manage the International. The address itself was another masterpiece of revolutionary politics. Marx could not transform the International into a new Communist League, but he could, at least, move it verbally toward the league's objective. He had written Engels in his original letter about the International: "Time is necessary before the revived movement can permit itself the old audacious language. The need of the moment is: bold in matter, but mild in manner."[21]

The Inaugural Address gave the implicit rationale for revolution, trusting that its readers would draw the proper conclusions at the proper moment. Making apt use of his research for *Capital*, and having clearly in his mind its thesis of the self-destruction of capitalism, Marx announced his argument in his first sentence: "It is a great fact that the misery of the working masses has not diminished from 1848 to 1864, and yet this period is unrivaled for the development of its industry and the growth of its commerce."[22] With a watchmaker's deftness Marx inserted in his logic an indestructible, jewellike lie which is repeated every time the address is reprinted, efforts to question it having been easily smothered. He quoted the chancellor of the exchequer as having crucially qualified his report on the nation's prosperity in his budget speech of 1863: "'This intoxicating augmentation of wealth and power,' adds Mr. Gladstone, 'is entirely confined to classes of property.'"[23]

Actually, Marx had attributed to Gladstone a truncated and altered statement that was in absolute contradiction to the sense of what he had said, which was: "I should look almost with apprehension and with pain upon this intoxicating augmentation of wealth and power if it were my belief that it was confined to the classes that are in easy circumstances." While expressing his regret over the extent of poverty, Gladstone went on to say that "the average condition of the British laborer . . . has improved in the last twenty years in a degree which we know to be extraordinary, and . . . unexampled."[24] Gladstone could point to the tripling of British trade in the last twenty years and the greatest improvement in national well-being in a period of that length.

In the address Marx, using the false quotation, nullified the chancellor of the exchequer's wordy good cheer and mass of triumphant statistics: "Everywhere the great mass of the working classes were sinking down to a lower depth."[25] It was untrue, as was *Capital*'s doctrine of progressive impoverishment from which it was derived. Hidden behind that, however, was the entirely reasonable argument that the workers were not getting their fair share of the new wealth and power. But then reasonableness could not reach Marx's great objectives. But then, constrained by the mediocrity of his situation, Marx had to be reasonable himself. Marx and the moderate-minded could agree on the conclusion of the address: "To conquer political power has therefore become the great duty of the working men's party. . . . Proletarians of all countries, Unite!"[26] This last command, however, echoed the *Communist Manifesto*.

The Inaugural Address, serving Marx in the same way as the *Manifesto* had served him in the Communist League, was important in establishing his leadership of the International. The provisional committee, which accepted the address with trivial changes, soon transformed itself into the leading organ, the General Council. Marx's position on the General Council was strengthened when he became corresponding secretary for Germany. He accomplished this with his old skill: he suggested that the

German Workers' Educational Association in London elect the corresponding secretary, and the association, where his prestige and influence had been rising, elected him.[27] Corresponding secretary for Germany and, on occasion, for another country requiring one, was the only title he held, but he preferred the substance to the appearance of leadership. In 1864 George Odger, the English labor leader, had been elected president, but he was never more than a figurehead. In 1866 Marx refused the nomination to the president's office and supported Odger's reelection.[28] The next year Marx suggested that the office be abolished; the collectivity of the General Council thereupon formally assumed the leadership.[29] The result of Marx's suggestion showed Marx's power: Marx was making the decisions for the collectivity.

Marx's power derived from his unqualified genius for leadership, the appropriateness to the International's situation of that genius, his rich experience in radical organizations—and hard work. Other General Council members like Odger had duties that meant more to them; nothing was more important to Marx than making revolution. This also required completing *Capital*, and Marx, suffering increasingly from the strain and cheating now one, now the other, concentrated on both *Capital* and International. For the latter, the conscientious bureaucrat Marx attended to a multiplicity of boring details that included corresponding with affiliates, collecting dues, and seeing to the printing and mailing of membership cards. A change in his behavior, the great achievement of his later maturity, provided the quintessence of his effectiveness: he contained his dominating nature. In the minutes of the General Council, Marx appears as patient and accommodating, reaching his ends through persuasion except for intermittent acts of trickery.[30]

Marx had one more source of strength that permitted him to avoid overt displays of power. The rules which he had written for the International let him make use of co-optation, the selection of additional members of a governing body by that body itself and not by a general election of all the organization's members. Marx, with the General Council's distracted approval, could name new General Council members whenever he thought fit; the candidates were always his old revolutionary friends. A life-and-death necessity in an illegal organization, when congresses could not be held and arrests tended to eliminate leaders, co-optation was inevitably a way of perpetuating the power of the original leadership, but it could be justified in an organization that did not know its own mind. Marx gave the International a mind. In 1867, his old enthusiasm reviving, he wrote Engels, "In the next revolution, which is perhaps nearer than it seems, *we* (i.e., you and I) have this powerful machinery *in our hands*."[31]

As a revolutionary with specific ideas, Marx found himself the leader of a legal and nonrevolutionary organization. Within two years more than a hundred societies, including, besides trade unions, mutual aid groups, free thinkers, language reformers, and artisanal guilds, had affiliated themselves to the International. This brought membership to several hundred thousand. Success increased the problems. Marx had to limit the organization's interventions to carefully selected matters that, like the Inaugural Address, did not offend too many of the various affiliates. In the welter of contradictory aims one activity united nearly all the members without disturbing the others. This was Odger's original idea of defending wage levels. The International energetically collected funds to support strikes and made use of publicity to warn off strikebreakers. From 1866 to 1868 it aided striking weavers, basket makers, bronze workers, bookbinders, cigar makers, tailors, and bakers.[32] The strike of the bronze workers in Paris in February 1867 gave the International its first success, the employers capitulating when the British Hatters' Union promised their French comrades a loan.[33] The promise was better than the money itself, since the International was pitifully poor. At a meeting of the General Council of February 9, 1869, the German Workers' Educational Association of London solemnly presented £2/6 for the locked-out weavers of Basel, and two months later Marx complained that the Geneva affiliate "allowed itself to get too deeply entangled in every little strike without having prepared any means to support it; it could only tend to compromise the *Organization*."[34] The International could seldom claim that its help had brought success in a given case, but the efforts were always excellent propaganda.

For Marx the point was clearly not economic gains, and once again he sought a proper economic-political balance. That was why he worked so hard to persuade the International's first congress to pass a resolution demanding the eight-hour day. Behind the specific economic demand, of course, was his theory of surplus value, which saw the capitalists getting rich only in the last hours of the working day, after they had paid for the workers' subsistence, that is, labor power. Behind *that* was the political objective, as he wrote some time later to a comrade in New York. Marx said he wanted to develop something much greater than increased well-being out of strike action in individual plants. "In this way, out of the isolated economic movements, there arises everywhere a *political* movement, i.e., a *class* movement . . . in a form possessing general, socially coercive force."[35] In this way, trying to change the retrograde ideas of the International's members in the process, Marx sought to lead its un-comprehending or half-comprehending membership to revolution.

During the first half-dozen years of the International's life, Marx was extraordinarily successful in combining idea and organization. His man-agement from London of the first congress of the International, meeting in Geneva on September 3–8, 1866, was a flawless example of that com-bination. Marx began by persuading the General Council to co-opt friends of his, including Karl Schapper, and to call a preliminary conference in London, the conference to decide upon the agenda of the congress. With the agenda, he could thus set its direction. He had made doubly sure of his control of the conference by giving delegates' mandates on his own authority to more friends. Marx thereupon drew up the agenda plus in-structions for the General Council's delegates to the congress; the con-ference approved agenda and instructions. The latter placed the necessary emphasis on the eight-hour day. Also consistent with *Capital*, the dele-gates approved of child labor, although they demanded that it be regu-lated by law. Many cooperatives had affiliated themselves with the Inter-national, and Marx's instructions tactfully urged a wider development of the cooperative movement, but, he specified, only as a stage leading to something more important.

The essence of the instructions lay in their definition of trade unions as "*an organized force for superseding the very system of wage-labor and capital rule itself.*"[36] Meaning no less than revolution, the words were now part of a statement of purpose of a considerable organization of workingmen, and not just a passage in an article or book. A poor speaker, Marx himself did not attend. He had prepared the ground so well, however, that the majority of the Geneva delegates accepted the program with minor changes, his supporters overriding the vigorous resistance of the French followers of Proudhon. With similar techniques and while remaining in London, Marx dominated the decisions of the next three congresses, in Lausanne (1867), Brussels (1868), and Basel (1869). It was the Brussels Congress that passed a resolution attaching the International to *Capital*. Marx's combination of theory and *praxis*, compromising graciously when necessary, was advancing in good order.

Marx had to use all his skills to maintain his leadership. The Proud-honians fought and refought their battles for free credit and against statist policy at each congress. In 1869 Marx's followers won approval of his two main demands, resolutions committing the International to ownership in common, that is to say, socialism, and, again, to the need for political action. But the Marxists had to permit the use of qualifying phrases in the final drafts.[37] The presence of the anarchist Mikhail Bakunin also qualified the victory. The Revolution of 1848 had flung him into Russian captivity and exile, but he had escaped from Siberia in 1861. Challenging Marx's position, he was winning supporters among the International's members in Western Europe, particularly in Switzerland, Italy, and Spain. Bakunin wanted the congress to call for abolishing inheritance. Marx rejected the idea, as he had the Proudhonian prescriptions, because he said it diverted attention from the one issue, socialism.[38] Bakunin, seeking power in the revolutionary movement, hardly took his idea seriously, or any idea, for that matter, but it gave him a useful ideological weapon. Marx's men, however, succeeded in getting the congress of 1869 to leave the question undecided. Bakunin remained a threat to Marx's ascendancy when the Franco-Prussian War radically changed the character of Europe and of the International.

The International and the Commune

When, on July 19, 1870, the Franco-Prussian War broke out, Marx and the International found themselves very nearly helpless. A war enthusiast in 1848–49, Marx had since become more aware of the uncontrollable forces released by arms. Now, Bismarck dominated Prussia after having led it through two successful wars, and he promised to unify Germany as a greater Prussia. Despite the threat of violent unknowns and authoritarianism, Marx nevertheless could see hopeful opportunities, while he continued to indulge his hatred of Louis Napoleon. The International had to take a position on the war, and he spent five days producing a statement, the first of three "Addresses" of the General Council in his formidable Marxian English. At this time he was writing Engels: "The French need a thrashing. If the Prussians are victorious, then the centralization of the state power will help the centralization of the working class. German preponderance will shift the center of the working-class movement in Western Europe from France to Germany. . . . The superiority of the Germans over the French in the world arena would mean at the same time the superiority of *our* theory over Proudhon's."[39]

On July 28 the First Address appeared as a flier which was reprinted in the *Pall Mall Gazette*, a conservative daily newspaper with which Engels had a connection. Marx first administered a thrashing to Louis Napoleon. "The war plot of July 1870 is but an amended edition of the coup d'état of December 1851." But the International's need for statesmanship was more important than this settling of old scores. Marx had to counter the increasingly frenzied patriotism of both the French and the Germans. He hopefully quoted a manifesto issued by a few of the Paris members of the International, which pleaded for brotherhood with the German workers, but he had to explain away the chauvinist statements made by a number of French trade unions. He could only characterize the unions as composed of the *Lumpenproletariat*, wretches "masqueraded into workers' blouses," who had originally helped Louis Napoleon in his coup d'état. As for Germany, Marx quoted ambiguously peaceful statements of German unions, but insisted that "the war is a defensive war as far as Germany is concerned." Now reality justified his old Russophobia and he could warn, "In the background of this suicidal strife looms the dark figure of Russia."[40] Engels presently reflected Marx's ideas back to Marx. If France won, Germany and its independent workers' movement would be "*kaputt* for years." If Germany won, so would "Bismarck & Co.": "very unpleasant, but not to be changed." Still, "Bismarck is doing . . . some of our work for us." The best policy would be to support Germany, but Engels caught himself: such a policy would obtain only in a defensive war.[41] The qualification was important.

The swift Prussian successes astounded Marx and Engels. Marx gave himself time to rethink his position and restricted himself to the three addresses. Engels, indulging himself as a military expert, said too much and said it often. He wrote fifty-nine military articles for the *Pall Mall Gazette* which were as wrongheaded as those he had written on the Crimean War. He was still seeing a near equality of forces as late as January 1871.[42] By early September 1870 Louis Napoleon, having surrendered at Sedan, was swept out of history, and bourgeois politicans, whom Marx despised on principle, had established a provisional republican government in Paris. Marx thereupon produced the International's Second Address, which appeared in full as a flier dated September 9. Again, only the *Pall Mall Gazette* of the English press took note of it, and this time published only excerpts a week later.

Now Marx shifted his weight against Prussia. He condemned it for turning the war into an offensive war by demanding Alsace and Lorraine. He insisted that the German workers wanted nothing but an "honorable peace" with France. As for the new French republic, Marx had his many suspicions, but he rejected the idea of an immediate proletarian revolution. "Any attempt to overthrow the new government now, when the enemy is already knocking on the gates of Paris, would be an act of desperate folly." The best the French workers could do was to support the national defense so that France might negotiate the best peace.[43] On September 6 Marx had apprehensively written Engels that he had sent an emissary to Paris to stop the International's French members from "committing . . . follies in the name of the International. . . . They want to overthrow the provisional government, set up a Paris Commune . . . etc."[44] On October 31 Auguste Blanqui, enjoying one of his rare periods of freedom, confirmed the wisdom of Marx's advice by joining other radicals in a feeble attempt at a coup d'état. Their objective was to set up a Commune with a Committee of Public Safety appropriate to a new Robespierre. The attempt proved to be an act of desperate folly. Blanqui, escaping when the plot failed, went into hiding but was arrested and removed to a prison outside of Paris. On January 18 Wilhelm I, king of Prussia, became emperor of all Germany, the coronation ceremony taking place in the Hall of Mirrors in Louis XIV's palace in Versailles. With Germany thus unified, the authoritarian Bismarck had succeeded where good German democrats had failed. On January 28 a newly republican France agreed to an armistice and admitted it had been defeated. Marx published nothing.

The situation was a practical-ideological conundrum which Marx could not solve for the moment. The French leaders of the left, members of the International or not, continued to act in a way he found irresponsible, even contemptible. They met defeat with shriller patriotism, words. The reality was simple: Paris, cut off from the rest of the country since September 25, was then encircled by German siege lines. Bismarck's generals, hoping to avoid the heavy casualties of house-to-house fighting, made no effort to storm the city. The members of the new government had slipped out of Paris to Tours, later moving to Bordeaux, and the French armies were virtually *hors de combat*. After the armistice, Bismarck permitted France, occupied or not, to elect a representative body which would have a clear mandate to make a decision on a peace treaty, an affirmative one, he trusted.

The elections to the National Assembly, held in early February 1871, produced the necessary mandate, but it was entangled in old French problems. Paris and the rest of the nation were divided on both the peace and France's political character. The majority of the 43 Parisian delegates was republican or socialist, and demanded that the war be continued in the old patriotic revolutionary tradition. The nation as a whole returned a total of 200 pro-war radicals (including the Parisians) as against 475 others, most of the latter members of two monarchist parties willing to negotiate the inevitably humiliating peace. Actually the monarchists were elected in such numbers not so much because they were monarchists, but because most Frenchmen agreed with them that the war was lost. Adolphe Thiers, predecessor to Guizot as Louis Philippe's chief minister, became chief executive of the government and accepted the German terms, loss of Alsace and Lorraine, and payment of an indemnity of five billion francs. Paris, removed all the more from reality by the siege lines, dreamed of setting an example and rousing new armies to drive out the invader.

The National Assembly, meanwhile, gave all radicals in and out of Paris good reason for righteous indignation. It abruptly ended a war moratorium on debt and rent payments. The effect was financial distress and the threat of ruin to many Parisians, most particularly workers and members of the lower middle class. Furthermore, another abortive Paris rising took place in January. This made the National Assembly increasingly suspicious of the city's radicalism, and it proposed to disarm and stop the pay, a wretched one-and-a-half francs daily, of the National Guardsmen there. Again, this meant hardship for many Parisians, chiefly workers whose regular employment had vanished during the war. Anachronistically, these measures united Parisian workers and large segments of the middle class. It seemed to be 1789 once again.

So began the episode of the Commune. Thiers had moved the seat of government from Bordeaux back to Paris in March. He thereupon ordered the regular army units to seize some 230 artillery pieces of the National Guard during the night of March 17–18. The troops were slow, and a suspicious Paris mob, given a cutting edge by National Guardsmen, overwhelmed them. With some of their officers taken as hostages and others, officers and men, joining the Parisians, the troops abandoned the guns and began to retire from Paris. Some persons were caught up in mob frenzy, and killed two generals and other victims of circumstance.[45] The Thiers government slipped out of Paris and established itself at Versailles, where the National Assembly, which had adjourned at Bordeaux on March 11, resumed its meetings on March 20. The Germans, opening their siege lines when necessary, let the French—*Communards* against *Versaillais*—settle matters amongst themselves. It was hungry Paris against fat Versailles, the poor against the rich, city against country, patriots against peacemongers. Such radical simplifications were of the kind with which Marx worked so familiarly.

The Commune was, strictly speaking, the municipal government of Paris. It took as its model the revolutionary city administration that had ruled Paris and strongly influenced the entire country from 1792–94, during the most radical period of the original French Revolution. The word *Commune* has also come to mean the Communal Assembly of ninety-one seats, never entirely filled, which was elected on March 26. Before that date, and after the Thiers government had departed on March 15, the Central Committee of the National Guard governed the city. In Paris the Communal Assembly was then generally accepted as the legal or most nearly legal authority, but the National Guard's Central Committee, after properly arranging for the elections, refused to give up all its civil responsibility. The Communal Assembly itself functioned with the inevitable eloquence and inefficiency. One of its committees failed in its function as Executive Commission and, as urgencies mounted, on May 1, the Assembly gave away most of its limited powers to a new executive named the Committee of Public Safety. Another revolutionary-traditional revival, it looked back to Robespierre's national governing committee of the great Revolution. Still another authority was the military commander of the moment, the Commune appointing a swift succession of five, who frequently ignored Commune and Committee of Public Safety. The effect was anarchy.

The Commune had little time to define its purposes in the seventy-two days of its life. The Communal Assembly's leading parties were Neo-Jacobins, totaling two dozen representatives, who used Robespierreist slogans although they did not want a Robespierreist dictator, and Blanquists, half their number, who wanted Blanqui as Robespierre.[46] One could say little more than that the Commune was patriotic, egalitarian, and friendly to suggestions of socialism.[47]

Marx's actions expressed the International's weakness. According to its records, Marx took few initiatives besides dispatching an emissary to Paris, inserting a few articles in the English press, and writing the addresses.[48] Most of the Communal Assembly's Blanquists and a few of the Neo-Jacobins, about seventeen together, were also members of the International, but only because their local organizations were affiliates. Committed to a wildly patriotic effort, they ignored Marx.[49] Only two of his letters or drafts of letters to members of the Commune survive. The most important of Marx's correspondents was not even French. He was the Hungarian Jew Leo Frankel, who had joined the International in London and had now become head of the Commune's Commission of Labor and Commerce. In one letter, Marx told Frankel he had written hundreds of letters in support of the Commune, doubtless an exaggeration by a considerable multiple. If letter-writing was the best Marx could claim, moreover, it shows how little the International was able to do. Marx could not forbear to give advice. He urged that the Commune increase its efforts to get support outside of Paris, as if Paris were not surrounded.[50] In a letter which does not survive Marx urgently asked Frankel to send him statistics on French agriculture, evidently for the last volume of *Capital*.[51] Yet in all his thrashing about and distractions, Marx was brooding over the shape of a victory he alone could see in the coming defeat. The victory, however, would not save the Commune itself.

Overwhelming Marx's earlier prudence, a passionate adherence to the Commune had ignited in him instantly. He was responding to his natural bias for *action* and his instinct for political verity and metaphor. The Commune's cause was his cause and the International's, whether or not the Commune knew it or even knew what it was.

Despite all the frenzy the *Communards* could still be *raisonnables* in the French manner. At its first meeting, on March 29, the Communal Assembly canceled rents from October 1870 to April 1871. The Commune was obliged to spend three weeks dealing with the more complicated problem of debts. On April 18 it decided that creditors would be repaid in three interest-free installments. The Commune's financial rectitude, assisted by the common sense of some of its leaders, furthermore, was such that it left the Bank of France inviolate. In return the bank, disarming the hotheads, loaned the Communal administration nearly 17 million francs ($3.4 million). These actions, none of them an attack on private property and the last a confirmation of property's purist form, sketched the real limits to the social policies of the Commune. At heart, clutching its purse, it was petit bourgeois.

Within these limits, the Commune did begin to undertake, more often began to discuss or prepare to undertake, a few measures of reformistic coloration. One promising area for change was education, which was dominated by the Church, and an energetic leader began ejecting the old teaching staffs and secularizing schools wherever he found it convenient. Resolutely Catholic parents frequently responded by invading these schools and attacking the new teachers. There were egalitarian gestures: the Commune limited official salaries to a modest 6,000 francs, and ordered the free restitution of humble pawned articles like household goods and work tools up to the value of 20 francs. It tried to do something for the workers. It permitted workers' cooperatives to occupy ten deserted workshops; it encouraged the organization of thirty-four new trade unions, which had a doubtful claim on real existence, and forty-three producers' cooperatives, the last in anticipation of work that never arrived. One measure also attempted to abolish the bakers' night work, but the bakers conspired with their employers to evade the law. One sympathetic study of all these efforts concluded that the results were insignificant.[52]

As in all such revolutionary actions, violence and repression accompanied idealism. Paris was at war with France, and more killings succeeded those of the first days. The Commune also authorized arbitrary requisitions, anarchistic outbursts appropriate to the temper of the city. A twenty-five-year-old journalist and follower of Blanqui managed to become public prosecutor, took hostages, and persuaded the Communal Assembly to create a revolutionary tribunal with no judges or other protection for the rights of the accused. This was an important element in the frightfulness of the Commune's last days. The press had won freedom when Louis Napoleon fell, and many new journals appeared. The Commune found some of them suspect along with a number of the older newspapers and suppressed a total of twenty-seven. Among them was its own official organ, *La Commune*, which was found to be too critical.[53] If the Commune distrusted its own journal, it could not fail to turn its suspicions in on itself as new distresses befell it. When the law creating the Committee of Public Safety was passed, the minority opposing it was accused of treasonable motives and some members were arrested and nearly executed. It was a vicious imitation of the conflict between Jacobins and Girondins of the great Revolution. The issue arose, however, at the beginning of May, and the Commune fell that month.

The Commune was greatly superior to its nonsense and crimes. If it looked too much toward the past, it also saw, if dimly, a future to which conservatives and even moderates were blind. At least the Commune suggested something better for the lower middle class, the workers, and the poor, while they, refusing to remain the shuttlecocks of bourgeois society, gave their lives for their cause. Naturally they made up the majority of the victims.

The Commune and its various military commanders possessed nothing approximating a plan of war. Some regret, including that of Marx himself, was wasted on the *Communards'* failure to pursue the Versailles troops when they escaped from Paris,[54] but that could have produced an ephemeral victory at best, as Thiers, with Bismarck's approval, brought in regular troops from other parts of France. On April 2 the *Versaillais* tested out the defenses of Paris by taking a northwestern suburb. The Communal Assembly, fearful of losing the Parisians' support, ordered a counteroffensive the next day. Its forces were pitifully inadequate, and the result was slaughter. The Commune fell passive. Thiers was patient.

On May 1 his artillery began shelling the western sections of Paris, and Thiers concentrated more troops in the area. The attack began on Sunday, May 21. It was Bloody Week; the last shot was fired on the next Sunday, May 28. Between the two Sundays, as the beauty of Paris suffered disfigurement,[55] some 20,000 *Communards* and about 800 *Versaillais* died. The regular troops, many of them peasant boys, shot many prisoners out of hand, although it had been expressly, if perhaps not too sincerely, forbidden. They were reacting to the *Communards'* desperate fighting methods and reports of excesses. Earlier, the Commune had taken more than 100 hostages, chiefly priests and gendarmes, and on Thursday, May 25, the *Communards* retaliated by killing 70 of them, including the archbishop of Paris. In the end, about 36,000 men *and* women *Communards* were taken prisoner, of whom half was eventually freed, while more than 10,000 were condemned to prison, forced labor, banishment, or deportation to New Caledonia. After due process, 26 were executed.[56]

"The Commune has passed out of history and into the realms of ritual and symbol," an historian reflected a few years ago. "On Whitsunday wreaths are laid to commemorate the *Communards* . . . while above Paris rises the cupola of Sacré-Coeur as an expiation for the sin of the rising and a thank-offering for the deliverance of France from its scourge."[57] Marx deserves much of the credit for the wreaths.

Marx's instinct refused to endure what his intelligence told him of the Commune's quality and viability. Three weeks after the episode began, on April 6, he wrote to Wilhelm Liebknecht, "It seems that the Parisians are going down to defeat." But then Marx, casting about for a negation of the negation, went on to take defensive action against the facts. He warned Liebknecht against believing the newspapers. "It is all lies and more lies."[58] Six days later, in a letter to another German friend, Marx went over to the offensive. He referred to an antistatist pronouncement of the Commune which neither he nor the Commune took seriously,[59] and misrepresented his *18th Brumaire of Louis Napoleon* as having predicted a French revolution on precisely that principle. "This is also the objective of our party comrades of Paris." Marx was too cautious to promise success for the Commune, but he saw inspiration in it. "What flexibility, what historic initiative, and what a spirit of sacrifice!"[60] He had begun to adjust the Commune's features to serve a greater cause than its own or, for that matter, that of the International itself.

Remaining officially silent after having written the International's addresses of July and September 1870, Marx published nothing about the

Commune as long as it lived. Before the end of March 1871 he did indeed volunteer to write another address, but more than a month later, on May 2, Engels was explaining to the General Council that his absent friend was ill and the work not complete.[61] Three weeks later it was still not ready, and Marx excused himself in person before the General Council. On May 30, two days after the Commune fell, Marx read the Third Address, subtitled *The Civil War in France*, to the Council. The members present approved it unanimously. Marx had written two earlier drafts, but he was justifiably dissatisfied with them.[62] First, the Commune had to be safely immobilized in historical amber.

In the name of the proletariat the Third Address laid claim to the true meaning and best hope of all the events of Paris from the founding of the Provisional Government to the last shot fired. Marx began, "On the 4th of September 1870, when the working men of Paris proclaimed the republic, which was almost instantaneously acclaimed throughout France, without a single voice of dissent, a cabal of place-hunting barristers, with Thiers for their statesman . . . took hold of the [government]."[63] Marx denied the bourgeois character of the Communal Assembly. "The majority of its members were naturally working men, or acknowledged representatives of the working class."[64] In his next sentence Marx conceived of a government more democratic than any parliamentary government. "The Commune was to be a working, not a parliamentary, body, executive and legislative at the same time."[65] Just what "working . . . body" meant was left to the reader's imagination, while the statement baldly denied the existence of the Commune's redundant executives. As for the Commune's scattering of social or pseudosocial measures, Marx overwhelmed their triviality with the grand statement, "The great social measure of the Commune was its own working existence."[66] He would later write privately and reasonably that the "majority of the Commune was in no sense socialist, nor could it have been."[67] The address, however, had insisted, "It aimed at the expropriation of the expropriators."[68] The address concluded, "Working men's Paris, with its Commune, will be forever celebrated as the glorious harbinger of a new society."[69] At a symposium in 1967 Isaiah Berlin remarked, "Marx saw quite correctly that it was necessary to bless this workers' movement as the first rising of workers as workers, and that it therefore had to be assimilated, integrated into what might be called revolutionary hagiography."[70] In simply calling the Commune "this workers' movement" Berlin had shown himself not entirely impervious to Marx's genius for creating legends.

The Civil War in France helped solve one of the greatest difficulties inherent in the character of the Commune, its extravagant and regressive patriotism. In the address itself Marx ignored the patriotism and concentrated on the socialist aims he had discovered. His major argument was the fact that the International itself had issued the address: the cloak of international unity was flung around the Commune. Within the city limits of Paris Marx had seen the model, imperfect and a failure, of successful revolution on a national *and* international scale. His achievement was to transform the model into myth—and make it real.

AFTER THE COMMUNE

The Civil War in France, argued with his superb disdain for the facts, was the last of Marx's polemical masterpieces. It was marred only by his vulgar use of the argumentum ad hominem and his paranoid sensing of conspiracy. Thiers was a "monstrous gnome" and a "virtuoso in perjury and treason."[71] Jules Favre, the foreign minister, lived in adultery with the wife of a drunkard.[72] Thiers and his military commander had plotted to surrender Paris from the beginning.[73] Unlike the first two addresses, *The Civil War in France* won wide notice. Published as a pamphlet, it went through three editions in two months and was immediately accepted as a classic of radical literature.

If Marx had internationalized the meaning of the Commune through the International, the Commune, for its part, made Marx and the International splendidly infamous. Marx boasted that the address "is making the devil of a noise and I have the honor to be at this moment the most abused and most threatened man in London."[74] That was another exaggeration, but newspapers in London and New York found Marx newsworthy enough to request interviews, which he graciously granted. The London correspondent of the New York *World* published his report of a talk with Marx on July 18. To the question, "just what is the International?", Marx replied, "You have only to look at the people who make it up—they are workers." Marx denied any conspiratorial activities, but, like a revolutionary statesman, admitted to "confidential . . . relations." The aim of the International, he said, was "the economic emancipation of the working class through the conquest of political power."

The effect of the interview was to make the International seem as important as possible, without being so dangerous to the established order that it should be suppressed. But the suggestion of a threat—the shadow

of power—was there.[75] Some conservatives found it convenient to believe in the danger represented by the International, and the effective
connection of International and Commune. On June 6 Jules Favre, for
the French government, issued a circular letter of warning, which said
that the International was a "society breeding war and hatred. Its foundation is atheism and communism. Its aim is the destruction of capital
and those who possess it. Its medium is the brute force of the masses."[76]
Here we have the beginning of the Red scare—not in the 1840s, as Marx
had boasted in the *Communist Manifesto*. It was the greatest moment in
the lives of Karl Marx and the International.

Immediately after the Commune, with the Commune contributing
greater force to them, the International had to face postponed and new
problems. The success represented by the Third Address had made matters much more difficult. Nationalism had become more intense, as Marx
had feared, and governments and patriots found more to suspect in an
international organization. Within the confines of their countries, moreover, socialists and labor leaders found new opportunities or problems
demanding all of their time. In a newly united Germany the socialists
concentrated on the domestic activities that would make them a major
political party in less than a generation. In France, socialism and the labor
movement found that the events of the Commune had lamed them badly.
In March 1872 the French government, following upon Favre's warning,
forbade its citizens to join the International. Other governments discouraged membership more or less absolutely. A harder nationalism pre-
vailed, and workers, the French workers themselves refusing to forget
Alsace and Lorraine, entered into it as well. The world had turned hostile
to the internationalism of the International.

Within the International itself Bakunin threatened again. In 1868 he
had built an organizational base in the form of the Alliance of Social
Democracy, composed of a coterie of supporters. Bakunin had tried to
affiliate his alliance with the International, but Marx got the General
Council to refuse. Bakunin thereupon broadcast the message of his
harmlessness by officially dissolving the alliance. In 1871, however, it
seemed to be alive. In Switzerland Bakunin won the support of James
Guillaume, editor of a radical newspaper and leader of a group of anarchistic building workers and watchmakers in the Jura Mountains. Marx
prepared to counterattack.

In London itself Marx saw his position weaken. There, George Odger,
the former president, and another English member of the General Council resigned indignantly from it in June. Marx had published the Third

Address with their names appended, but without their approval.[77] They would doubtless have objected, and Marx had felt the matter was important enough to risk the consequences. The break with the English members had become inevitable: the working classes of Britain rejected socialism and revolution. At the London conference in 1865 Odger had apologized for his English followers, explaining, "English workmen were seeking for the franchise and it was difficult to make them think of anything else."[78] If the English workers would not begin to become Marxists, Marx would not stop being Marx. It had been a combination of English apathy in international matters and vague goodwill that had permitted Marx to move the International to do what he found most important. Goodwill was not enough now. Marx's initiatives had hardened the English apathy into rejection.

Marx dealt with Bakunin and Britain in the usual manner. As he had before, he persuaded the General Council to call a conference, which he would dominate, to prepare for the next congress, which he would then also dominate because he would have persuaded the conference to give him the necessary powers. Of the twenty-three delegates to the conference, which met in London from September 17 to 23, thirteen were members of the General Council, including Blanquist *Communards* escaped from Paris whom Marx had won to his tactics and co-opted. Most of the other delegates from the Continent had similarly demonstrated obedience to Marx. The conference's resolutions, all proposed by Marx and Engels, showed Marx's weakness as well as his strength.[79] While they tightened Marx's control, one of them provided for the founding of the English Federal Council of the International: it meant that the English had withdrawn from the International. The other resolutions rephrased Marx's ideas and, by implication, rejected those of Bakunin. Resolution II forbade sectarian names such as Positivists, Mutualists, Collectivists, and even Communists. Resolution IX permitted Marx once again to insist upon a proper balance of the economic and the political.[80] As for Bakunin, Marx expressed his doubts that the alliance was really dissolved, and accused Bakunin of trying to win control of the International with it. The result would be disaster, Marx argued.[81] The London conference, despite the damaging loss of the English affiliates, confirmed Marx's command of the machinery of the International.

With his power, Marx used the London conference to name the majority of the delegates to the congress and write the agenda of subjects they would discuss. Meanwhile, in the year between conference and congress, he defended and attacked. James Guillaume, Bakunin's ally, broadcast a circular in November 1871 accusing Marx of dictatorial methods. Responding with a circular early the next year, Marx and Engels charged that Bakunin, working through Guillaume, wanted to make *himself* dictator of the International and the world, for that matter. Furthermore, Bakunin was an extortionist.[82] Marvelously irrelevant, the latter charge permitted Marx to flourish an incriminating-seeming document in the manner he had practiced during the Cologne communist trial and his war with Karl Vogt. In fact, a murderous friend of Bakunin's had written a letter threatening the life of a student acting as a publisher's emissary; the student had been trying to get the return of an advance Bakunin had received some time ago. Bakunin, who evidently knew nothing or little of his friend's action, had been, at worst, guilty of consorting with characters who belonged in a Russian novel as much as he did himself, and, like Marx, of consuming an advance without doing the promised work. But Marx had his document, the threatening letter, when the Congress of The Hague met, from September 2 to 7, 1872.[83] He also was in possession of his majority.

It was the first congress Marx had attended. He had to come this time, since quick, crucial decisions had to be taken. He had not improved as a speaker, and the audience had to wait interminably while he retrieved a repeatedly dropped monocle and reinserted it into his eye, but his leader's instincts were still impeccable. Marx could trust no one, not even Engels, to act with the necessary authority and speed. The real issue was whether he could maintain his leadership. As before, Marx had arranged to send as many mandates as possible to supporters, even if the mandates represented nonexistent affiliates. Well aware of Marx's tactics, his opponents resisted so stubbornly that the congress devoted three of its six days to the examination of credentials. Marx and Engels, controlling the votes on the Credentials Committee, simply ruled in favor of their followers. Thus Engels, who had himself paid the fare of five obedient delegates from England, admitted five sympathetic Spaniards while rejecting five of their anarchist countrymen.[84] When the mandate of an English delegate, the journalist Maltman Barry, was questioned by another Englishman, Marx returned, "It is to Barry's credit not to belong to the so-called leaders of English workingmen, for they have all more or less sold out to the bourgeoisie and the government."[85] The insult was the argument, particularly effective when voting power supported it. In this way Marx assured himself of a majority among the sixty-one delegates recognized.

The congress then dealt with the International's fundamental character.

Bakunin himself was ill; more important, he realized that he could not defeat Marx. He simply stayed away and saved himself public humiliation. The Italians had organized themselves into the Italian Federal Council of the International, and opting for anarchism, had refused to send any delegates. In this manner they assisted Marx's purposes. At The Hague the leader of the opposition was the Swiss, James Guillaume, who knew he could not capture the International under any circumstances. His solution was impotence: he would withdraw all power from the General Council, which would become simply an informational exchange center. On the afternoon of September 5 Guillaume argued: "Two great ideas run side by side in the movement, that of centralization of power in the hands of a few, and that of a free federation. . . . The movement cannot represent the conception of a single brain."[86] Everyone knew whom he meant, and Marx accepted the challenge. "We would rather abolish the General Council than . . . transform it into a letter box." Superbly denying his own identity, Marx continued, "The leadership of the association would fall into the hands of journalists, that is, mainly nonworkers."[87] The congress then voted on a motion giving the General Council the power to suspend the federal councils in the various countries if they violated the spirit of the International. The vote was thirty-six against six, with fifteen abstentions.[88] Marx was in command.

In the next moment Marx and Engels carried out a prearranged action that was a shocking surprise to almost everyone and seemed to throw away everything they had just achieved. Engels took the floor. Speaking for Marx and himself, he proposed that the General Council be transferred to New York for a year. He argued incredibly that the International's documents would be safer in New York, but then more pertinently, "Party frictions have become so bad in London that the seat must be moved."[89] This time, the Blanquists among his supporters rebelling, Marx did not have an easy majority. The vote was dangerously close: twenty-six to twenty-three, with nine abstentions.[90] Marx was doubtless aware of the risk, but had no alternative. He had to force his will on the International or see it lose its place in history.

Marx had betrayed the Blanquists, who were so unhappy that they departed the congress. That desertion, however, did not matter. Marx had become increasingly dependent upon them in the General Council, but he knew that they had remained conspirators who would inevitably seek to lead the International into dangerous adventures. The organization had to be saved from its friends as well as from its enemies.

Marx did not rest content. Another action was necessary to secure the two motions. A committee of inquiry had been studying charges which Marx had brought against Bakunin. Repeating his earlier accusations, Marx formally accused his old enemy of conspiring to capture the International illicitly through his alliance. Also, there was the matter of fraud, the Russian letter providing Marx's evidence against Bakunin. On September 9, in the afternoon and evening of the last day of the congress, the committee found Bakunin guilty on both counts, although it admitted that the alliance's existence was not conclusively proven. The congress thereupon, similarly disposing of Guillaume and another associate as co-conspirators, voted to expel Bakunin from the International.[91] Marx had accomplished all he had set out to do.

A year later Marx suffered the nervous collapse that ended his active career.

The transfer of the International meant its death, as everyone knew. No one believed that it would, as Engels' motion permitted, return to Europe in a year. Marx made sure that it would die appropriately, since the members of the new General Council, composed of German immigrants in the United States, were beholden to him. In 1876, after four quarrelsome but harmless years, the International formally dissolved itself in Philadelphia.[92]

Marx extinguished the International for the same reason that he had twice dissolved the Communist League. In all three cases he was eliminating organizations which had arrived at a point where they had now become a danger to the revolution they had once served.

The expulsion of Bakunin might seem a sadistic humiliation of a defeated enemy, but Marx had a better reason, whatever his private pleasure might have been. He wanted to cripple Bakunin's standing in the labor and revolutionary movements. Many thousands of old members of the International were without leadership, and Bakunin might very well revive the International as an anarchistic organization. Actually, Bakunin joined Guillaume and other anarchists at a meeting in St. Imier, Switzerland, a week after the Congress of The Hague; claiming to represent the International redivivus, they set up a shadowy executive that won recognition from the International's Belgian and Dutch federations.[93] Bakunin himself was too sick and disorderly to give stable leadership to this effort and he died, like the International, in 1876, but he was a real danger even after his death. His inspiration dominated an anarchist movement that began committing violent acts in the 1870s. In 1881, while Marx was still alive, an anarchist international congress held in London solemnly advocated simple and unqualified violence as nec-

essary to destroy unjust authority. Beyond the violence an era of socialism would begin; meanwhile no great amount of thought need be applied to its shape. During the next generation anarchists assassinated
beggars, presidents, and royal personages. Marx had been correct to dis-
sociate his International from the anarchists with such cruel publicity.
Like the Communist League, Marx's International remained inviolate as
an example for future action.

Even without the anarchist danger, the International could not exist
under the new conditions, particularly in the face of the new nationalism.
In September 1873, writing to his representative in the New York area,
Marx advised him to let the "official organization of the International
move into the background for the while." The point was to keep the
General Council out of the hands of "idiots . . . who would compromise
its character." Future events would provide for its resurrection.[94] In 1874
the New York leader, disgusted by the petty quarrels, resigned from the
International. Engels, approving his action, wrote him that the International had belonged to the period of Louis Napoleon's Second Empire,
when domestic action was virtually impossible. Success had to defeat it
after the Commune gave it "moral power in Europe. . . . It was really
on its deathbed at the Congress of The Hague . . . its prestige exhausted."[95]

Marx's leadership of the International was his last great contribution
to the revolutionary cause. The memory of the First International composed itself as a Hegelian-Marxian dialectic of internationalism transcending the nationalism that had led to its death. The dialectic was, like
other formulas of Marx, both truth and illusion. It could no more lead
to the end of nationality and war than his economic theory could lead to
the elimination of classes and all internal conflict. Yet, in the real world,
with its facts and dreams, the dialectic of internationalism worked much
like the economic theory, that is to say, very well.

TEN

THE MARXIAN REVOLUTIONARY MACHINE

By HIS IDEAS AND ACTIONS Marx had been constructing a machine for manufacturing revolution and administering the power thereafter. The complex of ideas (and organizational suggestiveness) of *Capital* and the organizational example (and conceptual suggestiveness) of the First International had provided the last important parts. Actually, the machine was not absolutely required to make revolution, although Marx and his early followers thought so. Unlike Bakunin, Marx did not seek an ultimate revolutionary chaos but the just social order beyond. His acute sense of reality, firmly gripping his long-range objective, made him accept an interminable truce—betray his revolutionary's temperament. Unconsciously adapted by Marx himself, his revolutionary machine proved it could generate power without revolution as well as with it.

On first view the Marxian revolutionary machine appeared to be a monstrous agglomeration of unrelated, in fact, mutually rejecting parts—tender human being and clanking apparatus, the real and ideal, conflict and peace, the profound and the simplistic, truth and lie. But Marx had often enough shown how effectively he could manage Hegelian-Marxian contradictions.

Marx was the First Cause, alone and absolute, of the machine. He determined everything—every conception, every initiating action. Marx, his hierarchy of professional associates, and, ultimately, the workers were the revolutionary machine as personnel. The Marxian cadre, which could be called an order, had mastered a range of skills in such disciplines and activities as philosophy, Marxian social-economic-political theory, administrative theory and practice, military theory (mark well Engels' self-appointment, with Marx's approval, as military expert), military operations (Engels in action in the Revolution of 1848; the potentials suggested by his commander, Willich), journalism and propaganda, manipulation of art (Marx's effort to improve Heine's poetry, *Capital* as literary-humane), and industrial management (theory by Marx, practice by Engels). With improvements, the order of revolutionaries would be a mirror image of established authority. Marx saw the world as workshop to be captured and managed, and the leadership of the revolutionary order as a combination of military general staff and industrial board of directors. Like the Jesuits in their time, when they revived the faith, proselytized, educated, advised princes, and managed colonies, the order could accomplish any task of social engineering.

Marx's order of revolutionaries was ringed about by many other groupings. With its followers the order formed a party that was frankly revolutionary but patient: its words promised everything and committed nothing. When expedient, the party doubled itself by maintaining both a secret and an acknowledged membership engaged in secret and public activities. All manner of combinations were possible; secret members could act publicly and known members could carry out secret assignments. Beyond, as it made its power and dreams known, the revolutionary order attracted opportunistic allies and idealistic sympathizers.

The revolutionary mechanism had to relate sanely to the circumstances. Its personnel was not a community of logical psychotics, correct according to mad standards. Marx always seized hungrily upon the real for his party, thus the anticipation, definition, discovery, and championship of the working class as proletariat, and his realization of the need for economic leadership and stability. The machine was manufacturing an essential product.

While the machine as described so far has all of its physical parts, it lacks one element to come to life: spirit. Another word for it would be "faith," a necessary part of any such radical action as revolution. Marx provided for that as well. Only a belief going beyond fact and arguments could accept all the contradictions in Marxism. Faith had innumerable vital uses. It exhilarated as mere understanding could not. It encouraged and even demanded sacrifice. It solved the great problem of socialist leadership: how to justify giving the command of the proletariat to an elite order. With faith the problem vanished. The elite *believed* it was the proletariat, more, the essence of the proletariat. Faith solved all the problems one of the world's greatest thinkers left unsolved.

This was why Marx the revolutionary politician had so brutally and absolutely rejected religion as received. Jealous of his power, he would concede nothing to any faith that would distract his followers from total commitment. His atheism was calculation as well as piety.

The revolutionary machine was very simple and its effect would be crude. This was a great advantage, whatever the stresses or losses occurring in those cases for which it was not designed. In its simplicity it was less likely to break down. Furthermore, its simple parts could be replaced by approximate substitutes. Although Marx would have disbelieved it, Marxism does not even require a working class.

The absolute authority of the leadership, the boundlessness of the task, the element of faith, the simplicity of the operations—all this required absolute intolerance. The leadership would enter every area it thought required change. Its decisions were correct and final. Anyone resisting the proper speed of change was a traitor to humanity, an absolute criminal to be eliminated.

Not surprisingly, the machine refused to function quite according to design: its ideal components remained persistently ideal. Most of its operations can be studied in the cases of Germany and Russia, since Marx himself made the originating connections. This can lead to identifying the most important aspects of the contemporary machine.

In Germany

With *Capital*, Marx had returned to Germany in greater force. He had already been exerting a certain influence through his followers as organized in two lively, if small, parties, but the book provided a solid theoretical base upon which real power could be mounted. Marx's power, however, would be tightly circumscribed, a situation which he understood more easily than accepted.

Capital had insultingly few readers and reviewers when it appeared in 1867, but its greatness was inexorable. Year after year more and more persons found their way to it and readjusted their thinking accordingly. In 1865 Wilhelm Liebknecht, back in Germany physically and carrying out his socialist mission, had correctly and urgently commanded Marx with Marxian underlings, although through Engels, "*Marx must finish up his economics—and do it soonest.*"[1] Upon its publication, Liebknecht immediately began to publicize *Capital* in the German press and use it as a text in his speeches.[2] It was *Capital* that made a Marxist of August Bebel, Liebknecht's partner in the socialist movement. Bebel, an excellently self-educated former lathe operator, had earlier given up on the *Critique of Political Economy* as incomprehensible. His distinguished career has shown how well he understood *Capital*.[3] The rival of the Liebknecht-Bebel partnership, Ferdinand Lassalle's successor, was operating in the same way with *Capital*. Marx's biographer, Franz Mehring, said that Johann Baptist von "Schweitzer set about his parliamentary operations with the first volume of *Capital* under his arm."[4] Schweitzer's newspaper, *Der Social-Demokrat*, published a series of articles on *Capital* from January to April 1868[5] and drew heavily upon Marx's ideas in developing its editorial policy. As in the case of the First International, the book helped Marx's followers and Marx's followers helped the book. With the appropriate adjustments, the politics of *Capital* began to function as effectively in the specifics of Marx's homeland as it had in the vastness of the International's area of responsibility.

In the year of *Capital* the German socialists became nationally visible and officially honorable: seven of them, including Liebknecht, Bebel, and the competitive Schweitzer, were elected to the Reichstag, the lower house of the new North German Confederation and, from 1871, of a united Germany.[6] German socialism drew its strength from a rich ideology as given manageable shape and tremendous force by *Capital*, but not limited by it, the ghosts of the two Communist Leagues, a network of personal loyalties comprising the Marx Party, and the direct and indirect propagandistic effects of Marx's various operations from the Brussels Communist Correspondence Committee to the First International. Most historians have overlooked one other important way by which Marx's influence spread, namely the initial broadcast of his ideas by the friendly heretic Stephan Born in 1848–49. Those ideas "entered into the real workers' movement . . . only through the organizational work of [Born's] Brotherhood."[7] Economic reality also encouraged German socialism. From 1848 to 1857, as the true proletariat began to appear in the new factories, the production of capital and consumer goods tripled in the German Customs Union:[8] the course of the Industrial Revolution converged with the line of development of *Capital*.

In the 1860s Marx's presence had become corporeal in Germany in the form of the two political parties acknowledging his intellectual patronage. Marx, characteristically, was happy with neither, since, among other reasons, they were effective and thus stood for more reality than he could endure. One of them was the socialist party founded by the questionable and unmanageable Ferdinand Lassalle in 1863, and the other, under the Liebknecht-Bebel leadership and closer to Marx, was not even socialist when it was organized in 1866. Whipped about by envy and not unreasonable suspicion, Marx intrigued *against* Lassalle[9] (and his successors) and *for* Liebknecht and Bebel. Yet Lassalle served Marxism better than Marx would ever admit.

The Marx-Lassalle relationship, with its entanglement of mutual aid and exploitation, began during the Revolution of 1848. At the time Lassalle, in his early twenties but already an overpowering personality, was chief attorney in a divorce case, a *cause célèbre* that neatly divided left and right. The *Neue Rheinische Zeitung* published at least five lead articles supporting Lassalle's aristocratic client, the injured wife, who was known for her radical sympathies.[10] Lassalle, becoming a political leader in Düsseldorf, brought a delegation of his followers to the Marx Party's great protest meeting in Worringen in September 1848. Two months later, in Düsseldorf itself, Lassalle then led a rising, which was gently put down after a week.[11] The authorities, weighing his popularity and the political uncertainties, found it best to release him after six months of investigative arrest. Lassalle had a genius for luck; he was the only revolutionary leader of stature left free in Germany. The Marx biographer paid tribute to him in romantic idiom. "He stood like an immovable rock in the middle of the froth-bedecked breakers of the counterrevolution."[12] Legally, prosperously, Lassalle continued to help the cause—and Marx.

A brilliant negotiator among ideas as he was among men, Lassalle derived most of his superficial but seductive proposals from Marx's writings.[13] The blurry counterfeiting that resulted inevitably angered Marx, but he had to remain silent because Lassalle was indeed introducing Marxism to increasing numbers of increasingly receptive Germans, particularly workers. Furthermore, Lassalle performed various personal services for Marx, thus arranging the journalistic assignments that brought Marx some small additions to his income. And more: Lassalle got his publisher to take Marx's *Critique of Political Economy*. In 1859, when the book appeared, Marx wrote Lassalle at least seventeen letters.[14] The connection was important enough to lead to their exchange of visits of 1861 and 1862.

In Leipzig, on May 23, 1863, Lassalle founded the All-German Workers' Association (Allgemeiner Deutscher Arbeiterverein) as a frankly socialist *workers'* party. He made a point of rejecting the middle-class help upon which other labor groups were still dependent. The AGWA achieved a membership of almost 5,000 in a year with the adherence of several Workers' *Educational* Associations, which had been springing up as reaction receded during the late 1850s. The members were artisans; the

German industrial proletariat would not become conscious of itself and enter organizational life in any great force until the 1880s. For Marx the AGWA was another ambiguous gift of Lassalle's. Its program insisted on going beyond Marxism and solving the problem of Ricardo's Iron Law of Wages, the tendency of wages to fall to bare subsistence under capitalism. Marx had accepted the law as insoluble and used it as another major argument for revolution; Lassalle had a solution. His idea, all too reminiscent of proposals of Louis Blanc and Proudhon, was state-aided workers' cooperatives, which would coexist with private enterprise. Lassalle's logic, promising immediate betterment under capitalism, insolently discarded an essential part of Marx's theory and opened up the possibility of delaying the revolution forever. He was making Marx's position unbearable. In August 1864, however, Lassalle resolved matters by provoking a duel and getting killed. Marx could now use his services without his interference.[15]

Two weeks after Lassalle had created the AGWA, labor leaders and anti-Lassallean socialists set up a counterorganization, the loose Union of German Workers' Associations, some fifty-eight of them, in Frankfurt. August Bebel, already established as a leader of the Leipzig Artisanal Educational Association, was one of the union's founders. He had kept the Leipzig Association out of the AGWA on the argument that the workers still needed their bourgeois connections and were not even ready for universal suffrage.[16] The union operated on those principles. Marx was not embarrassed to back Bebel. Liebknecht, who had been enthusiastically sabotaging the Lassallean organization in Berlin, was expelled by the police in 1865, and came to Leipzig, where he began his great partnership with Bebel. In August 1866, consorting with both particularism and capitalism, Liebknecht and Bebel founded the anti-Prussian Saxon People's Party as a union of the Union of German Workers' Associations and several Democratic groups. The partners were soon strong enough to eliminate the middle-class Democrats, and in 1869 the party changed its name to the Social Democratic Workers' Party and adopted a cautiously understated Marxian program.

Under their various names and following their various leaders, the two rival, more or less socialist groupings strained against each other healthfully for a dozen years—through and beyond the period of the wars of German unification. Marx knew very well that all the German socialists together were still a small minority in a powerful and expanding state, still far from revolutionary effectiveness. Too much of his revolutionary machine, around which the socialist movement was organized, remained theory and potentiality. Distracted, furthermore, by the demands of the International, Marx could only shunt his hopes for Germany another few years into the future.

Another frustration was the limit on Marx's power among the German socialists themselves. In 1867, following a weak interregnum, the Frankfurt patrician Schweitzer became president and provided the AGWA with a masterful and artful leadership. Liebknecht, no longer a runner of errands in exile, became his own man in Germany. Both men set Marx his limits. Liebknecht wrote Marx, again through Engels: "I agree with you in everything important; it is only in the matter of practical considerations that there can be a difference of opinion. I admit that you two have a better view of the whole . . . but as far as the details of the struggle are concerned, you must inevitably miss a lot."[17] Earlier, Schweitzer had written Marx in precisely the same sense: "If you would like to explain . . . theoretical questions to me, I shall always accept your instructions thankfully. But as far as the practical questions of tactics of the moment are concerned, I beg you to consider that a person must be right in the middle of things properly to evaluate the details."[18]

Marx had one irreducible power deriving from his character as founding leader of scientific socialism, the threat of repudiation, but, like papal excommunication, the threat was more effective than the act. Marx threatened repeatedly and never repudiated. He intrigued; he played off one party against the other. On one occasion, while encouraging Liebknecht and Bebel to attack Schweitzer, he composed a letter warning Schweitzer that he was in danger of "being more or less wiped out" and offering his honest brokership: "I promise you the impartiality [*Unparteiischkeit*] which is my duty."[19] Schweitzer, making his good use of Marx, knew better than to depend on Marx's impartiality. As for Liebknecht, be did more than reject gratuitous counsel. In 1869 Marx was wrathfully complaining to Engels over Liebknecht's "colossal . . . shamelessness"— in asking him to denounce Schweitzer. Marx reported, "Right off . . . I wrote him a very rough [*saugrob*] letter in which I reminded him how often he has compromised me, and told him straight that I will *publicly repudiate* him, the minute he attempts a similar act of insolence." Marx finished weakly, "He . . . betrays us if it suits him, and identifies us with himself whenever he can't do better." Two days later, referring to Schweitzer, Marx was demanding why Liebknecht "*has made peace* with the monster?"[20]

Within a half-dozen years, even as socialism in general, and, more specifically, his own doctrine prospered, Marx had lost his position as arbiter of the German movement. Schweitzer, with all his ability, could not compensate for the ideological poverty in the Lassallean heritage. Meanwhile, the idea of unification asserted itself, and Schweitzer, a party dictator like Lassalle, represented an obstacle. In the face of rumors of a connection with the police, Schweitzer solved a number of problems by resigning his position abruptly in March 1871.[21] Although the AGWA was still somewhat larger than the Social Democratic Workers' Party, his mediocre successors could not compete with the political skills and Marxian fundamentals of Liebknecht and Bebel. In 1875, during Marx's declining years, the two parties united to form a greater Social Democratic Workers' Party, that is to say, the AGWA leadership surrendered. Marx was furiously unhappy.

Marx's distress was compounded by humiliation. Liebknecht, maneuvering around his opposition, had not consulted him on the unification agreement, and Marx, humiliatingly, learned of it in the press. Moreover, Liebknecht suppressed Marx's comments on it—the *Critique of the Gotha Program*, which remained unknown except to a few socialist leaders until 1891.[22] As Marx's power increased, his ability to control that power had diminished comparably.

The *Critique* was an impotent denunciation of reality.[23] Marx could not dispute the fact that the Gotha Program itself was fundamentally Marxian. He could, however, refuse to recognize the great triumph that it meant. He made much of the program's impurities, fading Lassallean ideas retained to make submission easier for Lassalle's followers. The political Marx understood compromise, but now he refused to understand. He even attacked his own ideas as reflected back accurately enough in the program, thus the attribution of all wealth to labor (discussed in relation to the economics of *Capital*, ch. 8). It seemed as if the Gotha Program were too Marxian as well as too Lassallean for Marx. Beyond this real success he could too clearly see another reality, the further deterioration of the best components, as he felt them to be, of his revolutionary machine.

The *Critique* was much more than impotence verbalized: containing valuable revolutionary materials that would inspire and guide new action, it was a last flaring up of Marx's revolutionary genius. Among the materials, besides its magic-lantern image of the socialist future, was the operational formula, with its powerful phrase rationalizing violence: "Between capitalist and communist society lies a revolutionary transformation from the one to the other. There is a corresponding period of transition in the political sphere and in this period the state can only take the form of a *revolutionary dictatorship of the proletariat.*"[24] The *Critique* was too great in its conceptions to be able to speak to the contemporary German situation.

The *Critique*, another example of Marx's incessant drive toward revolution, came less than three years after a frequently quoted statement of his that seemed to qualify that drive. But the statement could be interpreted in that sense only when torn from its context. It was made in Amsterdam at a meeting of the Dutch section of the International on September 8, 1872, the day after the International's last congress had closed in The Hague. Easy with success, Marx used his best public-relations talents to bury the International decently. To the Dutch members he remarked that "allowance . . . must be made for the institutions, manners, and traditions of different countries." He continued, "We do not deny that there exist countries like America, England, and, if I knew your institutions better, I would add Holland, where the workers may be able to attain their ends by peaceful means." But the statement, all in the conditional mood in any case, did not stop here. It continued in the next sentence, "If that is true we must also recognize that in most of the countries of the Continent force must be the lever to which it would be necessary to resort for a time." Moreover, Marx had begun his talk by claiming that one of the most important results of the International's congress was the decision to continue the politico-economic struggle, that is, revolution, against "the old, decaying society."[25]

If Marx had seemed to make a conditional exception of two or three countries, they were on the periphery of what he regarded as the world's heartland. Were the Continent to have its revolution, and it must, Holland and Britain could not very well resist. That left only the United States, isolated and vulnerable, on Marx's map. The exceptions, on closer view, were more likely to be tardy members of the same international revolutionary union. The circumstances had dictated that Marx disguise the spectral features of the International, but he had firmly, and just as skillfully, broadcast his revolutionary message once again. A fine stroke by a master politician, it was, for the while, only words.

However Marx tried, the weight and direction of events were pressing him further and further backward—away from the battle lines where the revolution could be launched. In the 1870s, the influence of the eclectic socialism of Eugen Dühring, a blind lecturer at the University of Berlin, "took on a significant, to some extent . . . dangerous magnitude," according to the Soviet editors of Marx's writings. The danger lay in Dühring's attack on the revolutionary spirit through his denial of the class-war thesis. In 1872 Bebel was sufficiently impressed to publish two articles praising Dühring in Liebknecht's newspaper.[26] Yet Dühring had mocked Marx for using "demi-sciences and dwarfish philosophy."[27]

By 1875 Liebknecht recognized the danger, and correctly identifying the man for the task, wrote Engels, "You must make up your mind to give Dühring's hide a tanning."[28] Urged thus by Liebknecht, and, in effect, assigned by Marx, who was incapable of the labor, Engels thereupon wrote a series of articles expounding a modish scientism that offered a rebuttal to Dühring's conceptions without being too different. The articles were published in a Social Democratic organ in 1877–78 and in a book in 1878. Known as the *Anti-Dühring*, the book became one of the most popular writings in the Marxian canon.[29] More widely read than any of Marx's difficult works, it efficiently commenced the public burial of Dühring. Engels, even more eclectic than Dühring, had thickened his facile arguments with the positivism deriving from Auguste Comte (1798–1857), the monistic philosopher who had succeeded to the dominant position once held by Hegel. Marx refused to be disturbed, although he detested Comte and had always fought or ignored positivism, with its strict unitarian view and its rejection of the doublings and syntheses of the dialectic. Still the cool-headed revolutionary statesman, Marx approved the use of hostile conceptions to solve an immediate tactical problem; he could always reject responsibility for the theoretical errors of a subordinate. The successful solution of the Dühring problem made good a loss, however, and represented no advance at all.

Once again, five years after the episode of the Gotha Program, Marx tried to impose his will on the leadership of German socialism. At the end of 1880, further removed from events and seriously failing, Marx struggled now for a symbol and not even a fragment of the real. He insisted upon his choice, an intriguer of unproven capacity named Karl Hirsch, as editor of the new Social Democratic party organ.[30] Marx was opposing the Liebknecht-Bebel candidate, Eduard Bernstein. In this last desperate fantasy Marx gave his man the role of guarantor of the revolution. But Hirsch, on second thought, thought better of it and withdrew. It was too easy to see that Liebknecht and Bebel, in complete command in Germany, could make matters impossible for him.[31] Bernstein, confirmed as editor, advocated a policy of moderation that suggested more and more delay before arriving at revolution. As a theoretician, he would do worse.

In the last years of Marx's life the Social Democrats had become a serious force in German politics. In 1877, two years after unification, they won almost a half-million votes, 9 percent of the electorate. In 1884, in the year after Marx's death, the party got 550,000 votes, reaching a total of 800,000 in 1887 and 1.4 million in 1890. Its progress took place through a period of mild but enlivening martyrdom from 1878 to 1890, when Bismarck had it declared illegal and its newspapers suppressed. Persecution led away from revolution, since the state power was overwhelming and its electoral expectations too great. The 1890 elections, held after the Reichstag refused to renew the antisocialist laws, then established the Social Democrats as the German Empire's second largest party. Marx, demanding revolution from his revolutionary machine, would have despised these later victories, which Engels lived to celebrate.

The German Social Democrats, drawing heavily on Marx's teachings, had made themselves much more than a political party. They were the Social Democracy—a way of life. In the tradition of the Workers' Educational Associations the German Social Democracy continued to give lectures and courses for the workingman's self-improvement and, for the complete man, organized clubs for such activities as choral singing, chess-playing, acrobatics, and hiking, as well as mutual-aid societies. It was these auxiliaries that kept the party organization functioning during the period of illegality. Another major component, much in Marx's spirit, was the press. The Social Democracy had seventy-five newspapers by 1878[32] and many more after 1890. Its expanding publishing empire, appealing to every kind of reader from housewife to intellectual, produced magazines, books, and all kinds of mass-circulation and specialized publications. The good Social Democrat, reading his party newspaper with its sports supplement, going to French class one evening a week and an outing on Sunday, need never leave the party's all-satisfying embrace. At the center of that satisfaction was spiritual comfort. Liebknecht had said correctly enough that "the great advantage of the German movement" lay in a "program founded on firm principles, a *scientific* outlook, and realistic tactics." Liebknecht's phrase, "firm principles," however, masked the nonscientific, panreligious side of Marxism: the Old Testament morality, Christianate worship of the oppressed, the leaps of faith. With the other elements that were truly scientific, the Marxian apparatus was splendidly equipped to manage the old human longings and the huge new industrialism.[33]

But reality demanded something other than the announced product of the machine, which found itself being shaped by the materials upon which it worked. Disarmingly, government and society thrust concessions on the Social Democracy, which soon began to include more and more true proletarians as the swiftly expanding numbers of factory workers joined the party and party-sponsored unions. In the 1880s Bismarck introduced the most advanced social legislation in the world. Academic socialists held professors' chairs. In these exorbitantly favorable conditions the military-staff and conspiratorial elements in the Social Democratic leadership deteriorated from disuse and fell away. The board of directors, imprisoned by reality, became a respectable, bourgeois hierarchy. In Germany, against Marx's will but according to his operational principles, the revolutionary machine efficiently manufactured not revolution but generalized, legal power.

Eduard Bernstein spoke out the truth of the German situation in a series of articles published from 1896 to 1898, and appearing as a book in 1899. In the English translation, the book's title is, precisely, *Evolutionary Socialism*.[34] Bernstein was arguing that the condition of the workers, contrary to *Capital* (and, before that, the International's Inaugural Address), was steadily improving; that they had something to lose in a revolution, "a sudden catastrophe."[35] But the Social Democracy could not give up a conception that was central in its doctrine: Bebel got the party to denounce Bernstein's view officially at its congress in 1903 (Liebknecht[36] had died in 1900)—and went on pursuing the long-established policy of evolutionary socialism.[37] "Revolution," no longer an objective, had to serve as a piety. At the preceding congress, in 1900, Bebel had been obliged to smother the Revolt of the Young Ones, opposition by intransigent young Social Democrats to that policy. Every generation would have its Young Ones:[38] the German Social Democracy, evolutionary to this day, encapsulated but nourished the pure idea of revolution.

In Russia

Like Jenny von Westphalen, Russia had been ready for Marx long before he was ready for her. Russia had welcomed his earlier writings. Untranslated, *The Misery of Philosophy* and *The Condition of the Working Class in England* (this latter by Engels) were known to intellectuals in Russia before 1850. The books, for example, were in the library of the Petrashevsky Circle, the Fourierists of St. Petersburg, who were arrested in 1849.[39] In 1865 the populist Peter Tkachev made the first mention of Marx's *Critique of Political Economy* in the Russian press. Emphasizing the idea of materialism and going on to translate the book's famous passage on it, he added, "This idea has now become common to all thinking and honest men, and no intelligent man can find any serious objection to it."[40] Presently all of *The Misery of Philosophy* and the *Critique* were translated into Russian and selling well.

It was therefore not extraordinary that a Russian publisher should commission the translation of *Capital* within a year of its publication in German. Referring to the translation project, Marx deprecated in a letter to a friend: "But all this should not be overestimated. In its youth the Russian aristocracy is schooled in the German universities and in Paris. It always chases after the extremes found in the West. . . . This doesn't prevent the same Russians from becoming scoundrels the instant they enter state service."[41] Marx was trying to deny the pleasurable flattery at the prospect of the translation, but he could easily hide his new feelings under his old hatred and suspicion. The carelessness of his remark, which suggested that only the aristocracy among the Russian population was worth mentioning, showed how distant Russia remained to him.

"A rapid and widespread success," *Capital* "for a brief time enjoyed greater renown in Russia than in any other country."[42] Russia was the first country to receive *Capital* after Germany, before France of revolutionary tradition and England, Marx's domicile. The translation of volume I went on sale in St. Petersburg on April 8, 1872, and 900 copies of the edition of 3,000 were sold in six weeks. The great majority of the reviews, in conservative as well as radical journals, was favorable when not enthusiastic. The critic of the semiofficial organ *Sanktpeterburgskie vedomosti* called it "one of the magisterial works of modern economic literature." Even if readers disagreed with the writer's philosophy, the critic said, "the thinking minority of the reading public [would find in it] instructive lessons not only of a purely scientific character but also of a social character."[43]

Thinking Russia accepted *Capital* as a handbook on Western European capitalism, the Russian readers using "that aspect of Marx's work that seemed to support [their] a priori assumptions."[44] Among the revolutionaries, one populist argued that *Capital*, with its description of the horrors of the English experience, showed "how not to industrialize."[45] In general, the populists, oriented to the peasant interest, tried to graft *Capital*'s industrial aspect onto the green bough of Russian agriculture. Russian capitalism welcomed the book. The St. Petersburg industrialists actually drew upon its denunciation of low English wages. This gave them an argument for higher minimum wages in Russia. The point was that the St. Petersburg area's labor shortage forced them to pay their workers more than their Moscow competitors, and the measure would have reduced Moscow's advantage.[46] If much of this was contradictory to *Capital*'s explicit sense, it was consistent enough with its contradictions—its powerful, covert sense.

The publishing of *Capital* was the most revolutionary act in Russia since the serf emancipation of 1861. No one, whether he accepted any of *Capital*'s arguments or not, realized it then. The book's publication had originally been suggested by a scholarly group of populists interested in theory and patient about action, who read *Capital* as a plan for slow construction according to scientific principles.[47] The Russian censorship that had approved its publication had forbidden Hobbes's *Leviathan*, Lecky's *History of European Morals* and Spencer's *Social Statics* between 1865 and 1872.[48] *Capital* seemed no threat at all. One censor said that it was "a difficult, inaccessible strictly scientific work." Two others brushed past the book's explosive potential by remarking that its arguments did not apply in an agricultural country like Russia.[49] Marx's great ambiguities and *Capital*'s truly scientific aspect had deceived the censors and all its readers. For Russia there was infinitely more to the book than science, scholarship, and economics. Russia, the censorship included, was unknowingly responding to the great revolutionary forces in its depths.

Marx's relations with Russia had always been difficult. Primitive and reactionary, she had been the perfect antithesis to civilized, progressive Western Europe in Marx's Hegelian foreign policy, and Marx could see the country concentrated in the persons of Czar Nicholas, the Great Aggrandizer, and Bakunin, who threatened to Russianize the First International. Another Russian whom Marx chose to hate hugely was another radical émigré, thus a rival and also unforgivably rich. He was Alexander Herzen, the Great Dissident of the nineteenth century, publisher of a newspaper-in-exile that excoriated the Russian regime as vigorously as Marx could have wished. Marx's hatred had been perfectly a priori; he had made a point of never meeting Herzen, a resident of London from 1852 to 1864. In 1855 Marx went so far as to protest Herzen's election to an émigré organization, explaining to Engels, "I have no desire to see old Europe renewed by Russian blood."[50] Herzen was elected over Marx's objections, and Marx resigned.[51] Yet "Herzen was the true founder of populism,"[52] a movement that was commendably revolutionary even if Marx could not predict it would be so welcoming to his theory. Marx would see Herzen dead before he would appreciably change his attitude toward Russia.

Marx had always been as inconsistent in his Russophobia as he was in everything else. His cordiality to Pavel Annenkov, the witness to the liquidation of Weitling in Brussels, had been a minor example. Annenkov arrived with a letter of recommendation from a Russian friend, who had known Marx in Paris, and Marx, in his contorted way, later boasted of such relationships: "It is an irony of fate that the Russians whom I have uninterruptedly fought for twenty-five years . . . were always my 'patrons.' In 1843–44 the Russian aristocrats couldn't do enough for me."[53] But, as Marx's book on Palmerston and his articles for the New York *Daily Tribune* showed, Russia had been too thoroughly satisfactory as antithesis, most completely so during the Crimean War. Marx was not mollified by the death of Czar Nicholas in 1855, Russia's defeat the next year, or even Alexander II's emancipation of forty million serfs, the greatest act of liberation in world history. In 1864 the Inaugural Address Marx wrote for the International was eloquently paranoid about Russia, "this barbarian power with its head in St. Petersburg and its hand in every cabinet in Europe."[54]

It was Bakunin, the Russian threat from another flank, who inadvertently encouraged the beginnings of a rapprochement between Marx and Russia. The connection, antedating the theoretical relation represented by *Capital*, was personal but, not unexpectedly, maintained at a distance.

As in the case of *Capital*, Marx's new personal associations, which began in the late 1860s, were made on Russian initiative. Russia approached him as respectfully. In November 1868 one Alexander Serno-Solovevich, a member of a populist group in Swiss exile, wrote to Marx. He wanted Marx to contribute to a weekly newspaper the group was planning. Serno-Solovevich and his friends made themselves interesting to Marx because they announced themselves his supporters against Bakunin, then resident in Switzerland and active among the International's members. Marx did not trouble to promise any articles and the newspaper never appeared, but he sent the young Russian a copy of *Capital*.[55] There followed a contretemps produced by the interaction of the intriguer's reflexes of Marx and the Russian's revolutionary idealism. Marx had wanted, as he told Engels, "to use Serno to keep an eye on Bakunin." Then, "since I trust no Russian," Marx made a point of inquiring about "his old friend" Bakunin. Serno-Solovevich however stood Marx's precaution on its head. Giving the advantage to Bakunin and enraging Marx, he showed Marx's letter to Bakunin to try to reconcile the two men and their philosophies.[56] Serno-Solovevich was not even a good target for

Marx's anger. In August 1869, after a Swiss doctor tactlessly assured him he was going mad, the young man committed suicide.[57]

The Russian connection maintained itself more promisingly than Marx realized. A few of Serno-Solovevich's populist friends persisted in Marx's theoretical sense, and one of them, Nikolai Utin, organized the Russian section of the International, comprising a bare dozen members at most, in Geneva in March 1870. On March 12, 1870, Utin sent Marx his group's program and asked him to be the Russian section's representative, thus corresponding secretary for Russia, on the General Council. The program set as its objective "a strong link between the working classes of Russia and those of Western Europe," while Utin assured Marx in his covering letter that he had "absolutely nothing in common with Bakunin."[58] Utin set himself up as a rival to Bakunin after a brief association with him. An active revolutionary leader in Russia since 1861, he had then established a position for himself in exile through his virtual control of the populist newspaper, *Narodnoe Delo–La Cause du Peuple*, which published a few issues in Geneva from September 1868 to September 1870. Marx needed the kind of help Utin was offering, but he did not simply accept the gift, he seized it in a way that would have crushed it. In his reply he demanded that the Russians set Polish freedom as their first objective, since it was "an absolutely indispensable preliminary condition for the general liberation of the European proletariat." Marx articulated his suspicions and hostility to Engels: "*Drôle de position* for me, to function as representative of Young Russia! You never know where you'll end up, and what strange fellowship you'll experience." He would be happy to enter into the fellowship, but "I . . . emphasize that the prime task of the Russian section is to work for Poland (that is, free Europe from their [country's] proximity)."[59]

Engels could fill in the rest of the logic: When Alexander Herzen had fraternally supported the 1863 Polish rising, his newspaper lost four-fifths of its readers by the end of that year and its influence among Russians had fallen precipitously and irrecoverably.[60] The tiny Russian section of the International committed suicide not quite according to Dr. Marx's prescription, but in his service. Utin, successfully countering Bakunin's influence, won the support of the majority of the International's members at a Swiss regional conference in April 1870. As the section's leader, Utin then attended the preparatory conference of the International in London in 1871 and aggressively supporting Marx against a representative of Bakunin's, drove the man away from the conference.

But the struggle with Bakunin alienated the Russian colony in Switzerland, where Utin was accused of having sold himself to Marx and the
International's "German dictatorship." As a result, the Russian section
disintegrated some months *before* the climactic Congress of The Hague
in September 1872, and Utin, without an organizational base, did not
attend the congress.[61] A few other Russians approached Marx in person
or by mail, but little came of it.

The Russians, meanwhile, were acting more and more in a way to
recommend themselves to Marx. At home the populists discarded Alexander Herzen as too moderate for the cruel work ahead[62] and turned
activist by 1860, when the brother of Alexander Serno-Solovevich founded
the country's first operational group. Arrests wiped it out by 1862, but
a series of increasingly effective ones followed. The "Go to the People"
movement of 1873–74, a students' invasion of the countryside to en-
lighten and radicalize the peasants, provided a resonant context for revolutionary action, and the populists were presently assassinating hated
officials and stirring up peasant revolts. In September 1879 a group of
thoroughly professional revolutionaries condemned Czar Alexander II to
death; on March 13, 1881, having mounted an operation in military style,
they closed in and assassinated him.[63] Marx celebrated their act in a letter
to his daughter Jenny, still a member of his revolutionary staff. The as-
sassins, he wrote, were "brave people with no melodramatic poses,
straightforward, realistic, and heroic." They were teaching Europe that
"their method of operations is specifically Russian and historically unanswerable, and that there is as little point in moralizing argument for
or against as there is in the case of the earthquake in Chios."[64] For the
first time in his life Marx had responded to something Russian with unqualified approval. He felt more than that: the act flooded his consciousness with new illumination. But still this very Russian operation had to
be fitted to Marx's theory and the theory had to allow for it. In the event,
Marx had adjusted the theory a few days earlier.

A great problem of theory as relating to Russia lay in the very essence
of *Capital*—its definition of economy as essentially industry, denying life
to agriculture. This was clear enough from a reading of volume 1 (supported by other Marx writings) before the appearance of the more explicit volume 3. The populists were champions of peasant and agriculture: how could their activities be made acceptable in *Capital*'s model of
the world? If all men manipulate theory according to the compulsions of
practice, and if Marx was particularly expert in manipulating theory *and*
men manipulating theory, he had nevertheless made matters extraordi-

narily difficult for himself vis-à-vis a Russia that was 90 percent agrarian. *Capital* suggested that she was overwhelmingly engaged in retrograde, futile economic activity. Progressive-minded Russians attracted by *Capital*'s marvelous promise sought a route that would lead them around its repellent side.

Marx and the Russian revolutionaries agreed both on revolution and socialism. Revolution was no problem, but socialism was. Here, also, agriculture interfered. Marx, as the *Communist Manifesto* showed in detail, could be more severe with socialists than with liberals or conservatives, and the populists advocated a socialism that was pre-Marxian and agriculture-oriented. They would generalize the *obshchina*, the peasant commune, already existing and socialist in a primitive way: as members, the peasants owned the land in common. The obshchina, moreover, seemed to suggest a way of avoiding the evil side of progress, which *Capital* itself had so mordantly described. In January 1871 a populist woman, a member of the International in exile in Geneva, asked Marx what he thought of it. Disagreeing with most of her friends, she volunteered the opinion that the peasant commune would be a victim of advancing capitalism.[65] There is no record of a response from Marx, but, withdrawing and delegating more and more, he had permitted Engels to denigrate the obshchina in correspondence.

This called up the rebuttal of an "Open Letter" by Peter Tkachev in 1874: Tkachev was the populist who had quoted the *Critique of Political Economy* in Russia so enthusiastically. He accused Engels of ignorance of Russian conditions. Contrary to what Engels claimed, "our people . . . in its great majority . . . is permeated with the principles of common ownership; it is . . . instinctively, traditionally communist." By way of Tkachev the Russian revolutionary movement was pressing Marx to review his position. Marx would not: in 1874–75 Engels published a series of articles as a counterattack on Tkachev in a German Social Democratic newspaper.[66] Adding anthropological conceptions with which he and Marx were taken, Engels simply and coolly drew out the implications of volume 1 of *Capital*. The obshchina-centered agricultural society of Russia was the "natural basis for *Oriental despotism*," the fundamental characteristic of the Russian state. Engels envisaged the rise of a bourgeois society in Russia, and this "would destroy the communal property little by little." He concluded with more doom-saying and a faint, patronizing flicker of hope: "Communal ownership in Russia is . . . to all appearances moving toward its disintegration." The hope was a proletarian revolution in the West which would come to the aid of the Russian peasant.[67]

The question of the viability of the obshchina—the viability of Russian agriculture—persisted. Once again, a decade after the first recorded inquiry—and two weeks before the czar's assassination—it was put directly to Marx, this time in a letter from a female populist in exile.[68] The new correspondent was worthy of maximum respect. She was Vera Zasulich, who had attempted assassination herself, and shot and wounded the military governor of St. Petersburg. She was a member of a group of distinguished émigrés responsive to Marx's ideas and thus all the more distressed by the negative components in them. The question of Vera Zasulich, validated by years of Russian revolutionary action, was one of the hardest Marx ever faced. She was inviting Marx to disavow his associate Engels and himself as well. Everything that Engels had said, except the hope, derived directly from Marx himself. In 1868, in a letter to Engels, he had been absolute and explicit; he remarked on the "undemocratic, in fact *patriarchal* character of the communal executive" and concluded, "The whole pile of shit is collapsing."[69] Now, delicately, Marx obliged Vera Zasulich.

Marx took the question so seriously that, condensing and excising possibly troublesome themes, he wrote four drafts before he was sufficiently satisfied to send a reply. (The reply was dated March 8, 1881, five days before the czar's death.)[70] The *Werke* edition identifies no other instance of repeated rewriting of letters by Marx. In the first draft he had leaned toward the pessimism Engels had expressed: "[The obshchina] had already been brought to the very edge of ruin." But Marx drew back. He was willing to speculate that a Russian revolution, but only a revolution, could save it.[71] In a second draft he reemphasized the need for a revolution, which, he said, would draw Russia out of her isolation from Western Europe, the mainstream of progress. Otherwise, if Russia remained isolated, the obshchina would die in accordance with the inexorable laws of history.[72] The third draft remained trapped in near hopelessness. The final draft, however, executed the necessary strategic maneuver. *Capital* itself, Marx wrote, provided neither proof nor disproof of the obshchina's viability. "But special research [in the] . . . original sources" later had convinced him of something more positive. He did not explain what it was that he had discovered or reasoned out. Guaranteeing the statement with his "special research," Marx asserted that "this village commune is the foundation of the social rebirth of Russia."[73] In this manner, contrary to his fundamental ideas and writings, his sense of reality, and his taste, Marx led the Russian revolutionaries around his massive rejection of their country and its social formation.

Central as it had been, the problem of the obshchina vanished as soon as it was solved: the new Russian Marxists, Vera Zasulich among them, had no place for the obshchina in their new view of the world. Once again Marx, one of the world's greatest thinkers, showed that he did not take ideas seriously when the needs of action conflicted with them. As usual, the politician dominated the thinker. Doubtless the totality of Marx's life and works would have won over the Russian revolutionaries eventually, but he had made it easier at an important moment in both Russia's and his own history. His living touch in the final months of his life quickened appropriate Russian action as nothing else could.

Marx's enthusiastic letter to his daughter half-articulated a new logic based upon the czar's assassination. He could see that the "straightforward, realistic, and heroic" terrorists had something to teach Europe. Surely this associated itself closely to his own aims. Marx pursued the thought in his last writing for publication, which was brought into being by another friendly Russian initiative. Vera Zasulich's group was publishing a second Russian edition of the *Communist Manifesto*, and requested Marx to write an introduction. He obliged in collaboration with Engels. In the introduction, dated January 21, 1882, Marx remarked on the effect the assassination had produced. With a new czar a "prisoner-of-war of the revolution" in his heavily guarded palace, Marx said, "Russia forms the vanguard of revolutionary action in Europe." Linking the obshchina with thrilling revolutionary deeds, Marx returned to the question: "Can the Russian obshchina, though greatly undermined . . . pass directly to the higher form of communist common ownership? Or, on the contrary, must it first pass through the same process of dissolution as constitutes the historical evolution of the West?"

Marx's reply was a perfection of circular reasoning and ambiguity. "If the Russian revolution becomes the signal of a proletarian revolution in the West, so that either complements the other, the present Russian common ownership of land may serve as a starting point for a communist development."[74] It was best to leave the question of the obshchina there, in total but amicable confusion. Only an exalted idealist, preferably Dostoievskian-Russian, could see the peasant commune as more than a collectivity of ignorance, lack of incentive, and rejection of progress. How could such a "precapitalistic formation," a phrase Marx had used frequently in his *Grundrisse*, support a modern industrial society? But Marx, a former ally of the German bourgeoisie, had less difficulty with Russian populists, who, at least, could *act*. The ultimate theoretical adjustment, as the "Theses on Feuerbach" posited and the czar's assassination proved, could come after the revolutionary deeds.

It is too facile to find Marx inconsistent or simply wrong on the question of *where*, advanced or retrograde region, to make revolution. If the reflective Marx of *Capital* conceived of revolution as a highly sophisticated social product, he was much more than a thinker. The instinctive Marx, unerringly guided by his sensual affinity for violence, had seen the future in the light of the assassination; the act's revolutionary sense had transcended chronology and logic. Furthermore, the preindustrial Germany which was the only Germany he really knew and the Russia he enjoyed despising were by no means dissimilar. In his critique of Hegel in 1843 (discussed here, ch. 3), Marx had placed his homeland emphatically *"beneath the level of history."* His contempt had united both countries as fellow inhabitants of the category of the least who would be first.

Marx remained ill at ease in the new Zion. A letter written just three months before he died reports on the thinker's accelerating conquest of Russia and the strategist's laggard, perhaps reluctant, perception of it. He was writing in English, probably since the letter was going to his daughter Laura, another revolutionary staff member, and her husband, still another, who knew no German. Marx began with satisfaction: "Some *secret Russian publications*, printed in Holy Russia, not abroad, show the great run of my theories in that country. Nowhere my success is to me more delightful;—" But he ended the sentence by ignoring the constructive character of his own influence on Russia: "It gives me satisfaction that I damage a power which, besides England, is the true bulwark of the old society."[75] Nevertheless, the Marxian and the Russian revolution had made their connection and Marx did not deny it, just as he had refused to deny his German following with its softening of his message.

The translator of the second Russian edition[76] of the *Communist Manifesto* was Georgi Plekhanov, who led the revolutionary group to which Vera Zasulich belonged. Plekhanov, a trained engineer and former officer, had been active in the populist movement in Russia. In June 1879 he had resigned from the organization which was planning the czar's assassination, although he was not against violence on principle, because he opposed concentration on terrorism as politically sterile. He began publishing a newspaper expounding his revolutionary program, but police discovered it while the first number was being published in January 1880. Plekhanov was able to escape from Russia. He settled in Geneva and, recognizing the *Capital*'s constructive side, set about studying it in Swiss security. In Geneva in September 1883, five months after Marx's death, Plekhanov founded the Emancipation of Labor, the first Russian Marxian party.

Beginning with Plekhanov, there was a laying on of hands by Marx and Engels. Marx himself never met any of the Emancipation of Labor group. To him Vera Zasulich had been just a correspondent who happened to formulate an important problem demanding solution, and Georgi Plekhanov was still another correspondent, also deserving of a measure of attention. Certainly the republication of the *Communist Manifesto* in Russian was worth the labor of collaborating on a brief introduction: the results would be useful in Russia and elsewhere, but the project did not require his personal association with Plekhanov. Marx disappeared. Thereafter, the elderly Engels, acting as personal patron to the Emancipation of Labor, implemented Marx's new Russian policy splendidly.[77]

From 1890 to 1892 the leaders of Emancipation of Labor published four issues of the Russian-language periodical *Sozial-Demokrat* in London. Engels contributed a long article on Russia that skillfully rationalized Marx's Russophobia and made him a comrade of the Russian revolutionaries as an enemy of czarism.[78] The old man received Plekhanov frequently and gave him the use of his library, particularly interesting to the Russian with its copies of the *Neue Rheinische Zeitung* and the *NRZ-Revue*.[79] In the last year of his life, in 1895, Engels was fussing over Vera Zasulich, a sufferer from chronic bronchitis and a heavy smoker, who had stayed on in London.[80] In the spring of 1895, as Engels was dying, the twenty-five-year-old Lenin came to Western Europe to establish his connection with the leaders in exile of Russian socialism. He achieved a meeting with Plekhanov in Geneva, and as a self-converted Marxist and an already experienced activist, his blessing. Plekhanov had one reservation: Lenin seemed too narrow in his revolutionary zeal.[81] By 1902 Lenin had won others to his interpretation of the revolutionary Marx and superseded Plekhanov as the outstanding (but far from dominant) leader among the Russian Marxists. Thus the line of succession: Marx and Engels—Plekhanov—Lenin—Stalin . . .

In 1902 Lenin published the book *What Is to Be Done?*, which advocated the creation of an uncompromising, disciplined, militant—fighting—party of professional revolutionaries united in ideology and strategy: the Marxian revolutionary machine. Four years earlier the All-Russian Social Democratic Labor Party had been organized in Russia as a loose, quarreling union of Marxian groups. Lenin's proposal led to the schism of 1903, when the party divided into his Bolsheviks and the more numerous, less single-minded Mensheviks (including Plekhanov eventually).[82] Lenin and his twenty-odd immediate followers were the general staff and board of directors of the revolutionary mechanism. Most of it was in Russia, more or less dormant but waiting to be roused to action by Lenin's decisive leadership: those persons who had the attitudes and personalities that would make them the field officers and foot soldiers of the revolution, or, at least, sympathizers willing to help these activists. Like Marx's *Neue Rheinische Zeitung*, a newspaper was operational head-quarters, and Lenin, in Western European exile from July 1900, had founded one in Germany before the end of the year. For Lenin his news-paper had an additional function: the clandestine party organization in Russia was developed around its distribution network. The newspaper distributors were all party agents whom he ordered, in the unrelenting war on authority, "to dissemble, to lie and deceive, threaten and ap-pease."[83]

Lenin's policy of unremitting action to overthrow the government re-quired such an organization. In 1906 Leon Trotsky, although more or less a Menshevik and alienated from Lenin, expressed the sense of Lenin's policy in an essay revising and adapting Marx's conception of the per-manent revolution.[84] While the Menshevik pedants assumed there had to be a pause for a bourgeois stage, Trotsky said the Russian revolution could drive directly from the prebourgeois period into the proletarian future. Mensheviks could correctly cite such statements of Marx as the Address of the Communist League of March 1850 which, still hopeful of revolution, nevertheless foresaw a period of bourgeois power (see ch. 6). But then the Mensheviks had to ignore the sense of the conception of the "revolutionary dictatorship of the proletariat" of the *Critique of the Gotha Program* of 1875. Even more to the point, the Mensheviks had to ignore the hard sense of Marx's life and works. Clearly, Marx had always wanted as much revolution as he could get and Trotsky was saying that the Russian situation in 1906 was objectively more promising for revo-lution than Marx had judged the German situation to be in 1850. Trotsky and Lenin, whatever their differences, were in agreement on this major issue with each other—and with Marx.

When the Revolution of 1905 broke out in Russia, the Bolshevik ap-paratus and policy showed themselves to be well adapted to the new demands. The Bolsheviks gained considerably more members and proved themselves to be a formidable, if small organization. Although it de-clined almost as considerably in the reform era that followed, the party, still an efficient revolutionary machine, could take maximum advantage of the opportunity created by World War I.

The opportunity came with the breakdown of government and society in Russia by 1917. Only Lenin's Bolsheviks had the necessary decisive-ness, shamelessness, and ruthlessness, the innocence and faith, to desire and seize power. The other major revolutionary parties, the Mensheviks and Socialist Revolutionaries, were more numerous and suffered for it; their numbers extended over too many opinions and humane inhibitions. The Socialist Revolutionaries, by far the largest, suffered from an additional difficulty related to their size: direct descendants of the populists, they represented agriculture and the peasants, that is, the past according to Marx and Lenin. Lenin was the brother of a populist executed for plotting Alexander III's assassination and himself a populist originally, but he accepted the industrial, hence urban, character of the Marxian revolution totally: no nonsense about the obshchina. His tactics could make the most of his principles. The decisive battleground in the struggle for power was the cities, particularly Petrograd, where the Bolsheviks could attract, organize, and arm the workers, while gaining the support of soldiers and sailors, who were mostly peasants separated from their origins for the moment. The total number of workers was insignificant as compared with the peasant four-fifths of the population, but it just sufficed. While Lenin could make the most of his urban proletariat, he made the least of the peasantry, to whom he assigned the role of an appendage of the working class. Yet he won over many of the peasants and neutralized them as a class by telling them to seize the land from the landowners; the revolution would take it back when it could.

In arranging the components of the situation in 1917, Lenin helped himself with the description he found in Marx's *Civil War in France*: "the organization of the armed workers after the model of the . . . Commune."[85] Translating Marx's fictions and creating his own about the Commune, Lenin got a firm grip on the realism he found in Marx and the realities of the Russian situation. Fortunate circumstances and great strategy were not enough: the Marxian principle was the foundation of the victory. However fantastic much of his program was, however many deadly mistakes he made, Lenin spoke the language of the future, and many persons, however threatened, understood it and submitted. The revolutionary machine, operating *en permanence*, as Marx would have it, had made its revolution in Russia, although not quite as he had conceived and, without hesitation, proceeded to manage the power.

Brilliantly, greatly, if approximately, Lenin suggested the further future: "Communism is soviet power plus the electrification of the whole country."[86] Forcing its way forward in ideology as much as in function, the new leadership provoked civil war and caused economic chaos and famine; it killed millions and martyred nearly everyone. Lenin died in 1924. Beginning in 1929 Stalin carried out his suggestions with the Five-

Year Plans: with the campaign against the peasants, labor camps, and with purges to eliminate or anticipate opposition—millions more killed, including two-thirds of a million Communist Party members and half of the officer corps.[87] In its single-mindedness the revolutionary machine, the revolution achieved, devastated, and continues to devastate, great areas of human activity which Marx had thought irrelevant or hostile: thought, art, individual initiative . . . The price for Russian progress has been infinitely greater than that measured in the lives lost. At a Harvard symposium on the Soviet Union's fiftieth anniversary, it was pointed out that the country had become almost 60 percent urbanized since 1917.[88] Soviet Russia was the second greatest industrial power in the world.[89] Screwing his monocle into his eye and peering at Russia's imperfections, could Marx repudiate the Russian Revolution and its works?

ELEVEN

MEMORIAL

MARX HAD BEGUN TO DIE when he suffered his nervous collapse of 1873. The last decade of his life was a darkening period of illness and family afflictions. Earlier, in 1860, when Jenny Marx was forty-six, she was stricken by smallpox. Her face scarred and her spirit deeply wounded, perhaps as a culmination of too much pain felt for too long, she began to withdraw from the world, and, somewhat later and more gradually, from her family. While she continued loyally to copy out Marx's manuscripts, she did not enter into his newer concerns. She did not interest herself in the affairs of the International as she had in the émigré politics of the 1850s. She took her holidays separately from her husband, and Marx found a companion in his youngest daughter.

But Eleanor and the other daughters gave cause for worry. Eleanor herself, entangled in unsatisfactory relationships and deeply dependent on Marx, underwent repeated nervous crises; Jenny, asthmatic and variously ill from childhood, felt abused by her French husband and mother-in-law. Laura's husband, also French, was ineffectual, a doctor who had practiced briefly and never found another vocation; Laura, suffering the loss of her three children, one as a boy of three and one-half and the others as infants, subsisted as an incomplete person. (Eleanor would take poison at the age of forty-three, in 1898; in 1911, Laura and her husband, aging and hopeless, would also commit suicide.) Although the ferocious boils had subsided, Marx was attacked by a series of ailments. Insomnia and his old liver complaint persisted. In the 1880s a cough caused him increasing pain and weakness. Before then, Jenny Marx fell ill and retired to her bed. On December 2, 1881, after prolonged agony, Jenny Marx died of cancer of the liver. Engels, on seeing Marx, said, "The Moor is dead, too."[1] Ill with pleurisy and probably tuberculosis, Marx could not attend the funeral.

Seeking relief from coughing spells, Marx spent much of the year 1882 in pursuit of a sun that perversely vanished upon his arrival in North Africa and several places on the Continent. Somewhat restored after a late-summer visit with his daughter Jenny, who lived near Paris, he returned to a chilly England in the fall. On January 10, 1883, Jenny Marx Longuet, mother of five surviving children, died of cancer of the bladder. Marx had an acute attack of bronchitis and coughed all the more. He could not eat solid food and often refused the milk that was his only nourishment. He died in his home in north London on March 14, 1883.

Marx had tried to go on until near the end, when Jenny Marx's death destroyed the life and meaning in his home. Before she died, he had wisely husbanded his declining powers. The *Critique of the Gotha Program* had been a scattering of words requiring no labor of research or of organization; the introduction to the second Russian edition of the *Communist Manifesto*, written, moreover, with Engels' collaboration, made up a page and a half of print. Marx's most important activity was make-work. The paralyzing difficulties in the logic of *Capital* and his health had prevented work on volumes 2 and 3, but in the early 1870s he busied himself unnecessarily overseeing the capable French translator of volume 1. Before then, by 1870, Marx had learned to read Russian because, as he theorized, Russian agriculture would best instruct him on the economics of land rent, so important in volume 3. (One of the first Russian books he read was Herzen's memoirs, which he had just finished when he heard that the author had died.)[2] Perhaps Marx expected to come upon a philosopher's stone that could only be found embedded in the most extreme difficulties and guarded by the great dragon, the czar.

All of this was part of a general study, another of Marx's boundless projects. It comprehended agronomics, American and Russian agriculture, banking and currency, physical sciences including geology and physiology, and mathematics—all of which Marx understood darkly or not at all. Engels said he found among Marx's effects 3,000 pages of notes on his readings and two cubic meters of Russian statistical reports.[3] Marx's last research project, begun as Jenny Marx was dying and kept up for a few weeks after her death, was a study of Russian peasant emancipation.[4] And yet, if the direct uses of these projects were nil, they made private sense as work therapy, and operational sense, particularly as relating to Russia. Surely Marx's Russian studies helped prepare him to establish his positive relations with that country after so much rejection. It is not at all unlikely that Marx's old revolutionary instinct had aroused his friendly interest in the first place. That instinct remained true to the very end.

One of Marx's finest accomplishments was the delegation of more and more functions to Engels, who redundantly proved himself to be one of the great deputies of world history. The most important task Marx did not even dare to delegate in so many words to his friend: the creation of the last two volumes of *Capital* out of his chaotic notes. Engels wrote in the preface to volume 2, "This is the material . . . out of which I was supposed 'to make something' as Marx remarked to his daughter Eleanor shortly before his death."[5] Although Engels had to leave the *Theories of Surplus Value* to Karl Kautsky, he managed to complete the assignment in the year before *his* death. Meanwhile, in the dealings with the German Social Democracy, Engels had been translating Marx's incoherent anger and unhappiness into letters of guidance, admonishment, and manipulation. Engels had turned into positivist philosopher with the *Anti-Dühring* and another, more intellectually ambitious study, the *Dialectic of Nature*.[6] He wrote numerous articles in the German Social Democratic press. Although unable to prevent its being bowdlerized, he forced publication of the *Critique of the Gotha Program* in a party organ in 1891.[7] Correctly selecting the correct attitude toward the Russians among Marx's ambivalences, Engels developed the filament of Marx-Russian relations into a strong, if still slender, axis of world revolution. With such help, Marx was able to adjust, enhance, and re-create the theory and praxis of revolution.

The change from the living to the dead Marx was virtually imperceptible even within the world of Marxism. It completed and made perfect Marx's last accomplishment. Marx deserves full credit: he had prepared the succession himself.

If a biographer had written the life of Marx at his death in 1883, he would have had to treat his subject as a minor figure, an exiled revolutionary leader of 1848 who had produced writings of a significance as yet undetermined but quite possibly considerable, and the chief personality in an ineffectual international organization, vanished some time ago, of artisans, radicals, and cranks. In his lifetime Marx never exercised more immediate power than a provincial politician, a field-grade officer, or the owner of a medium-sized cotton mill. Yet this comparative weakness permitted him to gain his world-historical power. He might, like some contemporaries, have committed himself to nationalism and, in the end, fallen in with Bismarck; he might, like the Willich group, have insisted upon immediate revolution, no matter what the real situation was, and

vanished. For that matter, the effective rulers of Marx's world like Bismarck himself, or Disraeli, Gladstone, Cavour, and many others were
trapped in their own time. Able only to complete and not to initiate,
they have not left behind magnitudes remotely comparable to Marx's.
Marx had shifted his weight forward onto the future.

How important has Marx's effect been on the future—our present?
The account of events in Germany and Russia, beginning with Marx's
initiatives, has already extended here beyond his lifetime. Other events
in other countries can now be attached to it in the movement toward the
present. Marx, as we have seen, worked with great, simplifying abstractions. He conceived of the proletariat as an ideal before he knew workers
or industry. Revolution, an abstraction doubled, could be the storm of
violence his temperament preferred, or, as his thinking in *Capital* suggested, the natural and peaceful sloughing off of a dead skin—"integument." His internationalism based itself on these abstractions and saw
the proletariat coming together, with or without violence, in a world-
wide unity. To try to find substance in these Platonic shadows or to condemn Marx for the lack of it would be a waste of time. Rather, one must
get behind the abstractions to the realities they represented so powerfully.

It would be useful to examine, along with Germany and Russia, the
three national cases England, France, and China. *All* cases defy Marx's
theory.

England, inventor of the Industrial Revolution, had the largest, most
self-conscious, most militant working class in the nineteenth century.
The workers had earlier got through the first horrors of industrialism
with comparatively little complaint. When they began to resist, they first
suffered humiliating defeats, but then the situation changed, and government and employers yielded encouragingly. The workers got the vote in
1867, the year of *Capital*. From the 1850s the trade unions had been expanding and winning higher wages and improvements in working conditions. The British economy, Marx to the contrary, was producing increasing amounts of wealth to be shared, and the British Empire sucked
in still more from the colonies and poorer countries. This increasing
strength and prosperity led the English workers to socialism. It was not
a reversal of wretchedness according to *Capital*, and the socialism was
not Marxian. Religion and the national pragmatism immunized the
workers against ideology. In his long residence there, Marx had never
accepted or understood England, and England had overlooked him.

During the last years of his life, Marx had nevertheless inspired the founding of a British Marxian party. This was the Social Democratic Federation, organized as the Democratic Federation in 1881. Its leader was Henry M. Hyndman, an arrogant, wealthy amateur of politics who had read the French translation of *Capital* on an American trip early in 1880, and got introduced to Marx that summer. For nearly a year Hyndman saw Marx, learned more, and became a proselyte. Hyndman then published a book that paraphrased passages from *Capital* without giving credit to Marx. Marx learned about the book when it was distributed at the Democratic Federation's founding meeting in June 1881. Hurt and enraged at having been exploited, Marx broke off with Hyndman.[8]

In 1900 the Social Democratic Federation joined with other left-wing and labor groups to organize the Labour Representation Committee, the forerunner of the Labour Party. Another founding organization was the Fabian Society, itself founded in 1884.[9] The Fabians, including such capacities as Sidney and Beatrice Webb and George Bernard Shaw, rejected Marx's economic theory as incorrect and advocated a piecemeal, pragmatic socialism that appealed to many middle-class people as well as workers.[10] Very soon, in 1901, the Social Democratic Federation withdrew from the Labour Representation Committee into insignificance, when the new organization refused to adopt a program of explicit socialism and class war. The Fabians went on to serve the Labour Party as its nonideological, nonrevolutionary intelligence. The posthumous Marx would have to pursue a slower, more devious route to influence in England.

France had taught Marx the art of revolution. No working class represented the class-war thesis so accurately and gallantly as the French in 1848 and in 1871; and Marx justly celebrated it. Yet events in France, promising in their beginnings, swung away from his theoretical pattern, another instance of anarchy in the historical data. The June insurrection of 1848 was an episode in the suicide of the Second Republic, and crushed the working-class aspirations associated with the republic. The failure of the Commune of 1871 then maimed left-wing action for still another generation. France preferred a more comfortable pace for her Industrial Revolution than England's or Germany's, and her factories and industrial working class grew more slowly. Moreover, her agriculture was prosperous, and not to be easily classified by the Marxists as a backward part of the economy. Among the workers, many still artisans, the ideas of Proudhon remained strong, and Marxism, represented at last by a political party in 1879, made slow progress and tended always to fall off into schism and heresy. Marx was incompetently represented by his French sons-in-law who, however, were operating on difficult terrain. Engels recorded that Marx, considering the character of the "so-called 'Marxism' in France," informed Laura's husband, " 'Ce qu'il y a de certain c'est que moi, je ne suis pas marxiste.' "[11] A stable and unified Marxian party was not established until 1906. Evolutionary and doctrinally careless, it would have evoked the same comment from the spirit of Marx.

Like Germany, thus, England and France took their industrial progress without revolution. Russia and China, to simplify not too much, violated Marxian theory in a perfectly symmetrical way: they achieved their revolution before their industrial progress. In all five national cases, the most important in Marxian history, theory and revolutionary praxis were absolutely opposed. A closer comparison of Russia and China can help explain the apparent paradox.

Lenin made his revolution with a scanty working class, 2.6 million in a population of some 140 million in 1917.[12] Mao Tse-tung made it with the peasants Marx had defined away as reactionary. Lenin and Mao were right; Lenin had known to what degree to violate Marxian theory, Mao had known to violate it absolutely. For Lenin, progress, as Marx had taught, was associated with industry and the urban community, where the necessary skills and attitudes were nurtured. Here, also, the workers were concentrated, giving a great tactical advantage to a policy oriented theoretically around their interests. Thus the workers, unlike the peasants, were available for strikes, the kind of action that could lead efficiently to revolution. By 1920 civil war, hunger, and flight to the countryside had reduced the Russian working class to 1.2 million. "The proletarian dictatorship was triumphant but the proletariat had nearly vanished," one Marxian scholar put it.[13] With the country forced to make extreme sacrifices, this thin, eroded base was just adequate for the great Russian industrial state. But the adequate, providing the necessary progressive nucleus, was miraculously successful.

Why then could Mao do without the workers—and with the peasants? The question is absurd: China simply did not have the workers. The Chinese Communist Party, obeying Stalin and Marxian theory, had once tried to operate with the few workers available, those in the large coastal cities where foreign capital had established some industry, but their numbers failed the theory. In 1927 Chiang Kai-shek easily put down a rising and wiped out the party as an urban organization. Mao the peasant's son and a few other surviving leaders then set up headquarters in the countryside and enrolled the peasants. Mao was able to use a class-war formula easily enough, since the peasants felt oppressed by their landlords and moneylenders, while he had another force which united all Chinese, nationalistic xenophobia in a proud country invaded by Western imperialism.

Chiang, without an ideology beyond nationalism and qualifying that by accepting aid from the West, could not withstand the fictions and efficiency of Mao's complete Marxian revolutionary machine. "Progress," as represented by a working class, was missing from the machine, but Mao had one great advantage over Lenin, Lenin's accomplishment itself. Mao imported his progress in the form of example, inspiration, and technical aid from a Russia become objectively progressive. In both national cases the active agent of modernization had been the elite—the board of directors and general staff of the revolutionary machine—using passive human material, the first time in the form of nascent working class (later supplemented by waves of confused, uprooted peasants), the second time in the form of a virtually homogeneous peasantry. In China the proletariat had been transformed back into Marx's original abstraction.

The need to use these national cases here suggests the problematic and rudimentary nature of Marxian internationalism. The difficulty is nationalism. Rising nationalism had been a compelling factor in Marx's decision to make an end of the First International. He had kept the idea pure, and it inspired the founding of the Second International in 1889. But the new organization was a loose union of *national* socialist parties, actually a ring of satellite parties attached to the great, motherly German Social Democracy. To make an issue of the Second International's failure to prevent World War I would be misleading. In a time of nationalism intensified by imperialism, German megalomania, and French obsession with revanche, the organization had represented a rather small fraction of the European population and an even smaller fraction of European opinion. It served well enough by helping carry Marx's internationalizing and socializing ideas into the twentieth century. World War I itself cruelly exposed and shattered the Second International, but the war produced tougher forms of both internationalism and socialism.

Like the internationalism of Marx, the newer forms of international action in our century are mixed with virulent strains of nationalism. The League of Nations and the United Nations, while Marx inevitably had an influence in their creation, can be dismissed as the dwarf products of other illusions that, compared with his, are empty and infertile. In direct line with Marx, however, Lenin made off with the Marxian internationalist heritage in 1919 by organizing the Third International, the Comintern or Communist International, which he used to found and control Communist parties throughout the world. By defining Soviet Russia as the workers' motherland, Lenin and his successors could rationalize commanding French, German, Chinese, Indians, and English in its national interest. The Russian leaders could also use the din of their internationalist sounds to cover the repression of the non-Russian half of the nation's population, another appropriate use of Marxian logic.

The foreign Communists, the Chinese as outstanding examples, were not always docile. Serving *their* national interests, they nevertheless enormously expanded the international presence of Marxism. Inevitably, Communist internationalism found itself facing the United States and the leading Western European nations using such agencies as NATO and other military alliances, the Marshall Plan, and the European Economic Community. With all the anomalies and the Russo-Chinese enmity, the world's internationalism works, although it remains fragmented and warlike. It is, of course, unable to assure peace and prevent a global disaster that could destroy most or all of life. But this is in Marx's sense, whatever he thought he thought. Marx was better at functioning in the real world with all its horrors and dangers than at imagining a happier, safer one.

Supporting and demanding the international arrangements is the intensification of economic contact throughout the world, expressed in everything from the multinational corporation and international investment to active governmental intervention in foreign trade and economic matters. Businessmen guiding governments and governments guiding businessmen; Communist officials acting as businessmen: the world moves closer toward the ultimate goal—whether it will arrive is another question—of organizing itself as a unitary workshop. It does so while compromising both its Marxism and its spirit of free enterprise.

Operating nationally and internationally in this way, Marxism continues to be adapted to a widening range of instances—prosperously to be violated. The national Communist parties, some of them quite large, have functioned as a second wave of Marxian influence in France, so resistant in the nineteenth century and only feebly receptive until World War II; Italy, where Marxism arrived late and then succumbed to fascism; England, but in a lesser way, and elsewhere. In England, as another example of the protean character of Marxism, it gets more results by way of the left-wing intelligentsia in and around the Labour Party than through the small, ineradicably alien Communist Party.

Germany is a somewhat special case. The great majority of West Germans, chilled by the prison atmosphere of East Germany, refuse to grant the Communist Party a serious political role, while the Social Democrats reject the class-war thesis and apply the lessons of Keynesian economics. Certainly West Germany represents violation more than adaptation, but the Marxian elements are irreducible. With all the shortcomings and strains, the Marxism of East Germany and the other captive nations of the Soviet Bloc is crudely effective, while it has been so deeply impressed upon their peoples' consciousness that it is now much more than an external force. This is only Europe.

Other Marxian applications have worked well in the very different conditions of the Middle and Far East, sub-Saharan Africa, and Latin America. What more need be said of the unspeakable horrors of Vietnam, Cambodia, and Laos? Marxism won out. In many countries nationalistic elites have won independence by organizing themselves around the military, the most efficient instrument of power and government, and using selected parts of Marxism. In some cases, Egypt and Algeria, for example, the Mohammedan religion rejects the ideology and grants Marxism a severely circumscribed field of operations, but every success means an addition to the Marxian sum. In general, revolutionary Marxism or independence movements influenced by Marxism have been most successful in countries that were technologically backward but modern in their aspirations.

There have been failures. Cuba is a trivial success within the general failure represented by Latin America, and the most expensive one, since Soviet Russia must support its economy; and there were the plain failures of tactical action in Chile and Bolivia. But that is only up to today: Central America is stirring and Marxism can reasonably hope to advance in a region with so much poverty and so many people. In Indonesia, Mohammedans massacred the Communists and wiped out the party. In India, socialism was a word of Nehru's that sank in the swamp of poverty, caste, religious divisions, and religious antipathy to progress; the Marxian parties continue to thrash about in that swamp. Still, new Marxian effects continue to arise, rebound, and criss-cross. The Marxian sum always mounts.

Part of the Marxian total is the fascist-Nazi phenomenon, which Marxists have disposed of as the purest expression of the capitalistic spirit. No one, however, has proved the point, and the bare, obscene bones of the question arrange themselves differently. Mussolini came out of the extreme left-wing of Italian socialism. Fascism used masses, propaganda, mystifications, and force according to Marxian prescription. As for Na-

Marx Memorial Headstone, Highgate Cemetery, London

zis, "Nazi" was the simplified acronym for National Socialist German Workers' Party. It was an accurate name for the party Marx would like to have led in Germany in 1848–49, nationalistic, socialistic, and as anti-Semitic as tactically useful. With all their non-Marxian and anti-Marxian elements, fascism and Nazism owed a great deal to Marxism. Their consequences, moreover, have moved the world all the closer to socialist internationalism.

Marx's failures suggest his human inability to conceive of all of the multifariousness of real existence. His system, like any other system a lie according to Nietzsche, assumed and then constructed a terribly simplified world. Marx left out or misrepresented innumerable factors which insist upon influencing events on their own terms, thus personality (including his own), the shape and changes in the world's wealth, governmental forms, population and population growth, wars, ideas, art, conscience, psychology, self-interest and altruism, religion, nationality and nationalism, science and invention, generalization of education, interactions among all these and interactions among individuals, classes, regions, races, cultures; freedom and the unknown. The list is as immense as Marx's presumption. Marx was not unaware of what he was doing. When, in *Capital*, he tried to collapse all phenomena into the material of materialism, he contradicted himself by investing the material with metaphysical qualities. But that was pitifully inadequate, and the Marxian system, unable to account for most of reality, is condemned to operate inefficiently in many areas, most particularly and painfully in those having to do with the integrity of the human being.[14]

Yet Marx did see greatly and correctly. He saw the agglomeration of industrial empire, the world as workshop to be managed. Since his time the forces controlled by the captains of industry, the Fords, Rockefellers, the anonymous bankers, have grown immensely. Their huge private establishments could manipulate governments while suffering reverses that gravely damaged national economies. The Great Depression and its nefarious consequences in unemployment, general suffering, and war, were unanswerable arguments for governmental coordination, which could also assure democratic control. John Maynard Keynes hypnotically rationalized such a policy in his *General Theory of Employment, Interest, and Money*, published in February 1936. If Marx had demanded infinitely more than that, the West would respond to him, although too slowly, with a sensible Keynesian half-measure. Meanwhile, in the 1930s, non-Communist countries like Mexico and Turkey imitated Stalin's Five-Year Plans. It was another kind of half-measure; the countries remained unsocialized and the results were not so tremendous, but the price was not so high as to require national suffering.

After World War II the ideas of Marx & Stalin and Keynes took united effect in the form of national economic planning plus subtly conducted fiscal and monetary policy. A classic example of the first was the Monnet Plan of France, introduced in 1947, to provide governmental direction for the nation's reconstruction. Examples of the second were the United States Employment Act of 1946 and similar measures in many other nations—all asserting in one way or another, as the British White Paper of 1944 put it, that "the government accepts as one of their primary aims and responsibilities the maintenance of a high and stable level of employment after the war."[15] In all these cases, production planning and Keynesian fiscal-and-monetary planning were fused. Today, planning is normal procedure in all nations. Marx had seen very well.

Marx, demanding the impossible, had shown the world how much was possible. A Marxist can look upon the Keynesian solution as only a temporary halting place. Larger corporations must obey governmental direction to such an extent that they are best described as semisocialized, and more increases in the concentration of private economic power lead to more political interventions. In the major Western nations, in Italy, France, and England, government has become, sometimes by plan, sometimes by unplanned circumstances, an important owner of great industrial firms. This means socialism, but then the real difference between governmental possession and governmental direction is hard to determine. In one way or another it all amounts to socialism; the only question is the rate. But the rate *is* important. If it does not change radically in the West, we can leave the question of the benefits and evils of the ultimate socialism to our grandchildren, if any, or theirs, if any, who would be living in circumstances too much changed for us to predict.

Now the Marxian ideal governs the Communist third of the world and pervades the West even as Western governments make overt war against Marxian states. Marxism, revolutionary or peaceful, shows no signs of retreating. On the contrary, the Third World wants the kind of progress it promises. In the West itself the businessman accepts the primacy of government. The government planner speaks Marx's language as his own. The Western intellectual, oriented instinctively to the left like the young Marx, indoctrinates himself and others. We are all Marxists in a Marxian world.

CHRONOLOGY
NOTES
BIBLIOGRAPHY
INDEX

CHRONOLOGY

KARL MARX IN ACT AND THOUGHT

1814
  November 2–June 11,   Congress of Vienna: Restoration.
    1815

1818
  May 5   Birth of Karl Marx in Trier, the Rhineland.

1824
  August 26   Baptism of Karl with brothers and sisters.

1835
  September 24   Karl Marx graduates from secondary school.
  October 15   Matriculates, University of Bonn.

1836
  Summer   Becomes engaged to Jenny von Westphalen.
  October 22   Matriculates, University of Berlin.

1837
  Early in year   Breakdown in health, convalescence outside of
                                   Berlin.
  November 10   Letter to father on studies, writings, travails,
                                   illness.

1838
  May 10   Death of father.

1841
  March 30   Marx withdraws from University of Berlin.
  April 15   Awarded doctorate by University of Jena for
                                   dissertation on philosophy of Democritus
                                   and Epicurus.

1842

May 5–19	First published article, on press freedom, in *Rheinische Zeitung.*
October 15	Named editor, *Rheinische Zeitung.*
October 25–November 3	Marx's article series attacking government on law against wood-gathering.

1843

January 15–20	Last important article, protest against impoverishment of Moselle winegrowers.
January 19	Prussian government decides to suppress *RZ*, effective April 1.
March 17	Marx resigns editorship.
Late May	Accepts offer of coeditorship of *Deutsch-Französische Jahrbücher.*
June 19	Marries Jenny von Westphalen.
Summer	Reads Hegel and historians of French Revolution.
September	Writes programmatic letter for *Jahrbücher*: its objective—unite German philosophy, French revolutionary experience, and socialist thought.
Mid-October	Arrives in Paris.

1844

End February	*Jahrbücher*'s first and last issue, which carries Marx's articles "On the Jewish Question" and "A Contribution to the Critique of Hegel's *Philosophy of Right.*"
April–August	Marx reads economics; writes the *Economic-Philosophical Manuscripts* (first published 1932); discovers idea of materialism.
May 1	Birth of Jenny Marx.
Late spring	Marx enters into association with Paris *Vorwärts!*
Summer	"Marx has dived into the local communism."
August 7, 10	Marx's article in *Vorwärts!* celebrating Silesian weavers' strike.
End August–early September	Ten-day visit of Friedrich Engels with Marx.
September–October	Marx writes first book, *The Holy Family*, attacking philosophy of withdrawal from world (published February 1845).

1845

Mid-January	Marx ordered to leave France.
February 3	Leaves Paris for Brussels.

Spring	Writes "Theses on Feuerbach": idea of super-seding philosophy with revolution (published 1888).
July–August	Marx and Engels visit England.
September 6	Birth of Laura Marx.
September–summer 1846	Marx writes *The German Ideology*: idea of materialism (published 1932).
December 1	Renounces Prussian citizenship.

1846

February	Marx organizes Communist Correspondence Committee.
March 30	Purge of Wilhelm Weitling.
August–January 1848	Engels in Paris attempting and failing to capture radical workers' groups for the CCC.

1847

January 3	Founding of *Deutsche Brüsseler Zeitung*, vehicle for CCC articles by summer.
January	CCC joins League of the Just, radical workers' group of London.
January–April	Marx writes *The Misery of Philosophy*, attacking Proudhon's economics (published July).
June 2–9	League of the Just transforms self into Communist League, London congress.
August 5	Marx transforms CCC into branch of Communist League.
Late August	Marx organizes German Workers' Educational Association of Brussels.
November 15	Elected vice president, Brussels Democratic Association.
November 30–December 8	Second Communist League congress; adoption of Marx's program.
December 17	Birth of Edgar Marx (d. April 6, 1855).

1848

January (–February?)	Marx writes *Communist Manifesto* (published late February).
February 22	Revolution of 1848 breaks out in Paris.
End February or early March	Central Committee of Communist League transfers powers to Marx, who organizes new Central Committee in Brussels, March 3.
March 4	Marx arrested, expelled from Belgium to France.

About March 12   Marx, formally named president, reconsti-
                                  tutes Central Committee of Communist
                                  League, Paris.
March   Revolutions break out in German Confedera-
                                  tion.
April 6   Marx and Engels leave Paris for Cologne.
April   Marx joins Cologne Democratic Association.
May 31   The editor Marx begins publishing the *Neue
                                  Rheinische Zeitung.*
June   Marx dissolves Communist League.
June   Joins Committee of Six, representing three left-
                                  wing Rhineland groups.
Mid-August   Attends Congress of Rhine Democrats.
September 13   Marx's associates organize mass demonstra-
                                  tion, Cologne; elect Committee of Public
                                  Safety.
September 17   Committee of Public Safety leads mass dem-
                                  onstration, Worringen, outside of Co-
                                  logne.
September 28–Octo-   State of siege and suspension of *NRZ.*
    ber 12

1849
February 8, 9   Marx acquitted of charges of libel and sedition
                                  at two trials.
April 15   Resigns from Rhine Committee of Demo-
                                  cratic Associations.
May 18   Publication of final issue of *NRZ,* the "Red
                                  Edition."
June 3   Marx arrives in Paris.
August   Ordered to leave Paris.
Late August   Arrives in London.
Late August or early   Joins reconstituted Communist League and
    September   German Workers' Educational Association;
                                  leads émigré aid committee of latter.
November 5   Birth of Heinrich Edmund, called Guido, Marx
                                  (d. November 19, 1850).
About November 10   Engels arrives in London.

1850
January   Marx orders organization of secret sections of
                                  Communist League in Cologne and else-
                                  where in southern Germany.
March   March Address of Communist League orders
                                  workers to carry out *permanent* revolution.
March–November   Marx publishes *NRZ: Politisch-Ökonomische
                                  Revue,* which carries his analysis *The Class
                                  Struggles in France, 1848–1850.*

Spring	Marx family moves to Soho after brief stay in Chelsea.
June	Marx obtains reader's ticket to Reading Room of British Museum.
July	Changes his mind about the possibility of immediate revolution.
September 15	Transfers powers of Communist League Central Committee to Cologne section Central Committee in order to hinder premature revolutionary action; retains leadership of small London section.
September 17	Resigns from German Workers' Educational Association.
November	Engels moves to Manchester to join father's firm, Ermen & Engels.
December	Marx family settles at 28 Dean Street, Soho.

1851

February 23	Follower of Marx ejected from émigré banquet.
March 28	Birth of Franziska Marx (d. April 14, 1852).
May 10	Members of Communist League Cologne section arrested.
May–December	Marx works in British Museum.
June 23	Birth of Frederick Demuth, Marx's illegitimate son.
August 7	Marx begins association with New York *Daily Tribune* as London correspondent.
December–March 1852	Writes *The 18th Brumaire of Louis Napoleon* (published in New York German-language weekly, May 1852).

1852

May–June	Writes *The Great Men of the Emigration* (first published 1960).
Beginning October– end December	Writes *Revelations on the Communist Trial in Cologne* (published January 1853).
October 4–November 12	Trial of Cologne communists: seven convictions, four acquittals.
November 17	Marx dissolves his London Communist League section.

1853

March	Marx ill with liver complaint.

1855

January 16	Birth of Eleanor Marx.
February	Marx protests election of populist Alexander Herzen to émigré committee.

March   Suffers eye inflammation.

1856
April 16   Marx's speech at anniversary of Chartist news-
                               paper; subject: inevitability of revolution.
Early October   Marx family moves to villa on Grafton Ter-
                               race, north London.

1857
January–July   Marx suffers series of illnesses reducing ability
                               to work.
August–March 1858   Writes manuscript later entitled *Grundrisse*
                               (published 1939–41).

1858
February–May   Marx ill with liver complaint, other ailments.
August–January 1859   Writes *Critique of Political Economy* (published
                               June 1859).

1859
December–February   Begins writing draft of *Capital*, but breaks off.
  1860

1860
February–mid-1861   Marx conducts quarrel with another German
                               émigré; writes *Herr Vogt* (August–Novem-
                               ber; published December 1860).
November   Suffers various distresses, including tooth-
                               aches.

1861
January   Marx ill with liver complaint.
January–October   *Tribune* suspends publishing Marx's articles.
March–April   Marx visits Ferdinand Lassalle in Berlin.
April 10   Requests restoration of Prussian citizenship;
                               refused.
August–June 1863   Marx writes manuscript comprising first draft
                               of *Capital* and *Theories of Surplus Value*.

1862
July   Lassalle visits Marx in London.
September   Marx visits mother for last time.

1863
February–May   Suffers from eye, liver, and lung ailments.
May 23   Lassalle founds All-German Workers' Associa-
                               tion (AGWA) as socialist workers' party,
                               Leipzig.
June 7–8   Founding of Union of German Workers' As-
                               sociations, Frankfurt.

September–December	Marx has attack of boils.
December 2	Death of Marx's mother, who wills him £700.

1864

March	Marx family moves to larger villa, at Modena Villas, later called Maitland Park Road, short distance from previous house.
May 9	Death of Wilhelm Wolff, who wills Marx £824.
August	Marx suffers from respiratory ailment and boils.
August 31	Death of Lassalle.
September 28	Marx attends founding meeting of First International.
October–November	Writes Inaugural Address of International.

1865

February–March	Marx ill with boils.
May–June; June 20	Writes and delivers lecture "Wages, Price, and Profit" before International's General Council.
September	London conference of International, dominated by Marx, prepares Geneva Congress.

1866

January	Marx begins to prepare manuscript of volume 1 of *Capital* for publication; suffers bad attack of boils: "I hope the bourgeoisie will remember my boils as long as it lives."
April–December	Ill with most of his usual ailments.
August 19	August Bebel and Wilhelm Liebknecht organize Saxon Peoples' Party.
September	Geneva Congress of International.

1867

February	International helps Paris bronze workers win strike.
May 20	Johann Baptist von Schweitzer elected president of AGWA.
August 31	Seven socialists elected to North German Reichstag.
September	Lausanne Congress of International.
September 14	Publication of volume 1 of *Capital—Das Kapital*—in Germany.
November	Marx suffers from attack of boils after period of remission.

1868

January–May	Marx suffers from renewed attack of boils.
Spring	International helps Geneva building workers win concessions.

April 2	Laura Marx marries Paul Lafargue.
September	Brussels Congress of International.
November	Russian populists in Swiss exile make contact with Marx.

1869

January–May	Marx variously ill.
June 30	Engels retires from Ermen & Engels.
August 7–9	Bebel and Liebknecht found Social Democratic Workers' Party.
September	Basel Congress of International.
Late October	Marx begins to study Russian.

1870

January–April	Marx variously ill, undergoes two operations for abscessed boils.
February	Marx begins to draw annuity of £350, purchased for him by Engels.
March 12	Marx becomes corresponding secretary for Russia in International's General Council.
July 19–23	Writes International's First Address on Franco-Prussian War.
September 6–9	Writes Second Address.
Late September	Engels settles near Marx in north London.

1871

January	Marx experiences onset of virtually continual illness, including bronchitis.
March 18–May 28	The Paris Commune.
March 24	Schweitzer resigns as AGWA president.
April–late May	Marx writes three drafts of Third Address, *The Civil War in France*, published June 13.
September 17–23	London conference of the International to prepare The Hague Congress.

1872

April 8	Publication of Russian translation of *Capital*.
Spring–November 1875	Publication in installments of first French edition of *Capital*.
September 2–7	The Hague Congress of International: de facto dissolution.
September 8	Marx speech suggesting possible instances where revolution could be avoided.
October	Jenny Marx marries Charles Longuet.

1873

| Spring | Marx suffers intensification of his ailments. |
| May–June | Corrects parts of French translation of *Capital*. |

November	Suffers nervous collapse: end of ability to do sustained work.

1874

August	Requests British citizenship; refused.
August–September	Marx at Karlsbad for the cure, first of three annual visits.

1875

March	Marx family moves to another house on Maitland Park Road.
Early May	Marx writes *Critique of the Gotha Program* (published 1891).
May 22–27	Unification congress of AGWA and Social Democratic Workers' Party to found greater Social Democratic Workers' Party.

1876

July 15	International formally dissolved, Philadelphia.

1877

January 3–July 7, 1878	Engels' *Anti-Dühring* published serially in newspaper *Vorwärts!*, Berlin; published as book, 1878.

1878

October 18	Antisocialist law passed by Reichstag.

1879

October	Union of the Party of Socialist Workers of France founded; adopts Marxian program in consultation with Marx, May 1880.

1880

Summer–June 1881	Association of Marx with Henry M. Hyndman.
November	Bebel and Eduard Bernstein visit Marx and Engels, retain their support.

1881

February 28–March 8	Letter exchange of populist Vera Zasulich and Marx on Russia's route to socialism. Russian populists assassinate Czar Alexander II.
June	Hyndman founds Democratic Federation (future Social Democratic Federation), first British Marxian party.
December 2	Death of Jenny Marx.
End 1881–early 1882	Marx carries out research on Russian peasant emancipation of 1861, last research project.

1882

January 21   Marx's introduction to second Russian edition of *Communist Manifesto*: Russia as "vanguard of revolutionary action."

February–September   Marx on trip for health, North Africa, Europe.

1883

January 11   Death of Jenny Marx Longuet.

March 14   Death of Marx.

March 17   Burial of Marx.

September   Georgi Plekhanov founds Emancipation of Labor, first Russian Marxian party, in Geneva.

1885

May   Engels publishes *Capital*, volume 2.

1889

July   Founding meeting of the Second International, Paris.

1890

January 25   Reichstag refuses to renew antisocialist law.

February 20   Social Democrats win 1.4 million votes, become second largest party in Germany.

1894

October   Engels publishes *Capital*, volume 3.

1895

Spring   Lenin meets Plekhanov in Geneva, wins his patronage.

August 5   Death of Engels.

1896

October   Bernstein begins publishing two-year article series with evolutionary conception of Marxism in Social Democratic journal (published as book, March 1899).

1898

March 31   Suicide of Eleanor Marx.

1902

March   Lenin publishes *What Is To Be Done?*, with idea of professional and uncompromising revolutionary party.

1903
July   Second Russian Social Democratic congress:
                              Lenin splits party and organizes Bolshe-
                              viks.

1905
October–December   Revolution of 1905.

1911
November 20   Suicide of Paul and Laura Marx Lafargue.

1917
March 8–12   Russian czarist government overthrown.
November 7–8   Russian Provisional Government overthrown
                              by Lenin's Bolsheviks.

1919
March   Lenin founds the Third International, Mos-
                              cow.

1929
January 28   Death of Frederick Demuth.
April   Stalin begins first Five-Year Plan.

1949
October 1   Proclamation of the Chinese People's Repub-
                              lic.

NOTES

PREFACE

1. *The Marx-Engels Reader*, ed. Robert C. Tucker, 2nd ed. (New York, 1978), pp. 681, 682.

CHAPTER I. BEGINNINGS

1. See the "Note on Sources," in the Bibliography. Details of Marx's life chiefly from the three German-language editions of the collected works: *Historisch-Kritische Gesamtausgabe* (hereafter *MEGA*), which was never completed, the *Werke*, and the *Gesamtausgabe (MEGA)* (hereafter *New MEGA*); the English-language *Collected Works* (hereafter *Works*), which is in process of being published; *Karl Marx: Chronik seines Lebens in Einzeldaten*, published by the Marx-Engels-Lenin Institut (Moscow, 1934), *Mohr und General: Erinnerungen an Marx und Engels*, published by the Institut für Marxismus-Leninismus ([East] Berlin, 1964), Heinz Monz, *Karl Marx: Grundlagen der Entwicklung zu Leben u. Werk* (Trier, 1973), and Maximilien Rubel and Margaret Manale, *Marx without Myth: A Chronological Study of His Life and Work* (New York, 1976); the biographies: Franz Mehring, *Karl Marx: Geschichte seines Lebens* (1918; reprint ed., Frankfurt, 1964) and, in English, *Karl Marx: The Story of His Life* (Ann Arbor, 1962); Boris Nicolaievsky and Otto Maenchen-Helfen, *Karl Marx: Man and Fighter*, tr. Gwenda David and Eric Mosbacher (Philadelphia, 1936); Isaiah Berlin, *Karl Marx: His Life and Environment* (London, 1939); Robert Payne, *Marx: A Biography* (New York, 1968), David McLellan, *Karl Marx: His Life and Thought* (London, 1973), and Saul K. Padover, *Karl Marx: An Intimate Biography* (New York, 1978).

2. Monz, *Karl Marx*, pp. 245–47; quotation, p. 245. The Monz work is the product of a search in the Trier archives of 1814–48, ibid., p. 23.

3. Ibid., pp. 247–48, 34.

4. Ibid., p. 245.

5. Ibid., p. 245. A note appended to the baptismal record said that Henriette had not joined her children because her parents were still living. But they were living when she then underwent baptism on Nov. 20, 1825. Eduard, a son born later, was baptized in 1826.

6. A recent study by a regional historian concludes that the Trier Jews resented Heinrich Marx's conversion. There was no evidence of social intercourse and another negative suggestion in the fact that Heinrich Marx represented the authorities in a suit against the Jewish community for allegedly unpaid taxes, Richard Laufner, "Heinrich Marx und die Regulierung der Steuerschulden der trierschen Judenschaft," in Richard Laufner and Albert Rauch, *Die Familie Marx und die Trierer Judenschaft*, Schriften aus dem Karl-Marx-Haus, booklet 14 (1975).

7. In the newspaper *Vorwärts!*, issue of Aug. 7, 1844, attacking the views of Arnold Ruge, *MEGA*, I, 3:4; *Werke*, 1:393; *Works*, 3:190. The *MEGA* edition is divided into series I and III. "I, 3:4" means page 4 of volume 3 of series I.

8. Letter from Bad Ems, Aug. 12–14, *MEGA*, I, 1(1):206; *Works*, 1:675 (not in *Werke, Ergänzungsband*, 1). The first *MEGA* series begins with two separate volumes called "half-volumes." "*MEGA*, I, 1(1):206" thus means page 206 of the first half-volume of the first series.

9. Letter of Nov. 10, 1837, *MEGA*, I, 1(2):220; *Werke, Ergänzungsband*, 1:11; *Works*, 1:20.

10. For a carefully documented and clearly reasoned psychoanalytical study of Marx's life and works see Arnold Künzli, *Karl Marx: Eine Psychographie* (Vienna, Frankfurt, Zurich, 1966); on relations with his parents, see especially pp. 33–140. Another psychological study, compounded with an intellectual biography, is Jerrold Seigel, *Marx's Fate: The Shape of a Life* (Princeton, 1978); parent-son relations, pp. 43–59.

11. Letter, Dec. 15, 1863, *Werke*, 30:643–44.

12. According to his youngest daughter, Eleanor, who got the story from her elderly aunts, *Mohr und General*, pp. 272–73.

13. According to Eleanor Marx, quoted in McLellan, *Karl Marx*, p. 10.

14. Preserved and reprinted, along with the schoolmasters' comments, in *MEGA*, I, 1(2):164–84. Essays without comments, *Werke, Ergänzungsband*, 1:591–601; *Works*, 1:3–9, 636–42.

15. *MEGA*, I, 1(2):164, 166; *Werke, Ergänzungsband*, 1:591, 593; *Works*, 1:3, 7.

16. *MEGA*, I, 1(2):166, 167; *Werke, Ergänzungsband*, 1:593, 594; *Works*, 1:7.

17. *MEGA*, I, 1(2):167; *Werke, Ergänzungsband*, 1:594; *Works*, 1:8.

18. Letter, Nov. 18–29, 1835, to Karl, at the University of Bonn, *MEGA*, I, 1(2):186; *Werke, Ergänzungsband*, 1:617; *Works*, 1:647.

19. For more details and documentation see Nicolaievsky and Maenchen-Helfen, *Karl Marx*, pp. 10–15.
20. The essay, *MEGA*, I, 1(2):168–70; quotations, pp. 169–70. Also *Werke, Ergänzungsband*, 1:595–97; quotations, pp. 596–97. *Works*, 1:639–42; quotations, 640–42.
21. Essay and quotations, *MEGA*, I, 1(2):171–74; *Werke, Ergänzungsband*, 1:598–601; *Works*, 1:636–39.
22. *MEGA*, I, 1(2):174. The pastor had added in his comment on the religious essay, "It merits commendation even though the essential of the union in question is not at all indicated, its basis conceived only from one aspect, and its necessity only imperfectly demonstrated." Similarly, the headmaster found the German composition rich in ideas, but only "fairly good" in sum, and suffering from Karl's "exaggerated desire for rare and imaginative expressions," ibid., p. 167.
23. McLellan, *Karl Marx*, p. 10.
24. *MEGA*, I, 1(2):184; *Works*, 1:644.
25. Heinrich to Karl Marx, letter of March 2, 1837, *MEGA*, I, 1(2):202–5; quotations, p. 202. Also *Werke, Ergänzungsband*, 1:626–29; quotations, p. 626. *Works*, 1:670–73; quotations, p. 670.
26. *MEGA*, I, 1(2):205–8; *Works*, 1:674–77 (not in *Werke, Ergänzungsband*, 1). This was the letter in which Heinrich referred to "your admirable mother."
27. *MEGA*, I, 1(2):223–28; *Werke, Ergänzungsband*, 1:635–40; *Works*, 1:685–91.
28. Heinrich to Karl Marx, *MEGA*, I, 1(2):228–30; *Works*, 1:691–94. In a letter from Henriette Marx dated Feb. 15–16, 1838, Heinrich added: "Dear Karl, I send you a few words of greeting, I cannot do much yet. Your father, Marx." *Works*, 1:694.
29. The letter was dated May 10, 1838, the day of Heinrich's death. Writing to Karl in Berlin, she had one subject: a recent face-to-face quarrel with him. If correctly dated, the letter would suggest that Karl had indeed been in Trier, the most likely place for a meeting, but would be clear evidence that Karl was not at the deathbed. *New MEGA*, III, 1T:331. This means page 331 of volume 1 of textual material (as compared with the accompanying volume 1 of notes) of series III. For more details see the "Note on Sources."
30. *Karl Marx: Chronik*, p. 3.
31. *Werke*, 27: endnote 309; letters of Marx to Arnold Ruge, his future associate, Feb. 10 and Mar. 5, 1842, ibid., pp. 266–67, 268–69; *Works*, 1:381–83.
32. Letter, Marx to Ruge, July 9, 1842, *Werke*, 27:405; *Works*, 1:389–91.
33. Letter of Nov. 10, 1837, *MEGA*, I, 1(2):213–21; quotation, p. 218. Also in *Werke, Ergänzungsband*, 1:3–12; quotation, p. 8. *Works*, 1:10–21; quotation, p. 18. Marx actually said he had written the preface on printers' sheets (galleys), which would be much larger than normal pages, but that is unlikely.

34. Poems, play, and the novel fragments, *MEGA*, I, 1(2):4–89; quotation, pp. 68–69. Also *Works*, 1:517–632; quotation, p. 599. A few of the poems, but not the celebration of Prometheus, also in *Werke, Ergänzungsband*, 1:602–15.

35. *Werke, Ergänzungsband*, 2:301; *Works*, 2:336. The lecturer, Edgar Bauer, was a brother of Marx's friend Bruno Bauer, and a member of the Doktorklub (see text, below). Friedrich Engels, who had not yet met Marx, collaborated on the poem, which described various members of the group.

36. Letter of Friedrich Köppen (who later wrote a well-regarded study of the Tibetan religion) to Marx, June 3, 1841, *MEGA*, I, 1(2):257. About the dedication, see Helmut Hirsch, "Karl Friedrich Köppen: Der Intimste Berliner Freund Marxens," *International Review for Social History* 1(1936):323–26. Köppen's pamphlet was a polemical defense of Frederick the Great as a ruthless destroyer of medieval survivals.

37. Dated Sept. 2, 1841, *MEGA*, I, 1(2):261.

38. Dissertation and notes (plus the editors' German translations of Greek and Latin passages), *Werke, Ergänzungsband*, 1:260–373; Marx's research notes (with translation), ibid., pp. 16–255. Also *Works*, 1:25–106, 405–509. This material, but without the translations, also in *MEGA*, I, 1(1):3–144. Chapters 4 and 5 of the ten chapters of the dissertation are missing from the copyist's manuscript, the source of the published versions. We must assume they were lost, although Marx, as in the case of *Capital*, could leave a work unfinished and trust it would be acceptable.

39. *Werke, Ergänzungsband*, 1:267; *MEGA*, I, 1(1):18; *Works*, 1:35.

40. *Werke, Ergänzungsband*, 1:305; *MEGA*, I, 1(1):52; *Works*, 1:73.

41. *Werke, Ergänzungsband*, 1:305; *MEGA*, I, 1(1):52; *Works*, 1:73.

42. *Werke, Ergänzungsband*, 1:284; *MEGA*, I, 1(1):33; *Works*, 1:52.

43. Letter of Nov. 18–29, 1835, *MEGA*, I, 1(2):186; *Werke, Ergänzungsband*, 1:617; *Works*, 1:647.

44. *Werke, Ergänzungsband*, 1:372; *MEGA*, I, 1(1):144; *Works*, 1:104–5.

45. Marx's covering letter and reproduction of doctorate, *Werke, Ergänzungsband*, 1:374, 377; the dean's letter, *MEGA*, I, 1(1):254–55. Dean's letter and reproduction of doctorate, *Works*, 1:705–6, opposite p. 703.

46. On his sympathies and intellectual interests see his letter to his brother, Otto, Jan. 25, 1843, *Rheinische Briefe und Akten zur Geschichte der politischen Bewegung 1830–1850*, ed. Joseph Hansen (Essen, 1919), 1:411.

47. According to a letter of the Prussian minister of the interior to the chief administrative officer (*Regierungspräsident*) of Cologne, Jan. 31, 1842, ibid., p. 318; editor's account of background, 318n.

48. Published, May 5–19, 1842, *Werke*, 1:28–77; *Works*, 1:132–81.

49. Letter of Otto to Ludolf Camphausen, May 26, 1842, Hansen, *Rheinische Briefe*, 1:344.

50. Letter to Arnold Ruge, July 9, 1842, *MEGA*, I, 1(2):279; *Werke*, 27:407; *Works*, 1:391.

51. *MEGA*, I, 1(2):280; *Werke*, 27:409; *Works*, 1:392.

52. Letter to Ruge, Nov. 30, 1842, *MEGA*, I, 1(2):286; *Werke*, 27:412; *Works*, 1:394.
53. *Rheinische Zeitung*, Oct. 16, 1842, *MEGA*, I, 1(1):263; *Werke*, 1:108; *Works*, 1:220.
54. *Rheinische Zeitung*, Oct. 25–Nov. 3, *Werke*, 1:109–47; *Works*, 1:224–63.
55. *Werke*, 1:172–99; quotations, pp. 188, 190; *Works*, 1:332–58; quotations, pp. 347, 349.
56. Letter of Ludolf to Otto Camphausen, Jan. 25, 1843, and report of the *Ministerialsekretär* Wilhelm von Saint-Paul to his superior in Berlin, *Regierungsrat* (Government Councillor) Bitter, in the Ministry of the Interior, Jan. 31, 1843, Hansen, *Rheinische Briefe*, 1:410–11, 418–21.
57. An important source for details of the whole episode is Hansen, *Rheinische Briefe*, pp. 401–506 passim.
58. Published in the *RZ*, Jan. 4, 1843. See Nicolaievsky and Maenchen-Helfen, *Karl Marx*, pp. 60–64.
59. Marx retaliated by punishing the censor personally. Years later Marx happily recalled that the man, invited with wife and daughter to the governor's ball, waited in vain for the newspaper's proofs. Desperately late, the censor at last had his carriage driven to Marx's lodgings, where Marx had the satisfaction of telling him that there were no proofs since the paper was not appearing the next day. Marx's account, as given to Wilhelm Blos, a young Social Democrat, "Karl Marx in Leipzig," in *Mohr und General*, p. 352.
60. Letter (mentioned above, n. 56) to *Regierungsrat* Bitter, Jan. 31, 1843, Hansen, *Rheinische Briefe*, 1:418–21. Saint-Paul said he had arrived the day before.
61. Ibid., p. 402*n.*, pp. 402–5; quotation, p. 402. The Prussian government, according to its correspondence, had not been as certain as the language of its stop order. On Feb. 4 the editor of the *RZ*'s rival, the *Kölnische Zeitung*, warned Saint-Paul that everybody in the area was unhappy about the suppression (ibid., pp. 424–25). Besides being concerned about local ill feelings, the government held to the policy that had led it to support the *RZ*'s founding. In a letter to his chief on Feb. 10, Saint-Paul analyzed the *Kölnische Zeitung*'s monopolistic position and emphasized the need for another newspaper (ibid., pp. 429–30). On Feb. 27 he was hopeful that the *RZ*'s shareholders, who had given off signs of restiveness, might yet remove its directors and editor. On Mar. 2, discussing Marx and his situation, Saint-Paul refused to be discouraged about the considerable problem of replacing him with an acceptable and effective editor (also in letters to his superior, ibid., pp. 466–69, 472–73). On Mar. 27, however, the three Prussian ministers responsible for censorship, giving detailed reasons in the sense of the original order, upheld the decision to suppress the *RZ* (government communication to *RZ* shareholders, ibid., pp. 492–97).
62. Minutes, ibid., pp. 436–47; *Works*, 1:712–24.
63. Quoted, Hansen, *Rheinische Briefe*, 1:441; *Works*, 1:717.

64. Hansen, *Rheinische Briefe*, 1:433; not in the *Works*.
65. Petitions, Hansen, *Rheinische Briefe*, 1:414–16, (in part) 448*n*.; *Works*, 1:710–11, 725–26. Quotation, Hansen, *Rheinische Briefe*, 1:448*n*.; *Works*, 1:725. Accounts of petitions, Hansen, *Rheinische Briefe*, 1:414*n*., 448*n*., 463*n*.
66. Hansen, *Rheinische Briefe*, 1:472–73.
67. Letter to superior, dated (by the editor) "a few days after" Mar. 2, ibid., p. 473*n*.
68. Marx's statement, published in the issue of Mar. 18: "The undersigned makes known that he has withdrawn from the editorial staff of the *Rheinische Zeitung* as of today because of the *present censorship situation.* . . . Cologne, March 17, 1843. . . . Dr. Marx." *MEGA*, I, 1(1):393; *Werke*, 1:200; *Works*, 1:376.
69. To his superior, Hansen, *Rheinische Briefe*, 1:490.
70. Letter to Ruge, Jan. 25, 1843, *MEGA*, I, 1(2):294; *Werke*, 27:415; *Works*, 1:397.

Chapter 2. The Revolutionary Materials

1. See Lucien de La Hodde, *Histoire des sociétés secrètes et du parti républicain de 1830 à 1848* (Paris, 1850). Some details here are taken from La Hodde, who joined one of the societies early in the 1830s, became a police agent and, by the 1840s, had risen to the rank of a republican leader. His *Histoire* is detailed, generally credible, and confirmed on important issues by other sources. See also Gabriel Perreux, *Au Temps des sociétés secrètes* (Paris, 1931); George Morange, *Les Idées communistes dans les sociétés secrètes et dans la presse sous la monarchie de juillet* (Paris, 1905), and M. Gisquet, *Mémoires*, 4 vols. (Paris, 1840). Gisquet was prefect of police in Paris from 1831 to 1836.
2. Quoted in Paul Thureau-Dangin, *Histoire de la monarchie de juillet*, 7 vols. (Paris, 1884–92), 1:209.
3. La Hodde, *Histoire des sociétés secrètes*, p. 38.
4. The earlier names suggested the importance of revolutionary inspiration; the names Families and Seasons emphasized the *organization*. The Society of the Seasons, thus, was divided into four major divisions, seasons, which were divided into the subgroups months and, finally, weeks. How much of this structure was actually realized is unclear.
5. La Hodde himself, author of *Histoire des sociétés secrètes*.
6. The republicans once entered into a social issue. In fact it was the connection that had been established with the silk weavers of Lyons, who were resisting lower piecework rates, that caused the disastrous insurrection of the Rights of Man in 1834. The weavers carried out a much superior operation, which became a five-day street battle in which 170 weavers and 130 soldiers died. The Paris rising had been meant to be coordinated with the Lyons action, but started the day after it was over.

7. See Samuel Bernstein, *Auguste Blanqui and the Art of Insurrection* (London, 1971), and Edward S. Mason, "Blanqui and Communism," *Political Science Quarterly* 44 (Dec. 1929):496–527.

8. See, e.g., Paul Louis, *Histoire du socialisme en France, 1789–1945* (Paris, 1946), pp. 24–36.

9. See, e.g., Henri Saint-Simon, *Textes choisis*, ed. Jean Dautry (Paris, 1951); Charles Fourier, *Le Socialisme sociétaire*, ed. Hubert Bourgin (Paris, 1903); and Frank E. Manuel, *The New World of Henri Saint-Simon* (Cambridge, Mass., 1956) and *The Prophets of Paris* (Cambridge, Mass., 1962).

10. Flora Tristan, *Union ouvrière* (Paris, 1843), pp. 4, 80–85.

11. Quoted in Alexandre Zevaès, "L'Agitation communiste de 1840 à 1848," *La Révolution de 1848* 23 (1926):975.

12. Pierre-Joseph Proudhon, *Qu'est-ce la propriété?* (Paris, 1849).

13. On Proudhon see the conveniently brief Denis W. Brogan, *Proudhon* (London, 1934).

14. *Rheinische Zeitung für Politik, Handel und Gewerbe*; photograph of first page of issue of Oct. 16, 1842, *Werke*, 1: opposite p. 106; *Works*, 1: opposite p. 216.

15. David S. Landes, "Technological Change and Development in Western Europe, 1750–1914," in H. J. Habakkuk and M. Postan, *The Cambridge Economic History of Europe*, 6: *The Industrial Revolutions and After: Incomes, Population, and Technological Change* (Cambridge, 1965), part 1:327–28; table, p. 449.

16. Walther G. Hoffman, *British Industry, 1700–1950* (Oxford, 1955), p. 33; table, p. 38.

17. W. O. Henderson, *The Industrialization of Europe, 1780–1914* (New York, 1969), pp. 135–36.

18. Gustav Mayer, *Friedrich Engels: Eine Biographie*, 2: *Engels und der Aufstieg der Arbeiterbewegung in Europa* (The Hague, 1934; English trans., New York, 1936), p. 61; W. O. Henderson, "The Firm of Ermen & Engels in Manchester," *Internationale Wissenschaftliche Korrespondenz*, no. 11–12 (Apr. 1971):1–10.

19. G. W. F. Hegel, *The Phenomenology of Mind: The Science of the Experience of Consciousness*, tr., J. B. Baillie (New York, 1931), pp. 75–76.

20. Ibid., p. 245.

21. Ibid., pp. 375–76.

22. Ibid., p. 513.

23. Ibid., p. 789.

24. Ibid., p. 797. But Hegel peers beyond the ultimate. "Spirit is engulfed in the night of its own self-consciousness. . . . Here, it has to begin all over again. . . . Yet at the same time it commences at a higher level" (ibid., pp. 807–8). Consistently contradictory, Hegel's dialectic extends through all eternity.

25. Ibid., p. 142.

26. Ibid., p. 789.

27. Ibid., p. 797.

28. Herbert Marcuse, *Reason and Revolution: Hegel and the Rise of Social Theory* (New York, 1941), p. 19.

29. Hegel placed the conceptions of the *Phenomenology* in different contexts in his *Philosophy of Right* (1821) and the *Philosophy of History*, the latter a series of lectures which was published from students' notes after his death. Both works were more explicitly political. A suggestion of their sense is given in this sentence from the first: "The state is the actuality of the ethical idea" (*Philosophy of Right*, tr. T. M. Knox [Oxford, 1942], p. 155 [para. 257]). Hegel looked upon the Oriental, Greek, and Roman civilizations as inferior stages to the one represented by Prussia and the Protestant peoples of northern Europe.

30. August von Cieszkowski, *Prolegomena zur Historiosophie* (Berlin, 1838), pp. 131, 172.

31. Quoted in Karl Löwith, *From Hegel to Nietzsche: The Revolution in Nineteenth-Century Thought* (Garden City, N.Y., 1967), p. 89.

32. Ministère des Affaires Étrangères, Paris, Correspondence politique, Archives des affaires étrangères, vol. 800; Allemagne, 1842–43. The journal was *Einundzwanzig Bogen aus der Schweitz*, edited by Georg Herwegh, poet and future friend of Marx.

33. Letter, Jan. 25, 1843, *Werke*, 27:414–15.

34. Letter of Feb. 2, 1843, *New MEGA*, III, 1T:389–91.

35. In his letter of Feb. 2 (cited above), Ruge proposed an annual salary of 550 to 600 (Prussian) thalers, plus about 250 thalers in royalties (the thaler was equivalent to 75 cents; see ch. 3 on comparative values).

36. Mar. 13, 1843, *Werke*, 27:416–17; *Works*, 1:398.

37. See letter of Heinrich to Karl about Karl's lack of discipline, which also mentioned his failure to write to Jenny, Dec. 9, 1837, *MEGA*, I, 1(2);226; *Werke, Ergänzungsband*, 1:639; *Works*, 1:689–90. Also Jenny's letters to Karl, May 10 and June 24, 1838, and letter dated 1839 or 1840 by the editors, *New MEGA*, III, 1T:331, 332–33, 337–39. Other letters of Jenny to Karl, Aug. 10, 1841 and Mar. (no day) 1843, *Werke, Ergänzungsband*, 1:641–43, 644; *Works*, 1:707–9, 727.

38. List of books read and notes on most readings, *MEGA*, I, 1(2):107–36; notes on Hegel's *Philosophy of Right*, *MEGA*, I, 1(1):403–553, *Works*, 3:5–129.

CHAPTER 3. MARX IN PARIS: THE PRACTICE AND THEORY
OF REVOLUTION

1. Letter, Mar. 1843, published in the *Deutsch-Französische Jahrbücher*, *MEGA*, I, 1(1):557; *Werke*, 1:338; *Works*, 3:134.

2. Letter to a friend, July 9, 1844, Arnold Ruge, *Arnold Ruges Briefwechsel und Tagebuchblätter aus den Jahren 1845–1880* (Berlin, 1886), 1:361.

3. Pamphlet, in the file of *La Réforme* preceding the first issue (Aug. 26, 1843), Bibliothèque nationale, Paris.

4. Wolfgang Schieder, *Anfänge der deutschen Arbeiterbewegung* (Stuttgart, 1963), pp. 110–11, 111*n*.
5. Ibid., pp. 97–101. Schieder discounts larger figures for the number of Germans in Paris. In *Karl Marx* (London, 1973), David McLellan gives "almost 100,000" for German workers in Paris alone (pp. 86–87), an impossible magnitude in view of Paris's total population of 800,000. In 1851, Schieder points out (p. 98) that the census, which identified foreigners for the first time, counted 57,000 Germans in all France, including many close to the German frontier.
6. Dr. Paul Hammer, Institut historique allemand, Paris.
7. For the details of their history see especially Schieder, *Anfänge der deutschen Arbeiterbewegung*, and Ernst Schraepler, "Der Bund der Gerechten: Seine Tätigkeit in London, 1840–1847," *Archiv für Sozialgeschichte*, 2 (1962): 5–29. An account by Engels is a valuable document in the history of Marxism, but its character as information is subordinate to its propagandistic purposes: "Zur Geschichte des Bundes der Kommunisten," *Werke*, 8:577–93; Marx and Engels, "History of the Communist League," *Selected Works* (London, 1942–43), 2:3–27.
8. Letter of Ruge to Marx, Sept. 2, 1843, *MEGA*, I, 1(1):315.
9. Letter of Aug. 11–12, 1843, Ruge, *Arnold Ruges Briefwechsel*, 1:323, 324.
10. Arnold Ruge, *Zwei Jahre in Paris* (Leipzig, 1846), 1:69–77, 93–102, 141, 147–48, 151–59.
11. Ibid., p. 159.
12. As Ruge quoted him, ibid., p. 147.
13. Ibid., p. 148.
14. *Karl Marx: Chronik seines Lebens in Einzeldaten* (Moscow, 1934), p. 21.
15. In a letter published in the German newspaper, *Der Social-Demokrat*, Feb. 1, 3, and 5, 1865, *Werke*, 16:27.
16. Pierre Haubtmann, *Marx et Proudhon* (Paris, 1947), pp. 22–23.
17. Letter to a friend, May 20, 1844, Ruge, *Arnold Ruges Briefwechsel*, 1:353.
18. Lucien de La Hodde, *Histoire des sociétés secrètes et du parti républicain de 1830 à 1848* (Paris, 1850).
19. Marx, *Herr Vogt*, *Werke*, 14:439.
20. Account based on primary sources Gustav Mayer, "Der Untergang der *Deutsch-Französischen Jahrbücher* und des Pariser *Vorwärts!*", *Archiv für die Geschichte des Sozialismus und der deutschen Arbeiterbewegung*, 3 (1913): 415–38.
21. According to the Prussian Minister to France, letter to the minister of foreign affairs, Apr. 1, 1844, quoted ibid., p. 423.
22. Auguste Cornu, *Karl Marx et Friedrich Engels* (Paris, 1958), 2:331.
23. Letter of Ruge to Marx, Feb. 2, 1843, *New MEGA*, III, 1T:389–91.
24. Letter of Ruge to the philosopher Ludwig Feuerbach, May 15, 1844, Ruge, *Arnold Ruges Briefwechsel*, 1:344.
25. In the letter to Feuerbach, ibid., p. 342.

26. According to the friend's letters dated June 26 and July 31, 1844, quoted in *Marx: Chronik*, p. 22.
27. Mayer, "Der Untergang," pp. 420, 421.
28. Heinrich Börnstein, *Fünfundsiebzig Jahre in der alten u. neuen Welt* (Leipzig, 1881), 1:350.
29. Account and quotation, ibid., pp. 351–52.
30. Ruge, *Zwei Jahre in Paris*, 1:139–40.
31. Letter to the philosopher Feuerbach, May 15, 1844, Ruge, *Arnold Ruges Briefwechsel*, 1:344–45.
32. Ibid., p. 350; Ruge, *Zwei Jahre in Paris*, 1:140.
33. Issue of July 27, 1844, *MEGA*, I, 3:587–89.
34. *MEGA*, I, 3:16, 19, 23; *Werke*, 1:403, 406, 409; *Works*, 3:200, 203, 206.
35. *MEGA*, I, 3:18; *Werke*, 1:404–5; *Works*, 3:201
36. Letter to a friend, Dec. 6, 1844, Ruge, *Arnold Ruges Briefwechsel*, 1:381.
37. Letter to a friend, Feb. 2, 1870, ibid., 2:346.
38. Heinrich Heine, "The Weavers," *Sämtliche Werke* (Berlin, n.d.), 2:116.
39. The poem, ibid., pp. 202–61; quotation, p. 203.
40. Auguste Cornu, *Karl Marx et Friedrich Engels* (Paris, 1962), 3:34*n*.
41. *Geständnisse, Sämtliche Werke*, 9:182. Heine felt "an uncanny horror" at the sight of the proletariat, "this completely raw mass . . . half-witted sovereign." Yet, referring to their leaders, he added: "These philosophers of revolution and their merciless and determined pupils are the only men in Germany who are alive. The future belongs to them." Ibid., pp. 171–72, 176. On the Marx-Heine relationship see also Jeffrey L. Sammons, *Heinrich Heine: A Modern Biography* (Princeton, N.J., 1979), pp. 260–65.
42. "Die Lage Englands" and "Umrisse zu einer Critique der National-ökonomie," *Werke*, 1:525–49, 499–524; *Works*, 3:444–68, 418–43.
43. "*Geniale Skizze*," in the preface to *Zur Kritik der politischen Ökonomie* (published in 1859), *Werke*, 13:10; *The Marx-Engels Reader*, ed. Robert C. Tucker (New York, 1978), p. 5.
44. The philosopher Ludwig Feuerbach, *Werke*, 27:426; *Works*, 3:355.
45. *MEGA*, I, 3:135; *Werke, Ergänzungsband*, 1:553–54; *Works*, 3:313.
46. *Die Heilige Familie*, *MEGA*, I, 3:256; *Werke*, 2:89; *Works*, 4:84.
47. Schieder, *Anfänge der deutschen Arbeiterbewegung*, pp. 124, 56–57.
48. Letter to a friend, July 9, 1844, Ruge, *Arnold Ruges Briefwechsel*, 1:359.
49. Report to the Ministry of the Interior, Geheimes Staatsarchiv, quoted in Cornu, *Karl Marx et Friedrich Engels*, 3:7–8*n*.
50. Ibid.
51. *Werke*, 1:203–333; *Works*, 3:5–129. For another interpretation see discussion in McLellan, *Marx before Marxism* (New York, 1970), pp. 107–10.
52. Feuerbach then expanded his article, "Preliminary Theses for a Reform of Philosophy," into a book published later in 1843 and translated

as *Principles of the Philosophy of the Future* (New York and Indianapolis, 1966).

53. *Werke*, 1:209, 211; *Works*, 3:11, 12.
54. *Werke*, 1:209–17; *Works*, 3:11–19.
55. As quoted by Marx, *Werke*, 1:243; *Works*, 3:41.
56. *Werke*, 1:230–31; *Works*, 3:29.
57. *Werke*, 1:248; *Works*, 3:46.
58. *Werke*, 1:248, 249; *Works*, 3:46, 47.
59. *Werke*, 1:253; *Works*, 3:50.
60. *Werke*, 1:284; *Works*, 3:80. I have slightly readjusted this hasty sentence of Marx's so that it better expresses his meaning.
61. Discussion, *Werke*, 1:301–18; *Works*, 3:94–111.
62. *Werke*, 1:304–5, 307; *Works*, 3:99, 102.
63. *Werke*, 1:304–5; *Works*, 3:100.
64. *Werke*, 1:326–27; *Works*, 3:121.
65. *MEGA*, I, 1(2):107–36; not in other editions to date.
66. Ibid., pp. 128, 137.
67. *MEGA*, I, 1(1):572–75; *Werke*, 1:343–46; *Works*, 3:141–45.
68. *MEGA*, I, 1(1):557; *Werke*, 1:337; *Works*, 3:133.
69. *MEGA*, I, 1(1):573; *Werke*, 1:344; *Works*, 3:142.
70. *MEGA*, I, 1(1):573; *Werke*, 1:344; *Works*, 3:142.
71. *MEGA*, I, 1(1):576–606; 607–21; *Werke*, 1:347–77, 378–91; *Works*, 3:146–74, 175–87.
72. *MEGA*, I, 1(1):601, 603; *Werke*, 1:372, 374; *Works*, 3:170, 171–72.
73. E.g., McLellan in his *Marx* and an earlier book, on which more later.
74. *MEGA*, I, 1(1):601, 603, 604; *Werke*, 1:372, 374, 375; *Works*, 3:170, 172, 173.
75. *MEGA*, I, 1(1):582; *Werke*, 1:352; *Works*, 3:151.
76. Herbert Marcuse, *Reason and Revolution* (London, 1941), p. 312.
77. *MEGA*, I, 1(1):586, 587; *Werke*, 1:357; *Works*, 3:156.
78. *MEGA*, I, 1(1):618, 617–18, 620; *Werke*, 1:389, 388, 391; *Works*, 3:186, 185, 187.
79. *MEGA*, I, 1(1):609, 611, 614; *Werke*, 1:380, 382, 385; *Works*, 3:177, 179, 182.
80. *MEGA*, I, 1(1):621; *Werke*, 1:391; *Works*, 3:187.
81. Letter of May 5, 1844, Ruge, *Arnold Ruges Briefwechsel*, 1:361.
82. According to a report by the prefect to the head of the government, François Guizot, dated Feb. 17, 1846, Fonds Guizot: Rapports du Préfet de Police, 1843–46, Archives Nationales, Paris, Côte 57.
83. *MEGA*, I, 3:433.
84. Ibid., p. 425.
85. *MEGA*, I, 3:18; *Werke*, 1:404; *Works*, 3:201.
86. *Ökonomisch-Philosophische Manuskripte aus dem Jahre 1844*, *MEGA*, I, 3:33–172; *Werke*, *Ergänzungsband*, 1:467–588; translated under the title *Economic-Philosophical Manuscripts of 1844*, *Works*, 3:231–346. First published in the *MEGA* edition in 1932.

87. *MEGA*, I, 3:466.
88. Ibid., p. 556.
89. Ibid., p. 81; *Werke, Ergänzungsband*, 1:510; *Works*, 3:270.
90. *MEGA*, I, 3:63; *Werke, Ergänzungsband*, 1:494; *Works*, 3:256.
91. *MEGA*, I, 3:504.
92. Robert C. Tucker, *Philosophy and Myth in Karl Marx* (Cambridge, 1961), pp. 204, 219.
93. *MEGA*, I, 3:124; *Werke, Ergänzungsband*, 1:545; *Works*, 3:305.
94. *MEGA*, I, 3:125; *Werke, Ergänzungsband*, 1:546; *Works*, 3:305.
95. *MEGA*, I, 3:91–92; *Werke, Ergänzungsband*, 1:520; *Works*, 3:279–80.
96. Besides Marcuse's *Reason and Revolution*, see Georg Lukács, *Geschichte und Klassenbewusstsein* (1923; reprint, Berlin, 1962), and Karl Korsch, *Marxism and Philosophy* (1923; reprint, New York, 1970). Writing these books, Lukács and Korsch were unaware of the *Economic-Philosophical Manuscripts*, but both emphasized, as has Marcuse, the Hegelian idealism in Marx. In his *Der junge Hegel* (Zurich and Vienna, 1948), Lukács takes account of the *Manuscripts* and sees his older views confirmed in its Feuerbachian Hegelianism.
97. The sixth thesis, *Werke*, 3:6; *Works*, 5:7. The special character of the Feuerbachian-Marxian "humanism" was recognized and emphasized by one Marxist. He was the French Communist intellectual Louis Althusser, who discussed its implications in a series of articles published as a book, *Pour Marx* (Paris, 1965). In his preface Althusser argued that Lukács and Korsch were not only wrong about Marx's humanism but also heretical in their anti-Stalinism and *"gauchisme"* (p. 13). In the article "Marxism and Humanism," published originally in the *Cahiers de l'ISEA* in June 1964, Althusser insisted that Marx's materialism was a denial of humanist man as defined by the Renaissance and specified that Marx had dissolved man into a "social structure" (p. 236).
98. *MEGA*, I, 3:83; *Werke, Ergänzungsband*, 1:511–12; *Works*, 3:272.
99. *MEGA*, I, 3:83; *Werke, Ergänzungsband*, 1:512; *Works*, 3:272.
100. *MEGA*, I, 3:112; *Werke, Ergänzungsband*, 1:534–35; *Works*, 3:294–95.
101. *MEGA*, I, 3:114; *Werke, Ergänzungsband*, 1:536; *Works*, 3:296.
102. *MEGA*, I, 3:118; *Werke, Ergänzungsband*, 1:539; *Works*, 3:299–300.
103. H. M. Hyndman, *The Record of an Adventurous Life* (New York, 1911), p. 251.
104. The earlier materialist was the radical democrat Wilhelm Schulz, who wrote *Die Bewegung der Produktion* (Zurich, 1843), mentioned and quoted, e.g., in the *Manuscripts*, *MEGA*, I, 3:47–49, 61, 62, 65; *Werke, Ergänzungsband*, 1:478–80, 492, 497; *Works*, 3:242–43, 254–55, 258. Also, *Das Kapital*, 1 *(Werke)*:392n.; *Capital*, 1 (New York, 1947):366n.
105. Preface, *Zur Kritik der Politischen Ökonomie, Werke*, 13:8–9; *Marx-Engels Reader*, pp. 4–5.
106. *Die Heilige Familie oder Kritik der kritischen Kritik: Gegen Bruno Bauer und Consorten, MEGA*, I, 3:175–388; *Werke*, 2:7–223; *Works*, 4:7–211. In his sympathetic biography McLellan found that *The Holy Family*

"consisted of hair-splitting and deliberate misrepresentation which distorted their opponents' articles to the point of absurdity," *Karl Marx,* p. 133.

107. *Die Deutsche Ideologie.*

108. *MEGA,* I, 3:192, 339–87; *Werke,* 2:21, 172–221; *Works,* 4:21, 162–211.

109. *MEGA,* I, 3:376–77; *Werke,* 2:211–12; *Works,* 4:199–200.

110. E.g., *MEGA,* I, 3:249–55; *Werke,* 2:82–91; *Works,* 4:78–87.

111. *MEGA,* I, 3:211–12; *Werke,* 2:43; *Works,* 4:41.

112. *MEGA,* I, 3:253; *Werke,* 2:85; *Works,* 4:81.

113. *MEGA,* I, 3:294; *Werke,* 2:126; *Works,* 4:119.

114. See Mayer, "Der Untergang," pp. 426–37; Börnstein, *Fünfundsiebzig Jahre,* 1:347–54; Ruge, *Zwei Jahre in Paris,* 1:394–99; *Werke,* 27; endnote 24. Carl Bernays was also on the expulsion list, but the French government had found an excuse to imprison him in December 1844, and he remained in the country when he was released two months later.

CHAPTER 4. BRUSSELS: ANTICIPATING REVOLUTION

1. *Werke,* 3:5–7; *Works,* 5:5–8. Reprinted in many anthologies, e.g., *Marx-Engels Reader,* pp. 143–45.

2. *Die Deutsche Ideologie, Werke,* 3:26–27, 38, 45, 34–35, 33; *Works,* 5:36–37, 54, 41, 49, 47.

3. Philosophy (in general and in direct reference to Feuerbach and Bruno Bauer), the Young Hegelian (Max Stirner), and True Socialists, *Werke,* 3:13–100, 101–436, 441–520; *Works,* 6:23–116, 117–452, 455–530.

4. Draft of a letter to Karl W. Leske, Aug. 1, 1846, *Werke,* 27:448–49. Marx offered him the astonishing hope that the publisher of the second book, i.e., *The German Ideology,* would compensate Leske for the advance. Leske was trying to get the money back as late as 1871, McLellan, *Karl Marx,* p. 152.

5. *Werke,* 3:13; *Works,* 5:23.

6. It was first published in Moscow in 1932.

7. Introduction (dated Jan. 1859), *Zur Kritik der Politischen Ökonomie, Werke,* 13:10; *Marx-Engels Reader,* pp. 5–6. It was in this introduction that Marx gave his final definition of materialism.

8. Marx, *Misère de la philosophie* (Paris and Brussels, 1847). Section on materialism, pp. 92–120. Translations in *Werke,* 4; *Works,* 6. Sections in these translations on materialism, respectively, pp. 125–44 and 161–78.

9. *Misère de la philosophie,* p. 99; *Das Elend der Philosophie, Werke,* 4:130; *The Poverty of Philosophy, Works,* 6:165.

10. *Misère,* pp. 97–98; *Elend, Werke,* 4:130; *Poverty, Works,* 6:165.

11. *Misère,* p. 99; *Elend, Werke,* 4:130; *Poverty, Works,* 6:165.

12. *Misère,* pp. 27, 25; *Elend, Werke,* 4:82, 81; *Poverty, Works,* 6:125, 123.

13. Discussion of practical value of strikes, *Misère,* pp. 167–78; quota-

tion, p. 175. *Elend, Werke,* 4:175–82; quotation, p. 180. *Poverty, Works,* 6:206–12; quotation, p. 211.

14. McLellan, *Karl Marx,* p. 166; *Werke,* 4:endnote 43.

15. In 1885, "Zur Geschichte des Bundes der Kommunisten," *Werke,* 8:583; "History of the Communist League," *Selected Works,* 2:9.

16. Letter to Marx, *Werke,* 27:7; *Selected Correspondence,* p. 21.

17. Letter to Marx, *Werke,* 27:19–23; quotation, p. 20.

18. *Die Lage der Arbeitenden Klasse in England, Werke,* 2:229–506; *The Condition of the Working-Class in England, Works,* 4:297–583.

19. Letter, Oct. 19, 1844, *Werke,* 27:10.

20. See analysis and account of the book's impact, W. O. Henderson, *The Life of Friedrich Engels,* 2 vols. (London, 1976), 1:67–73.

21. Engels' history of the Communist League (see n. 15, above) is eloquent in what it elides. See also Julius Braunthal, *History of the International* (New York, 1967), 1:50–52.

22. Letter of Marx (and Engels) in the form of a communication of the Communist Correspondence Committee to Gustav Köttgen, a painter and poet, in Elberfeld, June 15, 1846, *Werke,* 4:20–21; quotation, p. 21. *Works,* 6:54–56; quotation, p. 55. Köttgen was a heretical True Socialist, but Marx found it politic to ignore the fact at the time.

23. For the period Jan. 1845–Apr. 1846 see *New MEGA,* III, 1T:450–533.

24. Letter of Oct. 31, 1845, ibid., pp. 489–90.

25. E.g., letters of Mar. 10, 1845; Jan. 21, Mar. 3, and Apr. 7, 1846, ibid., pp. 455–57, 498–99, 509–10, and 529–31.

26. Letter of Mar. 3, 1845, ibid., pp. 458–59.

27. Letter of Jan. 30, 1846, ibid., p. 500. The signal was correct: Jung fell away from Marx's life. During the German Revolution of 1848, Jung became a member of the Prussian Assembly as a left-wing Democrat, but he was insufficiently radical for Marx. Nevertheless, they had an amicable meeting in Berlin in 1848. Jung later joined the National Liberal Party as a supporter of Bismarck.

28. Letter of Feb. (no day given) 1846, ibid., pp. 506–8. Bürgers had been Marx's companion when he was expelled from France in Feb. 1845.

29. Ibid., p. 517. Another sign was Engels' broadcasting of grimy stories about Hess's wife, suspected of being a former prostitute (Henderson, *The Life of Friedrich Engels,* 1:88–89).

30. E.g., letters of Ewerbeck, Dec. 28, 1845, *New MEGA,* III, 1T:496–97, in which he reported on the regrettable success of Ruge's recent book *Zwei Jahre in Paris,* and its "*echt* German, so-called progressive position"; Wilhelm Weitling, Sept. 22–27, 1845, ibid., pp. 485–86, and the poet Georg Weerth, Oct. 23, 1845, ibid., pp. 487–88.

31. Pavel V. Annenkov, *The Extraordinary Decade: Literary Memoirs,* ed. Arthur P. Mendel (Ann Arbor, 1968), p. 167. The account was first published in a Russian periodical in 1880, according to Mendel, p. xi.

32. Annenkov, *The Extraordinary Decade,* pp. 167–70.

33. Moses Hess, *Briefwechsel* (The Hague, 1959), pp. 150–51; also in *Der*

Bund der Kommunisten: Dokumente u. Materialien, 1: *1836–1849,* Ed. Herwig Förder et al. ([East] Berlin, 1970), pp. 307–8.

34. Letter of May 20, 1846, *New MEGA,* III, 2T:208.
35. Letter of May 29, 1846, ibid., p. 211.
36. Minutes of meeting and resolutions, circular letter, *Werke,* 4:3, 4–17; *Works,* 6:35, 36–51.
37. In a letter of Marx to Proudhon, May 5, 1846, *Werke,* 27:442, 443; letter without postscript, *Selected Correspondence,* pp. 28–29.
38. Letter of May 17, 1846, quoted in Pierre Haubtmann, *Marx et Proudhon* (Paris, 1947), p. 63.
39. Letter of Aug. 14, 1846, Förder et al., *Der Bund der Kommunisten,* p. 395.
40. "Committee Letters" Nos. 2, 3, *Werke,* 27:40, 60–64; "Committee Letter" No. 3, *Selected Correspondence,* pp. 31–32. The correspondence from Aug. 19, 1846, to Jan. 21, 1848, *Werke,* 27:36–114.
41. *Werke,* 27:68–69, 81.
42. Stephan Born, *Erinnerungen eines Achtundvierzigers* (Leipzig, 1898), p. 49; for the full story of the Engels-Born activities, pp. 38–66.
43. Förder et al., *Der Bund der Kommunisten,* pp. 214–38; debate on action, pp. 218–22.
44. Ibid., pp. 347–50; postscript, p. 350.
45. Ibid., pp. 376–82; quotation, p. 380. Marx's second letter, to which this was a response, has also not been found.
46. Letter, no precise date given, ibid., pp. 402–3.
47. "Ansprache der Volkshalle," Nov. 1846, ibid., pp. 431–36.
48. Letter, dated "December 1846" by the editors, *Werke,* 27:68–72; quotations, pp. 69–71.
49. Reproduction of Moll's credentials, Franz Mehring, *Karl Marx* (London, 1936), p. 137; not in the German edition. Signers included Schapper, Bauer, and five other league members.
50. Marx, *Herr Vogt, Werke,* 14:439. Marx thought (also p. 439) that his CCC's polemics, and the solid materialist theory behind them, had persuaded the league's leadership to invite him to join. See also Schraepler, "Der Bund der Gerechten," pp. 25–26; and McLellan, *Karl Marx,* pp. 170–72.
51. Letter of May 14, 1847, *Werke,* 27:82.
52. Quoted in McLellan, *Karl Marx,* p. 172.
53. Reprinted, *Werke,* 4:593; *Works,* 6:601.
54. Letter, dated "before Sept. 14, 1847," by the editors, *New MEGA,* III, 2T:98.
55. Ibid., pp. 368–70.
56. Article 1 and complete statutes, *Werke,* 4:596, 596–601; *Works,* 6:633, 633–38.
57. Dossier Bornstedt, Archives Générales du Royaume de Belgique, Brussels, items 63, 108.
58. See detailed accounts of Bornstedt's activities in Nicolaievsky and Maenchen-Helfen, *Karl Marx,* pp. 133–35, and Gustav Mayer, "Der

Untergang der *Deutsch-Französischen Jahrbücher* und des *Pariser Vorwärts*," *Archiv für die Geschichte des Sozialismus und der Arbeiterbewegung*
3 (1913):424–25.

59. See (with caution) *Werke*, 4:endnote 86.
60. Letter to Georg Herwegh (in Paris), Aug. 8, 1847, *Werke*, 27:466–67;
quotation, p. 467.
61. All articles, *Werke*, 4:191–530 passim; *Works*, 6:92–558 passim. "Revolution in Paris," *Werke*, 4:528–30; *Works*, 6:556–58.
62. Some of Marx's lectures were written up as an article series entitled
"Lohnarbeit und Kapital" ("Wage-Labor and Capital") and published
in the *Neue Rheinische Zeitung*, the newspaper he would command during
the Revolution of 1848, Apr. 5–11, 1849; *Werke*, 6:397–403; *Works*,
9:147–228.
63. *Werke*, 4:416; *Works*, 6:388. On Harney's objectives, see Schraepler,
"Der Bund der Gerechten," pp. 16–20.
64. Letter (in French) to Marx from Wilhelm Schmalhausen, husband of
Marx's elder sister, Sophie, Oct. 12, 1847, *New MEGA*, 2T:368–70.
With a meticulous accountant's array of figures, Schmalhausen demonstrated that Marx had no further claim. But Marx soon won partial
satisfaction, ibid., 2N:910–11.
65. The president was the Belgian lawyer and editor of a progressive
Brussels newspaper Lucien Jottrand, and the other vice-president was
a French radical exile.
66. See Engels' Byzantine letter to Marx of Sept. 28–30, 1847, *Werke*,
27:84–92; his letter to Jottrand of Sept. 28, 1847, ibid., p. 469, and
endnotes 84, 86; indirect quotation from the letter to Jottrand, ibid.,
p. 91.
67. Letter reprinted, Robert Payne, *Marx* (New York, 1968), p. 162.
68. References will be to the *Manifest der kommunistischen Partei*, as reprinted in *Werke*, 4:461–93, and *Works*, 6:481–519. The translation
(published in 1888) is by Samuel Moore, the English translator of vol.
1 of *Das Kapital*, as edited by Engels.
69. Compare with the programmatic statement written by Engels,
"Grundsätze des Kommunismus," ("Foundations of Communism"),
Werke, 4:363–83; *Works*, 6:341–57. Engels wrote it, as he wrote everything, very quickly, at the end of October 1847, in the form of a catechism of twenty-five questions and answers. He wrote Marx (letter of
Nov. 23, 1847, *Werke*, 27:197), however, that, on second thought, he
did not like the catechism form and he suggested that they produce a
statement under the title "Communist Manifesto." Engels had brought
his catechism to the second London congress, where it served, at least,
to counter the infinitely worse efforts by the Schapper group and by
Moses Hess. Engels was then wise enough to let his talent yield to
Marx's genius, and Marx, making some use of the catechism as raw
material, wrote the *Manifesto* himself. The "Foundations of Communism" is better organized, more complete, and more reasonable, but
it is facile, flat with the commonplaces which Engels used too easily,

and deadly in its lack of the inspiring vision or even phrase. In passing on the task to Marx, Engels proved again that he was one of the greatest of the second-rate figures in history.

70. *Werke*, 4:461; *Works*, 6:481.

71. *Werke*, 4:463; *Works*, 6:485.

72. *Werke*, 4:462–74; *Works*, 6:482–96. Quotations, *Werke*, 4:463, 464, 465; *Works*, 6:485, 486, 487.

73. *Werke*, 4:472; *Works*, 6:494.

74. *Werke*, 4:482–92; *Works*, 6:507–17.

75. *Werke*, 4:482–84; *Works*, 6:507–8.

76. *Werke*, 4:482, 487; *Works*, 6:507, 512.

77. *Werke*, 4:488–89; *Works*, 6:513–14.

78. *Werke*, 4:484–85; *Works*, 6:509.

79. *Werke*, 4:491; *Works*, 6:516.

80. *Werke*, 4:474; *Works*, 6:497.

81. *Werke*, 4:492–93; *Works*, 6:519.

82. According to a statement of a Communist leader, quoted in full in Werner Blumenberg, "Zur Geschichte des Bundes der Kommunisten: Die Aussagen des Peter Gerhard Röser," *International Review of Social History* 9 (1964):88. A surviving document, dated Mar. 3, 1848, confirms the transfer of power. It recorded the decision of a group calling itself the "Central Committee of the Communist League." The document, signed by Marx, Engels, Gigot, and two others, began with legalistic specificity. "The Central Committee of the Communist League, meeting in Brussels, after a study of the decision of the former London Central Committee, according to which the seat of the Central Committee has been transferred to Brussels and the London Central Committee itself has been dissolved, through which decision thus the governing committee of the leading branch of the Brussels area has been constituted as the Central Committee." The document then went on to transfer the new Central Committee physically to Paris, and also give Marx full "discretionary authority" to take all the necessary decisions, *Werke*, 4:607; *Works*, 6:651–52.

Chapter 5. Cologne: Making Revolution

1. Mar. 8, 1848, *Werke*, 4:536–38.

2. Oscar Hammen, *The Red '48ers* (New York, 1969) is a detailed study of Marx's activities during this period. It does not always cite its sources, and while I made grateful use of it as a guide, I preferred to depend upon other sources, either original or referring specifically back to the original.

3. Memorandum by an official of the Belgian Ministry of Justice, mentioned in Horst Schlechte, "Karl Marx und sein Wirkungskreis in Brüssel: Dokumente aus belgischen Archiven," *Beiträge zur Geschichte der deutschen Arbeiterbewegung* 1 (1966):113. That document was miss-

ing when I searched the file in 1970. Jenny Marx mentioned Marx's donation, although not the amount, in her memoir, "Kurze Umrisse eines bewegten Lebens," in *Mohr und General: Erinnerungen an Marx und Engels* ([East] Berlin, 1964), p. 207.

4. Details of Wolff's expulsion in letter of Engels to Marx, Mar. 9, 1848, *Werke*, 27:115.

5. The actual expulsion order, dated March 2, is reproduced in Robert Payne, *Marx* (New York, 1968), p. 177; the undated order is in Dossier Karl Marx, Archives Générales du Royaume de Belgique, file 73,946, item 24.

6. According to Marx's letter in *La Réforme*, noted above (n. 1).

7. Dossier Karl Marx, Archives Générales du Royaume de Belgique, file 73, 946, item 34, Mar. 7, 1848. Jenny Marx was also held by the police briefly, and then expelled over the French border, leaving before Marx did. See especially Stephan Born, *Erinnerungen eines Achtundvierzigers* (Leipzig, 1898), p. 89.

8. Dated Mar. 1: "Brave and loyal Marx, the soil of the French Republic is a place of refuge for all friends of freedom. Tyranny has banished you, a free France opens her doors to you. . . . *Salut et Fraternité*," *Works*, 6:649.

9. Quoted, Samuel Bernstein, "Marx in Paris, 1848: A Neglected Chapter," *Science and Society* 3 (Summer 1939):348.

10. Herwegh escaped; Bornstedt, captured and imprisoned, went insane and died.

11. *MEGA*, III, 1:96; *Werke*, 27:118.

12. "Forderungen der kommunistischen Partei in Deutschland," *Werke*, 5:3–5; *Works*, 7:3–7.

13. According to Röser's statement (cited in ch. 4, n. 82), quoted in Werner Blumenberg, "Zur Geschichte des Bundes der Kommunisten; Die Aussagen des Peter Gerhard Röser," *International Review of Social History* 9 (1964):89–90. Röser was not a member of the league at the time Marx made the decision to dissolve it, and his statement (on Dec. 30, 1853) was evidently made to get better treatment in prison, to which he had been sentenced for six years on a charge connected with communist activities. The statement, however, accords well with all the other known facts, which will be given in text below when those "communist activities" are treated in detail.

14. *Der Bund der Kommunisten: Dokumente u. Materialien*, I: *1836–1849*, Ed. Herwig Förder et al. ([East] Berlin, 1970), pp. 783, 784.

15. Born, *Erinnerungen*, pp. 196–99.

16. Engels, "Marx und die *NRZ*" (originally published in 1884), *Werke*, 21:19; "Marx and the *NRZ*," *Selected Works*, 2:32.

17. *Werke*, 21:20–22.

18. McLellan, *Karl Marx*, pp. 202, 221.

19. Marx was penniless when he left Cologne for the last time, and his wife had pawned her silver, ibid., p. 223. Marx later claimed to have contributed 7,000 thalers, an impossibly huge sum, to the *NRZ*, ac-

cording to a letter of his in 1853, *Werke*, 28:endnote 578. The exaggeration probably smothers the honorable truth that he gave a few hundred thalers, which, considering his incompetent management of money, was all that he might have had left.

20. Engels, "Marx und die *NRZ*," *Werke*, 21:19; *Selected Works*, 2:32.
21. Herbert Kümhof, *Karl Marx und die "Neue Rheinische Zeitung*," (Berlin, 1961), pp. 151–52.
22. Quoted in Nicolaievsky and Maenchen-Helfen, *Karl Marx*, p. 181.
23. Franz Mehring, *Karl Marx: Geschichte seines Lebens* (1918; reprint ed., Frankfurt, 1964). On p. 175 Mehring first mentions the "Workers' Association at the head of which were Moll and Schapper." That is true enough, but Mehring does not say that Gottschalk founded the Association, and that Moll and Schapper succeeded him later—only after Gottschalk had been imprisoned.
24. Quoted in Nicolaievsky and Maenchen-Helfen, *Karl Marx*, p. 182.
25. Carl Schurz, *The Reminiscences of Carl Schurz* (New York, 1907), 1:139–40.
26. Article of June 29, 1848, *Werke*, 5:133, 134, 136; *Works*, 7:144, 144–47, 149. Ferdinand Flocon, the French republican who had welcomed Marx to France, supported the troop action, which was led by the republican general Godefroi Cavaignac. Flocon, who was briefly minister of agriculture and commerce in the Provisional Government, fled to Switzerland when Louis Napoleon seized power in the coup d'état of Dec. 2, 1851. He was repudiated by radicals for his *"vote terrible"* supporting the action against the Paris workers, and after subsisting wretchedly as a translator and losing his eyesight, died in isolation in 1866. *Dictionnaire bibliographique du mouvement ouvrier français*.
27. Issue of July 12, 1848, *Werke*, 5:202; *Works*, 7:212.
28. Issue of Sept. 10, 1848, *Werke*, 5:394; *Works*, 7:422.
29. W. O. Henderson, *The Life of Friedrich Engels* (London, 1976), 1:149.
30. See "Protokoll der Komiteesitzung des Kölner Arbeitervereins," Förder et al., *Der Bund der Kommunisten*, pp. 902–4.
31. *Werke*, 6:12; *Works*, 8:19.
32. Issue of Nov. 7, 1848, *Werke*, 5:455; *Works*, 8:503.
33. *Werke*, 5:457; *Works*, 7:505–6.
34. *Werke*, 6:102; *Works*, 8:154.
35. *Werke*, 6:148–50; quotation, p. 150. *Works*, 8:213–15, 215.
36. *Werke*, 6:233–34; *Works*, 8:316–17. See Saul K. Padover, *Karl Marx: An Intimate Biography* (New York, 1978), p. 272. Engels and another *NRZ* staff member were tried and acquitted with Marx. Engels also spoke, characteristically with facility but much less power.
37. *Werke*, 6:257, 245; *Works*, 8:339, 327.
38. There were also two other defendants, Schapper and Karl Schneider, the latter a Democrat and a lawyer by profession. Schneider had, with Marx, signed the *NRZ*'s call to arms.
39. *Werke*, 6:195; *Works*, 8:266.
40. In an open letter in February, quoted in McLellan, *Karl Marx*, p. 217.

When the German Revolution ended, and quiet had been reestablished in Cologne, Gottschalk returned—and returned to his old profession. Later in 1849 he died while caring for his working-class patients in a cholera epidemic.

41. Statement of Röser, in Blumenberg, "Zur Geschichte des Bundes der Kommunisten," pp. 90–91. Röser did not specify a more precise date than "the spring of 1849."

42. *Werke*, 6:397–403; *Works*, 9:197–228.

43. *Werke*, 6:397; *Works*, 9:197.

44. *Werke*, 6:426; *Works*, 9:282.

45. The Red Edition, *Werke*, 6:503–19; photograph of front page with Freiligrath's poem, p. 521; Marx quotations, pp. 504, 505. Red Edition, *Works*, 9:451–67; photograph of front page, p. 469; Marx quotations, pp. 452, 453.

46. *MEGA*, III, 1:113; *Werke*, 27:142.

Chapter 6. The Permanent Revolution

1. Marx, "Nachwort," *Enthüllungen über den Kommunisten-Prozess zu Köln*, *Werke*, 8:574–75; "Postscript," Marx and Engels, *The Cologne Communist Trial*, ed. and tr. Rodney Livingstone (London, 1971), p. 131. Marx wrote the book from October to December 1852 and published it the next year. He wrote the "Postscript" for a later edition.

2. Werner Blumenberg, "Zur Geschichte des Bundes der Kommunisten: Die Aussagen des Peter Gerhard Röser," *International Review of Social History* 9 (1964):91. For the history of the Communist League activities on the Continent during this period, besides Marx's splendidly partisan account, see also Shlomo Na'aman, "Zur Geschichte des Bundes der Kommunisten in Deutschland in der zweiten Phase seines Bestehens," *Archiv für Sozialgeschichte* 5 (1965):5–82, of which pp. 43–46 are specifically on the leadership of the Cologne league; and Karl Bittel, *Der Kommunistenprozess zu Köln im Spiegel der zeitgenossischen Presse* ([East] Berlin, 1955). The latter carries detailed accounts of the trial of the Cologne defendants, including their testimony.

3. "Ansprache der Zentralbehörde an den Bund vom März 1850," *Werke*, 7:244–54; "Address . . . ," *The Cologne Communist Trial*, pp. 237–45. The editors of the *Werke* ascribe the authorship to both Marx and Engels, but the style is Marx's.

4. *Werke*, 7:248, 249–50, 250, 254; *The Cologne Communist Trial*, pp. 241, 242, 245.

5. *Werke*, 7:553–54.

6. In the *Neue Rheinische Zeitung: Politisch-Ökonomische Revue* (see text, below), *Werke*, 7:273.

7. Published in *Werke*, 7:415.

8. "Ansprache . . . ," *Werke*, 7:306–12; "Address . . . ," *The Cologne Communist Trial*, pp. 245–50.

9. According to a hurt letter from the Central Committee of the Cologne section, July 18, 1850, published in Wolfgang Schieder, "Der Bund der Kommunisten im Sommer 1850: Drei Dokumente aus dem Marx-Engels-Nachlass," *International Review of Social History* 13 (1968):54–57. Marx's letter has not survived. The Central Committee, defending itself, claimed it was indeed energetically pursuing organizational action.

10. According to Röser, Blumenberg, "Zur Geschichte des Bundes der Kommunisten," pp. 98–99.

11. McLellan, *Karl Marx*, pp. 247–48, among other accounts.

12. Minutes of the "Sitzung der Zentralbehörde vom 15. September 1850," *Werke*, 8:597–601; *The Cologne Communist Trial*, pp. 250–53.

13. *Werke*, 8:597; *The Cologne Communist Trial*, p. 250.

14. *Werke*, 8:598–99; *The Cologne Communist Trial*, pp. 251–52.

15. *Werke*, 8:599; *The Cologne Communist Trial*, p. 252.

16. *Werke*, 8:600; *The Cologne Communist Trial*, p. 253.

17. This conduct by Willich, his follower, and Schapper was duly recorded in the minutes, *Werke*, 8:600–601; *The Cologne Communist Trial*, pp. 252–53.

18. *Die Klassenkämpfe in Frankreich 1848 bis 1850*, *Werke*, 7:9–107; Marx, *Political Writings*, Ed. David Fernbach (New York, 1974), 2:35–142.

19. *Der achtzehnte Brumaire des Louis Napoleon*, written from Dec. 1851 to May 1852, *Werke*, 8:113–207; Marx, *Political Writings*, 2:143–249. The title refers to Louis Napoleon's coup d'état: the 18th Brumaire was actually the date of his uncle's coup—according to the revolutionary calendar in effect in 1799.

20. In Engels' introduction to the third edition of *Der achtzehnte Brumaire*, published in 1885, *Werke*, 8:561.

21. *Werke*, 7:11; Marx, *Political Writings*, 2:35.

22. *Werke*, 7:89; Marx, *Political Writings*, 2:123.

23. *Werke*, 7:98; Marx, *Political Writings*, 2:131.

24. *Werke*, 8:118; Marx, *Political Writings*, 2:150.

25. *Werke*, 8:115; Marx, *Political Writings*, 2:146.

26. *Werke*, 8:559; Marx, *Political Writings*, 2:143–44.

27. Marx and Engels withdrew formally from the association in a one-sentence note, signed also by nine others, on Sept. 17, 1850, *Werke*, 7:414.

28. E.g., letter paraphrased in testimony of Röser (Blumenberg, "Zur Geschichte des Bundes der Kommunisten," p. 109).

29. *Werke*, 8:599; *The Cologne Communist Trial*, p. 252.

30. *Werke*, 27:184–85. Note Marx's innocent assumption that what happened in the émigré underworld was of great notoriety.

31. Letter of Feb. 24, 1851, ibid., p. 198. Wilhelm Pieper, a former student, sometimes served Marx also as a secretary and received excellent returns in the form of hospitality and even money. He presently fell away from the Marx group. The other young man, Konrad Schramm, had been Marx's surrogate in the duel with Willich. Schramm main-

tained his relations with Marx, but later settled on the island of Jersey and died there in 1858.

32. Mar. 10, 1853, ibid., 28:224.

33. Letter, Marx to Engels, Jan, 29, 1853, *Werke*, 28:209.

34. McLellan, *Karl Marx*, p. 286.

35. Letter of Apr. 5, 1852, *Werke*, 28:48–49.

36. Bittel, *Der Kommunistenprozess zu Köln*, p. 30.

37. *Werke*, 8:414; *The Cologne Communist Trial*, p. 64.

38. Bittel, *Der Kommunistenprozess zu Köln*, p. 60.

39. Wilhelm Stieber was one of the authors of *Die Communisten-Verschwörungen des neunzehnten Jahrhunderts*, 2 vols. (Berlin, 1853–54), a sober study of communist conspiratorial action that refused to see cause for great alarm and carefully examined workers' grievances.

40. And became a storybook success: journalist for the German-language press and major general in the Union armies during the Civil War.

41. The social character of that revolutionary activity was hardly proletarian. Of the eleven defendants only three could be assigned to the working class, two tailors besides the cigarette worker Röser, thus artisans at best or worst. The others were a store clerk, a chemist, a journalist, a student, a lawyer and publisher, and three doctors. The poet Ferdinand Freiligrath had also been indicted, but he escaped and settled in London, where he resumed his successful business career. Marx, undeterred, never ceased to emphasize the proletarian character of the Cologne operations.

42. As Marx recorded the action: "The league [i.e., Marx's group] *dissolved* itself on my motion and declared the continuance of the league on the Continent to be *no longer opportune*." Letter to Engels, Nov. 19, 1852, *Werke*, 28:195.

43. McLellan, *Karl Marx*, p. 252. See Marx's letter of Oct. 28, 1852 to Engels, *Werke*, 28:168–74.

44. *Werke*, 27–190.

45. Letters of Jan. 7 and 27, 1851, ibid., pp. 157–62, 169; letter of Jan. 7 in *Selected Correspondence*, pp. 52–54.

46. *Werke*, 28:434–35.

CHAPTER 7. THE PERMANENT REVOLUTIONARY

1. Karl Heinzen, *Gesammelte Schriften*, 4: *Nach Meiner Exilirung* (Boston, 1864), p. 424. A radical Democrat, Heinzen had known Marx in Brussels.

2. Letter to a friend, quoted in Karl Vogt. *Mein Prozess gegen die "Allgemeine Zeitung"* (Geneva, 1859), pp. 151–52. Techow, who emigrated later to Australia, acted as Willich's second in the duel with Marx's young friend, recounted also in the letter.

3. The spy's report quoted in Gustav Mayer, "Neue Beiträge zur Biographie von Karl Marx," *Archiv für die Geschichte des Sozialismus und der*

Arbeiterbewegung, 10 (1922), pp. 58–59. The greater part of the article consisted of a reprint of the spy's report, which Mayer, who was Engels' first biographer, said he found in the police records in the Prussian archives. The spy also reported, "Washing, combing his hair, changing his linen are rare occurrences for Marx" (p. 57).

4. Wilhelm Liebknecht, *Karl Marx zum Gedächnis* (Wörlein, 1899), p. iv.
5. Letter, Apr. 12, 1855, *Werke,* 28:444.
6. Recent accounts in Robert Payne, *Karl Marx,* pp. 256–68 and 533–45; and Saul K. Padover, *Karl Marx: An Intimate Biography* (New York, 1978), pp. 523–24. Payne found the birth certificate of Frederick Demuth, as he was named; no father was given. Demuth died in 1929. The story was originally told by the first wife of Karl Kautsky, Louise Freyberger, who had been Engels' secretary and housekeeper during his last years. She gave the details originally in a letter of September 2, 1898, to August Bebel, the head of the German Social Democrats, quoted in Werner Blumenberg, *Karl Marx in Selbstzeugnissen und Bilddokumenten* (Hamburg, 1970), pp. 115–18.
7. Evidently written in 1865, when Jenny Marx was forty-three, the memoir was entitled "A Short Outline of an Eventful Life"—"Kurze Umrisse eines bewegten Lebens," published in *Mohr und General,* pp. 204–36; quotations, pp. 204, 212.
8. Liebknecht, *Karl Marx zum Gedächnis,* pp. 27, 30, 35.
9. Eleanor Marx, "Karl Marx: Lose Blätter" (article originally published in Austria in 1895), *Mohr und General,* pp. 271–72.
10. Arnold Künzli, *Karl Marx: Eine Psychographie* (Vienna, Frankfurt, and Zurich, 1966), pp. 86–96 et passim.
11. Letter to Ferdinand Freiligrath, Nov. 28, 1859, *Werke,* 29:635. With the words "vulgar mob," Marx was referring to his enemies among the émigrés, but then he could think of nothing more expressive than the Latin pejorative for the proletariat of antiquity.
12. On Engels, see W. O. Henderson, *The Life of Friedrich Engels,* 2 vols. (London, 1976), and Gustav Mayer, *Friedrich Engels in seiner Frühzeit 1820–1851* (Berlin, 1920), and *Friedrich Engels: Eine Biographie, 2: Engels und der Aufstieg der Arbeiterbewegung in Europa* (The Hague, 1934). There is an English translation of the latter: *Friedrich Engels,* 2 vols. (New York, 1936).
13. The correspondence richly documents the Marx-Engels relationship as profoundly personal and efficiently professional. Letters provided release from conventional inhibitions, and the maturing gentlemen often appear as dirty-minded, foul-mouthed adolescents. Marx particularly was given to scatology and obscenity. From his research he reports on an apocryphal encounter of Peter the Great and his czarina with a statue of Priapus "dans une posture très indécente," and copies out French erotic verse (letters of Feb. 12, 1856, and Oct. 14, 1867, *Werke,* 29:15 and 31:369). But, except for such small self-indulgences, the correspondence kept to the main purpose, and the friends carefully saved it to serve that purpose. The letters were operational messages, a record

of those operations, and instructions for their followers. Often Marx or Engels would specify certain others as readers of a given communication. The letters were the business correspondence of manufacturers of revolution. The great bulk of the correspondence covers the two decades of Engels' residence in Manchester. Over long periods the friends wrote each other twice and three times a week. The *Werke* edition has published as many as 139 letters for a single year, 1868. There were more. Laura and Eleanor Marx destroyed embarrassing letters or parts of letters after Engels died, and other persons who have had possession of the letters, including the present Soviet Russian editors, have served other causes than scholarship. Most of the letters have not yet been translated into English.

14. Letter of Jan. 29, 1851, *Werke*, 27:170.

15. Letter of Feb. 3, 1851, ibid., p. 173.

16. Ibid., 30:310–11. Marx added that he would have preferred seeing his mother dead, since it would mean money for him.

17. Letter of Jan. 13, 1863, ibid., pp. 312–13; quotation, p. 312.

18. Letter of Jan. 24, 1863, ibid., pp. 314–16; quotation, p. 312.

19. Letter of Jan. 26, 1863, ibid., pp. 317–18. Sympathizing with Engels for the risk he had taken, Marx wrote, "If you had seen the joy of my children, it would have been a beautiful reward for you." Letter of Jan. 28, 1863, ibid., p. 319.

20. Blumenberg, *Karl Marx in Selbstzeugnissen*, p. 109.

21. Ibid., p. 109. According to his first employment contract, Engels got a salary of £100, plus 7.5 percent of the profits. In 1854 his profit share was £168; it rose to £408 by 1856 and £978 in 1859. The terms of Engels' association with the firm, Ermen & Engels, were improved when his father died in 1860. Four years later Engels became a partner in his own right. See Henderson, *The Life of Friedrich Engels*, p. 199.

22. Documented, e.g., in his letters of Aug. 3, 1881, and Jan. 12, 1882, *Werke*, 35:11–13, 34–36. In the first Marx mentioned (p. 11) "the anarchy which invaded the household in the last two years." In the second (p. 34), a year before his death, he simply asked for "some £" (Marx's English).

23. Blumenberg, *Karl Marx in Selbstzeugnissen*, pp. 109–10.

24. Letter of Lassalle to Marx, end of Aug. 1862, Ferdinand Lassalle, *Nachgelassene Briefe und Schriften*, 3: *Der Briefwechsel zwischen Lassalle und Marx*, ed. Gustav Mayer (Stuttgart and Berlin, 1922), pp. 402–5; quotations, pp. 404, 402.

25. *Werke*, 30:633.

26. Marx to Lassalle, letter of Nov. 7, 1862, *Werke*, 30:636–37. In all fairness to Marx one must credit the fact that he avoided repaying smaller sums he had borrowed earlier from Lassalle.

27. Marx-Engels letter interchange, Nov. 4 and 5, 1862, ibid., pp. 293–95.

28. Letter of Dec. 3, 1852, ibid., 28:200. Marx mentioned, incidentally,

Weerth's plan to go to the West Indies. Weerth departed soon and died there in 1856.
29. Letter of May 18, 1859, ibid., 29:431.
30. Letter, Marx to Engels, May 7, 1861, ibid., 30:164.
31. Born, *Erinnerungen eines Achtundvierzigers* (Leipzig, 1898), p. 199.
32. *Werke*, 12:4; *Marx-Engels Reader*, p. 478.
33. David McLellan, Marx's most recent major biographer, resists the word "anti-Semite" as descriptive of Marx. Referring to "On the Jewish Question" in an earlier work, *Marx before Marxism* (New York, 1970), he wrote: "It is largely this article that has given the impression that Marx was an anti-Semite. This is inaccurate" (p. 141). In *Karl Marx* McLellan expanded upon the discussion in *Marx before Marxism*, arguing (p. 86) that (1) Marx's willingness to help the Jews of Cologne—he promised his support for a petition on their behalf in 1848—"suggests that his article was aimed much more at the vulgar capitalism popularly associated with Jews than with Jewry as such," (2) the word *Judentum* (Jewry) has the secondary sense of commerce, and (3) Marx got his main points from an article of Moses Hess, "who was the very opposite of an anti-Semite." Point 1 does not deny that Marx's article did indeed treat the Jews negatively. Point 2 is possibly true of the vocabulary of an anti-Semite. Point 3 is untrue: Hess had indeed passed through an anti-Semitic phase. In any case McLellan restricted his discussion of Marx's anti-Semitism to the questions raised by the one article published in 1843. At that point in his discussion he made no effort to consider other evidences, which he himself mentioned. Thus McLellan had written earlier in *Karl Marx* (p. 6) that Marx's "letters contain innumerable derogatory epithets concerning Jews." McLellan, however, rejected the conclusion that seemed inevitable and completed the sentence: "—but this does not justify a charge of sustained anti-Semitism." One might inquire if spasmodic anti-Semitism would resolve the logic more satisfactorily. Following the analysis of "On the Jewish Question," McLellan made one more reference to the subject in connection with Marx, mentioning in a footnote (see n. 35, below) that anti-Semitism was a part of the *NRZ*'s editorial policy. McLellan thereafter did not recur to the question of Marx's anti-Semitism *an sich* and failed to note the powerful anti-Semitic denunciation in Marx's book, *Herr Vogt* (see text, below), although he gave the name of the person under attack.

A subtler, more philosophical defense of Marx is Henry Pachter, "Marx and the Jews," *Dissent* 26, no. 4 (Fall 1979): 450–67. Pachter ignores *Herr Vogt* and finds the anti-Semitic expletives of the letters to be expressions of a *general* bias. Compare with Isaiah Berlin, "Benjamin Disraeli, Karl Marx and the Search for Identity," in *Against the Current* (New York, 1980), pp. 252–86.

Also on Marx's anti-Semitism see Nicolaievsky and Maenchen-Helfen, *Karl Marx*, Appendix I; Edmund Silberner, "Was Marx an Anti-

Semite?" *Historia Judaica*, 11 (Apr. 1949), and Jerrold Seigel, *Marx's Fate: The Shape of a Life* (Princeton, N.J., 1978), pp. 112–19.

34. Not in the Marx biography but in his *Life and Opinions of Moses Hess* (Cambridge, 1959), p. 18.

35. McLellan, *Karl Marx*, n. 214; letter, Marx to Eduard Müller-Tellering, Dec. 5, 1848, *Werke*, 27:485: "Your articles are unquestionably the best which we are getting, entirely in accord with our policy . . . you have contributed much to the understanding of the European public." In 1850 Müller-Tellering published an anti-Semitic attack on Marx in a pamphlet, Seigel, *Marx's Fate*, p. 114.

36. Letter of Oct. 27, 1848, *New MEGA*, III, 2T:489.

37. *Werke*, 7:22, 24; *Political Writings*, 2:49, 51 (where, however, "Juden der Finanz" and "Börsenjuden" are translated as "financial sharks" and "stock-exchange sharks").

38. Letter, March 7, 1856, *Werke*, 29:31.

39. E.g., among many mentions, Marx to Engels, July 2, 1858, *Werke*, 29:336; Engels to Marx, Aug. 12, 1863, ibid., 30:270; Marx to Engels, Feb. 4, 1860, ibid., p. 26; Marx to Engels, June 3, 1864, ibid., p. 402; Marx to Engels, Feb. 25, 1859, ibid., 29:402 (and Engels' echo, March 4, ibid., p. 404); Engels to Marx, Feb. 6, 1861, ibid., 30:155.

40. Letter to Engels, July 30, 1862, ibid., 30:257.

41. *Herr Vogt*, *Werke*, 14:600.

42. Ibid., pp. 601–2.

43. Ibid., pp. 599–600.

44. Letter, June 10, 1869, *Werke*, 32:614. Marx was writing from Manchester, where he was visiting Engels.

45. Letter to Lion Philips in the Netherlands, Nov. 29, 1864, ibid., 31:432.

46. Aug. 8, 1875, ibid., 34:7.

47. *Das Kapital*, 1 (*Werke*, 23):93; *Capital*, 1 (New York, 1947):51.

48. Quoted in Erich Eyck, *Bismarck and the German Empire* (New York, 1967), p. 239.

49. *Das Kapital*, 2:133; *Capital*, 2 (New York, 1967):131.

50. *Das Kapital*, 1:127; *Capital*, 1:87.

51. Letter of Jan. 7, 1851, *Werke*, 27:157–62; quotations, p. 161.

52. *Grundrisse der Kritik der politischen Ökonomie (Rohentwurf) 1857–1858* ([East] Berlin, 1953), p. 232.

53. Quoted in Mayer, "Neue Beiträge zur Biographie von Karl Marx," p. 59.

54. Letter to Engels, Feb. 23, 1852, *Werke*, 28:28. Marx said Bangya was an agent of a Hungarian statesman elsewhere in exile. See also Roman Rosdolsky, "Karl Marx und der Polizeispitzel Bangya," *International Review for Social History* 2 (1937):229–45.

55. "Die Grossen Männer des Exils," reprinted, *Werke*, 8:235–335; Marx and Engels, *The Cologne Communist Trial*, ed. Rodney Livingstone (London, 1971).

56. *Werke*, 28:endnote 143.

57. Ibid., 8:272–73, 320, 269; *The Cologne Communist Trial*, pp. 173, 216, 170.
58. *Werke*, 8:272; *The Cologne Communist Trial*, p. 173.
59. *Werke*, 8:269–70; *The Cologne Communist Trial*, p. 170.
60. Vogt, *Mein Prozess gegen die "Allgemeine Zeitung,"* pp. 133–39.
61. *Herr Vogt*, reprinted, *Werke*, 14:382–702.
62. Marx to Engels, letter of Feb. 9, 1860, ibid., 30:29–35. Many other letters refer to the Vogt affair, including eight of Marx's letters to his German lawyer, a *Justizrat* Weber, in vol. 30. For another account see McLellan, *Karl Marx*, pp. 311–15.
63. The émigré was Karl Blind, a former member of the Baden provisional government, with whom Marx had been friendly earlier in London.
64. Marx insisted upon believing he had been vindicated, and most biographers, e.g., McLellan, as above, have agreed with him. The facts are these: Marx happily wrote to Liebknecht that a report in a French newspaper had published new evidence against Vogt, letter of (about) April 10, 1871, *Werke* 33:203–4. He wanted Liebknecht, now editor of the *Volksstaat*, a newspaper in Leipzig, to reprint the story. After Louis Napoleon's downfall, the French newspapers were publishing his papers and correspondence. Marx wrote that on March 25 of that year *Le Petit Journal*, which was listing imperial expenditures, carried this item: "Vogt, il lui est remis en août 1859 40,000 frs." On April 15 the *Volksstaat* thereupon reported that Karl Vogt had received 40,000 francs from the French imperial government. The *Volksstaat* felt obliged to publish Vogt's denial on May 3, according to *Werke*, 33:endnote 255. Marx's letter to Liebknecht had not been quite accurate. The item in *Le Petit Journal*, as I confirmed in the Bibliothèque Nationale in Paris, had carried a question mark after the name "Vogt". Furthermore, Vogt is a common name in German (it means "abbot"), and Alsace had its share of inhabitants named Vogt. In point of fact, on the same day *Le Petit Journal* listed the questionable Vogt, it also reported: "Wohl, constructeur à Strasbourg. En 1866 il a reçu une avance de 40,000 frs." After Liebknecht remonstrated with Marx for putting him in an embarrassing position, Marx admitted that he had improved his evidence: there had indeed been a question mark. He refused, however, to give up his proof. He argued that *Le Petit Journal* was a conservative newspaper and he insisted, "Out of spiritual affinity with Vogt it even put a question mark after his name." As for the absence of a first name: "Vogt *sans phrase*—that could only be the 'famous' Karl Vogt of Geneva!" letter of May 4, 1871, *Werke*, 33:220. None of these skewed arguments changes the fact that Marx had falsified the report and that a questionable last name was no evidence whatever of Karl Vogt's guilt. Once again, Marx had been caught improving reality.
65. W. O. Henderson, "The Firm of Ermen & Engels in Manchester," *Internationale Wissenschaftliche Korrespondenz*, no. 11–12 (Apr. 1971):1–

10. The firm had been founded as a partnership of Engels' father and one Peter Ermen.

66. Letters, Marx to Engels, March 2; Engels to Marx, March 4; Marx to Engels, March 5, 1858. *Werke*, 29:291–92, 293–95, 296–97.

67. May 7, 1867, ibid., 31:298.

68. The companion was Marx's friend and admirer, Ludwig Kugelmann, whom Marx had been visiting in Hanover when he made the tour of the foundry. Later during this stay in Karlsbad Marx quarreled with Kugelmann and broke off relations with him. The incident in the factory (but not the quarrel) was reported, with Marx's words being directly quoted, by Kugelmann's daughter, Franziska, in a memoir in *Mohr und General*, p. 314.

69. Letter to Engels, Oct. 19, 1867, *Werke*, 31:368.

70. Letter to Engels, May 22, 1854, ibid., 28:362.

71. Letter of June 27, 1867, ibid., 31:305.

72. Frequent references in his letters; see also Félix Regnault, "Les maladies de Karl Marx," *Revue anthropologique* 43 (July–Sept. 1933):293–317, and Padover, *Karl Marx*, Appendix XII.

Chapter 8. The Politics of *Capital*

1. On primitive communism see ch. 10 (problem of Russian *obshchina*), below; on Algeria, where Marx, who was very ill, went to escape the British climate, see his letter to his daughter Laura in which he reported on what he saw as a commendable social equality of the Algerians, but, "Still they'll go to the devil without a revolutionary movement." Apr. 13–14, 1882, *Werke*, 35:309.

2. See Engels' prefaces to vols. 2 and 3 of *Das Kapital* and endnote 1 (the latter written by the Soviet editors) of the *Werke* edition of vol. 1 (*Werke*, vol. 23). The endnote gives additional details on the whole effort, including the closely related works. As in the case of Engels, the anonymous editors must be read with caution. The three volumes of *Das Kapital* are numbered vols. 23–25 of the *Werke*. All references here are to that edition, but the original identification as vols. 1, 2, and 3 of *Das Kapital* will be kept. In English, references are to *Capital*, 1 (trs. Samuel Moore and Edward Aveling; New York, 1947 [original ed., 1887]); 2 and 3 (New York, 1967 [original ed., 1909]).

3. Letter of Feb. 22, 1858, *Werke*, 29:551.

4. Reference here will be to *Grundrisse der Kritik der politischen Ökonomie (Rohentwurf) 1857–1858* ([East] Berlin, 1953); *Zur Kritik der politischen Ökonomie*, in *Werke*, vol. 13; *Theorien über den Mehrwert*, *Werke*, vol. 26 (actually 3 vols.).

5. According to the anonymous editors, *Grundrisse*, pp. vii and 149n., who add that Marx returned briefly to the ms. at the end of May or beginning of June 1858. See, in English, *Grundrisse*, tr. Martin Nicolaus (New York, 1973), pp. 7–12.

6. McLellan, *Karl Marx*, pp. 290–303, 341–53, respectively (pp. 341–43, which reprint other material, contain actually less than one full page of text).

7. *Werke*, 30:248.

8. McLellan in *Karl Marx* minimizes the importance of the ms., which Engels, compounding confusion, named "The Critique of Political Economy," the most overused title in Marx's writings. In the text of *Karl Marx* (p. 335) McLellan unaccountably suggests that only "some of this [i.e., the 1861–63 ms.] contained material later incorporated in the three volumes of *Capital*." This misleadingly and mysteriously implies that there was other source material. All other attributions assert unequivocally that the 1861–63 ms. was the direct source of both *Das Kapital* and *Theorien über den Mehrwert*, although the ms. naturally drew on Marx's earlier studies. Furthermore, to show the progression of Marx's economic writings, McLellan includes in the appendix of his biography a diagram listing the works designated as such. In the diagram the *Grundrisse* is a large presence leading directly to *Capital* and *Theories of Surplus Value* through a blank where the great 1861–63 ms. should stand.

9. In his two prefaces (n. 2, above), but the prefaces themselves differ about just what part of the whole Marx was writing or rewriting. Furthermore, the known Marx-Engels letters for the period from the summer of 1863 to the summer of 1865 contain virtually no mention of *Capital*.

10. Letters, Marx to Engels, July 7, 1866, Feb. 25, 1867, *Werke*, 31:234, 278. Comte, he found, "wretched compared with Hegel." One of the two Balzac works he mentioned was the novel *Le Chef d'oeuvre inconnu*, the story of a painter who repaints his masterpiece so much that he destroys it.

11. In the early 1870s Marx expended some energy on the French translation and the second German edition of vol. 1. Engels said that Marx also wrote a few dozen new pages, which were incorporated into vols. 2 and 3. All that did not matter. Marx could let Engels and Kautsky take care of such details.

12. *Karl Marx: Essai de biographie intellectuelle* (Paris, 1957), p. 344. Rubel dropped the sentence, although not the sense of it, in the revised second edition (1971), to which all other references will be made here.

13. *Werke*, 13:8–9; *Marx-Engels Reader*, pp. 4–5.

14. Plekhanov was the founder of the first Russian Marxian party; the term "dialectical materialism" appeared in his essay on Hegel, published in 1891, according to Rubel, *Karl Marx* (edition of 1971), pp. 293–94, 293–94n.

15. Ibid., pp. 330, 341. I translate Rubel's "*éthicien*" as "moral philosopher," although the dictionary sanctions "ethician."

16. McLellan, *Karl Marx*, p. 299.

17. (London, 1952), pp. 5, 11, 55–57.

18. *Das Kapital*, 1:49; *Capital*, 1:1. The *Critique* had opened, "At first

view bourgeois wealth appears as a monstrous accumulation of commodities, the individual commodity as its elementary being [*Dasein*]," *Werke*, 13:15. In *Capital* Marx was referring back to this by putting quotation marks around "monstrous accumulation of commodities."

19. *Das Kapital*, 1:85; *Capital*, 1:41–42.

20. This occurs in the penultimate chapter (see text, below, where expropriators are expropriated). The final chapter, dealing with a new subject which Marx did not bother to pursue further, may have been added to persuade authority of the book's harmlessness, or it may be another example of the disorder in Marx.

21. *Das Kapital*, 1:533–34; *Capital*, 1:519.

22. *Das Kapital*, 1:790–91; *Capital*, 1:788–89.

23. *Das Kapital*, 3:828; *Capital*, 3:820. I have changed the order in this badly organized paragraph so that the time sequence is in accord with the logical development.

24. *Randglossen zum Programm der deutschen Arbeiterpartei*, *Werke*, 19:15–32; *Critique of the Gotha Program*, *Political Writings*, 3:341–59.

25. "[The individual] receives a certificate from society saying that he has furnished such and such an amount of labor (after society deducts labor done for the common fund), and with this certificate he draws from the social stock as much as the same amount of labor costs," *Werke*, 19:20; *Political Writings*, 3:346.

26. *Werke*, 19:21; *Political Writings*, 3:347.

27. Joseph Schumpeter, *Ten Great Economists* (London, 1952), p. 55.

28. Reprinted, *inter alia*, in Marx and Engels, *Selected Works in Two Volumes* (London, 1942–43), 1:282–337. It has also been published as an individual work, usually entitled confusingly *Value, Price and Profit* (instead of *Wages . . .*), e.g., the edition published by International Publishers (New York, 1955). This is because Eleanor Marx, who brought out the first printing in 1898, took it upon herself to change the title. The confusions are compounded when we recall Marx's talks in Brussels, published originally in the *NRZ* under the title "Wage-Labor and Capital."

29. *Selected Works in Two Volumes*, 1:282.

30. Paul Samuelson, "Wages and Interest: A Dissection of Marxian Economic Models," *American Economic Review* 47 (December 1957):911.

31. To Ludwig Kugelmann, July 11, 1868, *Werke*, 32:552; *Selected Correspondence*, p. 209.

32. *The Random House Dictionary of the English Language* (unabridged; New York, 1969).

33. Following is Smith's argument, which began by positing a primitive society: "In that early and rude state of society . . . the quantity of labor necessary for acquiring different objects seems to be the only circumstance which can afford any rule for exchanging them one for the other. If . . . it usually costs twice the labor to kill a beaver which it does to kill a deer, one beaver should naturally exchange for or be worth two deer" (*Wealth of Nations*, Book 1, ch. 6). Note the bald

assumption of how a primitive society functioned, and Smith's hesitancy and qualifications. But uses of the logic of supply and demand occur in the same chapter, where Smith attributes high prices to scarcity, and in ch. 4 where he explains the low "exchange value" of water by its abundance, and, again in Book 3, ch. 2, "Abundance, therefore, renders provisions cheap." Samuelson has pointed out that "supply and demand are still operating," arguing that if it required still more time to kill a skunk than a beaver or a deer, but if there were no demand for skunks, they would not be hunted and thus, in effect, would be defined as valueless (*Economics*, 10th ed. [New York, 1976], p. 735).

34. *Das Kapital*, 1:207; *Capital* 1:174. In a letter to Engels on June 23, 1868, thus less than a year after the first volume of *Capital* appeared, Marx sneered at Adam Smith for attributing value to the capitalist's function. Marx was satirizing Smith's self-contradictory definition of profit as both a production cost and an unearned return. Marx made his point by personifying the argument and calling Smith "that same man whose organ[s] of pissing and procreating also coincide intellectually" (*Werke*, 32:101).

Elsewhere Marx gave the capitalist credit for increased value. Thus, as we have seen, the *Communist Manifesto* said the capitalist served progress and well-being, since he had necessarily created new value by destroying inefficient feudalism and replacing it with a more productive economic system.

Marx might have had less difficulty here by making a distinction between the pure capitalist, i.e., the man who simply invests his money and never goes near the company in question, and the entrepreneur engaged in active "inspection and superintendence." Actually, Marx's capitalist is a capitalist-entrepreneur in this case and throughout most of *Capital*.

In vol. 3 (*Das Kapital*, p. 400; *Capital*, p. 382), however, Marx makes that distinction, but does little with it. Perhaps he realized that it would have been only a minor evasion, since the investor of money, if he is acting rationally, must do the *work* of determining the proper investment to be made. Thus the modern capitalistic economy requires the highly trained and appropriately paid functions of investment adviser and securities analyst. Of course the man-with-the-money may be an heir whose sole act of "work" consists in selecting an investment adviser to make his financial decisions for him, but our concern here is economics, not justice.

35. *Das Kapital*, 1:55; *Capital*, 1:7–8.

36. *Werke*, 13:23–24.

37. Ibid., 19:15; *Political Writings*, 3:341.

38. *Das Kapital*, 1:49–98 passim, and especially 1:200–213; *Capital*, 1:1–55 passim, and 1:156–80.

39. *Das Kapital*, 1:181; *Capital*, 1:145. Ricardo had begun his *Principles of Political Economy* with the conception of labor power but Marx gave it functions that would doubtless have astonished him.

40. In his own English in "Wages, Price and Profit," *Selected Works in Two Volumes*, 1:312.
41. Note that Marx began *Capital* by ignoring services and defining all economic values, including the split identity labor/labor power, as commodities. Thus he would call a massage or a taxi ride a commodity. If this strains meaning, it need not detain us, since it does not affect his reasoning significantly. It is, however, another example of the reductive character of that reasoning.
42. Marx's discussion, "The Buying and Selling of Labor Power," *Das Kapital*, 1:181–91, and *Capital*, 1:145–55.
43. *Das Kapital*, 1:224; *Capital*, 1:191–92. Marx's general discussion on the whole subject in the chapter "Constant Capital and Variable Capital," *Das Kapital*, 1:213–25; *Capital*, 1:180–94.
44. There are other confusing definitions which might be touched upon because Marx insists upon them. We may then safely leave them behind, since they are not, when examined carefully, found to be essential to this discussion. Marx divides constant capital into fixed capital, i.e., the instruments of production, and circulating capital, i.e., raw material, fuel, etc., thus those other capital components which other economists would call variable capital. This leads to the misleadingly named set of definitions: circulating capital (*zirkulierendes* or *flüssiges Kapital*), which is different from circulation capital (*Zirkulationskapital*), defined as money and goods used in *exchange* as opposed to *production*.
45. *Das Kapital*, 1:651; *Capital*, 1:636–37. See the long chapter "The General Law of Capitalist Accumulation" and especially the section "Relative Diminution of the Variable Part of Capital Simultaneously with the Progress of Accumulation and of the Concentration that Accompanies It," *Das Kapital*, 1:640–740, 650–57; *Capital*, 1:627–735, 635–42.
46. *Das Kapital*, 1:675, 674; *Capital*, 1:661, 660.
47. *Das Kapital*, 1:791; *Capital*, 1:789.
48. Marx tried to support this logic with an example, but he had to torture words into meaninglessness in order to make his example do the work. Thus he compared the production totals of a British and a Chinese spinner, one using a machine and the other a spinning wheel to produce cotton thread. Marx began by contradicting himself from one sentence to the next. He argued that since the English and the Chinese spinners "would work with the same intensity, they would produce the same values in one week." The next sentence continued, "Despite this equality there is a huge difference between the value of the weekly production of the Englishman, who works with a massive machine, and the Chinese, who has only a spinning wheel." Marx noted that the English worker produced "several hundred pounds," as compared with the one pound of his Chinese counterpart. *Das Kapital*, 1:632; *Capital*, 1:618. Once again, when Marx willed it, equality equaled inequality.
49. Marx and Engels, *Selected Works in Two Volumes*, 1:282–84.

50. *Das Kapital*, 3:836; *Capital*, 3:828.
51. Eugen von Böhm-Bawerk, *Karl Marx and the Close of His System* (London, 1898), pp. 49, 60. Böhm-Bawerk was minister of finances in the old Austrian Empire three times and a teacher of Joseph Schumpeter, who held the same position in the Austrian Republic.
52. Ibid., pp. 191–92. The defenders of Marx's economics have offered counter-arguments to Böhm-Bawerk's, and the debate continues.

The hundredth anniversary of the publication of vol. 1 of *Capital* inspired a number of new books and articles. This is a tiny fraction of the enormous Marxian literature, and only a small fraction of this fraction can be mentioned here. In it, at least, many of the major problems are recapitulated, with the surplus value of newer historical experience as a possible test of the theory. See, e.g., M. C. Howard and J. E. King, eds., *The Economics of Marx* (New York, 1976), and David Horowitz, ed., *Marx and Modern Economics* (New York, 1972). These are collections of articles by Marxists and others more or less sympathetic to more or less of the Marxian economic theory. Ernest Mandel, *Marxist Economic Theory*, 2 vols. (New York and London, 1970; 1st [French-language] ed., 1962) is a brave and massive effort to reconstitute the theory for contemporary application. Joan Robinson, *An Essay on Marxian Economics* (London, 1942) is a carefully sympathetic view by one of John Maynard Keynes's closest followers. Mrs. Robinson, who believed that Marx and Keynes had much more in common than Keynes himself would ever admit, avoided either rejecting or accepting Marx's labor theory of value while agreeing with Marx that "owning capital is not a productive activity" (p. 21). Michio Morishima, *Marx's Economics* (Cambridge, 1973) is a sophisticated study by a mathematical economist who takes Marxian economic mathematics seriously. Attempting a compromise between Marxian and non-Marxian economics, Morishima accepts such Marxian assumptions as "exploitation," but, in the end, rejects the labor theory of value. In general the Marxian and demi-Marxian scholars, for their part, used arguments based on Marx's premises, e.g., value theory and the corollary that capitalism meant exploitation, to rebut criticisms from outside the Marxian thought system. A dialogue has not been truly joined.
53. *Das Kapital*, 3:627–821; *Capital*, 3:614–813.
54. *Werke*, 4:466; *Works*, 6:488.
55. *Werke*, 8:198; *Political Writings*, 2:238–39.
56. *Das Kapital*, 3:821; *Capital*, 3:813.
57. *MEGA*, I, 3:11; *Werke*, 1:398; *Works*, 3:195.
58. *Das Kapital*, 1:660; *Capital*, 1:645.
59. *Grundrisse*, pp. 499–502; *Grundrisse*, tr. Nicolaus, pp. 604–7.
60. *Das Kapital*, 1:644–46n. (quotation, p. 644); *Capital*, 1:629–31n. (quotation, p. 630). Marx incidentally repeated the charge of plagiarism, which he had developed in another long footnote, *Das Kapital*, 1:529–30n .; *Capital*, 1:514–15n.
61. *Das Kapital*, 1:476–77; *Capital*, 1:456–57.

62. *Das Kapital,* 1:245–320; *Capital,* 1:214–88.
63. *Das Kapital,* 1:674; *Capital,* 1:660–61.
64. *Das Kapital,* 1:453, 509–10; *Capital,* 1:430, 491.
65. *Das Kapital,* 1:469; *Capital,* 1:447.
66. *Das Kapital,* 1:507–8; *Capital,* 1:489.
67. *Das Kapital,* 3:517; *Capital,* 3:501.
68. *Das Kapital,* 1:391–530; *Capital,* 1:365–515.
69. *Das Kapital,* 1:399–401 (quotation, p. 401); *Capital,* 1:373–76 (quotation, p. 376).
70. *Das Kapital,* 1:402; *Capital,* 1:377.
71. From an interview, quoted, Leonard Silk, *The Economists* (New York, 1976), p. 166, and the article by Leontief, "The Significance of Marxian Economics for Present-Day Economic Theory," in Horowitz, ed., *Marx and Modern Economics,* p. 98.
72. *Das Kapital,* 1:345, 351–52; *Capital,* 1:315, 322–23.
73. Dante Alighieri, *The Inferno,* John Ciardi, tr. (New Brunswick, N.J., 1954), Canto X.
74. *Das Kapital,* 1:85–98; *Capital,* 1:41–55.
75. We have already dealt with these subjects in text, above: the metaphysical character of the commodity, and use and exchange value.
76. *Das Kapital,* 1:95; *Capital,* 1:53.
77. *Das Kapital,* 3:823; *Capital,* 3:815.
78. *Das Kapital,* 1:146; *Capital,* 1:108–9. Marx used the world *Zirkulation,* which translators have usually taken directly into English, but I think it is better rendered by "commerce."
79. *Das Kapital,* 1:189–91; *Capital,* 1:155. Marx also attacked Bentham for Adam Smith's crime of elevating the idea of self-interest, the "invisible hand," as a dynamic principle of a beneficent capitalism. Probably Marx transferred the accusation from Smith to Bentham because he respected and even liked Smith too much.
80. *Das Kapital,* 1:302; *Capital,* 1:272.
81. *Das Kapital,* 1:636; *Capital,* 1:622.
82. *Das Kapital,* 1:342; *Capital,* 1:312.
83. *Das Kapital,* 1:677, 2:484; *Capital,* 1:664, 2:488.
84. *Das Kapital,* 1:96*n.,* 21; *Capital,* 1:53*n.,* xxiv. The second reference is from an additional note, dated Jan. 24, 1873, which Marx wrote for the second German-language edition.
85. *Das Kapital,* 1:220*n.*; *Capital,* 1:188*n.*
86. *Das Kapital,* 2:372, 1:94*n.*; *Capital,* 2:372, 1:52*n.*
87. Böhm-Bawerk, *Karl Marx and the Close of His System,* p. 220. His book was published originally in German in 1896.
88. Engels, understanding this in his character as world-historical masochist, could take his odd satisfaction from the blows accepted on behalf of Marx. He had prepared for this earlier by accepting punishment directly from Marx. Still later, Karl Kautsky could take his share of the blame for his part in editing *Theories of Surplus Value,* as well as for

other derelictions committed within the context of the German Social Democracy. That leads to blameworthy others, etc., etc.

89. Quoted in Julius Braunthal, *History of the International* (New York and Washington, 1967), 1:135–36.

90. One profound student of Marx, Robert C. Tucker, has emphasized the political content of *Capital*, although he conceived of the work as a *study* of power and did not directly consider it as an *instrument* of power. See Robert C. Tucker, in "Marx as a Political Theorist," paper given at an international symposium on Marx, held at the University of Notre Dame, April 1966, published in Nicholas Lobkowicz, ed., *Marx and the Western World* (Notre Dame, Ind., 1967). Tucker said of Marx: "His major work, *Das Kapital*, was in its special way a study in rulership. Its central theme was as much political as economic. . . . Marx's economics of capitalism was quite literally a 'political economy'—the phrase that he himself always used in referring to economics. To analyze it in these terms is to see Marx as the essentially political thinker that he was. His vision of the political saw the productive process itself as the prime field of power relations between man and man. And his position as a political philosopher was basically determined by this fact" (p. 126).

Power as a subject of direct concern is absent from the illuminating Shlomo Avineri, *The Social and Political Thought of Karl Marx* (Cambridge, 1968), which, moreover, places less emphasis on the political than the social. Marxian in its premises, the book ignores the politics in *Capital* and accepts Marx's official definition of the political as an inevitable and subordinate expression of socioeconomic reality.

CHAPTER 9. THE POLITICS OF INTERNATIONALISM

1. As early as 1843, in *The Holy Family*, Marx gave nationalism its precise coordinates in history: "The egoism that is essential to the very meaning of the phenomenon 'nation' is greater and purer than the egoism of a particular estate or community of economic interests [*Korporation*]." *MEGA*, I, 3:295; *Werke*, 2:127; *Works*, 4:120.

2. *Werke*, 5:202: *Works*, 7:212. The article was probably written by Engels, but Marx may have added a phrase or two. In any case it expressed the *NRZ*'s policy, as determined by Marx.

3. *Werke*, 4:479; *Works*, 6:502.

4. *Werke*, 4:479; *Works*, 6:502–3.

5. Issue of Nov. 3, 1848, *Werke*, 5;450; *Works*, 7:495. That did not prevent Marx from holding the opposite opinion, which he expressed three years later. Retroactively he joined *La Réforme* in regretting the enfeeblement of French patriotism: "The Republic, therefore, was not confronted by a *national* enemy—Thus no tremendous developments to kindle energy, accelerate the revolutionary movement." *Die Klassen-*

kämpfe in Frenkreich 1848 bis 1850, Werke, 7:21; *The Class Struggles in France, Political Writings,* 2:48.

6. Jan. 13, 1849, *W,* 6:168; *Works,* 8:230.

7. Letter of Feb. 7, 1882, *Werke,* 35:273, 270.

8. Letter of Feb. 22, 1882, ibid., pp. 279–80.

9. Recounted here, ch. 4.

10. *Werke,* 9:116; *Works,* 12:114.

11. *Werke,* 16:13: *Political Writings,* 8:81.

12. In the *Tribune* article of June 14, 1853, mentioned in text, above.

13. See Marx, *Secret Diplomatic History of the Eighteenth Century and the Story of the Life of Lord Palmerston,* ed. Lester Hutchinson (New York, 1969). Marx's more fantastic articles were not published in the *Tribune* but in the *Free Press,* a small London newspaper published by the M.P., David Urquhart. Actually, Engels wrote most of the Crimean War articles appearing in the *Tribune,* but as the military expert of the two, he kept to the more technical aspects. His military judgments were frequently as absurd as Marx's conspiratorial-political view of the war. Marx however, also communicated a sense of the underlying verities of power politics, while the articles of Engels lay drowned in the shallows of his mind.

14. The logic of Marx's Russian policy led to other twists as he fitted other countries to it. Thus he became a great Turkophile, and despite his detestation of peasants in general, found much to praise in the Turk, who was "one of the *ablest and most moral representatives of the peasantry in Europe,*" letter to Wilhelm Liebknecht, Feb. 4, 1878, *Werke,* 34:317. It followed, thus, that those Greeks still under Turkish rule were counterrevolutionary by definition. Marx took occasion to express his satisfaction when the Turks put down the Greek rebellion of 1854. The Greeks, he explained off-handedly, were a treacherous lot, and their Christian neighbors "despised them thoroughly," *Tribune,* Mar. 29, 1854, *Werke,* 10:132. Marx's paranoia never got quite out of touch with the practical politics of his revolution, however, whatever twists within twists were required. The point here and in all cases was to frustrate Russia and use her for the cause.

15. June 14, 1853, *Werke,* 9:95–102; quotation, p. 96; *Works,* 12:93–100; quotation, p. 94.

16. June 25, 1853, *Werke,* 9:127–33; quotations, pp. 128, 133; *Works,* 12:125–33; quotations, pp. 126, 132.

17. Published Sept. 9 to Dec. 2, 1854, *Werke,* 10:433–85; quotation, p. 444. Reprinted, Marx, *On Revolution,* ed. Saul K. Padover (New York, 1971), pp. 586–629; quotation, p. 594.

18. "Sir,/The Committee who have organized the meeting as announced in the enclosed Bill, respectfully request the favor of your attendance. The production of this will admit you to the committee room where the Committee will meet at half 7./I am, Sir, your very Respectfully,/ W. R. Cremer/To Dr. Marx," quoted in *The Founding of the First Inter-*

national: A Documentary Record, ed. Leonard E. Mins (New York, 1937), pp. 57–58.

19. Letter of Nov. 4, 1864, *Werke,* 31:13; the full letter, pp. 9–16. *Selected Correspondence,* p. 146; letter (without passages on other subjects), pp. 146–49.

20. Inaugural Address, *Werke,* 16:5–13; *Political Writings,* 3:73–81. Marx wrote it originally in English and later translated it into German.

21. *Werke,* 31:16; *Selected Correspondence,* p. 149. Marx expressed the principle of action in the original Latin phrase, "*fortiter in re, suaviter in modo.*"

22. *Werke,* 16:5; *Political Writings,* 3:73.

23. *Werke,* 16:7; *Political Writings,* 3:75.

24. London *Times,* Apr. 17, 1863. The German economist and academic socialist Lujo Brentano, writing in 1872, was evidently the first to call attention to the false quotation. Marx responded furiously and Brentano attacked again; their debate expanded to comprise a half-dozen articles in the German press. Soon after Marx's death, Eleanor Marx found herself defending her father against an attack in the English press. Then Engels, again tidying up after Marx, attempted to scotch the story in the foreword to the fourth German edition of *Das Kapital,* published in 1890, and, once again, in a long pamphlet in 1891. The documentation is collected in two pamphlets: Brentano, *Meine Polemik mit Karl Marx* (Berlin, 1890), and Engels, *In Sachen Brentano contra Marx wegen angeblicher Zitatsfälschung, Werke,* 22:95–185. Brentano, reprinting the truncated quotation (*Meine Polemik,* p. 24), was able to give its origin: the book *Theory of Exchanges* by the monetary crank G. Henry Roy. Brentano went on to reprint a number of other quotations (pp. 24–25), which Roy had similarly falsified. The Gladstone statement as given in the address is, in fact, a truncated version of Roy's initially truncated quotation. It is not credible that Marx had used the Roy quotation innocently, since it so clearly reverses the sense of the Gladstone speech. In any case, Marx falsified the falsification. Against Brentano's charges Marx asserted: (1) the quotation as he had given it appeared in an article on the International published by a radical English professor in 1870 and in the *Theory of Exchanges,* (2) that the *Times* and two other London newspapers quoted Gladstone in the same sense as the address, although with other words and phrases, and in a different order, (3) that the quotation was, it is true, not in Hansard (the published parliamentary minutes), but that Gladstone himself had personally suppressed it (*Volksstaat* [Social-Democratic newspaper, Berlin], June 1 and Aug. 7, 1872, *Werke,* 22:141–43; 149–56). It was a mixture of the irrelevant, the confusing, and the untrue. In his counter-reply Brentano quoted the passages from the *Times* (as given here in the text) and the *Morning Star* (but not the third London newspaper). In both cases he showed (*Meine Polemik,* pp. 26–28) that Marx's first quotation in the address and also the corrected one in his reply were

each false in its own way. Brentano also pointed out (p. 14) that Marx himself had said he had given the material on the International to the radical professor; the professor, whom Marx had given as an authority, had been quoting Marx as his authority. Later, Brentano wrote Gladstone to ask about Marx's accusation that he had changed the Hansard report (which, incidentally, agreed with that of *The Times*). Gladstone, taking the trouble to reply in two letters in 1890, denied it (*Werke*, 22:184).

The false quotation also appeared in *Das Kapital*, 1:681 and 681n. (*Capital*, 1:668), but with new discrepancies. In the German edition the German translation does not agree with the English quotation as given: it leaves out the "is" between "intoxicating augmentation of wealth and power" and "entirely confined to classes of property"— joining both phrases by the three dots indicating ellipsis. In both German and English editions the sentence continues beyond that point and follows the passage in Roy's *Theory of Exchanges*, which added a series of phrases softening the sense of "entirely confined to classes of property."

The objections to the quotation have subsided partly because people seldom doubt the printed word when it is often repeated. Another reason lies in the character of the disputants. On the one side were Marx and his defenders, who would not admit a flaw in his infallibility and integrity, and who were supported by the expanding masses of German Social Democrats and other Marxian parties. On the other side were isolated individuals raising a question about an obscure matter to resistant Marxists and indifferent non-Marxists.

One additional confusion was caused by Marx's manner of citing Gladstone. Marx began the address with a quotation from Gladstone's budget speech of 1864, so identified. The questionable quotation plus a genuine one to which it had been appended came from the budget speech of 1863, which was not specifically identified. The reader would normally assume that only one speech, that of 1864, was at issue.

25. *Werke*, 16:9; *Political Writings*, 3:77.

26. *Werke*, 16:13; *Political Writings*, 3:81.

27. Meeting of Oct. 5, 1864, *The General Council of the First International: Minutes* (Moscow, 1963), 1:37.

28. Meeting of Sept. 25, 1866, ibid., 2:36. Marx's demurrer was that he was a "head worker and not a hand worker."

29. Letter, Marx to Engels, Oct. 4, 1867, *Werke*, 31:354.

30. *The General Council of the First International: Minutes*, vols. 1–5 passim.

31. Letter, Sept. 11, 1867, *Werke*, 31:342–43; *Selected Correspondence*, p. 194. Marx's position was not affected by the fact that he had no organization with which to correspond in his character as corresponding secretary for Germany. The law forbade German groups from entering into international associations of this kind, and German members of

the International were only those persons who took the initiative of joining as individuals.

32. *The General Council of the First International: Minutes*, 2 passim.

33. Julius Braunthal, *History of the International* (New York and Washington, 1967), 1:114–15.

34. *The General Council of the First International: Minutes*, 3:65, 83.

35. Letter to Friedrich Bolte, Nov. 23, 1871, *Werke*, 33:332–33; *Selected Correspondence*, p. 271.

36. *Werke*, 16:197; the instructions in full, pp. 190–99.

37. Braunthal, *History of the International*, 1:136–41.

38. At a meeting of the General Council on July 20, 1869, Marx explained his theoretical position at length. "The working class who had nothing to inherit had no interest in the question. . . . Besides, if the working class had sufficient power to abolish the right to inheritance, it would be powerful enough to proceed to expropriation, which would be a much simpler and efficient process." *The General Council of the First International: Minutes*, 3:130.

39. Letter of July 20, 1870, *Werke*, 33:5. Marx then wrote a letter dated Aug. 22–30 with similar sentiments to the executive committee of the German socialist party adhering to his ideas, *Werke*, 17:268–70; *Selected Correspondence*, pp. 245–47. The committee published it, and the French members of the International were outraged.

40. *Werke*, 17:3–7; *Political Writings*, 3:172–76. The address was also published as a flier a few days later. Marx's addresses plus other writings on the Commune are also conveniently collected in one English-language volume, Marx and Engels, *On the Paris Commune* (Moscow, 1971). This also includes earlier drafts of the third and most important of the addresses (see text, below), but it leaves out other valuable material.

41. Letter of Aug. 15, 1870, *Werke*, 33:39–41; *Selected Correspondence*, pp. 241–43.

42. Engels' article of Jan. 7, 1871, three weeks before a thoroughly defeated France agreed to an armistice, said, "The forces on either side are nearly balancing off each other," *Werke*, 17:227. Engels' series of articles on the war, *Werke*, 17:11–264.

43. *Werke*, 17:176–77; *Political Writings*, 3:184–85.

44. *Werke*, 33:54.

45. Georges Clemenceau, the future premier and then mayor of the Eighteenth *Arrondissement* (Montmartre), later recalled the scene: The mob was "in the grip of some kind of frenzy. Amongst them were *chasseurs*, soldiers of the line, National Guardsmen, women and children. All were shrieking like wild beasts. . . . I observed then that pathological phenomenon which might be called blood-lust. . . . Children brandished indescribable trophies; women, disheveled and emaciated, flung their arms about while uttering raucous cries. . . . Men were dancing about and jostling each other in a kind of savage

fury." Quoted in Roger L. Williams, *The French Revolution of 1870–1871* (New York, 1969), pp. 113–14.

46. Blanqui himself, with his odd luck, had been safely transferred from a Paris prison to one elsewhere in France just before the rising took place.

47. On April 19 the Commune published the "Declaration to the French People," written by a Proudhonian journalist, which called for a federal union of completely autonomous, somewhat socialist communes, but the majority of the Communal Assembly was completely opposed to Proudhon's ideas of local autonomy and did not take the "Declaration" seriously. "Declaration" quoted in Stewart Edwards, *The Paris Commune, 1871* (London, 1971), p. 218. See also Williams, *The French Revolution of 1870–1871*, pp. 134–40.

48. *The General Council of the First International: Minutes*, 4:57–208 passim.

49. Some French members of the International disowned the Paris rising. Among them was Henri-Louis Tolain, a leader of the French worker delegation that founded the International in 1864. He was elected to the National Assembly in February, and stood by it—against the Commune.

50. Draft letter of May 13, 1871, *Werke*, 33:226–27; *Selected Correspondence*, pp. 264–65. The letter was addressed jointly to Frankel and Louis-Eugène Varlin, a bookbinder who had supported Bakunin against Marx at the International's Basel Congress in 1869.

51. According to a letter, dated April 29, 1871, to Marx from a mutual friend, the German lawyer Victor Schily, reprinted in Jules Rocher, ed., *Lettres de Communards et de militants de l'Internationale à Marx, Engels et autres* (Paris, 1934), p. 39.

52. Comprising the chapter "The Commune: Social Reform," in Edwards, *The Paris Commune, 1871*, pp. 249–76, from which most of these details are taken. See also Williams, *The French Revolution of 1870–1871*, pp. 113–52.

53. Edwards, *The Paris Commune, 1871*, p. 245.

54. Letter to Wilhelm Liebknecht, Apr. 6, 1871, *Werke*, 33:200; *Selected Correspondence*, p. 262.

55. The leaders of the Commune ordered the firing of the Palace of the Tuileries (its existence is now marked by the gardens), the City Hall, the Prefecture of Police, and the Palace of Justice. These last buildings survived, as did the Ministry of Finance, which was set afire by the regulars' artillery. Before the fighting, on May 16, the Commune festively and clumsily pulled down the Vendôme column, with its statue of Napoleon.

56. Details of Bloody Week in Edwards, *The Paris Commune, 1871*, pp. 313–50; Williams, *The French Revolution of 1870–1871*, pp. 145–52.

57. John Roberts, "The Myth of the Commune," *History Today* 7 (May 1957):290.

58. *Werke*, 33:200; *Selected Correspondence*, p. 262. This was in the letter in which he had also regretted the failure of the *Communards* to pursue the regular troops.

59. The "Declaration to the French People" of April 19, 1871; see n. 47, above.

60. Letter to Ludwig Kugelmann, Apr. 12, 1871, *Werke*, 33:205–6; *Selected Correspondence*, pp. 262–63. In this letter Marx paraphrased the passage from *The 18th Brumaire* in these words, "The next objective of the French revolution will no longer be, as before, to transfer the bureaucratic-military machine from one hand to another, but to *smash* it."

The *18th Brumaire*, rather, had vaguely foreseen the collapse of Louis Napoleon's "bureaucratic-military governmental machinery" as the peasants lost faith in it. The pamphlet had then specifically said: "The disintegration of the state machine will not endanger centralization. Bureaucracy is only the low and brutal form of centralization." It was another instance of Hegelian-Marxian splitting: the evil centralizing action of Louis Napoleon and a good, i.e., Marxian, centralization for the benefit of all. *Der 18te Brumaire*, *Werke*, 8:204–5; *The 18th Brumaire*, *Political Writings*, 2:245 and 245n.

In later editions Marx and then Engels, following his lead, suppressed the paragraph that began, "The disintegration [*Zertrümmerung*] of the state machine will not endanger centralization."

61. *The General Council of the First International: Minutes*, 4:184. The General Council had co-opted Engels, who had moved to London in September.

62. Ibid., pp. 200, 204; *Der Bürgerkrieg in Frankreich*, *Werke*, 17:313–62; *The Civil War in France*, *Political Writings*, 3:187–268. The earlier drafts were reprinted in *Werke*, 17:493–610; also, in English, *On the Paris Commune*, pp. 102–221. Each successive writing showed great improvement, the greatest following upon the fall of the Commune.

63. *Werke*, 17:319; *Political Writings*, 3:187.

64. *Werke*, 17:339; *Political Writings*, 3:209. The social composition of the Commune has been carelessly studied. Of the total of eighty-one members who actually served in the Communal Assembly, Edwards, for example, classified eighteen as middle class, thirty from the professions or arts, and some thirty-five who were either artisans or revolutionaries. These classifications are misleading and confusing, since professionals are also bourgeois. Furthermore, nearly all the revolutionaries, like Marx and Engels, were middle class in origin. As for the artisans, they could have been apprentices or master craftsmen who were employers at the same time. There were few, if any, industrial workers. The evidence is clear that the Commune was preponderantly bourgeois in composition and leadership, as was to be expected. See Edwards, *The Paris Commune, 1871*, pp. 205–10.

The confusions about the social character of the Commune were matched by those about the character of its political representation. The Commune was more radical than the city it claimed to speak for. Thus, twenty-one persons elected on March 26 refused to serve in a body that was revolutionary by definition. A supplementary election on April 16 returned seventeen new members. A total of eighty-one members actually took their seats, and maximum attendance at the sessions was estimated at about sixty.

65. *Werke*, 17:339; *Political Writings*, 3:209.

66. *Werke*, 17:347; *Political Writings*, 3:217.

67. Letter to Ferdinand Domela Nieuwenhuis, a Dutch socialist (later anarchist), Feb. 22, 1881, *Werke*, 35:160.

68. *Werke*, 17:342; *Political Writings*, 3:213.

69. *Werke*, 17:362; *Political Writings*, 3:233.

70. Richard Pipes, ed., *Revolutionary Russia: A Symposium* (Cambridge, Mass., 1968), p. 72.

71. *Werke*, 17:322, 326; *Political Writings*, 3:191, 195.

72. *Werke*, 17:321; *Political Writings*, 3:190.

73. *Werke*, 17:320; *Political Writings*, 3:188–89.

74. Letter to Kugelmann, June 28, 1871, *Werke*, 33:238.

75. The interview, *Werke*, 17:639–43; quotations, pp. 634, 640.

76. Quoted in Braunthal, *History of the International*, 1:158. Bismarck, going beyond Favre, tried to interest the European powers in taking action against the International, but Great Britain saw no danger in it, and nothing was done. The International's notoriety, however, inspired the British Home Office to inquire courteously of the International just what it was about. Marx accepted the responsibility for replying for the International and on July 12, 1871, sent the Home Office thirteen items, including his Inaugural Address, the statutes, etc. (covering letter, *Werke*, 33:246–47). The Home Office continued to neglect the International.

77. Braunthal, *History of the International*, 1:173.

78. *The General Council of the First International: Minutes*, 1:236. Marx also lost the support of Eccarius, his original protégé in the International, who had become too independent-minded to continue to follow his orders. But now Marx had Engels beside him in the General Council.

79. *Werke*, 17:418–26.

80. Ibid., pp. 418–19, 421–22.

81. At a committee meeting on the second day of the conference, according to notes of his remarks as written down by an unidentified person, ibid., p. 411.

82. *Les prétendues scissions dans l'Internationale*, original in French; German translation entitled *Die angeblichen Spaltungen in der Internationale*, *Werke*, 18:7–51.

83. Quoted in full in Payne, *Karl Marx*, pp. 436–37. The whole story is a concentrate of revolutionary materials and meanings. The work that

Bakunin had contracted to do was—a translation of Marx's *Capital!*
Bakunin's friend was Sergei Nechayev, already an experienced conspiratorial killer. Nechayev, who had won an ascendancy over Bakunin, also collaborated with his friend on the *Revolutionary Catechism*, a
tract advocating the use of crime by a monkish order of dedicated
revolutionaries. It was a remarkable anticipation of the character of
Bolshevik action. Nechayev, who boasted of the murders he had committed, was arrested in 1872 and delivered over to the Russian authorities. He died in prison ten years later. He was the model of Verkhov-
ensky, the nihilistic destroyer of Dostoeveski's *Possessed.* On Nechayev
see also Franco Venturi, *Roots of Revolution: A History of the Populist
and Socialist Movements in Nineteenth-Century Russia* (New York, 1966),
pp. 354–88.

84. Hans Gerth, ed., *The First International: Minutes of The Hague Congress of 1872 with Related Documents* (Madison, Wis., 1958), pp. xv–xvi
(introduction), 184–85 (minutes). Some of this material on the congress, *Werke*, 18:127–207. The story of the monocle as reported by
Theodor Cuno, a participant at the congress, Robert Payne, *Marx* (New
York, 1968), p. 445.

85. Gerth, *The First International . . . The Hague Congress*, p. 186.

86. Ibid., p. 207.

87. Ibid., p. 211.

88. Ibid., p. 212.

89. Ibid., pp. 213–14.

90. Ibid., p. 215.

91. Ibid., pp. 225–31.

92. Braunthal, *History of the International*, 1:191.

93. Ibid., pp. 190–91.

94. Letter to Friedrich Sorge, Sept. 27, 1873, *Werke*, 33:606; *Selected Correspondence*, p. 286. Giving personal reasons, Marx had written of his
approximate intentions more than three months before the congress
to a Russian friend: "I am so overworked . . . that, after September, I
shall *withdraw* from the *commercial* concern. . . . I can no longer afford
. . . to combine two sorts of business of so different a character," *Werke*,
33:477.

95. Letter of Sept. 12–17, 1874, *Werke*, 33:641–42; *Selected Correspondence*,
pp. 288–89.

CHAPTER 10. THE MARXIAN REVOLUTIONARY MACHINE

1. Letter, Mar. 25, 1865, Wilhelm Liebknecht, *Briefwechsel mit Karl Marx
und Friedrich Engels* (The Hague, 1963), p. 50.

2. Letter of Liebknecht to Engels, Dec. 11, 1867, ibid., p. 86.

3. August Bebel, *Aus Meinem Leben* (Berlin, 1953), 1:127–28. He had the
advantage of the leisure provided by a prison term in 1869.

4. Franz Mehring, *Geschichte der deutschen Sozialdemokratie* ([East] Berlin, 1960), 2:339. The "parliamentary operations" were in the North German Reichstag, for which see text, below.

5. Franz Osterroth and Dieter Schuster, *Chronik der deutschen Sozialdemokratie* (Hanover, 1963), p. 32.

6. The seven also included two AGWA followers of Schweitzer, and two members of a splinter group, which had left the AGWA but which returned presently. Also elected were two Democratic allies of Liebknecht and Bebel, all four—socialists and Democrats—as members of the Saxon Peoples' Party.

7. Shlomo Na'aman, "Zur Geschichte des Bundes der Kommunisten in Deutschland in der zweiten Phase seines Bestehens," *Archiv für Sozialgeschichte* 5 (1965):67. Na'aman was referring to the ideology of the Communist League, but the League got its ideas from Marx. Na'aman added that the Communist League could not have done what the Brotherhood did in reaching the workers. By itself, it "otherwise would have been written off as a sect of intellectuals" (p. 67).

8. See Theodore S. Hamerow, *Restoration, Revolution, Reaction* (Princeton, 1958), pp. 207–8.

9. Marx had been supporting potential rebels against Lassalle and building up a dossier against him since 1853. At that time a treacherous lieutenant of Lassalle's visited Marx in London, and began to recount vague calumnies and equally vague plans to revolt among Lassalle's followers. The visitor, one Gustav Levy, told Marx, as Marx put it, that some workers thought Lassalle "was exploiting the party for his *private crap* and wanted to use the workers [of Düsseldorf, where Lassalle was still living and wielding influence] for his *private crimes.*" Marx added, "I believe, after *very close* examination, that *they are right.*" The workers wanted the leadership of the "Marx Party" and Marx promised to join them "in case the circumstances permit." See Marx's letter to Engels about a later visit, May 3, 1856, *Werke*, 29:23–29; quotations, pp. 26, 28–29; also editorial note on original visit, ibid., endnote 39.

In fact, Lassalle and Bismarck had had talks vaguely exploring the possibility of cooperating against the middle-class liberals—from Oct. 1863 to Jan. 1864. Both were too realistic and clever as negotiators to come to any agreement in view of the negative factors: a political union of aristocrats and workers might appeal to the imagination but not to political sense in the contemporary realities. See Shlomo Na'aman, *Lassalle* (Hanover, 1970), pp. 35–39. When Marx heard about the talks (Bismarck later discussed them openly in the Reichstag), he saw his belief confirmed that Lassalle was betraying the workers. But then one might conclude without paranoia that Lassalle was leading German socialism toward an accommodation with the status quo.

10. The Countess Sophie von Hatzfeld, who became his long-enduring mistress and patroness.

11. Lassalle's action was an extravagant response to a cautious order from Marx. In a letter Marx had demanded that Lassalle have the Düsseldorf

Peoples' Assembly pass resolutions supporting the *NRZ*'s policy of refusing to pay taxes and of sending volunteer troops to Berlin; letter, dated Nov. 13, 1848, *Werke*, 39:520. Marx also asked for a personal loan of 200 thalers ($150). On Nov. 14, Lassalle put through the resolution, and then launched the rising on his own (and a Düsseldorf ally's) initiative. Details of the Assembly meeting and the rising, Na'aman, *Lassalle*, pp. 150–61, and *Werke*, 39:endnotes 528–30.

12. But not in the Marx biography. See Mehring, *Geschichte der deutschen Sozialdemokratie*, 1:571. One of Lassalle's first services after the end of the Revolution of 1848 was to collect money for Marx, arriving penniless in Paris. Marx was not grateful. Feeling that Lassalle had been too noisy about it, he was "quite unspeakably angered." Letter of Marx to Ferdinand Freiligrath, July 31, 1849, *Werke*, 27:503.

13. Lassalle was too hasty and physically active to pause long enough for complete and profound thought, but he could think on his own very well indeed. In 1844, at the age of nineteen, he wrote that "industry was itself nothing but the first still camouflaged form of communism." In a long letter, known in the Lassallean literature as the "Industry Letter," to his mother, Sept. 6, 1844, quoted in Na'aman, *Lassalle*, pp. 35–39; quotation, p. 38.

14. *Werke*, 29 passim.

15. In a letter to Engels Marx wrote that Lassalle's manner of dying was "one of the many tactless acts he has committed in his life." But Marx was shaken: "The misfortune of Lassalle has been damnably in my mind these days. After all, he was one of the Old Guard and the enemy of our enemies." Mixing in English words, given here in italics, he went on: "It is hard to believe that such a noisy, *stirring, pushing* person is now dead as a doornail and must *altogether* keep his trap shut. . . . *With all that* I'm sorry that relations were troubled in the last years, but of course it was through his own fault." Sept. 7, 1867, *Werke*, 30:432.

16. Osterroth and Schuster, *Chronik der deutschen Sozialdemokratie*, p. 22.

17. Letter of Dec. 11, 1867, Liebknecht, *Briefwechsel*, p. 82. This is the letter in which he also reported on using *Capital* (see text, above).

18. Letter, Feb. 15, 1865, quoted, *Werke*, 31:endnote 104.

19. Draft letter, Oct. 13, 1868, ibid., 32:568–71; quotation, p. 571.

20. Letters, July 22 and 24, 1869, ibid., pp. 343, 346.

21. Schweitzer had in fact made a special arrangement with the head of the Berlin police. A former lieutenant of his gave the details at a general assembly of the AGWA in May 22–25, 1872, and the members expelled Schweitzer from the party. Meanwhile, in 1871, his newspaper, *Der Social-Demokrat*, had stopped publication, leaving preeminence to Liebknecht's *Volksstaat*. In his new leisure, Schweitzer wrote a successful play and, on July 28, 1875, died.

22. Liebknecht did not even show the *Critique* to Bebel, in prison at the time and doubtless happy not to be troubled by it. It did lead the negotiators to make a few cosmetic changes in the final draft of the Gotha Program. See Mehring, *Karl Marx*, pp. 511–12. A year later, in

1890, the party dropped the "Workers'" from its name, becoming the Social Democratic Party, in order to attract nonworkers. The revolutionary Marx had been right to have been unhappy in 1875.

23. *Randglossen zum Programm der deutschen Arbeiterpartei, Werke,* 19:15–32; *Critique of the Gotha Program, Political Writings,* 3:341–59.

24. *Werke,* 19:28; *Political Writings,* 3:355. In 1850 Marx had expressed the conception but without all this force when conceiving of a "*class dictatorship* [one word in the German] of the proletariat as a necessary transit point on the way toward the *elimination of class differences.*" *Die Klassenkämpfe in Frankreich, Werke,* 7:89; *The Class Struggles in France, Political Writings,* 2:123.

25. Speech, meeting of the Dutch section of the International, Amsterdam, Sept. 8, 1872, *Werke,* 18:159–61.

26. Account and quotation, *Werke,* 20:endnote 1.

27. As quoted by Engels in the *Anti-Dühring* (n. 29, below), *Werke,* 20:118.

28. Quoted, *Werke,* 20:endnote 1.

29. Published in *Vorwärts,* which succeeded Liebknecht's *Volksstaat* in 1876, *Herrn Dührings Umwälzung der Wissenschaft* [Mr. Dühring's scientific revolution], *Werke,* 20:5–303. Dühring was so popular that many Social Democrats protested the publication of the *Anti-Dühring* in *Vorwärts* at the party congress of 1877. Bebel worked out a compromise: the article series was shifted from *Vorwärts* proper to its scientific supplement. *Werke,* 20:endnote 1.

30. This was *Der Sozialdemokrat,* founded in Zurich after the suppression of the party's newspapers in Germany (see text, below); not to be confused with *Der Social-Demokrat,* which halted publication in 1871 as its founder, J. B. von Schweitzer, withdrew from the socialist movement.

31. In his memoirs Bebel tactfully called the trip to London his "journey to Canossa," but he was covering the fact that it was Marx who surrendered. See Bebel, *Aus Meinem Leben,* 3:148–50; quotation, p. 148. Also draft of circular letter by Marx and Engels to Bebel, Liebknecht, and others, Sept. 17–18, 1879, *Werke,* 34:394–408, and (in part) *Selected Correspondence,* pp. 321–27.

32. Osterroth and Schuster, *Chronik der deutschen Sozialdemokratie,* p. 58.

33. Quoted in James Joll, *The Second International, 1889–1914* (London, 1955), p. 66. On the Marxian subculture and its demi-isolated position in German society see Guenther Roth, *The Social Democrats in Imperial Germany: A Study in Working-Class Isolation and National Integration* (Totowa, N.J., 1963).

34. The German title is in Marxian idiom: *Die Voraussetzungen des Sozialismus und die Aufgaben der Sozialdemokratie* [The Postulates of socialism and the tasks of the social democracy]. On Bernstein and his ideas see Peter Gay, *The Dilemma of Democratic Socialism: Eduard Bernstein's Challenge to Marx* (New York, 1962), pp. 73–78 et passim.

35. Gay, *The Dilemma of Democratic Socialism,* pp. 180–84; "sudden catastrophe," p. 76.

36. Of Liebknecht, George Bernard Shaw, observing him at a meeting of the Second International in 1896, four years before Liebknecht's death, wrote in an English journal: "He has become . . . a parliamentarian. . . . He still covers every compromise by the declaration that the Social Democrats never compromise." Quoted in Joll, *The Second International*, p. 76.

37. One socialist leader wrote Bernstein: "My dear Edi, one doesn't formally decide to do what you want, one doesn't say it, one *does it*," quoted ibid., p. 94.

38. One of the Young Ones of the next generation was the son of Wilhelm Liebknecht. In January 1919 Karl Liebknecht became a leader, with Rosa Luxemburg, of the rising of the Spartacists, as the newly organized Communists called themselves then, against the Social Democratic provisional government of Germany. Both were killed. Another Young One was Friedrich Adler, son of Viktor Adler, founder of the Austrian Social Democratic Party. Friedrich Adler assassinated the prime minister of Austria in 1916 as a protest against the war.

39. Franco Venturi, *Roots of Revolution: A History of the Populist and Socialist Movements in Nineteenth-Century Russia* (New York, 1966), p. 81. The circle, besides discussing Western ideas, was also making propaganda for reform and may have undertaken active, if very modest, resistance to the government.

40. Account and quotation, ibid., p. 395.

41. Letter to Ludwig Kugelmann in Hanover, Oct. 12, 1868, *Werke*, 32:567.

42. Albert Resis, "*Das Kapital* Comes to Russia," *Slavic Review* 29, no. 2 (June 1970):219.

43. Ibid., pp. 229–30.

44. Ibid., p. 228.

45. Ibid., pp. 231–32.

46. Ibid., pp. 230–31.

47 See ibid., p. 219; also excerpt from letter of Nikolai Danielson, an economist for the St. Petersburg Mutual Credit Society, inquiring about Russian rights, Sept. 30, and Marx's reply, Oct. 7, 1868, *Werke*, 32:endnote 209, and pp. 563–65. On other details see ibid.: endnote 559. The publisher specialized in "dangerous books," a risky but profitable business in an autocracy with an intelligentsia hungry for ideas. Danielson made the mistake of commissioning Bakunin to do the translating, thus serving Marx's intrigues so well in the International. Another Russian translated four chapters before dropping the work to try—vainly—to help the escape of a populist leader from Siberia. Danielson, remaining personally resistant to Marx's industrial emphasis but tolerant and loyal, thereupon translated the rest of vol. 1 *and* all of vols. 2 and 3, the last including Marx's greatest effort to eliminate agriculture theoretically. At this time more than 90 percent of the Russian population was engaged in agriculture.

48. Resis, "*Das Kapital* Comes to Russia," p. 219. In Highgate Cemetery Marx's funeral bust looks out of the corner of its right eye at the flat,

utilitarian tombstone of the sociologist Herbert Spencer (1820–1903), a defender of capitalism's morality.

49. Ibid., p. 221.

50. Letter of Feb. 13, 1855, *Werke*, 28:434. I am taking the liberty of correcting Marx's hasty sentence, which actually read, "I am not of the *opinion* to see Old Europe . . . "

51. Herzen, for his part, detested Marx and called his followers "Marxids." See his comments in Herzen, *My Past and Thoughts*, abridged and edited by Dwight Macdonald (New York, 1974), pp. 482–85, and "Appendix: Marx v. Herzen," pp. 677–84.

52. Venturi, *Roots of Revolution*, p. 1. It was the opening sentence of the book, which is an unqualified classic. It is also a classic account of populism. Another history of populism is Adam B. Ulam, *In the Name of the People: Prophets and Conspirators in Pre-revolutionary Russia* (New York, 1977), lucid, less detailed and profound than the Venturi book, but more convenient for that and for being rounded off more completely. On the intellectual background see another classic, Isaiah Berlin, *Russian Thinkers* (New York, 1978).

53. Letter, already quoted on the subject of Russians, to Ludwig Kugelmann, Oct. 12, 1868, *Werke*, 32:566–67.

54. Ibid., 16:13; *Political Writings*, 3:81.

55. See Venturi, *Roots of Revolution*, pp. 276–84; *Werke*, 32:endnote 261.

56. Letter, Jan. 13, 1869, *Werke*, 32:243.

57. Venturi, *Roots of Revolution*, pp. 284.

58. Utin episode, ibid., pp. 442–44; quotations, pp. 443, 444; also Woodford D. McClellan, *Revolutionary Exiles: The Russians in the First International and the Paris Commune* (London, 1979), pp. 83–104, 186–88, 200, 240–41.

59. Letter, Mar. 10, 1870, *Werke*, 32:466.

60. Herzen, *My Past and Thoughts*, n. xli. In 1864 Herzen left London and, continuing to publish his newspaper another three years, wandered restlessly about Europe.

61. Before deserting the cause to become a respectable engineer in Russia, Utin rendered it one more service. He pursued Bakunin with such vengeance that Bakunin's friends thrashed him on one occasion. The result of the pursuit, however, was a report on Bakunin's activities which strengthened Marx's case for expelling him from the International.

62. Herzen saw the new men: "Every one of them had some tic and apart from that personal tic they all had one in common, a devouring, irritable, and distorted vanity. . . . All of them were hypochondriacs and physically ill, did not drink wine, and were afraid of open windows. . . . They reminded me of monks who from love for their neighbor came to hating all humanity. . . . One half were constantly repenting, the other half constantly chastising." Ibid., p. 675. See also Dostoevski's *The Possessed*.

63. See accounts in Venturi, *Roots of Revolution,* pp. 627–720; and Ulam, *In the Name of the People,* pp. 297–356. Five terrorists, including a woman, were executed. A second woman was also condemned to die, but found pregnant and spared, she died of natural causes a year later.
64. Letter, Apr. 11, 1881, *Werke,* 35:179. The earthquake, taking place the previous week, had caused great devastation and loss of life on Chios, an Aegean island.
65. E. L. Tomanovskaia, mentioned in Resis, *"Das Kapital"* Comes to Russia," p. 228.
66. "Soziales aus Russland," *Werke,* 18:556–67; "On Social Relations in Russia," *Marx-Engels Reader,* pp. 665–75. Engels was quoting Tkachev in the articles: *Werke,* 18:556, 562; *Marx-Engels Reader,* pp. 665, 671.
67. *Werke,* 18:565–67; *Marx-Engels Reader,* pp. 672–73. Marx then tried to deal with a related question in an undated letter written apparently in 1877. He was commenting on a populist's article in a St. Petersburg journal objecting to the need, as he read Marx, for a mature proletariat to make a socialist revolution. Marx said that his own logic was not so absolutely negative, but he could not show an opening in it, and his new argument lost itself in learned references to Roman antiquity. *Werke,* 19: 107–12.
68. Letter of Feb. 28, 1881, quoted, *Werke,* 19:endnote 155.
69. Nov. 7, 1868, *Werke,* 32:197; *Selected Correspondence,* p. 217 (Marx's scatological expression rendered as "foul mess"). Marx's introductions, both to the *Grundrisse,* written in 1857–58, and the *Critique of Political Economy,* completed and published in 1859, and deriving from it, specifically categorized the commune as belonging to a primitive stage of social development associated with Oriental despotism. Vera Zasulich would have known of the *Critique's* view, but it was not as uncompromisingly specific as Engels' comments. The statement of Engels to Tkachev which made the connection between the obshchina and *"Oriental despotism,"* quoted in text above, based itself on those writings.
70. *Werke,* 19:389–95, 396–400, 401–6, and (the letter itself), 242–43; the letter also ibid., 35:166–67, and, in English, *Selected Correspondence,* pp. 339–40.
71. *Werke,* 19:394.
72. Ibid., p. 398.
73. Letter of Mar. 8, 1881, ibid., p. 243; ibid., 35:167; *Selected Correspondence,* p. 340.
74. *Werke,* 19:295–96; *Marx-Engels Reader,* p. 472.
75. Dec. 14, 1882, *Werke,* 35:408.
76. The first Russian edition was translated by Bakunin in 1869.
77. On Engels and the Plekhanov group, of which another important member was Paul Axelrod, see the relevant letters in the *Werke,* vols. 35–39 passim. See also, with caution, L. F. Ilyichov et al., *Frederick Engels: A Biography* (Moscow, 1974), pp. 441–46. The book, published

by the Institute of Marxism-Leninism and "written by" eight persons according to an introductory note, was published in Russian originally in Moscow in 1970.

78. "Die auswärtige Politik des russischen Zarentums" [The foreign policy of Russian czarism], *Werke*, 22:13–48.

79. Ilyichov et al., *Frederick Engels: A Biography*, p. 442; letter, Engels to Plekhanov, Nov. 1, 1894, *Werke*, 39:305.

80. Letters of Engels to Plekhanov, then back in Switzerland, Feb. 8 and 26, 1895, *Werke*, 39:405–6, 416–17.

81. See Adam B. Ulam, *The Bolsheviks* (New York, 1965), pp. 107–8.

82. The names represented a victory for Lenin of the kind that Marx won at crucial moments, thus over the Willich faction. "Bolshevik" means "member of the majority" and "Menshevik," "member of the minority." Those names derived from just one important vote at the second congress of the Russian Social Democrats, when Lenin had a temporary majority. The Mensheviks remained a much larger party until Lenin wiped them out after he took power. Lenin, who had dominated the conference which organized the congress had, like Marx, assured himself of the maximum possible number of supporters among the delegates. This recalls the London conference of the International which prepared for the climactic congress in 1872. Actually the largest group, the Jewish *Bund*, was very much underrepresented at the congress of the Russian Social Democrats. Most of its members became Mensheviks.

83. Harold Shukman, *Lenin and the Russian Revolution* (New York, 1967), p. 52.

84. The essay "Balances and Prospects—The Moving Forces of the Revolution," in the book *Our Revolution*. See Isaac Deutscher, *The Prophet Armed: Trotsky, 1879–1921* (London, 1954), pp. 149–63 (section of chapter 'Permanent Revolution'). Lenin evidently did not read the book until 1919 (p. 162), but there was no need.

85. V. I. Lenin, *State and Revolution*, in *Selected Works* (London, 1969), p. 345. *State and Revolution* was a short book Lenin wrote in Aug.–Sept. 1917, when he was hiding in Finland after his failure to seize power in the summer and before his successful effort of November.

86. Quoted, Ulam, *The Bolsheviks*, p. 580.

87. On the party purge see Leonard Schapiro, *The Communist Party of the Soviet Union* (New York, 1971), pp. 403–56. About the sense of the purges Schapiro wrote (p. 434): "Terror is useless, indeed dangerous to those who apply it, if it stops halfway and does not render harmless all who might, if left alive or at liberty, harbor thoughts of revenge. . . . Stalin did not stop halfway. . . . Stalin's revolution in agriculture and industry and his assault on the party which consummated this revolution must be seen as integrated parts of one and the same process."

88. By E. H. Carr, "A Historical Turning Point: Marx, Lenin, Stalin,"

in Richard Pipes, ed., *Revolutionary Russia: A Symposium* (Cambridge, Mass., 1968), p. 283.

89. On the economic achievement see Alec Nove, *An Economic History of the U.S.S.R.* (New York, 1975), table (from Soviet sources), p. 68.

CHAPTER 11. MEMORIAL

1. McLellan, *Karl Marx*, p. 448.
2. Letter, Marx to Engels, Jan. 22, 1870, *Werke*, 32:428. Marx wrote the abbreviated title with Russian characters. The book Marx had was actually an early part of Herzen's complete memoirs. Marx's comment was: "So Herzen's dead. Just about when I was finishing [the memoirs] etc." Marx then went on to other subjects, first, Bakunin's machinations.
3. Engels' preface, *Das Kapital*, 2:11; *Capital*, 2:3. Also McLellan, *Karl Marx*, p. 422. About the mathematics, in 1925–26 a German Communist, a trained mathematician, spent some months studying Marx's mathematical notes with a view to editing them for publication. Nothing came of the project. See E. J. Gumbel, *Vom Russland der Gegenwart* (Berlin, 1927), p. 7. In all his writings Marx never showed any competence in the physical sciences or mathematics. He usually avoided the first and his effort to deal with the second in vol. 3 of *Capital* illustrates his innocence of the subject too well.
4. Notes reprinted, *Werke*, 19:407–24. Marx also wrote the introduction to the second Russian edition of the *Communist Manifesto* at this time.
5. *Das Kapital*, 2:12; *Capital*, 2:4.
6. *Dialektic der Natur*, *Werke*, 20:307–570. It was begun in 1873 and interrupted in 1876 by the pressing assignment to write the *Anti-Dühring* and then by Marx's death. Resumed much later, it was finished in 1888. It was not, however, published until 1925, and then by the Soviet publishing organization.
7. *Werke*, 19:endnote 12.
8. H. M. Hyndman's account of the relationship, but not the rupture, *The Record of an Adventurous Life* (New York, 1911), pp. 246–65. It was to Hyndman that Marx told of his coming upon the idea of materialism in Paris. On the rupture see McLellan, *Karl Marx*, pp. 445–46.
9. See Norman MacKenzie and Jeanne MacKenzie, *The Fabians* (New York, 1977). On July 19, 1883, one of the founders, Edward Pease, wrote to his sister after attending a meeting of the Democratic Federation. It consisted, he said, of "the oddest little gathering of twenty characteristically democratic men with dirty hands and small heads, some of them with very limited wits, and mostly with some sort of foreign accent," ibid., p. 19. Attracted by "the spirit of the affair" but

not by the participants, he went on to organize another group that became the forerunner of the Fabians.

10. Shaw, who was a friend of Eleanor Marx, read *Capital* in the fall of 1883 and was temporarily convinced, but Sidney Webb, accepting the marginalist definition of value developed by the economist Stanley Jevons, brought Shaw around to his opinion. By 1888 the Fabians concurred as a group on neoclassical economics. In 1889 they published the famous *Fabian Essays*, which expounded the non-Marxian socialism they had fixed upon. Ibid., pp. 40–64.

11. Letter, Engels to Eduard Bernstein, Nov. 2–3, 1882, *Werke*, 35:388. The son-in-law in question was Paul Lafargue.

12. Alec Nove, *An Economic History of the U.S.S.R.* (New York, 1975), p. 67.

13. Isaac Deutscher, *The Prophet Unarmed: Trotsky, 1921–1929* (London, 1959), p. 7.

14. Mention should be made here of the monumental and profoundly humane Leszek Kolakowski, *Main Currents of Marxism: Its Rise, Growth, and Dissolution*, 3 vols. (Oxford, 1978). Kolakowski, a Polish political theorist who worked his way out of Poland and Marxism into the wealth of free Western thought, concludes, "The self-deification of mankind, to which Marxism gave philosophical expression, has ended in the same way as all such attempts . . . it has revealed itself as the farcical aspect of human bondage" (3:530).

15. Quoted, Robert Lekachman, *The Age of Keynes* (New York, 1966), p. 177.

BIBLIOGRAPHY

A NOTE ON SOURCES

The three German-language editions of the collected works of Marx and Engels comprise the great bulk of the primary sources. In chronological order they are: the *Historisch-Kritische Gesamtausgabe* (1927–35), the *Werke* (1959–68), and, not to be confused with the first, the *Gesamtausgabe (MEGA)* (1975–). In abbreviation the first edition has been known to scholars by its acronym *MEGA* (for Marx-Engels Gesamtausgabe), and will be so identified here. The last will be distinguished here from the original *MEGA* by the abbreviation *New MEGA*.

The original *MEGA*, a dozen volumes, broke off with the writings of 1848, although it carried some correspondence of the later period. Its first editor, David Ryazanov, was a former Menshevik who died in a labor camp during the Soviet purges. Ryazanov was guided, as his successors have not been, by rigorous scholarly standards, and the *MEGA* includes a few items the *Werke* has not and the *New MEGA* has not yet published.

The *MEGA* edition is divided into series I and III, series II never having appeared. Series I begins with two separate volumes called "half-volumes." The reference "*MEGA*, I, 1(1):206," as signaled in the first such reference here, means page 206 of the first half-volume of series I; a simpler example, "*MEGA*, I, 3:4," means page 4 of volume 3 of series I.

The *Werke*, forty-three volumes in all and extending over the entire lifetimes of Marx and Engels, was the most intensively used source here. The first twenty volumes of the *New MEGA* to appear have, however, provided invaluable new material on Marx's early years. This recent edition, which the editors say will total one hundred volumes, is evidently reprinting everything found in the *Werke* while adding notes made by Marx and Engels, manuscript drafts, variants of published writings, and letters by third persons. Both the *Werke* and the *New MEGA* contain extremely useful aids to research. Each volume of the *Werke* includes capsule biographies of every person mentioned (the biography section functioning as a convenient index of persons), a list of all periodicals mentioned with dates and descriptions, and meticulous endnotes on all points that might just possibly require elucidation. In the *New MEGA* edition each volume of textual material is accompanied by a separate volume of notes, the *Apparat*, which has similar data, although it is not so generous in biographical details. The Marx-Engels writings, it must be recognized, establish the moral basis of the Soviet regime, and the helpful information is shaped accordingly.

The *New MEGA* has been divided into four series, designated here by Roman numerals as in the case of the two old *MEGA* series. The *New MEGA* volume of textual material is indicated by the letter *T* and the accompanying volume of notes (the *Apparat*) by *N*. Thus, again referring to the first such mention, "*New MEGA*, III, 1T:331" means page 331 of the "text" volume 1 of series III.

An English-language edition of the writings, the *Collected Works*, hereafter *Works*, began to appear in 1975 and has recently reached its eighteenth volume. A fifty-volume edition is planned. Based on the Russian edition, and not a direct translation of the *Werke*, it has selected material on the basis of slightly different criteria. Consequently, a given item may appear in the one and not the other.

I have tried to refer the reader to the *Works* or to another convenient English translation as well as to the original, (usually) German-language source. Quoted passages in the text may differ in wording from the English-language source given as a reference, since, while making use of the published translations, I did my own translating.

Archival Sources

Archives des Affaires Etrangères. Ministère des Affaires Etrangères, Paris.
    Correspondence Politique.
        Vol. 218: Bavaria, 1843.
        Vols. 28, 29: Belgium, 1846–Feb. 1848.
        Vols. 796–804: Germany, 1839–Feb. 1848.
        Vols. 293–301: Prussia, July 1840–Feb. 1848.
        Vol. 56: Saxony, June 1843–Feb. 1845.
    Mémoires et Documents.
        France, 1847–48, vol. 350 bis: Bulletins du Préfet de Police sur l'état des esprits et sur les incidents journaliers à Paris.
        France et divers états, 1835–52, vol. 731.
        France et divers états, Allemagne, 1830–50, vol. 125.
        France et divers pays, Allemagne, 1848–49, vol. 129.

Archives Nationales, Paris.

Fonds Guizot.
   Dossiers Spéciaux: Rapports du Préfet de Police, 1843–46.
   Humboldt, naturaliste allemand, 26 lettres.
   Ministère de la Justice, Direction des Affaires Criminelles et des Graces.
   Association secrète formée à Paris sous le nom de Ligue allemande
   des proscrits.
   Dossier André Scherzer.

Archives Générales du Royaume de Belgique, Brussels.
   Dossiers, Adalbert von Bornstedt, Karl Marx.

Archive de la ville de Bruxelles.
   Réunions: rapports de police, 1841 à 1846.
   Biographes des suspects: dossier Marcx, Charles.

BY MARX

(Often with writings by Engels.)

General Editions

Collected Works. 18 vols. to date. New York: International, 1975–.

Gesamtausgabe (MEGA). 20 vols. to date. (East) Berlin: Dietz, 1975–.

Historisch-Kritische Gesamtausgabe. Ed. David Ryazanov. 12 vols. Frankfurt: Marx-Engels-Archiv, 1927–35.

Werke. 43 vols. (East) Berlin: Dietz, 1956–68.

Selections

The American Journalism of Marx and Engels. Ed. Henry M. Christman. New York: New American Library, 1966.

The Cologne Communist Trial. (The *Revelations* and other writings on the trial plus *The Great Men of the Emigration*). Ed. and Tr. Rodney Livingstone. London: Lawrence & Wishart, 1971.

Marx and Engels on Malthus. Ed. R. L. Meek. London: Lawrence & Wishart, 1953.

The Marx-Engels Reader. Ed. Robert C. Tucker. 2nd ed. New York: Norton, 1978.

On the Paris Commune. Moscow: Progress Publishers, 1971.

On Revolution. Ed. Saul K. Padover. New York: McGraw-Hill, 1971.

Political Writings. 4 vols. Ed. David Fernbach. New York: Random House, 1974–75.

Revolution in Spain. New York: International, 1939.

Selected Correspondence. 2nd ed. Moscow: Progress Publishers, 1965.

Selected Works in One Volume. New York: International, 1974.

Selected Works in Two Volumes. London: Lawrence & Wishart, 1942–43.

Writings of the Young Marx on Philosophy and Society. Ed. Loyd D. Easton and Kurt H. Guddat. New York: Doubleday, 1967.

Individual Works

(Vols. 1–3 of *Das Kapital* have been published as vols. 23–25 of the *Werke*.)

Capital, vol. 1. Tr. Samuel Moore and Edward Aveling. New York: International, 1947. (Reprint of 1887 edition as edited by Engels.)

Capital, vols. 2, 3. New York: International, 1967. (Based on Ernest Untermann translation, published by Charles H. Kerr, Chicago, 1909.)

Grundrisse der Kritik der politischen Ökonomie (Rohentwurf) 1857–1858. (East) Berlin: Dietz, 1953.

Grundrisse. Tr. Martin Nicolaus. New York: Random House, 1973.

Misère de La philosophie. Paris: A. Frank; Brussels: C. G. Vogler, 1847.

Secret Diplomatic History of the Eighteenth Century and The Story of the Life of Lord Palmerston. Ed. Lester Hutchinson. New York: International, 1969.

ABOUT MARX

Annenkov, Pavel V. *The Extraordinary Decade: Literary Memoirs.* Ed. Arthur P. Mendel. Ann Arbor: University of Michigan Press, 1968.

Becker, Gerhard. *Karl Marx und Friedrich Engels in Köln, 1848–1849.* (East) Berlin: Rütten u. Loening, 1963.

Berlin, Isaiah. "Benjamin Disraeli, Karl Marx and the Search for Identity." In *Against the Current.* New York: Viking, 1980. Pp. 252–86.

———. *Karl Marx: His Life and Environment.* 3rd ed. New York: Oxford University Press, 1963.

Bernstein, Samuel. "Marx in Paris 1848: A Neglected Chapter." *Science and Society* 3 (Summer 1939):323–55.

Blumenberg, Werner. *Karl Marx in Selbstzeugnissen und Bilddokumenten.* Hamburg: Rowohlt, 1970.

Born, Stephan. *Erinnerungen eines Achtundvierzigers.* Leipzig: G. H. Meyer, 1898.

Brentano, Lujo. *Meine Polemik mit Karl Marx*. Berlin: Walther u. Apolant, 1890.

Carr, E. H. *Karl Marx: A Study in Fanaticism*. London: J. M. Dent, 1934.

Cornu, Auguste. *Karl Marx et Friedrich Engels, 2: 1842–1844*. Paris: Presses Universitaires de France, 1958.

———. *Karl Marx et Friedrich Engels, 3: Marx à Paris*. Paris: Presses Universitaires de France, 1962.

Grünberg, Carl. "Urkundliches aus den Universitätsjahren von Karl Marx," *Archiv für die Geschichte des Sozialismus* 12 (1926):232–40.

Haubtmann, Pierre. *Marx et Proudhon*. Paris: Editions Economie et Humanisme, 1947.

Heinzen, Karl. *Gesammelte Schriften, 3: Vor Meiner Exilirung*. Boston: Selbstverlag des Verfassers, 1864.

Hyndman, H. M. *The Record of an Adventurous Life*. New York: Macmillan, 1911.

Karl Marx: Chronik seines Lebens in Einzeldaten. Moscow: Marx-Engels-Verlag, 1934.

Künzli, Arnold. *Karl Marx: Eine Psychographie*. Vienna, Frankfurt, and Zurich: Europa, 1966.

Laufner, Richard, and Rauch, Albert. *Die Familie Marx und die Trierer Judenschaft*. Schriften aus dem Karl-Marx-Haus. Booklet 14 (1975).

Liebknecht, Wilhelm. *Briefwechsel mit Karl Marx und Friedrich Engels*. The Hague: Mouton, 1963.

———. *Karl Marx zum Gedächnis*. Nuremberg: Wörlein, 1896.

McLellan, David. *Karl Marx*. New York: Viking, Modern Masters, 1975.

———. *Karl Marx: His Life and Thought*. London: Macmillan, 1973.

———. *Marx Before Marxism*. New York: Harper & Row, 1970.

———. *The Young Hegelians and Karl Marx*. London: Macmillan, 1969.

Mayer, Gustav. "Neue Beiträge zur Biographie von Karl Marx." *Archiv für die Geschichte des Sozialismus und der deutschen Arbeiterbewegung* 10 (1921–22):54–63.

Mehring, Franz. *Karl Marx: Geschichte seines Lebens*. 1918. Reprint. Frankfurt: Europäische Verlagsanstalt, 1964.

———. *Karl Marx: The Story of His Life*. Tr. Edward Fitzgerald. Ann Arbor: University of Michigan Press, 1962.

Mohr und General: Erinnerungen an Marx und Engels. (East) Berlin: Dietz, 1964.

Monz, Heinz. *Karl Marx: Grundlagen der Entwicklung zu Leben und Werk.* Trier: NCO-Verlag, 1973.

Nicolaievsky, Boris, and Maenchen-Helfen, Otto. *Karl Marx: Man and Fighter.* Tr. Gwenda David and Eric Mosbacher. London: Methuen, 1936.

Pachter, Henry. "Marx and the Jews." *Dissent* 26, no. 4 (Fall, 1979):450–67.

Padover, Saul K. *Karl Marx: An Intimate Biography.* New York: McGraw-Hill, 1978.

Payne, Robert. *Marx: A Biography.* New York: Simon & Schuster, 1968.

Raddatz, Fritz J. *Karl Marx: Eine Politische Biographie.* Hamburg: Hoffmann u. Campe, 1975.

Regnault, Félix. "Les Maladies de Karl Marx." *Revue anthropologique* 43 (July–Sep. 1933):293–317.

Rosdolsky, Roman. "Karl Marx und der Polizeispitzel Bangya." *International Review for Social History* 2 (1937):229–45.

Rubel, Maximilien. *Karl Marx: Essai de biographie intellectuelle.* Paris: Marcel Rivière, 1957. (2nd ed., 1971.)

Rubel, Maximilien, and Manale, Margaret. *Marx without Myth: A Chronological Study of His Life and Work.* New York: Harper & Row, 1976.

Schlechte, Horst. "Karl Marx und Sein Wirkungskreis in Brüssel." *Beiträge zur Geschichte der deutschen Arbeiterbewegung* 1 (1966):101–6.

Schurz, Carl. *The Reminiscences of Carl Schurz.* Vol. 1. New York: McClure, 1907.

Schwarzschild, Leopold. *The Red Prussian.* New York: Scribner's, 1947.

Seigel, Jerrold E. "Marx's Early Development: Vocation, Rebellion, and Realism." *Journal of Interdisciplinary History* 3, no. 3 (Winter 1973):475–508.

———. *Marx's Fate: The Shape of a Life.* Princeton: Princeton University Press, 1978.

Silberner, Edmund. "Was Marx an Anti-Semite?" *Historia Judaica* 11 (Apr. 1949):3–52.

Victor, Walther. *Marx und Heine: Tatsache und Spekulation in der Darstellung ihrer Beziehungen.* (East) Berlin: Bruno Henschel, 1951.

Vogt, Carl. *Mein Prozess gegen die "Allgemeine Zeitung."* Geneva: Selbstverlag, 1859.

PERSONS

Berlin, Isaiah. *The Life and Opinions of Moses Hess.* Cambridge: W. Heffer & Sons, 1959.

Dornemann, Luise. *Jenny Marx: Der Lebensweg einer Sozialistin.* (East) Berlin: Dietz, 1968.

Fleury, Victor. "Le poète Georges Herwegh (1817–1875)." Diss., University of Paris, n.d. (c. 1910).

Henderson, William Otto. "The Firm of Ermen & Engels in Manchester." *Internationale Wissenschaftliche Korrespondenz,* no. 11–12 (Apr. 1971): 1–10.

———. *The Life of Friedrich Engels.* 2 vols. London: Frank Cass, 1976.

Herzen, Alexander. See works under "Ideas."

Hess, Moses. *Briefwechsel.* Ed. Edmund Silberner. The Hague: Mouton, 1959.

Hirsch, Helmut. "Karl Friedrich Köppen: Der Intimste Berliner Freund Marxens." *International Review for Social History* 1 (1936):311–66.

Ilyichov, L. F., et al. *Frederick Engels: A Biography.* Moscow: Progress Publishers, 1974.

Lassalle, Ferdinand. *Nachgelassene Briefe und Schriften, 3: Der Briefwechsel zwischen Lassalle und Marx.* Ed. Gustav Mayer. Stuttgart and Berlin: Deutsche Verlagsanstalt, 1922.

Mayer, Gustav. *Friedrich Engels: Eine Biographie, 2: Engels und der Aufsteig der Arbeiterbewegung in Europa.* The Hague: Martinius Nijhoff, 1934. English trans., New York, 1936.

———. *Friedrich Engels in seiner Frühzeit, 1820–1851.* Berlin: Julius Springer, 1920.

Na'aman, Shlomo. *Lassalle.* Hanover: Verlag für Literatur und Zeitgeschehen, 1970.

Neher, Walter. *Arnold Ruge als Politiker und politischer Schriftsteller.* Heidelberg: Carl Winters Universitätsbuchhandlung, 1933.

Ruge, Arnold. *Arnold Ruges Briefwechsel und Tagebuchblätter.* 2 vols. Berlin: Weidmannsche Buchhandlung, 1886.

———. *Zwei Jahre in Paris.* 2 vols. Leipzig: Wilhelm Jurany, 1846.

Sammons, Jeffrey L. *Heinrich Heine: A Modern Biography.* Princeton, N.J.: Princeton University Press, 1979.

Weiss, John. *Moses Hess, Utopian Socialist.* Detroit: Wayne State University Press, 1960.

Zlocisti, Theodor. *Moses Hess*. Berlin: Louis Lamm, 1905.

POLITICS AND EVENTS

Bebel, August. *Aus Meinem Leben*. 3 vols. (East) Berlin: Dietz, 1953.

Bernstein, Samuel. *Auguste Blanqui and the Art of Insurrection*. London: Lawrence & Wishart, 1971.

Bittel, Karl. *Der Kommunistenprozess zu Köln im Spiegel der zeitgenössischen Presse*. (East) Berlin: Rütten u. Loening, 1955.

Blumenberg, Werner. "Zur Geschichte des Bundes der Kommunisten: Die Aussagen des Peter Gerhardt Röser." *International Review of Social History* 9 (1964):81–122.

Börnstein, Heinrich. *Fünfundsiebzig Jahre in der alten u. neuen Welt*. Vol. 1. Leipzig: Otto Wigand, 1881.

Braudel, Fernand. *Capitalism and Material Life, 1400–1800*. New York: Harper & Row, 1974.

Braunthal, Julius. *History of the International*. Vol. 1: *1864–1914*. New York: Praeger, 1967.

Der Bund der Kommunisten: Dokumente u. Materialien. Vol. 1: *1836–1849*. Ed. Herwig Förder et al. (East) Berlin: Dietz, 1970.

Carr, E. H. *The Bolshevik Revolution, 1917–1923*. 3 vols. New York: Macmillan, 1951–53.

————. *The Interregnum, 1923–1924*. New York: Macmillan, 1954.

————. *The Romantic Exiles*. London: Gollancz, 1933.

Caussidière, Marc. *Mémoires de Caussidière*. 2 vols. Paris: Lévy, 1849.

Checkland, S. G. *The Rise of Industrial Society in England, 1815–1885*. London: Longmans, Green, 1964.

Cohen, Stephen F. *Bukharin and the Bolshevik Revolution: A Political Biography, 1888–1938*. New York: Knopf, 1973.

Deutscher, Isaac. *The Prophet Armed: Trotsky, 1879–1921*. London: Oxford University Press, 1954.

————. *The Prophet Unarmed: Trotsky, 1921–1929*. London: Oxford University Press, 1959.

————. *The Prophet Outcast: Trotsky, 1929–1940*. London: Oxford University Press, 1963.

Dommanget, Maurice. *L'Introduction du Marxisme en France*. Lausanne: Rencontre, 1961.

Edwards, Stewart. *The Paris Commune, 1871.* London: Eyre & Spottis-woode, 1971.

Ewerbeck, Hermann. *L'Allemagne et les Allemands.* Paris: Garnier Frères, 1851.

Feuer, Lewis S. *The Conflict of Generations.* New York: Basic Books, 1969.

Fitzgerald, C. P. *Mao Tse-tung and China.* London: Hodder & Stoughton, 1976.

Flaubert, Gustave. *L'Education sentimentale.* 2 vols. Paris: Société Les Belles Lettres, 1942.

Freymond, Jacques. *La Première Internationale.* 2 vols. Publications de L'Institut Universitaire de Hautes Etudes, no. 39. Geneva: E. Droz, 1962.

The General Council of the First International: Minutes. 5 vols. Moscow: Foreign Languages Publishing House, 1963.

Gerth, Hans, ed. *The First International: Minutes of The Hague Congress of 1872 with Related Documents.* Madison: University of Wisconsin Press, 1958.

Habakkuk, H. J., and Postan, M. *The Cambridge Economic History of Europe, 6: The Industrial Revolutions and After: Incomes, Population, and Technological Change.* 2 parts. Cambridge: Cambridge University Press, 1965.

Hammen, Oscar J. *The Red '48ers.* New York: Scribner's, 1969.

Hansen, Joseph, ed. *Rheinische Briefe u. Akten zur Geschichte der politischen Bewegung 1830–1850. Gesellschaft für rheinische Geschichtskunde,* pub. no. 36: 1: *1830–1845.* Essen: Baedeker, 1919.

Herberts, Hermann. *Zur Geschichte der SPD im Wuppertal* (pamphlet). Elberfeld: Freie Presse, 1963.

Hoffmann, Walther G. *British Industry, 1700–1950.* Oxford: Basil Black-well, 1955.

————. *The Growth of Industrial Economics.* Manchester: Manchester University Press, 1958.

Joll, James. *The Second International, 1889–1914.* London: Weidenfeld & Nicolson, 1955.

Karnow, Stanley. *Mao and China.* New York: Viking, Compass, 1973.

Kümhof, Herbert. *Karl Marx u. die "Neue Rh. Zeitung" in ihrem Verhältnis zur demokratischen Bewegung der Revolutionsjahre 1848/49.* Berlin: Ernst-Reuter-Gesellschaft, 1961.

La Hodde, Lucien de. *Histoire des sociétés secrètes et du parti républicain de 1830 à 1848.* Paris: Julien, Lanier, 1850.

Lewin, Moshe. *Russian Peasants and Soviet Power: A Study of Collectivization.* New York: Norton Library, 1975.

Leys, Simon. *Chinese Shadows.* New York: Viking, 1977.

Liebman, Marcel. *The Russian Revolution.* New York: Random House, 1970.

McClellan, Woodford D. *Revolutionary Exiles: The Russians in the First International and the Paris Commune.* London: Frank Cass, 1979.

MacKenzie, Norman, and MacKenzie, Jeanne. *The Fabians.* New York: Simon & Schuster, 1977.

Mayer, Gustav. "Der Untergang der *Deutsch-Französischen Jahrbücher* u. des Pariser *Vorwärts.*" *Archiv für die Geschichte des Sozialismus und der deutschen Arbeiterbewegung* 3 (1913):415–38.

Mehring, Franz. *Geschichte der deutschen Sozialdemokratie.* 2 vols. (East) Berlin: Dietz, 1960.

Mins, Leonard E., ed. *The Founding of the First International: A Documentary Record.* New York: International, 1937.

Mohrenschildt, Dimitri von, ed. *The Russian Revolution of 1917: Contemporary Accounts.* New York: Oxford University Press, 1971.

Na'aman, Shlomo. "Zur Geschichte des Bundes der Kommunisten in Deutschland in der zweiten Phase seines Bestehens." *Archiv für Sozialgeschichte* 5 (1965):5–82.

Nettlau, Max. "Londoner deutsche kommunistische Diskussionen, 1845." *Archiv für die Geschichte des Sozialismus und der deutschen Arbeiterbewegung* 10 (1921–22):362–91.

Nicolaievsky, Boris. "Toward a History of the Communist League 1847–1852." *International Review of Social History* 1, pt. 2 (1956):234–52.

Nove, Alec. *An Economic History of the U.S.S.R.* New York: Penguin, 1975.

Osterroth, Franz, and Schuster, Dieter. *Chronik der Deutschen Sozialdemokratie.* Hanover: Dietz, 1963.

Pelissier, Roger. *The Awakening of China, 1793–1949.* Ed. and tr. Martin Kieffer. New York: Capricorn, 1970.

Perreux, Gabriel. *Au Temps des sociétés secrètes.* Paris: Hachette, 1931.

Pipes, Richard. *The Formation of the Soviet Union.* 2nd ed. Cambridge: Harvard University Press, 1970.

————, ed. *Revolutionary Russia: A Symposium.* Cambridge: Harvard University Press, 1968.

Plamenatz, John. *The Revolutionary Movement in France, 1815–71.* London: Longmans, Green, 1952.

Reichard, Richard W. *Crippled from Birth: German Social Democracy, 1844–1870.* Ames: Iowa State University Press, 1969.

Renard, Georges. "Cabet et les précurseurs de la Révolution de 1848." *La Révolution de 1848* 28 (Dec. 1931–Feb. 1932):181–92.

Resis, Albert. "*Das Kapital* Comes to Russia." *Slavic Review* 29, no. 2 (June 1970):219–37.

Rittiez, F. *Histoire du règne de Louis-Philippe 1er, 1830 à 1848.* Vol. 3. Paris: Société des Gens de Lettres, 1858.

Roberts, John. "The Myth of the Commune." *History Today* 7 (May 1957):290–300.

Roth, Guenther. *The Social Democrats in Imperial Germany: A Study in Working-Class Isolation and National Integration.* Totowa, N.J.: Bedminster Press, 1963.

Schapiro, Leonard. *The Communist Party of the Soviet Union.* 2nd ed., rev. New York: Knopf, Vintage, 1971.

Schieder, Wolfgang. *Anfänge der deutschen Arbeiterbewegung.* Stuttgart: Ernst Klett, 1963.

———. "Der Bund der Kommunisten im Sommer 1850." *International Review of Social History* 13 (1968):29–57.

Schraepler, Ernst. "Der Bund der Gerechten: Seine Tätigkeit in London, 1840–1847." *Archiv für Sozialgeschichte* 2 (1962):5–29.

Shub, David. *Lenin: A Biography.* New York: Doubleday, 1948.

Shukman, Harold. *Lenin and the Russian Revolution.* New York: G. P. Putnam's Sons, 1967.

Stein, Ludwig von. *The History of the Social Movement in France, 1789–1850.* Ed. Kathe Mengelberg. Totowa, N.J.: Bedminster Press, 1964. (1st [German] ed., 1850.)

Thureau-Dangin, Paul. *Histoire de la monarchie de Juillet.* 7 vols. Paris: E. Plon, Nourrit, 1884–92.

Tocqueville, Alexis de. *Recollections.* New York: Doubleday, 1970.

Tucker, Robert C. *Stalin as Revolutionary, 1879–1929: A Study in History and Personality.* New York: Norton, 1974.

———, ed. *The Great Purge Trial.* New York: Grosset & Dunlap, Universal Library, 1965.

Ulam, Adam B. *The Bolsheviks.* New York: Macmillan, 1965.

————. *In the Name of the People: Prophets and Conspirators in Pre-revolutionary Russia.* New York: Viking, 1977.

————. *Stalin: The Man and His Era.* New York: Viking, 1973.

Venturi, Franco. *Roots of Revolution: A History of the Populist and Socialist Movements in Nineteenth-Century Russia.* New York: Grosset & Dunlap, Universal Library, 1966. (1st [Italian] ed., 1952.)

Wermuth, ?, and Stieber, Wilhelm. *Die Communisten-Verschwörungen des neunzehnten Jahrhunderts.* 2 vols. Berlin: A. W. Hayn, 1853–54.

Williams, Roger L. *The French Revolution of 1870–1871.* New York: Norton, 1969.

Zévaès, Alexandre. "L'Agitation communiste de 1840 à 1848." *La Révolution de 1848* 23 (1926):971–81.

————. "Le Mouvement social sous la Restauration et sous la Monarchie de Juillet," Pts. 1 and 2: *La Révolution de 1848* 33 (Sept.–Nov. 1936), 34 (Dec. 1936–Feb. 1937):125–33, 209–40.

IDEAS

Althusser, Louis. *Pour Marx.* Paris: Maspero, 1965.

Avineri, Shlomo. *The Social and Political Thought of Karl Marx.* Cambridge: Cambridge University Press, 1968.

Barzun, Jacques. *Darwin, Marx, Wagner.* Boston: Little, Brown, 1947.

Berger, Martin. *Engels, Armies, and Revolution: The Revolutionary Tactics of Classical Marxism.* Hamden, Conn.: Archon, 1977.

Berlin, Isaiah. *Russian Thinkers.* New York: Viking, 1978.

Boersner, Demetrio. *The Bolsheviks and the National and Colonial Question (1917–1928).* Geneva and Paris: Droz-Minard, 1957.

Böhm-Bawerk, Eugen von. *Karl Marx and the Close of His System.* London: T. Fisher Unwin, 1898. (1st [German] ed., 1896.)

Bottigelli, Emile, *Genèse du socialisme scientifique.* Paris: Editions sociales, 1967.

Buret, Eugène. *De la misère des classes laborieuses en Angleterre et en France.* 2 vols. Paris: Paulin, 1840.

Carr, E. H. *Studies in Revolution.* 1950. Reprint. New York: Grosset & Dunlap, Universal Library, 1964.

Cieszkowski, August von. *Prolegomena zur Historiosophie.* Berlin: Veit, 1838.

Draper, Hal. *Karl Marx's Theory of Revolution*. Pt. 1: *State and Bureaucracy*. 2 vols. New York: Monthly Review Press, 1977.

Fourier, Charles. *Le Socialisme sociétaire*. Ed. Hubert Bourgin. Paris: Société Nouvelle, 1903.

Garaudy, Roger. *Les sources françaises du socialisme scientifique*. Paris: Editions hier et aujourd'hui, 1948.

Gay, Peter. *The Dilemma of Democratic Socialism: Eduard Bernstein's Challenge to Marx*. 1952. Reprint. New York: Collier, 1962.

Hammen, Oscar J. "Marx and the Agrarian Question." *American Historical Review* 77, no. 3 (June 1972):679–704.

Hayes, Carlton, J. H. "German Socialism Reconsidered." *American Historical Review* 23 (Oct. 1917):62–101.

Hegel, G. W. F. *Encyclopädie der philosophischen Wissenschaften im Grundrisse*. Leipzig: Felix Meiner, 1930.

———. *Phänomenologie des Geistes*. 1807. Reprint. Stuttgart: Frommanns, 1927.

———. *The Phenomenology of Mind*. Tr. S. B. Baillie. London: Allen & Unwin, 1931.

———. *Philosophy of Right*. Tr. T. M. Knox. Oxford: Clarendon Press, 1942. (1st [German] ed., 1821).

Herzen, Alexander. *My Past and Thoughts*. Abridged and edited by Dwight Macdonald. New York: Knopf, Vintage, 1974.

Hook, Sidney. *From Hegel to Marx*. 1936. Reprint. Ann Arbor: University of Michigan Press, 1962.

Horowitz, David, ed. *Marx and Modern Economics*. New York: Monthly Review Press, 1968.

Howard, M. C., and King, J. E., eds. *The Economics of Marx*. New York: Penguin, 1976.

Johnson, Christopher H. "Communism and the Working Class before Marx: The Icarian Experience." *American Historical Review* 76, no. 3 (June 1971):642–89.

Kamnick, Isaac. "Reflections on Revolution: Definition and Explanation in Recent Scholarship." *History and Theory* 11, no. 1 (1972):26–63.

Kolakowski, Leszek. *Main Currents of Marxism: Its Rise, Growth, and Dissolution*. 3 vols. Oxford: The Clarendon Press, 1978.

Korsch, Karl. *Marxism and Philosophy*. 1923. Reprint. New York: Monthly Review Press, 1970.

Lenin, V. I. *The Lenin Anthology*. Ed. Robert C. Tucker. New York: Norton, 1975.

―――. *Selected Works in One Volume*. London: Lawrence & Wishart, 1969.

Lichtheim, George. *Marxism: An Historical and Critical Study*. 2nd ed., rev. New York: Praeger, 1970.

―――. *The Origins of Socialism*. New York: Praeger, 1969.

Louis, Paul. *Histoire du socialisme en France, 1789–1945*. Paris: Marcel Rivière, 1946.

Löwith, Karl. *From Hegel to Nietzsche*. New York: Doubleday, Anchor, 1967. (1st [German] ed., 1941.)

Lukács, Georg. *Geschichte und Klassenbewusstsein*. 1923. Reprint. Berlin: Luchterhand, 1962.

―――. *Der junge Marx: Seine philosophische Entwicklung von 1840–1844*. Pfullingen: Neske, 1965.

―――. *Studies in European Realism*. New York: Grosset & Dunlap, Universal Library, 1964.

Malia, Martin. *Alexander Herzen and the Birth of Russian Socialism*. New York: Grosset & Dunlap, Universal Library, 1965.

Mandel, Ernest. *Marxist Economic Theory*. 2 vols. New York: Monthly Review Press, 1970.

Manuel, Frank E. *The Prophets of Paris*. Cambridge: Harvard University Press, 1962.

Marcuse, Herbert. *Reason and Revolution*. London: Oxford University Press, 1941.

―――. *Soviet Marxism: A Critical Analysis*. New York: Knopf, Vintage, 1961.

Mason, Edward S. "Blanqui and Communism." *Political Science Quarterly* 44 (Dec. 1929):496–527.

Meyer, Alfred G. *Marxism: The Unity of Theory and Practice*. 1954. Reprint. Cambridge: Harvard University Press, 1970.

Milibrand Ralph. *Marxism and Politics*. Oxford: Oxford University Press, 1971.

Mitrany, David. *Marx Against the Peasant*. 1951. Reprint. New York: Collier, 1961.

Morange, Georges. *Les idées communistes dans les sociétés secrètes et dans la presse sous la monarchie de Juillet*. Paris: V. Giard, 1905.

Morishima, Michio. *Marx's Economics: A Dual Theory of Value and Growth*. Cambridge: Cambridge University Press, 1973.

Morishima, Michio, and Catephores, G. "Is There an 'Historical Transformation Problem'?" *Economic Journal* 85 (June 1975):309–27.

Popper, Karl. *The Open Society and Its Enemies.* 2 vols. 1945. Reprint. London: Routledge & Kegan Paul, 1952.

Robinson, Joan. *An Essay on Marxian Economics.* London: Macmillan, 1942.

Rosdolsky, Roman. *Zur Entstehungsgeschichte des Marxschen "Kapital": Der Rohentwurf des "Kapital," 1857–58.* 2 vols. Frankfurt and Vienna: Europäische Verlagsanstalt, 1968.

Rothfels, Hans. *Bismarck und Karl Marx.* Sitzungsberichte der Heidelberger Akademie der Wissenschaften. Heidelberg, 1961.

Röttcher, Feodor. "Theorie und Praxis in den Frühschriften von Karl Marx." *Archiv für Philosophie* 11, nos. 3 & 4 (1962):246–311.

Rubel, Maximilien. "Gespräche über Russland mit Fr. Engels: Nach Aufzeichnungen von Alexei M. Woden." *Internationale Wissenschaftliche Korrespondenz* 11, no. 12 (Apr. 1971):11–24.

Saint-Simon, Claude-Henri. *Textes choisis.* Ed. Jean Dautry. Paris: Editions Sociales, 1951.

Samuelson, Paul A. *Economics.* 10th ed. New York: McGraw-Hill, 1976.

———. "Wages and Interest: A Modern Dissection of Marxian Economic Models." *American Economic Review* 47 (Dec. 1957):884–912.

Schaff, Adam. *Marxism and the Human Individual.* New York: McGraw-Hill, 1970.

Schumpeter, Joseph A. "Science and Ideology." *American Economic Review* 39 (Mar. 1949):345–59.

———. *Ten Great Economists.* London: Allen & Unwin, 1952.

Silk, Leonard. *The Economists.* New York: Basic Books, 1976.

Smith, Adam. *An Inquiry into the Nature and Causes of the Wealth of Nations.* Ed. Edwin Cannan. New York: Modern Library, 1937.

Somerhausen, Luc. *L'Humanisme agissant de Karl Marx.* Paris: Richard-Masse, 1946.

Tristan, Flora. *Union ouvrière.* Paris: Prévot-Rouanet, 1843.

Tucker, Robert C. "Marx as a Political Theorist." In Nicholas Lobkowicz, ed., *Marx and the Western World.* Notre Dame, Ind.: University of Notre Dame Press, 1967. Pp. 103–31.

———. *The Marxian Revolutionary Idea.* New York: Norton, 1969.

———. *Philosophy and Myth in Karl Marx.* Cambridge: Cambridge University Press, 1961.

Wolfe, Bertram D. *Marxism: 100 Years in the Life of a Doctrine*. New York: Dial, 1965.

Wolfenstein, E. Victor. *The Revolutionary Personality: Lenin, Trotsky, Gandhi*. Princeton: Princeton University Press, 1971.

Zagorin, Perez. "Theories of Revolution in Contemporary Historiography." *Political Science Quarterly* 88, no. 2 (June 1973):23–52.

Press (Paris)

La Démocratie Pacifique, (1843).

Journal des Débats, 1844.

Le Moniteur Républicain, 1837–38.

Le National, 1844–45.

Les Nouvelles du Soir, 1848.

Le Petit Journal, 1871.

La Phalange, 1836–40, 1845–46.

La Presse, 1845.

La Réforme, 1843–48.

La Réforme Industrielle ou Le Phalanstère, 1832–34.

Revue des deux mondes, 1842–45, 1848.

INDEX

David Felix is an intellectual historian addressing the interaction of ideas with politics, economics, and society. Author of two well-received books, one on an episode in the American social history of the 1920s and another on German political and economic history in the same decade, he has lately been writing a study of John Maynard Keynes and the political aspects of Keynesian economics. He is a professor of history at the Graduate Center and Bronx Community College of the City University of New York. He has also been a reporter for the Pittsburgh *Sun-Telegraph*, information officer in the United States Economic Mission to Austria, correspondent for the International News Service in Paris, a financial writer, and managing editor of a magazine of economic affairs. A recipient of research grants and fellowships from the Ford Foundation, the American Council of Learned Societies, the City University of New York, and the State University of New York, he carried out the initial research for his Keynes project as a senior fellow of the National Endowment for the Humanities. His scholarly articles and reviews have been published in *American Historical Review, American Scholar, Central European History, Columbia University Forum, European Studies Review, Foreign Service Journal, History Today, Journal of Economic Literature,* and *Journal of Modern History.*

MARX AS POLITICIAN

Designed by John DeBacher

*Composed by Graphic Composition
in Linotron Bembo*

*Printed by Thomson-Shore
on 50 lb. Glatfelter offset*

*Bound by John H. Dekker and Sons
in Holliston Roxite Vellum*